Spinoza, Right and Absolute Freedom

Against jurisprudential reductions of Spinoza's thinking to a kind of eccentric version of Hobbes, this book argues that Spinoza's theory of natural right contains an important idea of absolute freedom, which would be inconceivable within Hobbes' own schema. Spinoza famously thought that the universe and all of the beings and events within it are fully determined by their causes. This has led jurisprudential commentators to believe that Spinoza has no room for natural right – in the sense that whatever happens by definition has a 'right' to happen. But, although this book demonstrates how Spinoza constructs a system in which right is understood as the work of machines, by fixing right as determinate and invariable, Stephen Connelly argues that Spinoza is not limiting his theory. The universe as a whole is capable of acting only in determinate ways but, he argues, for Spinoza, these exist within a field of infinite possibilities. In an analysis that offers much to ongoing attempts to conceive of justice post-foundationally, the argument of this book is that Spinoza opens up right to a future of determinate interventions – as when an engineer, working with already-existing materials, improves a machine. As such, an idea of freedom emerges in Spinoza: as the artful rearrangement of the given into new possibilities. An exciting and original contribution, this book is an invaluable addition, both to the new wave of interest in Spinoza's philosophy, and to contemporary legal and political theory.

Stephen Connelly is Assistant Professor of Law at the University of Warwick.

First published 2015
by Birkbeck Law Press

Published 2016 by Routledge
2 Park Square, Milton Park, Abingdon, Oxfordshire OX14 4RN
711 Third Avenue, New York, NY 10017

First issued in paperback 2016

Routledge is an imprint of the Taylor and Francis Group, an informa business

British Library Cataloguing in Publication Data
A catalogue record for this book is available from the British Library

Library of Congress Cataloging-in-Publication Data
A catalog record has been requested for this book

ISBN 13: 978-1-138-24154-1 (pbk)

ISBN 13: 978-1-138-82689-2 (hbk)

Typeset in Baskerville by
Florence Production Ltd, Stoodleigh, Devon, UK

Spinoza, Right and Absolute Freedom

Stephen Connelly

Routledge
Taylor & Francis Group
LONDON AND NEW YORK

[This city] possesses not three dimensions, but four; the fourth is subject to obscurity and is not marked on maps at all, except as a dot, for a dot is the place where the plane of this existence touches against the spherical surface of the immense astral cosmos.

Andrei Bely, *Petersburg* (1995: 409)

Contents

Acknowledgements

Work on this book began as a part-time PhD thesis at Birkbeck College's School of Law. I am deeply grateful to the people and ethos at Birkbeck, which tolerated not only a break in research as I moved to Germany with my family, but also the openness to interdisciplinarity, which meant that I was permitted to stray far beyond the bounds of traditional legal research, something demanded by the very research itself. Following my move to Germany, the Goethe Universität Frankfurt am Main became a second academic home, and I would like to thank the Universtätsbibliothek for allowing me to use their resources.

Over the years, I have become indebted to several people who have contributed in different ways to the completion of this book. First and foremost has been my tutor, Dr Anton Schütz, who with great patience tolerated both the unwieldiness of many early drafts and guided me towards a text that was approachable to readers, who made very many stimulating suggestions and was open to my own tangential flourishes, and who practically accommodated my remoteness by meeting me both in London and in Paris, and by conducting a great deal of tutorial work by email and telephone. Further generous assistance and commentary has been provided by my *viva voce* examiners Étienne Balibar and Filippo del Lucchese, and variously by Tamara Caraus, Ben Dawson, Costas Douzinas, Peter Fitzpatrick, Piyel Haldar, Gilbert Leung, Elena Loizidou, Nathan Moore, Alberto Toscano, Illan Rua Wall, and Bald de Vries and Lyana Francot-Timmermans (who sponsored groundwork for this book at the Utrecht University Critical Legal Conference).

Finally, I would like to thank Fabienne, who let me take to sea knowing that the sea might take me.

Illustrations

Figures

Tables

Method of citation

Where references are by author and year of publication, full reference information may be found in the bibliography.

Spinoza's writings

The following common abbreviations have been used in referring to Spinoza's writings:

CGLH	*Compendium of Hebrew Grammar (Compendium Grammatices Linguae Hebraeae)*
DPP	*Descartes' 'Principles of Philosophy' (Renati Des Cartes Principiorum Philosophiae, Pars I et II, More Geometrico Demonstratae)*
E	*Ethics (Ethica Ordinae Geometrico Demonstrata)*
Ep	*Letters (Epistulae)*
KV	*Short Treatise on God, Man, and His Well-Being (Korte Vehandeling van God, de Mensch en des zelfs Welstand)*
TdIE	*Treatise on the Emendation of the Intellect (Tractatus de Intellectus Emendatione)*
TP	*Political Treatise (Tractatus politicus)*
TTP	*Theological-Political Treatise (Tractatus Theologico-politicus)*

References to the *Short Treatise on God, Man, and His Well-Being*, the *Treatise on the Emendation of the Intellect*, the *Political Treatise*, and the *Theological-Political Treatise* are by chapter and, within chapters, by the section numbers introduced in the Bruder edition of Spinoza's works and reproduced in many subsequent editions. Additionally, for the TTP, the line numbers of the Gebhardt edition of Spinoza's works are used, supplemented by those of the Akkerman edition.

References to the *Letters* are by letter number.

References to *Descartes' 'Principles of Philosophy'* and the *Ethics* begin with an Arabic number denoting the Part, and use the following common abbreviations:

App.	Appendix
Ax.	Axiom
Corol.	Corollary
Def.	Definition
Dem.	Demonstration
Ex.	Explanation
Gen. Def. Aff.	General Definition of the Affects (located at the end of EIII)
Lem.	Lemma
P	Proposition
PI	Physical Interlude (located after EIIP13 Sch.)
Po.	Postulate
Pref.	Preface
Sch.	Scholium

For example, 'EIP14 Dem., Corol.1' refers to Ethics Part I, Proposition 14, Demonstration and Corollary 1.

The following works of Spinoza were consulted:

(a) Texts in original language

Akkerman, F. (1999) *Spinoza: Oeuvres III – Traité Théologico-politique* (with trans.), Epimethée PUF, Paris.

Bruder, C.H. (1843–1846) *Benedicti de Spinoza Opera quae supersunt omnia, Ex editionibus principis denuo edidit et praefatus Editio stereotypa*, ex officina Bernhardi Tauchnitz, Lipsiae.

Gebhardt, C. (1925) *Spinoza, Opera*, im Auftrag der Heidelberger Akademie der Wissenschaften, Winter, Heidelberg.

Moreau, P.F. (ed.) (2009) *Spinoza: Oeuvres I – Premiers écrits* (with trans.), Epimethée PUF, Paris.

Spinoza, D. de (1677) *Opera Posthuma, quorum series post praesationem exhibetur*, J. Jelles (ed.), Rieuwertsz, J., Amstelodami, archived at: http://posner.library.cmu.edu/Posner/books/book.cgi?call=199_S75O.

(b) Translations

Bennett, J. (2007) *Translation of the Treatise on Theology and Politics*, archived at www.earlymoderntexts.com/pdfbits/spttp2.pdf.

Parkinson, G.H.R. (2000) *Spinoza: Ethics*, Oxford University Press, Oxford.

Shirley, S. (trans.) (2002) *Spinoza: Complete Works*, Hackett, Indianapolis, IN.

Wernham, A.G. (1958) *Benedict de Spinoza: The Political Works*, Clarendon Press, Oxford.

In addition, Akkerman and Moreau in (a) above have parallel translations into French.

Other commonly cited works

Aristoteles — Bekker Numbers are used, save in the case of the Pseudo-Aristoteles' *Mechanical Problems* or *Mechanica*, in which case the Problem number is referred to.

Descartes — We use the Adam and Tannery edition, referring by volume and page number (e.g. ATVIII p. 304). Where appropriate, we refer to the author's own titles (e.g. *Géometrie*) and, in the case of the *Principles of Philosophy*, use 'PP', then the part and [proposition number], so PPII[39] refers to the 39th Proposition of Part II of the *Principles of Philosophy*.

Stoa — We adopt the numbering provided in Von Arnim's classic *Stoicorum veterum fragmenta*, so SVF 2.17 is the 17th fragment in tome 2 of that work, save in the case of Seneca's *Letters*, were we refer directly to the standard Letter and line number.

Chapter 1

Introductory remarks

> [I]n turning my mind to political theory it was not my purpose to suggest anything that is novel or unheard of.
>
> Tractatus politicus I[4]

1.1 On the degree of jurisprudential confusion about Spinoza's intent

Perhaps it is useful if we begin our discussion of the trouble Spinoza's theory seems to cause the jurist by imagining a line on the Cartesian plane connecting existence or the now as 0 and running rightwards towards or into the ought-to-exist. Teleological conceptions of natural right might start on the far right, and as we move closer to 0 = actually existing, we find in some generality natural rights transferred and exercised for some greater purpose (security, as in Hobbes), permitted rights for limited purposes (one sense given by Grotius), rights issuing as volitions from a moral/just nature, which may encompass rationality about ends (Grotius, Hobbes), and rights issuing from whatever passing fancy one wills at all (Selden, Vaughan). All of these models, it is true, envisage a right as an endeavour or claim to a change in existence (= 0). The problem with Spinoza, as is universally remarked, is that he appears to take natural right as the difference between existence at 0 and the power (*potentia*) at 0. That is, he claims there is no difference between right and existence, and, so the jurist (usually implicitly) concludes, there is no *real* natural right theory worth talking about in Spinoza; the phrase being: there is no normativity. Spinoza becomes a limit case for seventeenth-century natural right theories. Yet if this is so, ought we not, like Spinoza's contemporary James Gregory, *pass to the limit*,[1] rather than dismiss an unusual result as an eccentricity? Is it not precisely Spinoza's argument that it is only by pursuing the bonds of mechanical determinism to the limit of God or Nature that we find that right and existence in act do indeed converge – that is, each passes into the other – at the zeroth instant, and that, consequently, here alone natural right amounts to 'performing any operation imaginable'.[2] For Spinoza, it is only by proving that the extent of natural right is necessary and determinate that he can lead us *as if by the hand* to the realisation that this necessity requires freedom as its condition, and that natural right is double: it is simultaneously the bonds of human fate and the inalienable source of human liberation.

The following quotation encapsulates the issue and why we have chosen a line to illustrate the above difference:

> The total equation of right with power has a number of interesting and provocative implications. The most fundamental of these implications is that Spinoza's doctrine of natural right is without normative content. In contrast to prior teleological conceptions, Spinoza's notion of natural right only looks at the given act itself, and then only to the degree of power manifested by that act.
>
> (Den Uyl 1983: 7)

It seems Spinoza, and thus we, must look at the power manifested by an act. In other words, we are apparently called upon to stare into the abyss of the One Being and despair (or rejoice). Now, if we look at our line again and see our natural right's extension into the ought-to-be reduced to the singular point that is zero, why would anyone stop at zero rather than keep going leftwards, as if the material conditions of the present were irrelevant? It is quite axiomatic for Spinoza that nothing is adequately conceived save through its causes; why should natural right be exempted from this and transposed into some magical realm? Spinoza has not simply adopted a 'provocative' (Den Uyl 1983: 7) and 'idiosyncratic' (Tuck 1979: 142) position by reducing the 'ought' of natural right to the zeroth limit; adopting an extreme position of complete scepticism about any form of natural right claim other than the state of the present. His theory continues to have content, but that content now pertains to an examination not of the degree of power manifested in a moment, but a thoroughgoing examination of the individual and particular things that are expressed through their power in the present. It is all too easy to regard power as some amorphous spirit that concretises itself as natural right, when Spinoza's whole aim is the unbounded knowledge of God and Nature, and thus knowledge of the determinate conditions that bring about equally determinate expressions of natural right. Perhaps M. Walther comes closest to this interpretation (from outside legal theory) when, in his critique[3] of Negri's well-known *Savage Anomaly* (1991), he contrasts Hobbes' legal positivism, whereby we examine the rules issued by those institutions exercising natural right, to what he terms Spinoza's 'sociological positivism', where we now examine all the diverse forces of 'life', which compose into a vector that is the 'law of life'. (In this perhaps Walther has in mind Weber's programme for an economic legal theory.)

As we shall see in the next section and in more detail over the course of this book, Spinoza's theory of natural right only makes sense, *and indeed only works (within its limits)*, because he sets the difference between the present expression of power and natural right to zero. It is this exasperating, deathly cold zero that anchors the very possibility of examining why people have this or that much right, why they make laws and in what form, and why they succeed and fail. Moreover, it is because this zero characterises the nature of every thing, that Spinoza is able to deduce a natural right capable of any operation conceivable. It is only by bounding natural right that he liberates it. Were this zero otherwise, as in the other natural right theories mentioned, right would necessarily be denatured, and so enter the dominion of belief and obfuscation. It is perhaps the overwhelming self-evidence of this point for Spinoza, just like the more difficult concept of the *idea Dei*, which explains why he does not take more care to explain himself to his juridically disposed readers, and misunderstanding occurs. Hence, in his *Political Philosophy of Spinoza* (1968: 139), McShea makes the signal declaration that Spinoza's theory of natural right is a theory of 'might-makes-right', a theoretical principle that follows from Hobbesian premises. As such, McShea continues, Spinoza may be treated as an eccentric Hobbesian, who said what Hobbes 'should have said had he been consistent' (ibid.: 138). This statement finds a partner in the following idealistic form of H. Steffen:[4]

> [A]bove all for Spinoza natural right can be nothing exemplary or normative, but rather only self-existent [*selbst Seiendes*].[5]

Apart from confusing Being and existence, one detects the recurrent theme of attacking Spinoza for lacking a value theory that only another theory of free choice can fill. In some cases, scholars have gone as far as imputing this missing link of 'choice'.[6] This interpretation leads to the same result, though, according to Windelband,[7] which is that natural right is 'die volle Entfaltung des Egoismus [the full unfolding of egoism]', or, as Steffen puts it, 'die Geltung des Faustrechts, des Rechts des Stärkeren [the validation of the law of the jungle, the right of the strongest]'.[8] Proceeding with rather more caution on this theme of absolute licence, Tuck (1979: 141–2) writes of Spinoza that 'a substantial part of his theory looks more like that of the early Hobbes or the Seldenians than that of De Cive', and quotes Spinoza in the following translation:

> [T]he right and law of nature, under which all are born and for the most part live, forbids nothing save what nobody desires and nobody can do; it forbids neither strife, nor hatred, nor anger, nor deceit; in short, it is opposed to nothing appetite can suggest.

Tuck draws parallels with the work of English theorists such as Jeremy Taylor and James Vaughan, both of whom regarded the state of nature in even more anarchic terms than the early Hobbes. It is suggested that Spinoza could have had access to these views through de la Court's *Polityke Weeg-Schaal* (which Spinoza did own at his death) or through Hobbes' *Elements of Law* or even Selden's *De Jure Naturali et Gentium juxta disciplinum Ebraeorum*, the latter two of which Tuck notes Spinoza did not own at his death.[9] Tuck admits, however, that Spinoza's view could have been arrived at by way of his 'idiosyncratic metaphysics' (1979: 142).

It is C.E. Vaughan (1960: II, 75), though, who pushes further and has it that Spinoza 'will have nothing [of Hobbes'] hybrid "law of nature", half prudence, half duty', which attempts to find some theory of duty over against selfish motivation. For Spinoza, writes C.E. Vaughan, 'the "law of nature" is . . . merely a convenient phrase for the results yielded by considerations of prudence and expediency. As a law of moral obligation he rejects it root and branch' (ibid.). As we have seen, similar conclusions are drawn by Den Uyl, who, for his part, draws on and expands Gail Belaief's treatment of *Spinoza's Philosophy of Law* (1971) in his own *Power, State and Freedom* (1983), which, insofar as it addresses natural right, follows Belaief closely in structure and intent. Our concern in each of these cases, as already expressed, is that little or no critical advance is taken into the 'considerations of prudence and expediency' whereby the content of Spinoza's thinking is revealed. Prudence and expediency appear to be thrown into the same basket as anarchic licence, thus denying Spinoza's complex ideas the room to express themselves.

Another scholar approaching Spinoza's theory of natural right from the angle of jurisprudence is Simone Goyard-Fabre (1987[10] and 2002). In both works, Hobbes and Spinoza are compared and distinguished helpfully at the level of their physics of the conatus, and the trap of homonymy is highlighted and largely avoided. Goyard-Fabre continues, however, to ascribe a little too much Hobbism to Spinoza in stating that: 'According to Spinoza it is not a power, but the essential capacity of each being to act according to Nature and its nature',[11] which appears a fair assessment of the opening to TTPXVI, but only on its own terms and not in light of the conclusions of the Ethics. One of the traps is to assume that one's own nature is lustful and that that is necessarily a bad thing; that, as we have seen above, the state of nature is one of anarchic licence. The Hobbist horror of reliance on human nature thus comes out in the stress Goyard-Fabre places (1987: 234–5) on the link between unreason and the state of nature, claiming that both Hobbes and Spinoza 'are in agreement on the necessity for man of leaving the state of nature'.[12] This is doubly surprising given Goyard-Fabre's quotation at the head of the 1987 article of Spinoza's letter to Jelles, which famously avers that, in opposition to Hobbes, the state of nature continues in the civil state. Surely this contradicts Spinoza's own distinction between the '*statu naturali*' and the '*civitas*' in EIVP37 Sch. 2, but even in the Appendix to EIV, Spinoza repeats that leaving nature is impossible. It is the manner in which one reconciles this apparent contradiction that is the key to avoiding certain errors. Evidently aware of this supposed problematic, Goyard-Fabre ingeniously approaches Spinoza's treatment of the social contract by distinguishing this creation of reason from a social pact that represents the desire to be in the state structure and locates its binding-ness in the utility thereof. The argument then runs that:

> pact and contract are not two distinct and successive stages of the passage of the state of nature to the civil state: they are both simultaneous and

> complementary figures of the act by which individuals transfer their essential rights in society.
>
> (ibid.)[13]

While putting emphasis on the 'discipline of reason' over against '*cupiditas*', Goyard-Fabre correctly notes that the idea of the pact and related Hobbesian concepts are jettisoned by Spinoza in Chapter II of the *Tractatus politicus*. One can already sense, however, in Ch. XVI of the TTP, that at some point, as Spinoza discusses the binding nature of utility, the philosopher himself has lost faith in the idea of the social contract. The second scholium to EIVP37 in connection with the Appendix to that Part offers an interesting *complexum* of the changing position. In view of this abandonment of the Hobbist apparatus of power, Goyard-Fabre concludes that Spinoza the metaphysician is quasi-revolutionary in his approach to questions of law, but seemingly only in the negative sense to which our metaphysicians would allude – that law is merely the expression of the power of the ruling class, be it one or many or all. In this, Goyard-Fabre seemingly fails to realise the different purposes that reason and its relation to law are playing in Hobbes and Spinoza's respective theories. In Hobbes, reason determines laws, which are used to at once limit and distribute maximally the pre-existing freedom of human bodies. As we shall see, in Spinoza's ideal schema, reason and laws are used to infuse transindividuals[14] with new freedom – freedom as yet not envisaged. We will discover that over and above the Hobbesian-style conatus to persevere in one's being, there is a specifically Spinozist conatus to mutate.

Part of the problem with the existing jurisprudential approaches seems largely to arise in the stress on Spinoza's theory of the social contract, which, it has long been known, he works out of his system. It may be that this stress comes from the ease with which comparisons with Hobbes may be drawn, but tends to lead to little time being granted to the innovative aspects of the *Tractatus politicus* (Negri being the notable exception) (1991: 192ff.), and indeed Spinoza's work on the divine law (TTPIV), which appears to be a working out of a legal theory almost entirely in the absence of Hobbesian influence.[15] One further feels that there is perhaps a lack of sensitivity to the wide and ancient abyss that separates the respective physics of Hobbes and Spinoza, something that repeatedly manifests itself in attempts to construe Spinoza's physics of bodies as grounded upon Hobbesian atomism (cf. among many others, Matheron, Goyard-Fabre). It does not seem to have occurred to jurisprudential critics in particular that Spinoza may be starting from metaphysical premises that actually have a greater ancestral resemblance to those implicitly maintained by the natural legal theorists of his time (Grotius, Pufendorf, whom they array against Spinoza). We would advance the conjecture that Spinoza concluded very quickly that those natural law theories substituted pseudo-theological fictions for a deeper understanding of the metaphysical nature of *Deus sive Natura*, a fate that had befallen Stoic philosophy in its late period. As such, Spinoza was moved to work out a more materialistic theory of law and the state, which he began by reinterpreting (in TTPIV) the classical Aristotelean structure of general and particular law, and justice, which was taught by Heereboord at Leiden. It is a matter of great debate whether Spinoza was already fully aware of the doctrines of Hobbes, but he almost certainly was aware of the politico-theoretical thrust when he began writing TTPXVI, which imports Hobbes' theory of the social contract. This issue, as Laerke writes, is certainly complicated.[16] We know that Spinoza owned a copy of Hobbes' *De Cive* at the time of his death,[17] and that Latin and Dutch translations of *Leviathan* were available to him from 1667 and 1668, respectively.[18] Lazzeri[19] and Balibar[20] severally believe that Spinoza studied Hobbes' political works to a great degree, and Curley goes as far as to declare that, despite some scholars continuing to deny any direct influence of Hobbes on Spinoza, he is 'virtually certain that Spinoza knew Leviathan' at least by the time he was composing the final draft of the TTP.[21] Yet just because Christian Huyghens, Isaac Newton or the Bernouillis were fully conversant with Descartes' analysis of curves and machines, this does not mean they deployed the same theoretical principles when pursuing research concerning the same problems.[22] So, we say, with Spinoza and his knowledge of Hobbes (as to which more shortly).

We agree with Wernham that in writing this chapter, Spinoza comes quickly to realise that Hobbes' system will not fit in any sensible way into his system, because the binding nature of a contract dissolves into a general theory of determinate desire for utility in Spinoza's theory of the passions.[23] As such, it seems Spinoza began slowly moving away from Hobbist natural right theory and parts of his Aristotelean instruction back to a position more consistent with his developing metaphysical principles. It is in fact, we maintain, easier to see what Spinoza intended if one works up from these principles, than if one tries either to push Hobbes to be consistent, or at least to dismantle the Hobbist social contract theory back to a more Spinozist conception. This is indeed the methodology this research proposes, to show the difference from Hobbes by taking us as if by the hand along Spinoza's very different path to his idea of natural right and its expression in the city, thereby in the result revealing and affirming a conception of right that stands alone, and not merely as a curious and misfiring offshoot of legal thought in the Early Modern period.

We think it important explicitly to underline that we are making no 'humanistic' claim of history or interpretation to the effect that Spinoza read little or no Hobbes, or misunderstood or did not particularly care about the *elements* of Hobbist philosophy. This book is not going to sift through contemporary evidence in search of proofs that *x* thesis of Spinoza is exactly the same as *y* thesis of Hobbes (or not) and, furthermore, Hobbes' intellectual fingerprint can be found upon the core of Spinoza's thought. Such research is valuable, but would it not be rather discourteous to a philosopher who collapses assent into determinate will to carve out a realm of probability where it is the necessary concept in itself that we are asked to consider. This book is interested in the standing forth of this concept. One might be tempted to oppose to such a humanistic methodology a playful hermetic stance, but if we are honest the approach we have adopted is that of attempting to 'get at' the concept at work in Spinoza's mind and to let this stand free and alone, liberated as it were from dependence on Hobbism – liberated in overcoming this dependence. This is after all what comes across at the politico-juridical level. As Hampshire has noted,[24] while Hobbes and Spinoza both oppose those who derive laws from supernatural first principles by arguing that it is for each to use her reason in a political setting, they separate on what using reason means. Hobbes ultimately devolves onto a calculus of probabilities in which rational men determine relative pros and cons in debate to settle on decisions that best keep down irrational but nevertheless mechanically determined desires. Spinoza on the contrary argued that settlement on rational political decisions is necessarily driven and derives solely from 'irrational' desire. Settling for the least worst is passivity; it does not express the laws of one's own nature and the resultant decision is not in common, does not express concord. For Spinoza, at the heart of every action there is the definite expression of the actor's law. A rational law under the second species of knowledge should aim to express laws common as between citizens to the greatest degree feasible.

A mathematical analogy might be in order: the physico-geometer David Hestenes tells the story of how one day he was working on an established mathematical description of a physical process, and realised that one of the terms of the equation was redundant: it added nothing to the description of what was occurring. Hestenes reported this to his father, himself a mathematician, declaring that he had deleted the obsolete term. His father's response was that the son had realised something that very many students fail to grasp, that the symbols used to represent mathematics are not at all the same as the concept they are trying to express. The symbols could take any form, the method could be other than geometrical, the concept was the goal; the concept should structure these expressions just as the location of the target structures the various possible tensions of the archer. Our view is that Spinoza grasped the concept – the formal essence of his natural right theory – in his mind (his beatific vision) and that his symbolic structure could have been otherwise had it so been determined. We want this concept to stand forth and will use in some modest way Spinoza's synthetic method to enable this; we shall endeavour to outline how the concept constructed itself in the eyes of Spinoza's mind.[25]

1.2 What is different about Spinoza's conception of right?

The claim that Spinoza's natural right theory lacks normative content has striking echoes with the severe criticisms early Stoicism suffered due to its alleged adherence to a similar doctrine of strict causal determinism. To accusations of inspiring defeatism, Chrysippos is reported by Eusebios[26] to have said: 'if a champion boxer enters the ring knowing he will necessarily win the fight, he does not therefore leave his hands by his sides'. A similar, mechanist's response can be imagined from Spinoza: *if I inform the dockworker that no matter what curses he utters the lever he is using will not exhibit sufficient natural right to lift a 100 lb load, he might rather put his energies into emending the lever – by extending the lever arm – so that it does have in the result the natural right to lift 100 lb even without being sworn at.* The 'moral' of this story is that machines are amoral; the Cartesian subtext is that we are all machines.[27]

At the heart of the jurisprudential confusion about Spinoza's theory of natural right seems to be the exasperation that the equation of right with that which exists effectively collapses natural right into 'anarchy', removing from it any normative content other than Job's acceptance, and thus rendering the concept a useless and peripheral outgrowth of an otherwise interesting metaphysics. Our argument is essentially that it is only because Spinoza reduces the difference between natural right and actuality to zero that any philosophical theory of *natural* right becomes possible; this zero or in-difference of natural right is precisely what permits Spinoza to posit a natural (physical) law about how right works, and to derive from this law all its necessary conditions. It is only by understanding this law that it is then possible to advance a theory of right in the city as an application of this physical law in the social space.

This research aims to illustrate the sources that drove Spinoza to this theory of right, and then to establish that theory's content and application by Spinoza from the simplest case to the idea of the city. Let us first, however, elaborate on our interpretation of Spinoza's theory of right, beginning with a key quotation:

> [W]hatever each man does from the laws of his own nature, he does by the highest right of Nature, and he has so much right over Nature as his power extends. [. . . *quicquid unusquisque homo ex legibus suae naturae agit, id summo Naturae Jure agit, tantumquae in Naturam habet juris, quantum potentia valet.*]

The false interpretation of this phrase would have it that might makes right, and that each person (or thing) has as much right as it has power at any given moment. In fact, we will argue, this fails to see the fundamental distinction Spinoza is drawing between power and power exercised, which amounts to the asymmetric distinction between cause and effect. If one approaches the question of right from a jurisprudential angle, and wishes to determine right as that which declares the ought of a situation, this is to take the right as a starting point, draw out its possibilities or facultative potential, and then to assess these potentials against what has actually been permitted to happen. It is a method reliant on ignoring the prehistory of a right and either guessing at what may be 'naturally' a right as in the case of Aquinas or Pufendorf, or by simply assuming a void of free will that spontaneously sends forth new effects into the world between which we must mediate, as in Hobbes and even more so Selden. It seems as if Spinoza cuts both of these routes out by permitting absolutely anything, but then declaring it natural only as far as this right extends or prevails. In other words, Spinoza's theory of natural right proceeds nowhere. This, however, is not at all how Spinoza approaches the question – as in so many aspects of his thinking he rather outrageously considers matters once preserved for moralists and theologians by means of geometry and physics. For Spinoza, right is indeed a kind of terminal point, but this is because he is interested entirely in what led up to this point. This, as we shall show, is the methodology of the mechanist and physicist; specifically, an autodidact physicist fascinated primarily by the statics and nascent kinematics of *machines*.

Insofar as we consider its common notions, a machine placed under the same conditions does the same thing every time; to permit a variation in outcomes would defy the divine or natural order and no finite thing could ever change this – *for against necessity not even the gods make war.*[28] Yet this is not a recipe for the fatalism or juridical nihilism (think of Nietzsche). It is precisely *because* the possibility of variation in effect is set exactly to zero for any given body that Spinoza believes we are in a position to treat matters of right as matters of geometry and mechanics. Put simply, if we cannot lift a weight, let us build a tool that assists our power of acting. If we build a lever and this is insufficient, let us emend the lever, and our conception of it, perhaps by extending the arm and adding a weight. By conceiving of a series of interconnected machines, we can increase our power of acting – our natural right – without ever defying the basic rule that no thing has more right than its power extends. It is immediately seen that the interconnected system of bodies that increases a human's power of acting is nothing other than the city: politics, grounded in the theory of natural right, becomes a massive constructivist exercise in right emendation.

We cannot ask *what is natural to a thing whereby we can determine its right* because we do not yet know what a body can do. Wittgenstein argued[29] that rules-as-machines or symbolic machines are the mythologising of machines such that we treat rules (and so laws) as the machines themselves – as their inner determinations to work. With this myth we fool ourselves about the nature of rules' formulation and about how in fact we apply them. We think we have grasped the future as it ought to be, but we have only grasped the future as it must be. Spinoza does not deny the last sentiment, but nor does he accept the inapplicability of his method. Wittgenstein, he could plausibly argue, is attacking the myth of the machine and the response to this myth ought not to be its abandonment but critical engagement with it. Spinoza 'went further than anyone else' because he rigorously followed the logic of the machine to its end, establishing an absolute freedom that Hegel would argue is the condition for rule-making. *Pace* Wittgenstein, Spinoza will show that it is because his machines are not permitted the least degree of play, even between pin and socket,[30] that the full circle of creation emerges from the system. Spinoza constructs freedom positively; he does not tell us what does not work and name the leftovers 'liberty'.

We cannot pretend that the will simply 'swerves' motive forces into existence because this introduces superstition into the world and, Spinoza believes, makes our knowledge of its fixed and immutable laws unattainable. Quotations of select parts of Spinoza's work that seem to support the 'anarchic licence' interpretation completely ignore his militant commitment to the efficient causes – to common and particular natures – a libel that is inexcusable even among jurists given that Spinoza carefully and consistently through his works defines natural right by reference to the laws of each thing's nature; not laws of nature, but the physical characteristics of the thing in question that are fed into the general laws of nature to produce particular effects. For Spinoza, the drunk who runs raving through the streets does not act by the highest right of nature, nor, necessarily, does Genghis Khan.[31]

Rather than a simple acceptance of might as right and the fact as the highest good, Spinoza is asking us to *work back* from natural right to emendation of power. The proper ethical question here is thus referred back to power, with the hierarchy of goodness now determined by reference to the infinite power of God or Nature expressed as the eternal return of the present. Not a bland, empty power, but a power that Spinoza believes to be within our cognition as intuition. Yet this third cognition can only arise from the second kind; only from working back from natural right. It is only by establishing precisely how our changing world is chained by the bonds of finite power that we can discover power enough to free ourselves.

Thus it is most important to begin correctly with natural right. For instance, we believe that that which has not adequately been distinguished is the difference between power/right, on the one hand, and the very precise phrase '*quantum potentia valet*': as far as [this] power extends or prevails. The meaning of this statement is clear enough to Spinoza: natural right is power projected onto a line. This is the inverse sense ascribed to it in the literature, where, for example, Curley summarises[32] his discussion of the doctrine as 'the co-extensiveness of right and power', and indeed Spinoza's meaning will be less clear to most readers possessing a legal perspective.

An example, drawn from Descartes:[33] a small child lifts a weight of 1 lb by 1 ft. A grown man then lifts the same weight the same distance. Finally, an army, by means of a simple pulley, lifts the same weight the same distance. What Descartes calls 'force*'[34] and we would call 'work' is the same in every case; no matter who did the work (or force*), the amount of work done is the same (one unit of work). Descartes has a simple geometric understanding of what has happened: he takes the effort needed to move the given weight and projects it along a line as far as the weight is actually moved, thus giving us a rectangle. The area of this rectangle is the work or force* done – in Spinoza's words, the natural right a thing has is its power as far as it extends [along a line]. We humbly suggest that describing this concept as the co-extensiveness of right and power at least opens the door to miscomprehension, for it seems to suggest that power and natural right are the same, in a manner that would be akin to suggesting that a particle's acceleration and the distance it travelled are the same. They are linked – absolutely so – but they are distinguished by our temporal focus: what happened instantaneously/what happened over some relative time. The dimensional simplicity of present natural right – the product of two magnitudes is a scalar quantum – is perhaps the mischief Spinoza is seeking to address, for it is precisely this simplicity that disguises the theoretical components of natural right that make it up.

If we can understand this reasoning, we can see that it is quite absurd to believe that just because the child, man, or army all did the same work, they all have the same power. Evidently they do not, and Descartes makes this point. The extension of power in this case – the actuality of natural right – tells us nothing of what else child, man, or army could do. *Per* Spinoza, we do not yet know what a body can do (EIII Pref.). It will be objected, however, that Spinoza's determinism prevents him from contemplating what else a person could have done in a given moment; only what is actually done has right by Nature. Surely the army would have continued to lift the weight much farther or more quickly than the child, and it is false to assume that they stopped lifting without some special determination that did not act on the child. To this, Spinoza's doctrine also has a response: no thing endeavours to do what it actually did (save *Deus sive Natura*), but rather indeed endeavours to act indefinitely. The child, in endeavouring to lift the weight, does it no less indefinitely than the army; each lifts 'by the Highest Right of Nature' until determined to do otherwise (EIIIP4, EIVP37 Sch. 2). It is a question of the relative conditions in each case, for were the child operating within suitable conditions, they could lift the weight to the very edge of the universe in an instant. No one is a kingdom within a kingdom, all are subject to ambient conditions, but this does not at all deny that by the power a thing has, it endeavours to extend itself as far as it is permitted. Thus already in finitude a gap opens up between natural right as that which *actually* happened, and the finite consciousness of exerting a right, which always *formally* extends indefinitely but for external determination. The normative question for the individual – what should I do? – makes no sense; every individual has always already willed *formaliter* to do all necessary to escape destruction. And more than this, we will show in Chapter 5, the individual also endeavours towards its own mutation – the augmentation thus of its *potentia* and its *potestas*. Spinoza appears within the limits of the conatus theory as a prophet of unlimited growth, with all the consequences that follow for modernity.

This argument embraces determinism, but on condition that each finite thing *actualiter* performs the least possible action, a doctrine that *pace* Leibniz, is not simply plucked from thin air by Spinoza and Descartes, but that derives from the reciprocity of God or Nature's constancy (immutability) and His or Its infinite power distributed through each finite existing thing as its conatus to persevere in its being (inertia). The immutability of God or Nature is to be understood as the ability to remain the same in flux, to eternally return as the same, despite local variations. For a finite thing, the parts of which change, the sum total of all local changes must *balance out* such that the global change equals zero. Immutability thus ensures that the striving of each finite thing buffers up against each other thing – there is always some effect (EIP36) – and that if a new effect is to occur in the universe, the cause must act against a universe doing its utmost to prevent change. Least action results from this accommodation of Highest Rights. Accordingly, each finite thing, while expressing a nature, has not by virtue of that nature a special predetermined place in a pre-existing hierarchy of orders. The ethical hierarchy entirely devolves onto the chance encounters or variations of the universe, which determine an existing thing to produce effects of greater and greater power. Each finite thing is forever endeavouring to do everything it wills, but it is externally determined to produce very few of these. The ethical task turns from the false question of trying to change the actual expression of natural right to an investigation of the finite things and their formal rights – that is the question: *what else could this body do?* This question, however, rests on a more fundamental thesis: we can only begin to discover what else a body can do by increasing its power of working. Some jurisprudential interpreters of Spinoza will not even admit variations of power (cf. the discussion of Den Uyl in Chapter 5), but even those who will, do not even begin, we argue, to realise how seriously Spinoza took this thesis, this first principle of his method: *what happens when we pass to the limit of power?*

A final example: imagine a child can at best lift the 1 lb weight 1 ft, whereas the grown man could lift 3 lb 1 ft in equal time. Spinoza would say that the man has three times the natural right of the child. But to illustrate his point, Spinoza then erects a block and tackle (pulley) system – a machine that will aid the child to lift a weight of 4 lb in equal time. Now, as this occurs, the child has more natural right than the man, and we have learned a lesson about the natural right doctrine. As Spinoza makes abundantly clear in the TdIE, we must make tools to increase our power of working, and with these new tools make others, and so on in the endeavour to attain beatitude.

The city is such a tool. The analysis of natural right is the juridico-political dynamics that Spinoza undertakes, the object of which is the constitution of a social machine, or tool, that every citizen (or the most possible) is permitted to actualise their power to the greatest degree. The purpose of this book is to illustrate the theoretical origins of this conception and to reconstruct the outlines of the dynamics of natural right. In so doing, we hope to overturn those crude 'might makes right' interpretations of Spinoza in favour of a constructive, natural philosophical theory that liberates natural right even as it binds it to the unerring actual. For Spinoza, it is only because natural right could not have been otherwise that we can properly begin to understand what a body can do. This is Spinoza's wager: that 'right' as 'ius' can only be properly understood as 'right' as 'rectitude', and thus determine perfection and degree of power. We do not have to follow Spinoza in making this bet, but we can attempt to understand that which caused him to lay the wager. As we shall see in Chapter 3, which examines Spinoza's mechanics, it is a question of sympathetically realising that Spinoza is expressing one conception in the language of another, and problems arise because the interpreter assumes the language is ostensibly adequate to the conception it *signifies* rather than that which it *expresses*. If Spinozism is a language game, then its grammar has a powerful materiality to it. In physics, we will show how Spinoza states a theory of kinematics that signifies a conception of kinematics but actually expresses a conception of static forces. In legal theory, Spinoza's wager is that his conception of dynamic physical forces, of power, is the only adequate concept that an *ethical* legal theoretical language can express. It is a move that has parallels in the adopted cynicism of Zenon the Stoic: to take the signifiers of commonly held theories about the state, and subvert them with powerful concepts.[35]

1.3 The right-producing machines

We will show how Spinoza explicates his rich conception of natural right by applying his key methodological principle of taking power to the limit in five transitions through this work:

1 from the formal being to formal essence (Ch. 2);[36]
2 from power of moving to power of resting (Ch. 3);
3 from motion and rest to the machine (Ch. 4);
4 from finite machine to infinite machine (Ch. 5); and
5 from city-machine to imperium intuitivum (Ch. 6).

One will conclude from these transitions that, when we look at this conception of natural right, we must always refer any instance to the machine that produces it. Natural right does not begin and end with an idealised individual, any more than the motions of a pulley can be derived from the hauler's wishes about the loads he is trying to raise. The Spinozan doctrine that in a *union* each part communicates a fixed proportion of motion and rest to every other and thereby ensures a constancy in the whole, needs to be grasped. In short, this doctrine can be written symbolically such that parts P, Q, R . . . always maintain the same relation and that between them the total change must always be zero. Thus if we change P in some small way p, in order that zero be maintained, Q, R . . . must compensate for this motion with some q, r . . . Hence, $Pp + Qq + Rr + \ldots = 0$. Such symbolic representation, while clearly anachronistic, we claim nevertheless expresses Spinoza's intuition: when we consider any instance of natural right p, we must refer immediately to the machine in which it occurs. The machine thereby constitutes the surface on which the activity of the world is written.

Yet Spinoza's thought replicates this basic machine model across three orders depending upon the degree of expression considered. The highest degree of God or Nature's power put to one side, we are left with degrees of disposed motion and relatively disposed motion. As an example of relatively disposed motion, let us take an arbitrary cube of incompressible fluid. For Spinoza, whose letters document his hydrostatic experiments, anything can technically be considered an incompressible fluid relative to its surrounding medium. This cube of fluid is a machine, no less than a pulley or a lever. If we push one corpuscle P by some small variation p, then all the other corpuscles in the cube must accommodate this variation (by virtue of incompressibility) – they either get pushed out of the way, or move to fill the potential vacuum (Spinoza does not consider elasticity or shear stress, and denies the vacuum). Thus any natural right actualised in the cube – in this water machine – complies with a version of the rule $Pp + Qq + Rr + \ldots = 0$, whereby the parts of the machine move in a manner that retains the initial volume of the cube of water. Spinoza utilises this water machine when he constructs a rigid tube in which water weighing down at the upturned end instantaneously communicates its endeavour to the water at the other end. This, however, is only a matter of relatively disposed motion; of motion in equal times.

Spinoza's ingenuity is to raise this model by a power through his doctrine of transitions, whereby variations in motions also operate according to this mechanical principle. We are talking here about accelerations and decelerations in movement and rest. Over and above stating that changes in place (relative motion) may be linked to a machine such that the total change = 0, it is our view that Spinoza also holds that changes in acceleration linked in a machine also produce a global change = 0. Such a machine would communicate a tendency to motion – an inclination or desire – to all parts. It will endeavour to be, but also to produce some effect. And each such effect is modal, understood as an expression of a given machine's law through other machines. We will show that this is in fact Spinoza's solution to problems in Cartesian celestial mechanics, which is itself a model for Spinoza's political theory, but here a simpler example suffices. Spinoza tells us to think of a sling propelling a stone around a point.[37] The constancy of the sling communicates its rotational motion at every instant to the stone. This is a machine for the communication of inclinations (given that Spinoza regards even a stone as conscious of its conatus). We can perhaps discern how questions of natural right, fundamentally linked to questions of machines, are also linked to questions of consciousness. We hope to show how just as machines produce natural right (i.e. work), so they produce consciousness, and insofar as natural right is considered as tendency to motion imparted by a machine, natural right and consciousness are linked. Yet as the order of transitions indicates, Spinoza does not stop with finite determinations, for he then asks: *what would an infinite machine do? What natural right would it exhibit?* It is only in answering this question that we can begin adequately to assess Spinoza's contribution to natural right theory.

1.4 The mechanisation of right – the juridification of the world

The Spinozan theory of natural right can be seen as at once pushing the juridification of the world to extremes – a tendency in many natural right theories – but also demystifying that juridification. Natural right theories seeking to rest on the God-given light of reason as the *ought* of a situation refer back to an essence, or to some innate sense of justice, always ultimately resting on supposition, priestly prejudice or similar authority. Spinoza concretises natural right by placing it in specific and determined physical dimensions that, mark well, say nothing about what ought to happen at the cost of declaring *everything* about what is happening. For Duns Scotus it was sovereign power that was well-ordered, this power assisted by an inalienable absolute power that could intervene in the good order of the state.[38] This power is ultimately simple and mysterious. For Spinoza this excessive power is itself well-ordered as the infinite mechanical power of God or Nature.

This double well-ordered theory of right involves linking natural right to right-producing-machines, each with its common and particular laws determining its productions. If every right is a product of a machine, and every machine expresses its law, then Spinoza's juridification of the universe may be described as a reduction of everything to right-machines. This mechanisation of law heralds the Enlightenment's view of the man-machine. To coin De la Mettrie's infamous dictum, Spinoza's view of right conceives the juridical individual as just a tube, with a mouth at one end and an anus at the other. Yet furthermore, this mechanisation of divine and natural law heralds the God-machine, which may be placed in comparison to the Stoics: 'they say that God is an animal . . .'[39] and the Hegelian *Life* or *absolute concept*.[40]

This foundational linkage of natural right to a world of machines (and nothing but machines) can be approached in two ways – a critique of mechanist reductionism or an explication of machinic thinking. In this book, we pursue the latter path, partly because the former critique has had a venerable history, partly because we have always believed that the more practical way to test a machine is simply to set it running rather than speculate on its name. This is Spinoza's own thesis: we can only examine effects, and integrate causes that are expressed by them. Therefore, this research will proceed to build up the insights needed to comprehend why Spinoza should regard the couple *right-machine* named *thing* (*res*) as clear and distinct. We will then proceed to establish how this view of natural right is conceived in considerable detail: we will explore the nature of these right-machines, and, moving from the simplest to the most complex machines, we will establish the manner in which Spinoza regards the city itself, in the limit, as a right-machine.

As we undertake this analysis, it will be shown that this mechanical view of the world is not merely a metaphorical description, but in intent is regarded by Spinoza as programmatic. To know that natural right is produced by machines is *no* different from knowing that a lever can in determinate circumstances lift 1 lb by 1 ft. The right of the lever is related to its mechanical nature, and so in order to vary the right, we examine the mechanical nature and make changes here. *This is only possible if natural right is fixed and determined.* Rather than enslaving right to the determinate order of things, Spinoza liberates right by attaching it to a practical philosophy of machines. We look not to changing the right, which is now impossible, but to changing the conditions of right, that is the machine or machines that produced that effect. We will see that the constant striving of finite existence, the striving to continue to be (the *conatus*), must not be taken as the sum of Spinoza's position and that it is augmented by the infinite power within finite things that is expressed in them as a kind of *source* of an inexhaustible power to produce an infinity of infinitely many modes. To use a phrase from Spinoza's book collection, a power considered as a *fons vitae*. So to reiterate: the Spinozan right-machine not merely expresses and accepts in the manner of a vulgar Stoic the concrete power relations of the world, but is driven from within incessantly to carry out the primary[41] causal task of recombining power relations in the world into ever new forms (the combative Stoicism of Cleanthes). Given the intimate link between right and consciousness, this is a natural right theory of changing, or raising, consciousness of this innate power.

There is, however, a deeper reason for pursuing this constructivist approach to Spinoza's thought. This is for us one of the key features of the natural philosophical movement of the Early Modern and Enlightenment periods extending into today (though having Hellenic precursors). That is the pursuit of a 'method' such that this method begins to force results upon us that were neither sought nor necessarily desired. These 'monsters', as we term them, are perhaps hidden from Spinoza's view by his refusal of the nascent analytical tools available to him and the unavailability of the logical tools that could have pushed his thinking that all is machine to the limit. This preference for the circle rather than hyperbola, the line rather than the curve, this impatience of the motion to the God-concept, renders Spinozism beguiling; it is difficult in any one work to both treat of Spinoza's detailed innovations and undergo the task of adequately extrapolating the complex responses to this thought that bring out its limitations. We will endeavour to sketch such criticisms as best we can through the text.

Of necessity we will only be focusing on certain aspects of Spinoza's thought, primarily because we have sought to clarify those related to natural right and did not want to cloud the issue with argumentation concerning parallel issues. What we have specifically avoided here can be considered at least two ways depending on how one divides Spinoza's thinking. *First*, if we consider the epistemological division of (a) particular affects (b) general reason of the first kind (c) singular reason of the second kind (intuition), what we will do is focus on the generality to derive the singular, and will only point the singular in the direction of the particular in a broad manner in speaking of the social revelation of affects: the multitude. A more detailed analysis of the multitude is given in our work on the cosmopolis (2015, forthcoming). *Second*, the specific mechanistic interpretative tools we deploy do not exhaust the natural philosophy at play in Spinoza's work. The mechanistic interpretation is, as we believe we will show, at the heart of his doctrine of natural right, but affects/multitudes demand a different approach that pertains to the nature of the mode and its composition. *Third*, in the depths of Spinoza's thought there is a need to analyse the meta-mechanics of *Deus sive Natura*, by which I mean engage in the analysis of how the one substance in act is constructed according to the natural laws by which it is bound. This is a difficult task that would take us far beyond the scope of this work.

Notes

1 James Gregory (1638–1675), Scottish mathematician and astronomer, author of the *Optica Promota*, which Spinoza owned (cf. Appendix 1) defined, in his *Vera Circuli et Hyperbolae Quadratura* (1667), a new algebraic method of *passage to the limit*, which, in respect of a function, amounted to treating the function as performing 'any operation imaginable' (effectively an infinite series of operations) (cf. Kline 1972: 339).

2 Quoted in Kline n.1 *supra*.

3 'Negri on Spinoza's Political and Legal Philosophy' in Curley and Moreau (1990: 295).
4 Steffen, H. (1968: 99).
5 '. . . kann allerdings für Spinoza auch das Naturrecht nichts werthaftes, seinsollendes sein, sondern lediglich selbst Seiendes'.
6 Verbeek (2008: 269). Cf. the criticisms of Verbeek by Laerke in Garber and Rurtherford (2012: 114 n. 25). Laerke points out that Verbeek provides 'no textual evidence' for the claim that for Spinoza 'the power of all finite things is free' with the consequence that they may 'use the powers . . . given by nature in the way [they] choose . . .' (Verbeek 2008: 261). We seek in this work to provide precisely the arguments to support the claim that indeed finite things do express an infinite and free power, provided that 'free' is understood in a definite manner. We agree with Laerke, however, that the purported consequent cannot be ascribed to Spinoza: the 'free' power that is due to finite existing things does not necessitate a freedom of choice; rather, it is best considered an overflowing source of a power to emend or constant issuance of this free power into the world. To put it in simple terms, a tap once turned will release water into a basin until determined otherwise. It cannot choose how or how much water will flow. In the infinite case, the flow has already occurred everywhere, formally, such that the formal essences of the flow's occurrence are *there* to be actualised by finite relations.
7 Quoted in Steffen (ibid.).
8 Ibid.
9 Tuck suggests that Selden's work would have been 'particularly attractive to a Jew' (1979: 142), which perhaps suggests more about the state of Spinoza scholarship in the 1970s than anything about Spinoza.
10 'Hobbes et Spinoza ou La Différence des concepts – L'ampleur d'une litôte' (1987) 3 *Studia Spinozana* 229–258 at 232–233.
11 'Selon Spinoza, il n'est pas un pouvoir, mais la capacité essentielle de tout être d'agir selon la Nature et sa nature.'
12 'sont d'accord sur la nécessité pour l'homme de quitter l'état de nature'.
13 'pacte et contrat ne sont pas deux moments distincts et successifs du passage de l'état de nature à la condition civile: ce sont les deux figures simultanées et complémentaires de l'acte par lequel les individus transfèrent leurs droits primordiaux à la société'.
14 This concept is due to Balibar (1997).
15 Apart from the mirroring Hobbes distinction of natural law and right, TTP approaches Scholastic legal theories in its quasi-Thomistic legal categories, definitions of general and particular law, and theory of justice. This is not to say that Hobbes did not himself stray towards Aristotle's teachings.
16 Laerke, M. 'Leibniz on Spinoza's political philosophy' in Garber and Rutherford (2012: 111).
17 Cf. Appendix 1.
18 As noted by Curley in Garrett (1996: 336 n. 5).
19 (1987: 175). Cf. also his (1998).
20 (2007: 54).
21 Op. cit., n. 15 *supra*.
22 In fact, here we have three different theoretical conceptions in play, or more exactly, two different theoretical conceptions, and one conception that seemed almost wilfully untheoretical even as it was sound (that of Huyghens).
23 And see also Matheron (1988: 295) who advances the generally followed view that Spinoza adopts Hobbes' theory only to demolish it.
24 Hampshire (2005: 136–138).
25 In an earlier draft of this work, we were much more explict in our formal (re)construction of Spinoza's concept, especially in Chapters 4 and 5, but as Anton Schütz pointed out, this was both off-putting to many readers and out of keeping with a philosopher who so eschewed analytic formalism.

26 SVF 2.998.
27 Hence, this story's morality really is its utility.
28 Simonides quoted in Plato's *Protagoras* 345d.
29 (1958) at §§191–193.
30 (1958) at §194. Cf. also Mulhall (2001: 119ff.).
31 *Pace* Matheron (1985: 176).
32 In Garrett (1996: 318).
33 A detailed discussion of this example is undertaken in Chapter 3.
34 We will clarify Descartes' choice of words in Chapter 3.
35 E.g. there is only one city and all are fellow citizens, nurtured by a common law (SVF 1.262).
36 Alternatively, from the idea, which is determined not to be actualised, to the contraction around which modes coalesce in characteristic relations.
37 DPPIIP16.
38 For a discussion of the link between Duns Scotus and the development of the liberal political subject in the early modern period, see Muralt (2002).
39 SVF 2.1021.
40 *Logik* (1969: 279).
41 Primary in the sense of EIP16 Corol. 3.

Bibliography

Arnim, J. von. (1979) *Stoicorum veterum fragmenta* (4 vols), BG Teubner, Stuttgart.

Balibar, E. (1992) 'A note on "consciousness/conscience" in the *Ethics*' 8 *Studia Spinozana* 37–53.

—— (1997) 'Spinoza: from individuality to transindividuality' *Mededelingen vanwege het Spinozahuis*. Vol. 71. Eburon, NL.

—— (2007) *Spinoza and Politics*, Verso, London.

Belaief, G. (1971) *Spinoza's Philosophy of Law*, Mouton, The Hague.

Connelly, S. (2015 forthcoming) 'Cosmopolitanism for the love of multitudes' in T. Caraus and E. Paris (eds) *Post-Foundational Cosmopolitanism*, Routledge, London.

Curley, E. and Moreau, P. (1990) *Spinoza: Issues and Directions: The Proceedings of the Chicago Spinoza Conference*, E.J. Brill, Leiden.

Den Uyl, D.J. (1983) *Power, State and Freedom: An Interpretation of Spinoza's Political Philosophy*, Van Gorcum, Assen, The Netherlands.

Garber, D. and Rutherford, D. (2012) *Oxford Studies in Early Modern Philosophy VI*, Oxford University Press, Oxford.

Garrett, D. (ed.) (1996) *The Cambridge Companion to Spinoza*, Cambridge University Press, Cambridge.

Goyard-Fabre, S. (1997) 'Hobbes et Spinoza ou La Différence des concepts – L'ampleur d'une litôte' 3 *Studia Spinozana* 229.

—— (2002) *Les embarras philosophiques du droit naturel*, VRIN, Paris.

Grotius, H. (1625) *De jure belli ac pacis libri tres, in quibus jus naturae & gentium, itme juris publici praceipua explicantur*, Nicolaum Buon, Paris.

—— (1755) [1627] *De veritate religionis christianae, cum notulis J. Clerici* (2 vols), J. Nourse, London.

—— (1970) [1648] *De imperio summarum potestatum circa sacra*, 1690 Frankfurt/M. ed., reprint Scientia Verlag, Aalen.

Hampshire, S. (2005) *Spinoza and Spinozism*, Oxford University Press, Oxford.

Heereboord, A. (1654) *Meletemata philosophica, in quibus pleraeque res metaphysicae ventilantur, tota ethica explicatur, universa physica per theoremata et commentarios exponitur, summa rerum logicarum per disputationes traditur*, Neomagi: ex officina A. ab Hoogenhuysen, 1664, 1ère édition Leiden [Paris BNF R-2400].

Hegel, G.W.F. (1969) *Werke in zwanzig Bänden*, Suhrkamp Verlag, Frankfurt am Main. The Roman numeral following the year refers to the volume number.

Kline, M. (1972) *Mathematical Thought from Ancient to Modern Times* (3 vols), Oxford University Press, Oxford.

Lazzeri, C. (1987) 'L'economique et le politique chez Hobbes et chez Spinoza' 3 *Studia Spinozana* 175–227.

—— (1998) *Droit, Pouvoir et Liberte – Spinoza, critique de Hobbes*, PUF, Paris.

McShea, R.J. (1968) *The Political Philosophy of Spinoza*, Columbia, New York.

Matheron, A. (1988) *Individu et Communauté chez Spinoza*, Editions de Minuit, Paris.

Mulhall, S. (2001) *Inheritance and Originality: Wittgenstein, Heidegger, Kierkegaard*, Oxford University Press, Oxford.

Muralt, A. de (2002) *L'unité de la philosophie politique: Duns Scot, Occam et Suarez, au libéralisme contemporain*, VRIN, Paris.

Negri, A. (1991) *The Savage Anomaly: The Power of Spinoza's Metaphysics and Politics*, University of Minnesota Press, Minneapolis, MN.

Newton, Sir I. (1999) *The Principia: Mathematical Principles of Natural Philosophy*, I. Bernard Cohen and A. Whitman (trans.), University of California Press, Berkeley, CA.

Plato (1992) *Protagoras*, S. Lombardo and K. Bell (trans.), Hackett, Indianapolis, IN.

Steffen, H. (1968) *Recht und Staat im System Spinozas*, H. Bouvier u. Co. Verlag, Bonn.

Tuck, R. (1979) *Natural Rights Theories: Their Origins and Development*, Cambridge University Press, Cambridge.

Vaughan, C.E. (1960) *Studies in the History of Political Philosophy Before and After Rousseau Vol. 1*, Manchester, England.

Verbeek, T. (2008) 'Spinoza on natural rights' 17 (3) *Intellectual History Review* 257–275.

Wernham, A.G. (1958) *Benedict de Spinoza: The Political Works*, Clarendon Press, Oxford.

Wittgenstein, L. (1958) *Philosophical Investigations*, G.E.M. Anscombe (trans.), Basil Blackwell, Oxford.

Chapter 2

The role of the attributes in the generation of right

> [T]he more attributes we discover in the same thing or substance, the clearer is our knowledge of that substance.
>
> Descartes, PPI[11][1]

2.1 Introduction

In this chapter, we seek to elucidate the metaphysical basis of Spinoza's theory of power in the attributes. God's power is his essence (EIP34), and the essences fall categorically within the attributes. Therefore, we must pass directly to a full appreciation of the attributes and their function as organisers (or 'orderers') of natural right. Drawing particularly on Descartes' theory of forces, and the neo-Stoic tendencies abroad in the Low Countries as background influences on Spinoza, we will endeavour to show how the attributes may be properly considered *events* of God or Nature; a theoretical construct that is immanent to every singular thing in act, and the key to understanding power and thus right. A key aim of this chapter will be to show the importance of avoiding an interpretation of the attributes that (however implicitly) permits a raw, absolute, or free power in God or the modes. We will try to show why the essences are not little seeds or algorithms for bodies, or souls waiting to be actualised, but, following the Cartesian philosophy to its limit, just as quantifiable and determinate as are bodies themselves, and as such just as open to variable implication as explication. We thus seek to prepare the ground for establishing a distinction between a preformationist interpretation of natural right, in which everything is determined as right from some imagined 'beginning', and an immanent determinist interpretation of natural right, which opens the way to its cognition in constituting natural right.

For this purpose, we propose to examine: (a) the Cartesian problematic of the ontological status of force; (b) the framework of generation offered by Spinoza's Dutch contemporaries; (c) Spinoza's reworking of the Cartesian problem through the attributes; and (d) how the attributes of Thought and Extension operate as active organisers of the causal order of the world.

2.2 Force and generation

2.2.1 The Cartesian problematic

We wish to highlight three issues in the Cartesian philosophy of particular pertinence to Spinoza's theory of the attributes, namely:

(a) the role of Thought and Extension as a weapon in driving back occult qualities from the field of the new science;
(b) the problematic of force within the Cartesian structure of substance and mode; and
(c) the unsatisfactory explanation of the Cartesian surface, that is, the relation between the methodological power of (a) and the substantial and modal constitutions in (b).

As Garber notes (1992: 65–70), perhaps Descartes, with a view to making his philosophy teachable in the Schools, reframed his metaphysics within a more familiar language of substance, attribute, *proprium*, and mode, when preparing his *Principles of Philosophy* ('PP'). Within this structure (PPI[51, 52]), substance is simply that which has a capacity for independent existence, granted by God. We cannot know a substance as such; rather, through our relations to it, which are mediated through its attributes and its properties and qualities.[2] The key source for Spinoza's thinking on ideas as modes of an attribute of thought has been shown by Gueroult to be located in and around the 53rd Proposition of PPI. It reads in part:

> A substance can be known through any attribute at all; but each substance has one principal property that constitutes its nature and essence, all its other properties being special cases of that. The nature of corporeal substance is extension in length, breadth and depth; and any other property a body has presupposes extension as merely a special case of it . . . The nature of thinking substance is thought . . .
>
> (AT VIII 25)[3]

Garber (1992: 65) informs us that the conception of principal attributes is part and parcel of Descartes' coming to view substances as both that which exist and require nothing else in order to exist, but also, in a sense, utterly empty of interesting data for the use of the new science. It is perhaps less than surprising that Descartes installs the formal elements of the Cartesian plane as the essence of any corporeal substance. To do this extends the possibilities of knowledge so deep into substance itself, placing all qualities as subordinate to the attribute, that nothing is left of the 'occult' save the special differences between substances *qua* extended, thinking, or divine. We note here that Spinoza will go one step further and attempts to 'know' even substance itself, but he is careful to draw a fine and treacherous distinction between 'perceiving' a substance and 'conceiving' substance. In EI Defs.

3 and 4, Spinoza asserts quite deliberately that 'substance is that which is in itself and which can be *conceived* through itself Def. 3 (part)', but in Def. 4 that an attribute is that which 'intellect *perceives* of [a][4] substance'.

Descartes' prioritisation of two attributes over the others, namely extension and thought, is not without significance. Broadly speaking, his use of quantification and clarity to sweep back occult qualities is the raising of his colours in ostensible favour of mathematical physics. Garber makes a note of the context of Scholastic thought that would have received such a tactical strike, for at this time the Schools operated within the loose framework of accidents, essences, properties and modes, which would in Thomist fashion exclude certain properties as merely accidental to a thing's essence, then nevertheless deem them proper to that essence as '*accidentia propria*'.[5] This capacity for confusion and a proliferating 'theory of distinctions' must be seen, however, as part of a wider variety of explanatory theories deployed in the seventeenth century to explain physical phenomena. These included the Hermetic and alchemical tendencies to be found in the Dutch court (Helvetius), and all those theories of occult qualities and signs (*signatura rerum* being the name of texts by Paracelsus and by Jakob Böhme). Yet we should not crudely posit a battle of Descartes against anti-scientism; occult forces were also at work in the cosmologies of Kepler and Galileo in the form of 'gravity', which accounted, through action at a distance, for the regularity of planetary orbits. This was an unattractive position for many seventeenth-century natural philosophers of Descartes' mechanist mindset, and the theory of celestial vortices found in *Le monde* would have constituted a more acceptable explanation.[6] None of this means that Descartes refused to think in terms of forces privately. For the purposes of clarity, we can paint this problematic, as Gaukroger has done,[7] with the broad-brush division between two approaches to physical science:

(a) the hydrostatic view, which (unsuccessfully) relied on innate (or *internal*) forces, termed impetus and gravity, to describe, for example, how a cork returns to an equilibrium state (floating) in the medium of water; and
(b) a kinematic view, which (unsuccessfully) attempted to reduce all observable activity to relations of quantifiable motion and rest, such as attempting to explain the cork's movement by vortices of water molecules.

In a Whig version of history, one of the goals of seventeenth-century natural philosophy was the attempt to explain dynamics, the way motion and rest interacted with forces in the real world, using either (a) or (b) or usually some elusive combination of both approaches. We should note for the record that Newton's genius was to see that the quantifiable kinematic approach was the sole basis on which to build a theory of forces in relation (i.e. gravity could have a quantum), provided one passed quickly over an implicit acceptance that forces were *occult* in a certain sense and could operate at a distance. His approach involved treating forces as *external*, being applied (by God) as little cosmic 'pushes' at the beginning and end of movements. The Newtonian approach,[8] therefore, concerns forces *that are not the tendential (conative) forces of the hydrostatic view*; they supervene from *without*, a conjecture of no little coincidental interest for our interpretation of Spinoza.

Returning, however, to physical theories of innate force, the aether, and occult qualities, in view of these theoretical practices the Scholastics, may have regarded themselves as bastions of sanity, but from Descartes' perspective logical confusion likewise infected natural philosophy with doubt and error. The elevation of the attributes of thought and extension appears designed to invest these concepts with an absolute explanatory power, whereby a cut is incised in reality between that capable of being quantified within kinematics, and the remainder a 'metaphysical rump'. If we can imagine the face of the world as being covered with confused *propria* and occult qualities, Descartes' prioritisation of thought and extension can be seen as passing a very efficient brush across that surface, one that allowed modes to remain in good order and that swept up the confused and occult qualities into substance, where they were dissolved in the total but bare concepts of existence, unity and duration. In the case of the attribute of extension, the programme was particularly clear: almost everything that can be said about a body is ultimately determinable by reference to its attribute, that is, by quanta located within the Cartesian plane. We say 'almost' because precision requires us to note that the duration of a thing, its unity or its number, and its individuality, remain beyond the attributes at the substantial level. We must bear in mind, however, that in the case of duration, for example, that a substance endures is known from the fact that it is a substance, but that this duration ceases is known through the attributes (i.e. the relevant modes are affected by other modes of other substances such that the substance in question ceases to exist).[9]

Again if we sketch the immediate points of comparison, Gueroult (1968: 44–56 and App. III) argues at length that Spinoza's move in EI Defs. 3 and 4 is to accept Descartes' views that:

(a) substance is that which is independent (i.e. it requires nothing to exist but itself) (PPI, P51, AT VIII 24); and
(b) substance is that which is referred to but only ever known *through* its 'essential' attribute,

and then, in the initial Propositions of that Part, to establish by indirect argument that it is absurd to conceive of more than one substance as so defined: *God or Nature*. It is the sense of 'referral' as deployed by Descartes to indicate the mediation of substantial independence and primacy through its natural and essential property, which is transformed by Spinoza into the verb 'to perceive': EI Def. 4 'By attribute I understand that which intellect perceives of substance, as constituting its essence.'[10] Perception here is not, as Hegel thought, an admission of categorical limitation on the mind's power to perceive – the attribute of extension is not a spatial 'grill' in or of a mind, through which God's power is mediated and made sense of by *us*.[11] Here, however, we are not absolutely convinced by Gueroult's explanation of what perception is. Gueroult, perhaps by structuralist inclination, focuses too greatly on the essential element of extension in particular (three-dimensional representability) to conclude that 'substance is the reality of the attribute itself' (1968: 50) and that 'the reality of substance is its nature or essence' (ibid.: 49), that is, that which is 'donné à l'entendement comme constituant cette chose même dont celui-ci découvre qu'elle possède effectivement le caractère de la substance' (ibid.). While agreeing that 'perception' operates here to draw on the old idea of substantiality as evident being in the Parmenidean sense,[12] we do not think that the active nature of substance is sufficiently emphasised. Surely if Spinoza privileges conception over perception, then it is conception that is most attuned to the reality (perfection) of substance. Perhaps this interpretation derives in part from the understandable shorthand of naming Spinoza's attributes (and Descartes' primary attributes) as thought and extension, which brings with it the very ideas of static distribution and 'completion' that Spinoza in particular is trying to avoid. We believe that in order to be real, and thus be thought *of* substance, the attributes must *act* and cannot simply be passive or constitute a Scholastic structure in potency (*potestas*).[13] Thus Descartes is very clear that:

> Thought and extension can be regarded as constituting the nature of thinking substance and the nature of bodily substance; and then *they must be conceived as nothing other* than thinking substance itself and extended substance itself, that is, as mind and body.
>
> (PP PI[63], AT VIII, 30, our emphasis)[14]

Likewise, Spinoza introduces his two known attributes:

> an extending thing and a thinking thing are either attributes of God or . . . are affections of the attributes of God.
>
> (EIP14 Corol. 2)[15]

Thinking and extending – *not* thought and extended.

Within the context of Spinoza's metaphysics, we have substance enacting its attributes, that is substance is a thinking thing (not thought) and it is an extending thing (not extension). Any distinction between substance and attribute is entirely formal; that is, we *conceive* of God or Nature as substance in the abstract, but even this conception is *thought*, entailing the interesting idea that God's omniscience cannot comprehend God's substance directly, but only ever as an act of Thinking, Extension, or any other attribute. It is worth pausing here briefly to discuss Spinoza's usage of concept within the wider philosophical context. The Cartesian starting point is clear enough: that concepts are God-made and innate, but by Chapter 5 we will have established that the truth of immanence is that God-made is also machine-made, thus taking in also the nominalist position to a degree. Further, this God-as-machine-made status grants to concepts their reality, for each concept *qua* conceived is revealed as reality – it is realised – and so attains perfection in its existence (so taking in Aristotle and Aquinas). Concepts are no less metaphysical for being mechanically produced.

Yet what is a 'concept' and how does it relate to a 'conception'?[16] Wittgenstein and Dworkin would claim that a concept is an abstract symbol that refers to a number of more concrete instantiation or conceptions, concepts being differentiable inter se by whether they permit of more or less variance of conceptions under them (a circle is limited as concept; justice permits many conceptions of itself). Thus Dworkin can speak of a tree with a concept at the root and branches of conceptions. Spinoza, and there we, only use concept in the sense of conception (i.e. as another word for idea). Hence, EII Def. 3 'by an idea I understand a conception [conceptum] of the mind, which the mind forms . . .' and 'conception' is said to indicate action of the mind. Now while common notions are indeed constructed by similarity of interaction, and so a degree of physical interaction, it seems Spinoza is not holding that there are abstract concepts over conceptions. But there is a kind of deeper arboreal filiation. If individual thoughts are modes of the attribute of Thinking, then our concepts are these modes and have their form. This is why Spinoza speaks of the mind forming a conception, and it is this constructed form that provides as it were a vessel for other conceptions that are organised by it. As with all modes (and we return to this in Chapter 5), the relational operation here is not 'logical' identity, but formal composition: given two conceptions, do they compose well or poorly with each other? This provides for a very wide *open* range of conceptual interrelations; for not only will similar conceptions combine well, but seemingly heterogeneous ones may well combine in exciting ways to augment the resulting mode. Powerful concepts arise from a cacophonous conception, and are not condemned to a restriction under the sign of an inert governing 'concept'.

If there is a place, however, for a concept in something like the Dworkian sense, then this is the formal essence of ideas in God, to which we will turn in this chapter. For the reasons to be discussed, it would be wrong to term these formal essences concepts: they are neither modes nor subject to the same laws. They are, however, the necessary conditions for concepts of the geometric kind – a kind of surface that determines the diffusion and strange peaks of conceptions over and above the constant churn of modal life. They are closer in a loose way to Wittgenstein's grammars of the *Philosophical Investigations*. We thus also have a response to the distinction between *l'être* (the to be) and *l'étant* (being) if one adopts the position that *être* refers to the essential nature of beings, the latter being concrete instantiations of these essences. Again we will see that the essential conditions are not any less concrete than beings; indeed they are more concrete than concrete. Our trouble, however, is that setting up Spinoza in this way misses his classical point of placing being as emerging from his system (God is the cause of the being of things). In fact he makes existence prior to being, following Aristotle. The problem for you, dear reader, is to take on faith that while it seemingly ought to be the case that essences as 'concepts' in God are distinct from ideational conceptions of finite minds, which are expressions of those concepts, this metaphysical distinction only holds by virtue of Spinoza placing God's activity on the same level as every other things and considering variations of power. In other words, 'concepts' of God – God's conceiving of Himself – do not transcend conceptions of humans, but are special cases of the same thing. Thus, we will speak of concepts and conceptions in all cases, their power not their inner content determining their singularity.

As a further aside, in the case of extension, which will be discussed in greater detail in the next chapter, we should note the asymmetry between 'thinking' (*cogitans*) and 'extended' (*extensa*), but it would seem that 'extending substance' makes little sense unless absolute space is posited, which Descartes and Spinoza came to at least implicitly reject. It should be seen, however, that for Spinoza each attribute is to be considered as the evidence of intellection to itself, either as thought or consideration of extension, this evidence being God or Nature *enacting* its own reality, or, in other words, *defining itself* or (to abuse English as Spinoza abused the Latin) *'essentialising' itself* – the infamous *causa essendi* (EIP24 Corol.).

The metaphysical issue becomes also a physical issue when we come to the nature of force [*vis*] within Descartes' philosophy, for it appears that Descartes at least ascribed force to the act of creation of finite substances by God and to His ensuring, as with the quantity of motion and rest in the universe, their continued existence.[17] Consequently, we are faced with a danger (from the view of the new science) of leakage through the attributes of God's absolute force into the real and quantifiable world of the modes. Descartes may have been safe had his mechanics been able to explain all motion and rest according to metrics within the Cartesian plane, but already, as has been noted by Gueroult, Gabbey, and Garber,[18] he discerned that the metaphysical notion of God's force supporting the continued existence or perdurance of substances continued to have an 'imaginary' role to play in his account of motion, rather than no role at all. And though 'imaginary', the role seemed real enough, demanding some kind of explanation within Cartesian categories of being. Thus, quoting Garber:

> God will act on the world in such a way as to keep moving bodies moving, and resting bodies at rest. This can be described as saying that bodies, as it were, have a force to continue their motion, or exert a force to maintain their rest. But this is not to attribute anything real to bodies over and above the fact that God maintains their motion and as a consequence they obey a law.[19]

Garber notes Gueroult's conjecture, refined in Scholastic terms by Gabbey, that for Descartes force is modally ascribed to a substance insofar as it changes, but is utterly dependent on God, and it is a question of formal distinction as to sense, as of whom force is said.[20] Garber's own view is that force is neither in God nor in a created substance, but is rather 'attributed' by the *manner* in which an extended body is in motion or at rest.[21] How a body could move from *A* to *B* is capable of infinite degrees of variation, and Garber thinks that Descartes' view is that this variation is but the exact 'how' in how this body moves. This suggests that Descartes' decision to retain force as a kind of 'transcendental' in the Scholastic sense,[22] whereby God's force creates and sustains substances as such, thereby has opened a possibility for this physically irrelevant force to pass across the highest attributes into the physical world of the modes. This virtual movement is manifested either as an express extension of the language of force in physical events, or the addition of modes of being, which shores up the theory against the observed facts, or, in the absence of data, an insufficient modal explanation. If we consider PPIII[57–59], the use of force here does indeed seem to be nothing more than the 'how' of the motion communicated to the stone by the various things acting upon it, and the force is accounted for by the 'effort' eventually produced. If this is the correct interpretation, despite the apparent hydrostatic flavour of Descartes' fluid-based explanation for cosmology, it does seem to mean that Descartes is either wont to infer modes where he is forced so to do by his explanatory apparatus, or to assume modal characteristics wholly at odds with the facts. As to the former case, Descartes' wonderful letter of 9 February 1645[23] to Father Mesland elucidates 'in confidence' Descartes' theories on the host and transubstantiation, concluding in part that the bread we eat may even have passed through Christ's gut beforehand.[24] The initial part of the letter[25] discusses the idea that the bread has a surface, as does the air that surrounds it, and that a third notional surface may be posited as it were between the surfaces of bread and air. This is not an attempt to find force in the formation of the modes in question, but an attempt, as the reference to the Council of Trent implies, to restrain the new science from entering upon the domain of theology by finding a full explanation of reality in the status of the modes. This third surface is not a substance or a real nature, which could be destroyed by God's power, but only another mode that changes along with the substances on which it depends. Descartes is careful to clarify that the three surfaces are the same *realiter*, and differ only according to a certain manner of thinking. However, as an additional mode, the third surface is necessary to constitute the limit or boundary of the geometric dimensions taken on by the bread and the air. Descartes thus posits an additional 'unreal' mode in order to drag the spatial determination of real objects into the Cartesian plane that grounds extension as such. As regards ignoring modal characteristics in favour of supposition, unfair as it may be, it is instructive to consider Descartes' theories on cloud formation[26] in his *Meteorology*, where he concludes that moving air works on condensing and cooling water to form clouds with perfectly rounded icy 'crusts'. Here geometric abstraction forces the real into its own image. As we shall see, for Spinoza the problems of persistence in being and of the nature of the surface are intimately linked.

As a result of these theoretical contortions, the infinite set of variations in the modality of a body's movement between two points, and the status of (geometrical) 'surfaces' in this theoretical model, remain remarkably open questions for Descartes, and credit is due to the Frenchman for having attempted relatively openly to deal with the issue in his *Principles*. That force should find itself framed in terms of 'choice', whereby degrees of motion, like the variations of the conic sections that inspired Kepler, appear to lack an empirically supported ground for selection, clearly sets in train the Leibnizian philosophy, but constituted a significant challenge for any advocate of efficient causes who studied *The Principles of Philosophy*, notably Spinoza.

From his reading of Descartes' works, Spinoza would have been aware of the problem of the ontological status of force in the Cartesian philosophy. His reworking of the PP as the DPP no doubt caused him to consider PPII[43] and its discussion of the 'force [*vis*]' that a thing has to persevere in its motion and resist change in that motion. The term '*vis*' appears only intermittently in the *Ethics*,[27] and with a meaning that we will say is closer to Descartes resolution of force as *work*, rather than power. Nowhere does Spinoza say a conatus or an impetus is a mode of the one substance, although what each force actually does – its work – is a mode of God or Nature, and, as Garber has shown, the question of status appears to trouble the Cartesian philosophy too. We shall show in the next chapter that this apparent inconsistency is not the fault of Descartes, but rather the fault of his using the concepts of force and work in the opposite sense to his contemporaries (something that may have added weight to Spinoza's decision to deploy '*potentia*' as his preferred term). Whatever the correctness of Garber's interpretation of Descartes' view (and we believe it the better one), it certainly brings out the appearance of this problematic for Spinoza within the metaphysical context of substance and mode (rather than Hobbesian bodies) and thus the framing of possible metaphysical solutions. One such solution, as we have said, is to begin to consider the attributes as verbal 'events' – as performing thinking and extending. It is a solution that may partly have its inspiration in the advances of Dutch geometry and Cartesian logic in the seventeenth century.

2.2.2 The principle of the generatrix

There is a certain amount of disagreement in the literature as to the source of Spinoza's generative conception of the definition, which is intimately bound up with the troublesome nature of the definitions of the attributes. We discuss here how generative definitions are indeed cases in point of Spinoza's theory of the attributes as events. First, it should be recalled, as Schuhmann has said,[28] that:

> the geometry of the Dutch Cartesian mathematicians is in its totality [*insgesamt*] oriented towards the production of geometrical figures by movements.

Gueroult stands as the chief exponent of the view that 'Spinoza [is] Hobbes' disciple when it comes to the nature of geometry [and] agrees with him on the genetic method in question'.[29] Gueroult has it that 'mathematics . . . while it is conceived by Descartes according to the analysis of the ancients and the algebra of the moderns, is conceived by Spinoza according to the geometry of Euclid as reformed by Saville and by Hobbes'.[30] Gueroult is well aware of the contemporary research (*c.*1974) that indicated genetic definitional notions existed in Clavius and Tacquet, but takes the reasonable view that even if Spinoza was aware of this work, it was still quite an intellectual leap to move from genetic definitions in geometry to a genetic conception of the human understanding, a leap that Hobbes had made.[31] We share the scepticism of Audié[32] that Hobbes in particular constitutes the principal source for Spinoza's thinking of genesis and definition, primarily because the documentary evidence shows Spinoza's possession of works by Clavius, van Schooten, Tacquet and others (cf. Appendix 1), and his friendship with De Witt, whereas no explicit evidential link can be drawn from Hobbes' geometric work to Spinoza.

By way of example of the genetic definition in action in the work of Clavius, Audié draws our attention to the following discussion of the circle:

> Euclid also adds that line to the edge of the circle [. . .] which is called the periphery, or as it is expressed in Latin, circumference. Here, too, the ratio of a circle can be described. A circle is a plane figure, which is described by one finite straight line led by its tip around another point at rest [quiescens], until it has been restored to the same place again, and thus to begin to move once again.[33]

Here this particular circle is mechanically[34] constructed by attempting to draw the line segment AB using the line segment AC with C as a fixed point. With C so fixed, AC rotates producing the circle before us. Using a straight edge we can simply draw the chords D and E using the circumference of our circle as the determining boundaries,[35] but note the infinity of possible chords that could be drawn, the infinity of their intersections, and, Spinoza notes, the infinite possibility of equal rectangles that could be drawn using four chords.

We add as a further example, drawing on Audié's appended[36] collection of extracts from the sources, the following discussion of the construction of an ellipse by Jan De Witt, whose *Elementa Curvarum Linearum, Liber Primus* pointedly defines (Ch. III Def. 1) the *linea describens* as the *generatrix* or 'generator'.[37] The generatrix is used, for example, in the construction of an ellipse, where the *proportions* of right triangle ABC are varied (as to the ratio AC:AB), causing the line BH (the generatrix), extended from BC, to describe a curve from D to F (one quarter of the ellipse). If we extend AC, then the point where a line drawn from H intersects AC at a right angle is called K, and we have a right triangle HKC that is proportionate to ABC (hence, *AB*:*AC*:: *HK*:*CK*, which states that the two ratios are in a certain proportion). The remaining quarters of the ellipse are constructed in similar fashion.

We present these geometric examples to illustrate how far the genetic conception of definition had advanced in Spinoza's intellectual milieu, but the core thesis of Gueroult seems unshaken, namely, as Audié also concedes, that the above proofs are still further away from a genetic conception of cognition than Hobbes' thesis. It is our view that this debate could benefit from further evidence of a Dutch source for Spinoza's view that certainty is grounded in the capacity to generate a singular thing. This may have been missed in other research because of the tendency to focus on the wealth of geometric work to which Spinoza did have (or, in the case of Hobbes, may have had) access, and which seems sufficient foundation for an explanation of what is after all the *mos geometricus*. Yet if we turn to matters of logic we also find in Spinoza's Cartesian-inspired contemporary, Johannes Clauberg, a notion of genesis that is directly grounded in the working of the understanding.

Reviewing Clauberg's *Logica vetus & nova*, which Spinoza owned, we note the manner in which it draws heavily on Cartesian conceptions of clarity and distinction and the mind in motion to divide the new study of logic into generation and analysis, with generation being further subdivided into generation of inner meaning (*sermo (lógos) internus*), which is a study of the formation of ideas, and generation of outer meaning (*sermo (lógos) externus*), the study of which is named *hermeneutica*. Jacqueline Lagrée[38] has proposed an investigation of this hermeneutics as the basis for Lodewijk Meyer's *Philosophiae s. Scripturae Interpres* and the theological chapters of Spinoza's TTP, and concludes in a short article on the subject that Spinoza is the far more consistent expositor of Clauberg's central idea that to understand outer meaning, one must investigate the real causes that brought about the 'what is said'. We propose to make a similar move in examining the *sermo internus*, which Clauberg expounds in the *prolegomena* and first part of the *Logica*. Here (*Logica Prol.*: §107), Clauberg posits a difference between a person's own thoughts, necessary even if they lived alone on this earth, and the thoughts as expressed or communicated between people in society; a difference between *ratio* and *oratio* (ibid.: §118). The *Logica Genetica* turns the mind towards itself and upon its own thoughts (ibid.: §108), a process that demands a meditation on genesis (ibid.: §110). The *Logica Genetica* leads (*ducens*) the mind to the correct formation of its own thoughts and 'directs the care of self or his relation to himself, or, to knowing anything rightly' (ibid.: §111).[39] This distinction is necessary because 'sometimes they say with words what their mind denies, often they are aware of something which they do not know how to bring out [i.e. put into words]'[40] (ibid.: §118). Clauberg thus proposes to prescribe laws for knowledge, such that one shall abhor the confusion, and others will follow this example. This constitutes a natural movement to the treatment of ethics, where moral virtue is grounded in fortitude or, as to the mind, temperance, which is the moderation of our anger, and our desire for pleasures (*cupiditatem voluptatum*) (ibid.: §119). It is also this fortitude that grounds social living as justice:

> each will respect the other by applying justice, which is the use of virtue towards others, such that he will give each his due and conduct himself correctly with men.[41]

It must be said, however, that for all the discussion of 'clear and distinct ideas' and genetic logic, Clauberg primarily seeks to meld the new philosophy of Descartes into a neo-Aristotelian framework. Taking up again the nature of definition and the role of the essences in the first part of the *Logica*, we read that:

> Finally a thing's manner may sometimes be described from its cause, the genus not being considered. This is called *causal* definition, and *from the essence*, which is clearly distinguished from genus and differentia.
>
> (*Logica* I, Ch. VIII, §101, emphasis in original)[42]

Thus a causal definition and an essential definition continue to run side-by-side in this work as an example of the continued blending of the two philosophical creeds. It suggests that mode of comprehension that ultimately ends in repeating the mistake of Scholastic essentialism, whereby one definition is swapped for another but the 'flatness' or arbitrariness of the definition remains unchanged. One senses this 'flatness' in Gueroult's otherwise fine interpretation. Gueroult expounds a genetic theory of the essences, which appears close to Spinoza's text, and indeed it is the case that definitions are genetic and we have true ideas of things when we understand their genesis (i.e. that which when posited gives rise to the thing itself). But one does not get much sense of the actual and immanent power that posits certainty and the proper linkage between God and essence, whereby God's power is His essence. If Macherey's analysis of Hegel's interpretation of Spinoza's God is correct,[43] we might find Gueroult located somewhere between: (a) the view Spinoza was attacking when he called for definitions of God that are founded on his properties or capacities (e.g. *the causa sui*); and (b) the view he was supporting at the culmination of Part I *Ethics*, namely God's definition derives from his *potentia*, but can never equal it. Why? Because it is one thing to understand God or Nature by its definition (e.g. its essence is its power), and another thing to have an intuition of the essence of being God or Nature, which is precisely the *event* of God or Nature's self-creation. There is a sense, therefore, in which God or Nature exercises absolute power to define itself, whereas modes are always defined by external causes. There is precisely the deferral of truth to the idea of the idea which Spinoza warns against; we may have obtained a natural law understanding of how a thing came to be, but we do not ourselves intuit that coming to be, save insofar as we experience the power that is the essences.

Returning to Clauberg, we say that it is his *Logica Genetica* that bridges the gap between generative conceptions of geometry and the Cartesian attributes, with clear language explaining how Thought is to be considered as an act of the mind and generative of logic. It ties together a principle of generation that is simply productive of desired forms, with a notion of *quality* of generation whereby it is possible to emend the act of thinking – vary its power – to *produce* clearer and more distinct ideas. We believe that this logic feeds into the production of the TTP, but then also returns to physical geometry with the idea that the event of Extension likewise is capable of emendation – variation of its power. Let us now see how Spinoza undertook this re-conception of the attributes.

2.3 Redefining the attributes

2.3.1 A fine distinction

In his magisterial analysis of Part I of the *Ethics*, Gueroult proposes that the attributes be understood as that which makes substance what it is – that 'which constitutes the essence of substance' (1968: 47). In so doing, Gueroult criticises those (he cites Hegel and Brunschwicg)[44] who believe that Spinoza's definition of the attributes – as 'that which is perceived of substance as constituting its essence' – indicates that the finitude of the human intellect determines and limits the individual mind's appreciation of substance and somehow confers on that mind a false comprehension. This is too Kantian a conception: the mind is deemed somehow separate from and acting upon the ready-made data that it perceives, whereas Spinoza conceives Thought as absolute in God and conceptually prior to the ideas that ground finite minds. With such an analysis as might be ascribed to Hegel, one risks viewing the attributes as 'grills' through which the reality of substance passes and is somehow deformed from its true nature. We see this discussion in Macherey's notable reappraisal of Hegel's thinking of the attributes (1990: 97ff.). This objection turns again on the problematic meaning of EI Def. 4, noting that Spinoza's attempts to unify all within one substance fall flat as he tries to explain multiplicity, for in so doing Spinoza must draw on the finite point of view to explain the variety supposedly provided by the attributes. This is why Spinoza says an attribute is that which the intellect perceives of substance, a move that Macherey powerfully describes thus: 'he [Spinoza] thus recovers Cartesian dualism'.[45] Such a statement draws on the Hegelian subjectivist view of the attributes, which presumably is not a little influenced by the free (absolute) power of the Kantian categories as explanatory determinants of perspective, but this 'subjectivism', as Eisenburg has noted,[46] has its strongest advocate in no less than H.A. Wolfson, who went as far as to say that the attributes were wholly illusory products of passive human imagination. This debate, Eisenburg notes, seems ultimately irresolvable given the variation of Spinoza's own views on the attributes, especially in his correspondence, and the way in which words in the *Ethics* take on new meanings in different Parts. Yet we will seek to show that if the attributes are considered as 'events' of God, one can see how Spinoza would explain perception as a degree of power that may be varied up to a limit, that of conception. The alleged dualism of finite and infinite is resolved in a manner that characterises Spinoza's philosophy: first, by regarding apparent opposites as special cases of each other; second, by grounding the possibility of perception in the necessity of conception – in other words, every human mind is constituted primarily by its immediate conception of substance, and only then becomes a locus of further perceptions; and third, by assuming that every mind endeavours to conceive all else, yet fails to do so in proportion as its finite power is weaker than the other powers affecting it, this restraint from conception being named 'perception'. This is not such an unusual conception for Spinoza's time; the reconciliation of idea

examine within Spinoza's logic a clear distinction of terminology that seems to have been largely overlooked.

The only previous expression of the possibility of this reading can be found in Wolfson (1958: 292–293), who noted parenthetically in his discussion of the immortality proffered in Part V of the *Ethics*, that Spinoza does not use 'essence' in one sense, but in at least two senses that he identifies across several characterised uses of the term. Wolfson's schema may be tabulated as in Table 2.1.

The realisation that there are two 'essences' operating in Spinoza's work, and, as is apparent from the above, that the distinction is entrenched in Spinoza's final incomplete work the *Tractatus Politicus*[51] between *essentia actualis*/data and *essentia idealis*, is crucial for understanding the nature of the *scientia intuitiva* (i.e. knowledge of the third kind). However, Wolfson's note on the difference points to uses in Spinoza's texts that are perhaps neither the most revealing nor determinative of this difference. Indeed, Wolfson does miss several other uses of essence of (possibly) more (particular essence)[52] and less (essence of nitrate)[53] importance. Indeed, *essentia actualis* is used to introduce none other than the concept of *conatus* thus: *Conatus, quo unaquaeque res in suo esse perseverare conatur, nihil est praeter ipsius rei actualem essentiam*.[54] We have marked the attribution of *esse formalis* to category (A) as erroneous. With respect to Wolfson, in the cited EIIP5 Spinoza is speaking of the formal being, not the formal existence, of things. Categorically, we maintain that Spinoza regards being and existence as separate, with attributes and essences having being but not existence. The proper division is as ever one of power, as we shall see in the remainder of this chapter.

We propose to begin our clarification of these differences with Spinoza's pedagogic correspondence to Simon De Vries, dated conjecturally to around February or March 1663:

From Letter 9:

> Therefore a definition either explicates a thing as it exits outside the intellect – and then it would be a true definition, differing from a proposition or axiom

Table 2.1 Qualifications of existence and essence by Spinoza (based on Wolfson)

Ontological use	*Term (Latin)*	*Contexts noted by Wolfson*
(A) As to the existence of actual things insofar as they have place and time	*Existentia* *Esse formalis* (*sic*) *Essentia actualis* *Essentia data*	EIP24; EVP22 dem.; CM 12 EIIP5 TP Ch. 2 §2* TP Ch. 2 §2
(B) Conceived of as actual insofar as in God and following necessarily from His divine nature	*Essentia* *Ideae rerum non existentium* *Essentia idealis* *Essentia formalis*	EIP24; EVP22 dem.; CM 12 EIIP8 TP Ch. 2 §2 EIP17 sch.; EIIP8

* This reference, and the one below, seem to be incorrect, though this term is used by Spinoza in the sense suggested in EIII (see *infra*).

> only in that former is concerned only with the essences of things or the essences of the affections of things, whereas the latter has a wider scope, extending also to eternal truths – or it explicates a thing as it is conceived by us, or can be conceived.[55]

We find here, as Gueroult has noted (1968: 23), two senses of definition discussed: (a) a definition that amounts to an architect's conception of some project (say a temple), which is the act of thinking and does not correspond to a true idea of a thing; and (b) a definition that explicates a thing that exists outside of an intellect – a 'true definition'. Our review of Clauberg's *Logica* admits an important dimension to this division that is overlooked by Gueroult. The distinction divides along the lines of the sermo *internus & externus*, with one definition being the act of the mind in its conception (*ratio*), the other being a sign (*oratio*) that is communicated between humans. The question for the latter is whether it is adequate to the concrete object 'outside the mind' that is being discussed. Hence, with the Borelli example in Letter 9, we must take each of the limbs of the definition of the figural as having a definitive value proper to itself. As *sermo internus*, if Borelli, that great thinker of gravitation, means by 'straight line' what we mean by 'curved line', then his proposition that two straight lines enclose an area *a* is correct by definition. But for us, if straight line is to mean what we all think it means, then the thing is plainly inconceivable and the definition false (it does not qualify as a true definition insofar as it is a *sermo externus*).

Now Gueroult is quick to limit the definition of the inner word to the particularity of the mind's internal *potestas*, describing it as granting 'a priori' definitions such as of the circle, triangle and square. He calls this a '*définition concevable*' (ibid.: 26). This reduction to the 'a priori', however, is too great a limitation on the power of the human mind and at odds with the very examples Spinoza offers. The conception of a project to rebuild Solomon's Temple is almost as far removed from the geometry of the circle as Spinoza could have pitched his example. The categorical grid view of the attributes again seems to creep into Gueroult's understanding, as it affected Hegel. The mind that produces a 'conceivable definition' must not be viewed as possessing specific properties in the same way as substance, but as being an actually existing power that has generated something as its effect. This seems also to amount to a hierarchy of the two types of definition, privileging the 'true definition' and consigning the conceivable definition to the status of a spontaneous production of the mind, which seems akin to the imagination (ibid.). Gueroult maintains that the spontaneity of the mind is separable from the imagination, and it is only the confusion of the mind that equates the two, but this leads to a strange argument that confusion is both the cause and effect of itself, that imagination grants a confused and mutilated perspective on things, rendering the conceivable definition, despite its essential clarity, as being an act of Thought, itself confused. The role of the process of emendation in clarifying the mind and sanitising its productions is correct, but as we have said, no hierarchy is admissible. In line with Clauberg's *Logica*, we aver that Spinoza grants equal status to the internal and external definition, the two concepts of definition however being linked dialectically in the process of emendation. The TdIE is very clear immediately prior to its discussion of the genetic definition of the circle that emendation involves the building of instruments of the mind:

> with the tools they were born with, men succeeded . . . in making very simple things; and when these were made they made other more complex things with less labour . . . In just the same way the intellect by its inborn power makes intellectual tools for itself by which it acquires other powers [*potestatem*] for other intellectual works . . .
>
> (TdIE §31)

It is thus apparent that Spinoza sees a qualitative difference between (A) the definition of things outside the intellect, which may be termed the essences of the affections of things, this corresponding, for example, to *essentia actualis*; and (B) the definition of conceptions, being the formative power that constitutes becomings of the mind, this corresponding to an *essentia idealis seu formalis*. This already indicates that formality is a term that is signifying something best explicated through power and work, rather than a purely nominalist concept. It is to this division of knowledge that Spinoza refers in his TdIE as he discusses his method of definition in relation to essences:

> For neither is there any need to understand their series. For the essences of singular mutable things are not to be elicited from their series or order of existing, which would furnish us with nothing but their extrinsic characteristics, their relations, or, at the most, their circumstances. All these are far from the inmost essence of things.[56]

In this statement we see Spinoza's fundamental division between the series of mutable, finite things and the intimate essences of things that occupy the attributes. Yet even as we note the dissimilarity of these two orders, we should not pass quickly to consider the inmost essences as transcending the finite essences as mute forms. Spinoza continues to use the language of power both at the finite and infinite level, and likewise the language of essences (formal and actual) at both levels. This indicates also an intentional similarity of orders that one might usefully oppose to the essence/concept terminology of Hegel. The similarity of operation is differentiated by the power of the thing's nature in question. Consequently, Wolfson's tabulation might be further simplified and clarified as in Table 2.2.

The emphasis is clearly on degree of power being expressed, not on some divine language or mute form. The most difficult aspects are the continued pertinence of the difference between God's *potestas* and His *potentia*, and the bilateral generative relation between the finite and infinite powers that flows therefrom. This *potestas* is not at all the same as the *potestas* of finite things, which is their materially determined nature; their determination to be this way rather than that.

Table 2.2 Relation between essence and power

Type of essence	*Degree of power (potentia)*	
	Finite	*Infinite*
Formal	Formal being of modes, or *potestas* in God	Formal essence, or what *in Dei potestate est*
Actual	Given essence, or conatus	*potentia Dei*

We can, however, only know a thing's nature from the activity that expresses it, that is, causes it to exist. This finite *existing potestas* might be defined as follows: we make a notional distinction between the formal *potentia* that grasps a set I of ideas or bodies to constitute a thing distributed according to the order of the attributes, and an incoming enacting *potentia* T that determines this thing to act, then *existing potestas* at any moment is equivalent to the distribution of this enacting *potentia* across I, or formally *Existing Potestas* $= T/I$. Evidently as I increases the *potestas* expressed must fall, but in the case of God T is so infinitely great that all of I, being God's infinite nature, is expressed, and the *Existing Potestas* converges on unity (i.e. everything in God's *potestas* necessarily is) in an infinite limit case of *Necessarily Being Potestas*.[57] It is a correct appreciation of the importance of precisely these aspects that we hope to build upon in Chapters 5 and 6.[58] To begin to understand why Spinoza might be interpreted in this way, we will indicate a possible antecedent among the works of his library (cf. Appendix 1).

2.3.2 *A reader of Seneca*

What is the metaphysical nature of the genesis that grounds the mind's internal conceptions? The question is directly linked to Spinoza's restructuring of the problematic of the being of force, a restructuring that is frankly astonishing. However, to understand it we must understand the original senses of the terms he deploys, and how they become reconfigured within this structure. The point of departure is the metaphysical relation of substance, property and attribute.

If we take certain Hellenistic philosophies and their medieval interpretations, we are given a body that in its independent *thisness* constitutes a primary substance. What can be said of this substance is determined not by just anything, but by those aspects that do not change during time and without which there would be no this as opposed to that. These are termed properties. For example, it is a property of a knife that it can cut, though it does not need to be cutting for its entire existence to be a knife. It is a property of Cato that Cato can think, but he does not need to be thinking now (he may be unconscious) to still be Cato and have the property of being a thinking thing. In this schema these substances are real beings and the properties really *are* in the substances. Let us note for completeness that bodies can enter into relations, so that Cato is wearing a toga designates a relation of proximity between a toga-substance and a Cato-substance, and interestingly Cato has taken poison indicates a very intimate relation between the poison-substance and the Cato-substance. But what is the status of the knife actually cutting now and Cato actually walking or thinking now? Where is the second substance that stands in relation to Cato such that it makes Cato walk or think? For this special, transitory state of affairs, the Stoa used the term *katelogemata*, which would be translated by Cicero[59] and Seneca[60] as 'attribute'. The attribute of Cato, according to this Stoic logic, is quite clear in that rather than saying 'Cato has the capacity to walk', or bizarrely 'Cato and the walk walk together [*sic*]', we say 'Cato walks', which is a relation of subject and verb. Broadly, attribute is to substance as verb is to noun. There is a further consequence, which is characteristic of Stoicism,[61] and that is that attributes do not exist *in se*, that is, to the extent that attributes are states of affairs or events said about propertied substances, they are deemed not to add existence (or further substantiality) being to those substances. These attributes of bodies are called 'incorporeal'.

Let us use this scheme to interpret Spinoza. Now, we have *Deus sive Natura* as the one unique substance. Spinoza details God's properties in the first half of EI, and these properties are deemed total, infinite, immutable, and so forth, in keeping with the spirit of his deduction of God's nature in Part II of the *Cogitata Metaphysica*. We are then asked to consider God's attributes. Ignoring the definition of attribute in terms of perception for the moment, we propose that attributes properly be considered according to the scheme delineated above, such that each of God's attributes are nothing other than verbs of God. This makes sense when we note that the attribute of Thought is also stated by Spinoza as God being a thinking thing. From *Cato thinks* we now have *God thinks*. Nature also 'extends', though English is somewhat unhelpful in grasping precisely which verb should be deployed here. Note finally that there are infinitely many attributes, because God or Nature is capable of infinitely many events, or, it seems to us, the *propria* of God or Nature are like a set of operations on some *U*, there being infinitely many solutions to what qualifies as *U*. Observe that we say 'infinitely many actions' rather than 'in infinitely many ways', for the infinitely many ways are the modes of acting – they are almost adverbial. Thus *Cato walks quickly* becomes *God thinks vividly now* or *extends quickly here*. We should be careful, with Spinoza, not to ascribe too transitory a nature to God or Nature, in the same way that Cato may stop walking. God's act of thinking and Nature's act of extending are each immediate, eternal and immutable *per proprium*. When Nature *extends quickly here*, Spinoza wants us to understand that Nature's immediate adverb, or mode of being, is the immediate infinite mode, that is movement and rest.

In this regard we note Deleuze's review[62] of Gueroult's justly fêted tomes, in which he remarks quite accurately that one of the historian of philosophy's significant discoveries is that Spinoza does not begin with God, but rather God emerges from the order of reasons. Gueroult (1968b), in common with all commentators[63] of whom we are aware, however, seeks to begin with substances as if these are somehow prior in nature. Gueroult goes to some effort establishing quite brilliantly that the general substance concept is then narrowed down to substances of one attribute, before explicating how Spinoza establishes that there is only one substance with an infinity of attributes. Yet he must surely have noticed that Spinoza does not even begin with substances, but first defines a special type of *cause* (the *causa sui*) and then sets out his first Axiom as the difference between 'caused by itself' and 'caused by another'. Even EIP1, which relates to substances, is really a statement about causation in that it establishes that substances are not their effects, but can only be the cause of the effects, and so are prior in nature. It is only really at EIP7 that we start establishing things about substances rather than determining how causation is to be related to them.

Does this mean, therefore, that we should prioritise causality in the construction of Spinoza's metaphysics? Not at all, for the nature of the *causa sui* is inherently circular and has nothing 'existential', which assists in overcoming the problems of believing the self-evidence of EIP7 – *existence belongs to the nature of substance.* By prioritising causation we simply defer the ontological question by one step as we struggle to establish any reason why Spinoza's claim that God as substance necessarily exists should so whole-heartedly rest on so apparently flimsy a proposition. Is there more to the first Axiom than has been hitherto thought? Let us set it out in the Latin:

> Omnia quae sunt vel in se vel in alio sunt.

Each thing is either in itself or in another. Several commentators, as we have said, seize on the critical importance of the *in se* and the *in alio*, including notably Hegel. Yet important for the purposes of the ontological proof (and thus the whole system) is the rather modest third person plural of '*esse*'. We are put on notice of an almost imperceptible change of categorical level from Def. 1 '*existere*' to Ax. 1 '*esse*'.[64] We note further that Defs. 3 and 5 state also that substances and modes have being, rather than existence. However, it is EIP9 that provides the critical elaboration of the categorical structure Spinoza is advancing. This reads:

> Quo plus realitatis aut esse unaquaeque res habet, eo plura attributa ipsi competunt.

The more reality or being each thing has, the more attributes belong to it. Gueroult (1968b: 144) spots that reality of being indicates the degree of grace a thing has and that Spinoza, like Descartes, will use this idea to elaborate precisely the different degrees of thinking (and extending) potency that individual things possess. We aver that properly understood, each substance[65] of one attribute is more than simply existing, but exists and then increases its being by reference to the attributes it has, that is, being is natural right and is the measure of how an acting existing thing 'extends or thinks' in accordance with its power of working. Gueroult argues (1968b: 145ff.) that it is here a question of minimum being equated with nothing, maximum being equated with necessity, and any mediate degree of being as possibility. We believe that this interpretation slightly occludes the change in categorical register from existing substances to being that Spinoza performs. Is it not more precise to admit according to Spinoza's logic that substances exist that are not in act (= reality), that is, there exist substances that are not and so constitute a void, though they would be uncaused substances. And note how in this framework Spinoza has dropped being's status from encompassing substance, attribute, mode, to sitting alongside existing substance as its inflection of reality in its attributes. When we interrogate substance as to its being, therefore, we are properly asking about its initial conditions of existence from which it acts, if at all, and then also about the nature of its acts from those initial conditions of existence. To be is not simply to exist, but to exist *in actu*, or, to stress how existence is generated by power: 'posse non existere impotentia est et contra posse existere potentia est' (EIP11 Alt. Proof).

This determination reduces the load that EIP7 must bear, for it is not stating that substance is, but only that substance exists, which by definition is what substance does if it has being first. The weight is placed rather on EIP11, which unites the bare existence of substance with an infinitely intensive reality due to the attributes. This does not mean, however, that we must refer attributes to being. Def. 4 of the attributes involves no reference to being, thus marking it out from substance and mode (Defs. 3 and 5). Furthermore, EIP8 does not say that the attributes have being, but that substance 'has' more being the more attributes that comprise it. This is to exist more intensely by acting with infinite power; the attributes are not of their own right, they are the verb of some substance. The first Appendix to the *Korte Verhandeling* likewise considers whether, at Proposition IV, essences should be distinguishable *realiter*, and concludes first that they must be 'contained' in something else, which is distinguished *realiter*, and then insofar as they are actual/real, they are observed as distinctions *modaliter* in some other thing. Again, attributes are not of themselves being, but are the means of being (real) and the possibility, conceptually, of differentiating substances by intensity, were it not the case that only one substance can be conceived as existing. As such, while the Stoic categories are indicative in this respect (for they grant incorporeals being but not existence), we need to understand that Spinoza attempts to tie the attributes conceptually to the one substance such that the attributes can only derive therefrom, and not from some primordial distinction in the 'something', which would open the way back to a transcendent philosophy.

One should note the amount of work Spinoza is requiring the attributes to do: the verb of each event constitutes both its being and its power, which is either both one and the same (the Being of being) or infinitely differentiated (each being is Being differently). In this context, Leibniz's apparent criticism of all Averroeists and Spinozists,[66] that they believed the different notes of the organ were all constituted by the same breath, might seem particularly appropriate. These thinkers all failed to see, *per* Leibniz, that the breaths in the organ must all also be different to achieve the variety of sounds *but need not be infinitely different to do this* – the sum of the breaths is just that: the grouping of moderately diverse instances of breath.

This is actually a criticism that itself underlines the importance of immanent power. Creation and power do not come from a point at infinity, save only in an abstract sense. They are immanent to actual generation and actual power as cause is immanent to effect. This means that, while there remains a massive leap from God or Nature's absolute infinite power to the power that generates modal relations, we must credit Spinoza with attempting to localise causation as power under the name of the formal essence.

With Spinoza's model of the attributes, Descartes' problem of force is given a new twist, and new light is thrown on Garber's conjecture that (inertial) force is nowhere in Descartes' world. The event, considered as an attribute, is not present; it has no being and it adds no existence to the things that are, namely extending and thinking substance in the Cartesian scheme, and the one substance in Spinoza's ethics. 'Non-presence' is the most neutral term, we feel, because we regard one of the primary dividing lines over Spinoza's legacy is the ontological nature of the attributes. Are they, following Hegel and today Macherey,[67] non-being and the movement of the negative, or, following Bergson and Deleuze,[68] a positive being-something, a virtuality? We do not propose to examine this issue in this chapter, though our belief, briefly stated, is that Spinoza's apparent reduction of perception and duration to what amounts to an illusion in favour of truth and eternity, suggests a view that the acts of God or Nature are indeed lacking ontologically insofar as they are events, though each event does draw on the nature of that which acts (substance) and determines the degree of its being, power, reality. This hierarchical preference for existence being explains much of the *Ethics*' tenor. The *force* of a happening in both models is something that plays around the surfaces of existing things, though in Spinoza the degree of force (the adverb) is only insofar as the manner of acting is a mode of substance. As such, we are taken back to God or Nature, and the world of modes has reality or being to the extent that the adverb, as characteristic of effect, discloses substance in act. But the event itself, the attribute, this is non-existent. It is because God's event constitutes the conditions of thought, that ideas exist but thinking is non-existent.

From the inexistence of thought, one can see how many errors follow. Thought as event of God is inexistent, but constitutes our thoughts as inexistent. The relativity of our perception causes us to measure the immediate appearance of our thoughts 'in themselves' against the external world; to notice however confusedly a fundamental difference of character, and thus to conclude 'our' thoughts are substantively different from what is out there. We thus collapse into mind-body dualism. Furthermore, we look for some basic *ens* or substantiality in our thinking that cannot be found. We wish for our thinking to be 'things' and have properties with which we can then determine rectitude. One may as well ascribe truth to the abyss. But by realising that the reality in thought inheres not in the incorporeality of its acting, but the modality of its acting, we come to focus on the substantiality of the one substance acting in its various ways. Hence, Spinoza's theory of truth, of perfection, of reality, of power and virtue, these are all expressed as adverbial transitions. To describe this in purely metaphorical terms, the truth is not just anything that is thought, because only God thinks, but rather that which God thinks quickly, forcefully, with the most power. This forcefulness differentiates as the formal being of things and their completion in the actual. And what is it that God thinks with the greatest vivacity and force? The infinite idea of God's self. And how does He think it? With the greatest pleasure, this pleasure accompanying the idea of Himself being Love, the most powerful affection of the attributes. With this in mind, we must proceed 'as quickly as possible' to that idea, for to think that idea replaces the unreal standard of an individual's thought as verb with its most forceful modulation. From this idea's force all truth can be measured; the idea of God constitutes the epistemological 'event horizon' (cf. Deleuze 1998: 151). Our discussion of the inexistence of the attributes now prepares the way for the consideration of the instantiations known to us: Extension and Thought.

2.3.3 The appearance of the attribute of Extension (distinction)

Further support for this interpretation of the attributes is the full appreciation of the lessons of the so-called *Letter on Infinity*.[69] Our route to this understanding synthesises certain trends of neo-Stoic geometry abroad in the Dutch Republic during Spinoza's life and, significantly, present on his bookshelves (see Appendix 1). It involves a realisation, already indicated above, of Spinoza's awareness of the logic and metaphysics underlying this neo-Stoicism and also the constant refusal to cede to the temptation of imputing to Spinoza an infinitesimal calculus. This temptation can be found satisfied in Gueroult and Hegel, for example, and in any focus on Spinoza's second proof of DPPIIP16, which draws on the Archimedean definition of a circle as a polygon of infinite sides to establish infinitely many tangents to a curve.

The problems arise in attempting to locate in the *Letter on Infinity* a declaration that the differences between line segments moving from AB to CD within the torus are infinitely small and yet exist within the one substance. The conclusion drawn on the face of the letter's wider argument is that the mathematics of the time, employing as it does the beings of reason, is not up to the task of fully comprehending substance in all its compossible modulations. The two most immediate objections to this thesis are that:

(a) Spinoza does not talk about infinitely small variations or differences, but (slightly mysteriously) of the inequality of spaces;[70] and
(b) Spinoza's central claim, as Gueroult maintains, is that reason can know God or Nature – it thus seems uncharacteristic for him to place elements of God beyond reason.

How then to reconcile this language of spatial inequalities, modal insufficiency, and the bounds of reason?

At least hermeneutic assistance may be derived[71] from the Stoic theory of surfaces, which accords with seventeenth-century Dutch geometry in that it too appears to favour a generative or dynamic theory of geometric construction. The sources recount the debate between the atomists and Stoics over the divisibility of bodies. Debates turned to the example of the cone, with Demokritos having at an earlier time posed the problem thus: if we consider the cone as constituted of circular conic sections, each neighbouring the next, either they have unequal surface areas, and the surface of the cone is not smooth but will rather contain breaks or little holes, or the surfaces are equal, and the figure will as a matter of definition be a cylinder rather than a cone.[72] Demokritos' point is that in order for the surface between the base and the apex to constitute a continuous plane, it would be necessary that the cross-section at height x be smaller than that at height x' immediately below (otherwise the cone would never narrow, but would be a cylinder). However, if the difference $x' - x$ constituted any definite quantity, one could always posit a cross-section halfway between x and x' smaller than the given quantity, and so on *ad infinitum*. Either, at infinity, one had to accept that a cone was in fact stepped ('proving' that ultimately there existed metaphysical atoms), or one accepted the paradox that a cone was rationally a cylinder, or you accepted infinitesimal differences that were beyond measure (a conclusion abhorrent to Greek theories seeking to locate reason in the world as *logos*). Chrysippos does not fall into the trap of accepting the existence of what Berkeley called 'the ghosts of departed quantities'.[73] Plutarch reports[74] that Chrysippos' response was that the circles were neither equal nor unequal. A surprising conclusion perhaps, but, as Bréhier brilliantly if not a little controversially notes,[75] what if Chrysippos had actually intended precisely that which his conclusion implies, namely that the surface of a cone does not exist.[76] Such a claim is a specifically limited one within the context of Stoic categories, which posits the *ti on*, the something, as prior to that which is corporeal *and* to that which is incorporeal. To say that the surface of a cone does not exist is not to say that it is not something, but rather that the surface *is* something inexistent and incorporeal. Hence, Chrysippos claimed:

> that no limit existed in the division of space and that consequently one could not speak of the number of parts contained within diverse magnitudes, such as the world and the finger of a man, since there is no more or less in infinity.[77]

The question is then: what sort of incorporeal is the surface, and one possible answer is that of place. Already in Descartes' discussion of surfaces in his letter to Mesland, we can see how an unreal 'place' may be thought between bread and surrounding air, though this place remains a passive expression of the changes of the relevant substances and their modes. The Dutch geometers, on the other hand, provide us with a generative interpretation of geometry, whereby a line is a point extended in a desired direction, a surface a line likewise extended. Within this view, the cone's surface is constituted by rotating the line *AB* from *A* – the surface is constituted by the nexus of attributive power acting on the given corporeal to generate a new modal relation. Note that across the first three dimensions it is possible to use point, then line, then plane, each as a new modal relation – a new successive body – to build new modal relations (EIII Pref.). This is the model for understanding how modal bodies generate yet further modal bodies on the same level of finite modal existence.

Is this to rely overly on a Stoicism that Spinoza explicitly criticises? Spinoza's most pertinent criticism of the Stoic doctrines, insofar as he understood the materials available to him, is found at TdIE §74:

> certain Stoics perhaps heard the word 'soul', and also that it is immortal, which things they imagined only confusedly. They also imagined, and at the same time understood, that the most subtle bodies penetrate all other bodies and a penetrated by none. Since all these things were imagined together and were accompanied by the certainty of this axiom, they forthwith became convinced that the mind consists of those most subtle bodies, that those most subtle bodies were divided, and so on.[78]

It should be noted, however, that this discussion is not in fact a blanket rejection of Stoicism, but is produced as evidence of the specific case of thought wherein something that is understood as clear and distinct is nevertheless erroneously mixed with an imagination. Spinoza regards the contention that the most subtle bodies penetrate all others and are penetrated by none as 'axiomatic'. This acceptation of at least one Stoic doctrine suggests that the other criticism in the Preface to EV is likewise doctrine specific, not School-wide. It is even possible to argue that Spinoza is attacking a doctrine the Stoa did not actually hold, but we cannot support this here.[79]

If Spinoza was so critical of the Stoics, especially his interpretation of thought as accepting little holes filled with breath, this does not mean that his readings in Dutch geometry and the Cartesian problematic of force nevertheless led him to conclusions that seem closer to the reality of the early Stoic position on surfaces. To be clear, we do not suggest any direct positive influence of Stoicism on Spinoza, but note a certain confluence of reasons from today's vantage point, which allow a revealing interpretation of the *Letter on Infinity* and the wider role of the attributes. In this way, the Stoic problematic of the cone amounts to a fruitful hermeneutic tool for reading Spinoza's theory of the attributes; a fruitfulness that one strongly suspects has its source in neo-Stoic influences among the thinkers of the Low Countries from Justus Lipsius on. Thus if we proceed with this caution, we suggest that Spinoza's discussion of the inequalities of spaces within the geometrically constructed torus aims to show us not that the entities of reason in mathematics are exceeded by the being of God or Nature, but rather that we must understand that the existence of the ideas of mathematics may constitute the torus in question *only if they are put into motion*. Morfino argues[80] that this is all explained by passages or transitions considered as infinite variations. We would dare to qualify this by arguing, for the reasons we will detail in Chapter 3, that to all the various abstract points of the torus there may be assigned a (directed) speed and a transition, and that for the matter moving round the torus it is necessary that at each point a compensatory determination to motion occur (positive or negative transition). Talk of 'variations' implies a virtuality that we believe is not in play here. It is actually the case that the matter in motion is constantly transiting from one (directed) speed to another, as we say, by virtue of a smooth, mutual compensation.

In these terms, we must place a metaphysical distinction between things, which *are*, and their being in action, which is their actual essence. The difference between the two types of reason (common notions and intuition) falls either side of this ontological division of being and act. This is precisely Spinoza's point at the end of the TdIE when he explains his theory of definition as not seeking out properties but essences:

> For a definition to be called complete it must explicate the inmost essence of the thing and must take care not to substitute for this any of its properties.
> (TdIE §95)[81]

Spinoza takes as his example an abstraction, the circle, because it is indifferent to its manner of definition. If one accepts the definition that it is a figure the lines from the centre to the circumference of which are all equal, one merely has indicated a property of a circle, not its essence. When we speak of real and physical things, 'created things', our definition must take into account: (a) the proximate cause of this thing; and (b) that all the properties of the thing can be concluded from the definition. A perfect concept or definition is that which institutes a mental affirmation of truth when any given property is considered. Thus, in Spinoza's view, we intuit that the radii of a circle are all equal because we understand that the essence of a circle according to criterion (1) is its construction as a metaphysical surface by the passage of a line, one end of which is fixed, the other mobile (TdIE §96). Note that this is not the case for non-created things (i.e. God) (TdIE §97). This generative definition of the circle perhaps stands as a direct rebuke to Descartes, who, in his Letter of 27 May 1630 to Mersenne, proffers as an eternal truth freely created by God the equality of all the lines drawn from the centre to the circumference of a circle.[82]

Any reading of Spinoza that finds in him the infinitesimal calculus must bear in mind that Spinoza is not arguing for the existence of infinitesimals but actually the opposite: that they do not exist in a very technical and limited way. In fact we note that Leibniz, as Robinson reports,[83] secretly did not believe infinitesimals existed either, admonishing L'Hôpital in correspondence for proclaiming that they did. The calculus did not come to be because anyone discovered the infinitesimal, but because Newton and Leibniz discovered that one could usefully proceed by assuming a difference smaller than the required amount (and thus not infinitesimally small) – that is, by assuming the 'auxiliary' of the infinitesimal at the limit it was found that mathematics could be stretched into the description of dynamic occurrences. It is for this reason, we believe, that Deleuze warns that a philosophy of difference should not become mired in the search for the infinitesimal, which disappears in the relation.[84] This caution concerning the infinitesimal (which Descartes himself espouses in his letters with Desargues)[85] is not without parallel in early Stoic thought, where as we have seen already there can be no more or less within infinity. A critical, if confusing, feature of the Stoic incorporeal is that (unlike bodies) these lack properties or natures, and so it is not possible to speak of resemblance and dissemblance within them.[86] Void is just void as such; place is just place. Indeed, in the latter case we can see an important distinction that informs a dynamic conception of Extension as attribute: insofar as Nature extends it constitutes the having-place-as-such (disposition) of any body, but it does not *yet* grant a relatively disposed quantity of spatial magnitude, for in the absence of all else a thing will continue to act (extend/think) indefinitely (EIIIP4). Spatial magnitude is a matter of determination by the indefinitely many other modes, being the relativistic point Spinoza makes in the *Short Physics* and obliquely at EIV Ax. At the level of the finite modes we may correctly speak of more and less, but at the level of attributes there are no natures, or seeds, of which we can speak save the infinite power of extension itself. An 'intensive infinite' reading of Spinoza that claims that each thing has a corresponding formal essence as an infinite degree residing in the attributes of God or Nature is straying dangerously close to the view that the attributes have characteristics or properties capable of comparison. We have already seen that Spinoza can logically accept that a thing may exist, but not *be* due to restraint of power (EIP9), but there he is speaking of substances that exist by their nature, whereas here is speaking of essences, which are implicated in the attributes and so categorically do not exist by nature. We aver that Spinoza's position is no more the idea that seminal souls are residing patiently and ready formed in the attributes than the idea of a pot is in the potter on the day he was born. In other words, the essence of the pot is in the newborn potter insofar as this potter will be the principle cause of the pot's coming to be, but only formally potentially (*potentia*), and not really, actually, or in terms of determinate capacity (*potestas*),[87] such that on the day of birth we can point to some mode that is the nascent pot – not far from a kind of Leibnizian preformationism.[88] This is the lesson of the white wall in the TdIE, where the potential for a figure to be picked out from the general whiteness of the wall in no way constitutes a claim that a sign or premonition of this occurrence can be said to exist *before* the fact.

We must not, however, jump to the other extreme and suddenly claim that Spinoza is an atomist against all the evidence. Spinoza is a thinker of the continuum, but a continuum that must be located not in the perception of the modes in isolation, but as a great *plane of immanence* that drives the modes to constitute lines, surfaces, durations, all the singular things of the world.

Stepping back to our overall discussion of generation and the role of the attributes, the result, as is apparent from the above, is that singular things such as the torus, or a cone, or a human body, are constituted as singular not by the modes alone in a certain relation, but by the metaphysically prior intervention of the attribute of extension. Turning again to the Cartesian failure to explain how a given body should move in a certain manner given a range of possible speeds of movement between two fixed points, we see that Spinoza posits the attribute of extension as the agent that selects the actual movement by reference to a supposedly determinate and necessary degree of power. The attributes thus can be said to disclose a relation of attribution to substance (God or Nature acts) and to the modes: here the attribute of extension attributes singularity to the relations of motion and rest. The mechanics of this singularisation form the silent basis of Spinoza's *Short Physics*. For now we wish to note the general role of the attribute of extension in describing continua and 'picking things out' as singular. This 'picking out' has a further aspect: just as a quantity of modes is placed in action to describe a surface, and thus a geometric form, we must not lose sight of a simultaneous reordering, whereby the individuality of the modes and certain sub-relations between them disappear under the thus created form. Accordingly, if for argument's sake, the surface of the torus is taken as Extension, it is the specific torsion of that surface that determines the relations of the fluid bodies within, and causes them to express a surface forced upon them that is not, cannot be, derivable from considerations of discrete parts. But note well that very many corporeal relations could be placed in this form and adapt itself to the essential character open to it. For example, Spinoza's worm finds a life in the blood vessel; but does this make the blood vessel the seed, or Idea, or nature of the worm? Clearly not – the blood vessel as condition of the worm's life is in this analogous sense its essence, and consequently this essence is open to all kinds of lives. Bodies cluster around formal essences, express them, but these essences could be expressed in infinitely many ways, limited only at the attributive level by the appropriateness of *this* 'home' to *this* group of bodies. It is not without reason that Spinoza uses the verb *fovere* to describe the fostering of human activity in the city (EIV App. 7) and of everything in the body by the idea of God (EVP16 Dem.); *fovere* is linked to *foetus* and implies a sense of providing a dwelling place for growth or fostering. Plato's thought that the line is a middle that stands in front of its extremities returns with a certain vengeance, for the point in motion loses its point-like nature for the perceiver focused on the line it describes. Wholes become parts; the worm in the blood is lost in the body. That attributes, according to the modal level of application, pick out, constitute, but also occlude singular things, is one of the key lessons of Spinoza's teaching on the attributes. Another is that we must continue to see these attributes not as static, but involved in the very act of generation itself.

2.3.4 The appearance of the attribute of Thought (certainty)

What, then, would be the correlate in Thought of the extensive surface? Neither the *Letter on Infinity* nor the *Ethics* provide an express answer. Given our conclusion that modes are distinct from the surfaces they describe when in act, we must conclude that ideas, as modes of Thought, cannot constitute the equivalent of the surface or plane. This also rules out the idea of God, which remains, amusingly, an *effect* of the one substance. If we turn to the *Tractatus de Intellectus Emendatione*, we may discern a possible solution to this conundrum. Here, Spinoza's discussion of ideas, signs and certainty, maps very well onto our understanding of the *Letter on Infinity* (subject to the wider structural problematic of Thought's relation to the acts it conceives in Extension). Spinoza sets out his stall on the structure of cognition in the following terms:

> For example, Peter is something real. Now the true idea of Peter is the objective essence of Peter and is in itself something real, something entirely different from Peter. So since the idea of Peter is something real, having its own individual essence, it will also be something intelligible, that is, the object of another idea which has in itself everything that the idea of Peter has formally. And in turn the idea of the idea of Peter has its own essence, which can be its own idea, and so on without end. This anyone can experience for himself when he knows what Peter is, and also knows that he knows, and again knows that he knows, and so on.
>
> (TdIE §34)[89]

Although Spinoza is bringing to this theory revisions of much older doctrines concerning the mind of God (to which we will come), the language he uses of objective and formal ideas, and their relation to the real, clearly has as its inspiration and counterpoint Descartes' *Third Meditation*,[90] and by this route the Scholastic doctrines of Duns Scotus, William Occam and others.[91] To summarise the relevant features of the Cartesian doctrine: we are asked to consider the objective reality of a thing as that which is observed by us and which representation forms part of that thing's formal reality (the thing as it is known from God's point of view). The objective reality of an existing thing reflects its formal reality, and reality as with Spinoza is equal to perfection (i.e. power). However, for Descartes reality is ordered hierarchically by reference to metaphysical natures, such that God, being infinite substance, has the greatest formal reality, a horse, being a finite substance, has 'median' formal reality, and whiteness, being a mode, has the least formal reality. Now when we speak of the reality of the ideas of these things – their objective reality – the perfection of these ideas is equivalent: the objective reality of the idea of God is the highest, of the horse median, of the whiteness of the horse, lowest. Descartes has perhaps a problem explaining a winged horse, which is patently a representation of some sort, but not of the thing it represents. In its self-contained substantiality it seems that the idea of a winged horse does have a median objective reality even if it has no formal reality to which it relates. Finally, each idea of a thing is also a thing, and thus has its own formal reality, of which one may have an idea, and so on. These 'things', however, are not substances but modes of a thinking substance, and their formal reality is modal, or of the lowest perfection. This is the first consequence on which the above quotation turns: that each idea has its own objective reality (in Scholastic terms its own *esse objectivum*) distinct from its representative being (*esse repraesentivum*), such that this idea of a thing itself can be a thing about which a further idea can occur. With this we might conclude that Spinoza follows Descartes in believing that the power of ideas depends on the correlative power of the beings of which they are ideas; after all, does he not exhort us to think the *idea Dei* – an idea of preeminent objective reality? We believe this is only half the story, for Spinoza also pursues a different route to the nexus of the *idea Dei*.

Spinoza seizes the Cartesian theory and develops it in terms of ideas *formaliter, objective ac realiter*, in the TdIE and in the *Korte Verhandeling*, yet he does so with a technical distinction that it is very easy to overlook. In the TdIE §§33–37 we are informed that 'certainty is nothing else than the objective *essence* itself' (my emphasis). We have suddenly shifted from the *idea formaliter* to the *essentia formaliter*. Why? This first move indicates that Spinoza wishes to avoid regress into formal ideas as 'ideal' or 'abstract' models by which objective ideas are measured. When he writes 'it is no more necessary than, in order to understand the essence of a triangle, one needs to understand the essence of circle', we understand this to mean we should not catch hold of the first idea we imagine to be the formal idea and apply it to the objective idea. The example is quite extreme, but applies as much to Peripatetic categories as Platonic ideal forms, for constructing the formal idea from objective ideas alone at best leads to abstractions of variable utility (EIIP40 Sch.1). Spinoza has in fact introduced an additional concept into his model to which we must be sensitive, and this is formal essence. *Now formal essences are categorically not formal ideas*, nor even to be considered as the traditionally logical *sine qua non* of those ideas. If we note that the formal ideas of God are modes of substance whereas the formal essences of things are in the attributes, our discussion of the nature of the attributes of God or Nature already indicates the manner in which formal essences operate within knowledge. Spinoza declares in conjunction with his equation of certainty with objective essence that 'the way in which we become aware of formal essence is certainty itself'. This is the awareness of the *cogito* (in Spinoza's revision EIIP9–11) and the becoming aware of God; that is, it is intuition. We must first have a true idea if we are to have an idea of that true idea. When we know, we know that we know, and we know that we know that we know, and we may only in vain have recourse to imperfect infinity in an attempt to establish the ground of the truth of one idea (triangle) in another (circle). Clearly Spinoza wishes to avoid a conception of certainty by reference to some other idea, and thus we must interpret 'we become aware of the formal essence' against any tendency to regard a formal essence over against the objective idea it constitutes. We submit rather that the formal essence of an objective idea is the very act of becoming certain – the *causal* moment of certainty, even if (and precisely because) that means that God's conception of the formal essence of a thing is the same thing as the act of becoming certain of it. This is because God's mind is thought as the attribute of Thought and subject to the absolute certainty of the divine intuition, which cannot be exceeded. The method of reflexive knowledge (§38) is then understood not as the arrangement of two ideas such that they correspond in the abstract to each other, but rather the search for an objective idea the perfection which invariably causes the formal idea to 'seek' it out and as it were actualise it completely. In other words, to think God with certainty is to generate God. But what do we think with such certainty if not the Cartesian *cogito* become Spinozan *cogitans*? Hence, the first generative idea of the thinking thing is for Spinoza also the *idea Dei*; the truth of the idea of God is the necessity that in thinking the first idea one always generates this living thought as undeniably true, powerful and complete. This act of thinking adds nothing to the idea of God and is ontologically neutral, being a matter of the attribute of Thought. It is a constant striving for the one idea; it is, to turn Le Brun's phrase, *the impatience of the concept.*[92]

This accounts for the first idea (of the thinking thing) but what about ideas about the world as perceived? Here we transit from the infinite to the finite, from God's power of thinking, which must be certain, to our finite struggle to make certain. Such a generative theory runs against any Thomist-inspired[93] interpretation of Spinoza, which would see in the *essentia formaliter* an Aristotelian signifying essence to be read off from the mind of God. Such a trap opens easily enough given Spinoza's theory of definitions where it seems we must posit the elements that in *addition* constitute the thing, but is avoided once we understand the generative nature of definitions, that the verb is critical in constitution, and that true definition is a question of *producing* the thing. If certainty is not a sign of a true idea, what is it? Having followed the argumentation concerning the attributes we are in a position to understand that this question is badly formulated, or, if it can be correctly answered, we must treat it as one of the ancient riddles, and grant that certainty is indeed *inexistent.* Spinoza can say this because he is locating certainty not in bodies, but in the incorporeality of the attributes. Note that Spinoza shifts his language slightly in preferring to add certainty over against the true idea, and deploying the concepts of objective and formal essence as the grounds for certainty over against the Cartesian structure of ideas. The Cartesian model is thus not rejected as such, but rather turned and augmented by additional concepts that deal with the role of God's power in thought. It is helpful that Spinoza takes up a further geometrical example to explain his innovation in this regard:

> *A true idea* (for we do have a true idea) is something different form its object (ideatum). A circle is one thing, the idea of a circle another. For the idea of a circle is not something having a circumference and a centre, as is a circle, nor is the idea of a body itself a body.
>
> (TdIE §33, emphasis in original)[94]

Spinoza may have in mind Descartes' discussion of the true properties of a circle in his correspondence and is trying to analyse the immanent role of generation in bringing about certainty *of* a thing's true properties. Thus Spinoza continues by supplementing the nature of ideas with the essences of those ideas:

> And since it is something different from its object, it will also be something intelligible through itself. That is, in respect of its formal essence the idea can be the object of another objective essence, which in turn regarded in itself, will also be real and intelligible, and so on indefinitely.
>
> (ibid.)[95]

Descartes' *vérités eternelles*, whereby God has decided for all eternity that a circle's radii are of equal length, are not the grounds for certainty in Spinoza's model. To list *propria* and then posit a sign of certainty is to proceed 'in the wrong order'. The certainty that pertains to a circle consists in God or Nature having created this particular circle. The correct order in reality is that God or Nature generates the circle; its power forces certain modes to describe a line around a fixed point. Only *then* do we have something that happens to have infinitely many equal radii. The beauty of Spinoza's example is that even if we knew that the radii so arranged would indicate that something was a circle, no one would be able to generate a circle knowing only this, because one would have to lay down infinitely many equal line segments. This property of circularity (the equal radii) constitutes nonetheless an adequate idea about a circle, but it is to be understood as the correlate in Thought of the modes of Extension that would be grounded by an existing circle. In other words, one can consider all the adequate ideas about a circle as being described or ordered by a given circle in the same way as the modes of graphite are ordered by a pencil-drawing of a circle on a page. That which orders these modes is the act of generation. Hence, Spinoza's conception of essence, defined as that without which a thing cannot be, is properly to be understood as a cause of that thing. To understand the essence of something is to be able to do one of the infinite things that God or Nature can do, that is, generate it. In Spinoza's view, if someone can construct a circle, one intuitively knows that it has infinitely many equal radii without ever having to draw them (or even one of them). That is why essence is the ground for certainty, because certainty grounds the ability to order partial ideas within a conceptual whole. Ideas are modes and complex ideas are merely compositions of modes in a characteristic relation. Nothing of the parts binds them together and any mode may be replaced by another without actually destroying the characteristic relation. The search for unity in ideas themselves is vain. A consistent theme of Spinoza's doctrine, the priority of works over faith, here finds its epistemological expression in the reduction of the role of the formal idea before the power of the act. Knowledge becomes labour: to know is to act and to act is to be able to create the idea again: to construct a circle, to build the tools of science,[96] to exhibit right effortlessly.[97]

Here again the distinction between the formal being of ideas and the formal essences in the attributes is critical. Both are moments of the same operation, save that the former are acts that fail because their finite power is restrained by other acts, whereas the latter are unrestrained and if they do not shine through for finite things, it is because the finite power of the things in question is insufficient to express this infinite power through their still-nascent nature. The finite things could think so much more, were they in an appropriate relation to the infinite, which rests entirely on being in an appropriate relation to the self through the construction of a machine of concepts that has, as it were, a greater and greater surface open to the flow of power (EIIP14). These attempts to construct a machine, due to their inherent restraint, fall into the formal being of ideas and the actual ideas, as the experience of one's finite *potestas* and *potentia*, respectively.[98] The formal idea thus has two moments: its generation as a particular volition to think, which is itself forced upon the body, but also then as that which is linked to the *conscientiae morsus* of its failure[99] – as the 'what ought to have been' that is the basis for the vulgar conception of the norm. According to this continuum of power we pass through the actual idea as of bodily success, through intellections or volitions, to the second kind of knowledge and finite ideas that are clear and distinct.

Certainty of finite ideas is now experienced as an active encirclement or grasping of an idea with a kind of surface that closes off that idea from the rest of infinite understanding and renders it an individual. Yet there is no mark or element of the idea that *is* this surface. Care is required in explicating a further doctrine of Spinoza's theory of ideas: that of the apparent dismissal of signs. We are told (TdIE §35–36) that the truth needs no sign, a claim that derives again from the refusal to seek the measure of truth in what we believe to be formal ideas; ideas that may be corrupted by inappropriate modes suggested by the imagination.[100] Yet at the same time truth is grounded in certainty as act. Why, then, is certainty not the sign of truth? The answer, on my reading, is that '*sign*' is implicitly defined as that which is a mode of substance, that is, an objective idea that relates to an only partially and confusedly perceived idea. A sign, being a mode, *is* and is as part of an idea. Certainty, however, being grounded in the act of the attribute, lacks ontological presence: it cannot be pointed out. As a result, while it is terminologically correct that Spinoza rejects signs as signifiers of truth, it would be wrong to assume that ideas as modes are alone their own truth. There needs to be an act in relation to an idea that constitutes its truth, and this act is the expression of God's power of thinking. We can see certain similarities in this view of certainty and Leibniz's doctrine that joy consists in the grasping of a rule of perfection related to the divine understanding.[101] Indeed the question arises whether Spinoza has stumbled upon a certain kind of what Kretzmann calls 'dictism' (Kretzmann 1970: 771). If 'terminism' is the Occamist view that the truth of a proposition is discovered by an analysis of its terms and the correctness of their logical interrelations, dictism, as ascribed to the Augustinian Gregory of Rimini, denies the sufficiency of logical analysis to discover the truth of an enunciation, and thus delves into an analysis of the contents of judgement in order to access 'that which is said by the judgement' (hence, 'dictism'). On Gregory's model, which inspired both Bayle and especially Leibniz, judgement is analysed and proofs are accumulated according to *recta ratio*, and it is this process that engenders meaning and assent in a given proposition. Spinoza's unequivocal assertion that everything is assented to, even Descartes' winged horse, indicates to us, however, that judgement as 'method' plays no useful role in Spinoza's conception of truth and meaning, rather degree of power alone (assent simply follows power, and at the limit, will and intellection are meaningless) (EIP32 Corol. 2). *Recta ratio* remains useless without the measure of truth offered by the most perfect idea; this latter is surest guide to whether reason is exercised correctly. One might suggest that Spinoza's view of dictism is that it merely transposes Scholastic language games from propositions themselves to the minds that encounter them. In this he could have foreseen the genesis of the Kantian programme as the internalisation of rules of thought.

With this we hope to have clarified Spinoza's rethinking of the Cartesian problematic of force by means of the attributes as inexistent generating powers, operating at the finite modal level by means of formal and actual being of ideas. A key aspect of this operation is the way that the attributes do not present us with things or ideas, but rather reorder existing things and ideas in complex wholes and parts (or decompose them). To conclude this discussion, we wish to recover this territory from a new perspective, which will help us see how this reordering works and just how systemically critical it is for Spinoza's project of mechanising natural right theory.

2.4 Summation of the role of the attributes in constituting order as right

Having covered the ground necessary to understand that the attributes constitute the eternal events of God or Nature, and that as such they are constitutive of the appearance – the logic – of the world, we can now gather together these insights for the purposes of understanding how things acquire their perceived order. This is necessary because it is according to the attributes alone, albeit immanent to modal relations, that power is expressed as natural right.

The first thing to remark, and which follows from genetic definition, is that Spinoza claims a real or causal theory of order. In temporal terms, this means that the order of causes and of effects is the order constituted relatively *by* causes and effects and which is non-referable to some prior absolute order of time. In holding a Galilean relativistic theory Spinoza is being in the least bit radical among his contemporaries; if anything Newton was the radical for daring to posit abstract time and space in the *Principia*, though it appears only as an auxiliary of analysis (he did not believe in such abstractions). For Spinoza an effect is simply a perceived cause, and thus a badly analysed composite. He is clear that a properly perceived effect is conceived through its cause. It is wrong to synthesise a chain of causes and effects; there is a chain of causes, and an imagined chain of effects. Spinoza evidently regards 'time' as this imaginary chain of effects when he describes the past and future as mental concatenations of simultaneous causes as a mode of *habitus* (EIIP44 Corol.1 Sch.). The word he uses for the chains of causes is the 'series' in TdIE §100 and 'order of things' in EIIP7, and every existing finite thing is described as enduring or having a *duration* (EIP21 Dem.).

The anchor of order is the simultaneity of the present. What is this simultaneity? Leibniz struggled with this question, initially believing that it was enough to believe that two things could be simultaneous if their existence involved no opposition to the other. Evidently this is not enough, and Leibniz refined this definition so as to require that one thing be the absolute condition of another without intervening change if the two things are to be deemed simultaneous. The reason for this can be seen in Spinoza's deployment of God or Nature. Each thing once determined to exist is present, which is not restrained from so existing: each thing is present to the mind 'unless causes arise which exclude their present existence'.[102] It is wrong, however, to suggest that because God or Nature is unrestrained, God or Nature is eternally present. The premise is incorrect; God or Nature is restrained, and thus His purported will is not absolute in the Scotist sense,[103] but is only restrained by Him (freedom of necessity is freedom from servitude). There is nothing else that can restrain God or Nature, and because nothing can intervene to change this, God or Nature is restrained to be eternally present. Being the *per proprietates* immutable constant of the eternal present, God or Nature is the condition of all simultaneity – the first surface on which all durations appear to be inscribed. Note the circular nature of this present: God or Nature is constituted as the infinite substance acting upon itself. If we are being precise, we must make clear that God or Nature though constituted in this fashion is not a *tabula rasa*. Beneath God or Nature is the eternal circulation of His or Its necessary constitution – it is this eternal return that is the cause of the face of the world that expresses at any moment varying degrees of reality across itself as vectors towards perfection. The difference again is one of power. EIV Ax. follows not only from the unicity of God or Nature but from the necessity of the infinite finite mode that has consumed all already for God.

As God or Nature unbound by any other returns eternally to the present, so each thing, once determined to exist, endeavours to return eternally to the present (EIIIP4). We are not saying that each thing is *causa sui*, but, in expressing God or Nature, each finite thing has a corollary desire to endure, which in God or Nature attains the limit of tirelessness. To be *causa sui* is not reserved to God or Nature by whim, but is the limit case of the continuum of all natural right.

So as to stress the point, simultaneity for Spinoza is unsurprisingly nothing other than power, insofar as the surface is not simply a plane on which causes are inscribed, but an active topos, a topos that determines the order in which causes are to occur and interact. The difficulty is in conceiving that as the degree of power of simultaneity approaches the limit, so all causes indeed become simultaneous; are revealed to the infinite understanding (omniscience), but not simply because things are 'there' to be revealed to the infinite intellect, rather because the things are rendered 'there' by the infinite act of Thought.[104] The more interesting case, however, is that of the finite simultaneity produced by each individual thing, for whom this power is unable to conceive (create) everything at once. Here the order of things takes on its fascinating complexity, as the power of each thing endeavours to order its world according not to abstract and arbitrary categories, but according to its material conditions of consciousness. Thus in the *Metaphysical Thoughts* (I.4; Geb. I/244) Spinoza is already keen to stress that time is constituted as '*our* comparison of the duration of things by reference to things which have an invariable and determined motion'.[105] Duration is thus 'conceived as . . . composed of parts' being 'an attribute of existence, but not of essence'.[106] Bove (1996: 20) prefers to stress the role of *habitus* in this determination of duration and time, but we prefer to stress that the very condition of habitude is the surface of simultaneity that is created by consciousness *qua* act of Thought. As the *Metaphysical Thoughts* makes clear, we have three moments of power – eternity-duration-time – with the latter two 'expressing', as Spinoza puts it,[107] the first. It is all too Bergsonian to put the weight on duration as Bove does,[108] when Spinoza anchors his thought of finite things first in eternity. He thus writes that as you take away a thing's duration so you take away its existence; the corollary being that the eternity of the thing subsists.[109] Spinoza is, however, careful not to regard God in this text as solely eternal, and so completes the foundation of the present for finite things. God, by virtue of being self-caused, expresses eternal essence as enduring existence, albeit that this duration is 'without beginning and end' and passes as a special case of duration into the indefinite – there is no primary dualism.[110] It is this relation between eternity and duration that constitutes a continuum distributed according to the power of enduring in one's being. As the power of enduring increases, so finite things pass closer to the perspective, or rather conception, of eternity.

This is perhaps more easily explained with a little formality and a sole focus on temporality: we take an arbitrary singular thing A as the condition of simultaneity for various developments a, b, c. A is itself a duration, with a progression of enduring in being, but its relative immutability presents us with the appearance of a static surface on which the developments a, b, c are said to occur. In the primary case (substance), these unchanging characteristics are categorically termed *propria*, rather than attributes, but in every other case it is possible to at least hypothesise a finite thing of sufficient power such that some of its [actual essences of the] attributes approach *property*-like immutability for the purposes of considering fleeting affects. Indeed, Spinoza goes one step further by approximating the experience of eternity of finite consciousness of being with the infinite consciousness of God or Nature. What we have therefore is a primary ontological division of what we can *say* about particular things as follows:

$$\textit{Substance } S \quad \begin{Bmatrix} \textit{Propria } A, B, C, \ldots \\ \textit{Attributes } a, b, c, \ldots \end{Bmatrix}$$

where the attributes are specific occurrences of the properties (e.g. that God *thinks* is His attribute; that He thinks *infinitely* is due to His property of infinitude).

This in the finite case becomes relativised somewhat as:

$$\textit{Thing } A \quad \begin{Bmatrix} \textit{Pseudo} - \textit{propria } A, B, \Gamma, \ldots \\ \textit{Affects } \alpha, \beta, \gamma, \ldots \end{Bmatrix}$$

As we have been stressing, in the finite instance the priority of the pseudo-properties rests entirely on their relative lack of alteration with respect to the affects. When Spinoza speaks of a thing's 'nature', he means nothing more than the adequate knowledge of these pseudo-properties, without claiming that 'natures' are somehow eternal and incapable of mutation (quite the reverse). Importantly, the distinction between a 'nature' and the affects of that nature is evidently not an individuating distinction; rather, the affects are necessarily expressions of nature insofar as that nature is affected by some other nature. From the perspective of *A*, then, each of its affects is a function of its nature (and some other nature) and determines a duration of affects in various series. In other words, if three distinct series of events occur for *A*, then the order of these events partly expresses the nature of *A*, and, as *A* becomes more or less powerful with respect to one of these series, so this order of things varies.

For example, let us call the pseudo-properties of *A*'s nature Α, Β, Γ, each of which determine a distinct series[111] of affects α, β, γ, . . . according to parallel temporal orders of causes c_1, c_2 . . . Then let us propose an arbitrary initial state of *A*'s consciousness:

$$A = \begin{cases} A_1 = \mathrm{A}(\alpha c_1, \alpha c_2, \alpha c_3, \ldots, \alpha c_n) \\ A_2 = \mathrm{B}(\beta c_1, \beta c_2, \beta c_3, \ldots, \beta c_n) \\ A_3 = \Gamma(\gamma c_1, \gamma c_2, \gamma c_3, \ldots, \gamma c_n) \end{cases}$$

In the initial conditions we will assume that the causes in each series in *A* run in parallel, such that αc_1, βc_1, γc_1 all are present in *A* simultaneously. This order of causes is generated by the attributes. Yet just as the order of causes is set by generation, so it may be amended by generation. Now, in the case of a continuous transition in series A_2 to a greater power of acting, the series of A_2 will be tensed, and each cause raised closer to existence in the present. As such, we can posit an increase in power such that when αc_2 and γc_2 occur, βc_2 has already occurred and βc_3 occurs simultaneously. In simple terms, it is as if *A* has reached into the determinate future and pulled it like a fabric towards itself. Understanding this, one sees that as the power of *A* increases, so the infinite chain of causation is pulled towards the present,[112] rather than the present *A* transiting to infinity. Readers of Spinoza should disabuse themselves of any conception of eternity as a sempiternity, in the sense that the immortality of the soul is something that lasts as long as can be. As with God or Nature, eternity means that *forever has in fact already occurred* as the present and indicates a complete lack of restraint, experienced as the delay or effluxion of time. Thus:

> we sense that our mind, insofar as it involves the essence of the body under a species of eternity, is eternal, and that this existence that it has cannot be defined by time i.e. be explained through duration.
>
> (EVP23 Sch.)

The converse case, of diminution in the power of acting, might be thought of as a dilation of a series relative to the others, though Spinoza appears only to permit an extension, a negation, by means of the powerful determination of some other series. Only one, true, *active* dilation is permitted, namely the Creation of the immediate infinite mode, which is termed *extension*, and it is a true active extension because it is the product of a determination, which is God or Nature's necessary determination of Him or Itself. Consequently, we have at least two instances of the attributes:

(a) the infinite immediate generation of the order of causes as such (present as the conditions of the infinite mediate mode); and
(b) the finite emendation of that order by this particular *A*, which is ultimately but a partial act of the attributes of substance in the last analysis, to create new initial conditions.

With this prioritisation of the eternal present, it becomes clear that intensity, virtue, power and thus natural right are commensurate with this returning present. Natural right, as we shall see, is this power to determine the order of things and so the perception of substance. Not, however, to reveal an underlying truth, but rather by rendering true through being the cause of the present. The event of the attributes constitutes the order of the world, but in addition the determinate right that each finite thing has continues to endeavour to intervene in this order with the purposes of reorganising it. In its simplest case, finite natural right cannot be seen as a pseudo-Stoic desire to accept and affirm an existing divine order, but a constant struggle to will desired objects into the eternal present, to realise actively the entire divine order 'now', just as God or Nature thinks and extends it.

The relation between natural right and the incorporeal order of the attributes is evidently mediated by the finite nature of the particular things involved in any situation. Now that we have asserted that the attributes operate as powers that continuously organise the incorporeal order of substance and modes, it is now time to assess how the finite things contribute to this causal nexus. For this, we must examine Spinoza's mechanist theory of nature.

2.5 The passage from the incorporeal theory of the attributes to the dynamic theory of mechanics, and its juridical import

Before we step fully into the appreciation of Spinoza's mechanical theory, it is very much worth outlining a context in which the passage from certain geometric insights, through early modern mechanical theory, to an ethics, would make sense to someone such as Spinoza, whose work, library, and training at van den Enden's school have exposed him to ancient thought. We hope this will provide a thread through the next chapter for those juridically oriented readers who understandably feel discomfort when confronted with a discussion of pulleys, wedges, hydrostatics, and celestial mechanics that purports to be the sole road to a theory of natural right.

The thread may be posed as a question: *what is the juridico-ethical meaning of the geometric transition, a meaning instantiated in Nature by the geometric regularity of mechanics as the supposed basis of the man-machine?* It will be perhaps easier to come to this question through contextualisation.

This question of the geometric transition is one that we have already encountered as we deployed Stoic thought to interpret the attributes of Spinoza. Yet unsurprisingly the Stoa were not alone in Hellenic philosophy in treating of this problematic, as the addressing of the problem of Chrysippos' cone to Demokritos indicates. The ethical significance of Chrysippos' claims when he invites us to make the transition from the stepped atomic cone to the smooth cone surface as a key moment of unified Stoic philosophy is best seen under the light of the problem's vicarious addressees (Epicuros, and by extension Lucretius). Indeed, as a counterpoint to our claim of Spinoza's inspiration by (or reinvention of a form of) the Stoic doctrine of the incorporeal, we draw on Marx's doctoral thesis on the *Differenz der demokritischen and epikureischen Naturphilosophie*,[113] which *inter alia* treats of what we regard as the counterpart of Stoic transition, namely the declination of the atom.

Marx quotes[114] Cicero twice and then Pierre Bayle to report the Epicurean theory of the declination of the atom, and we note the latter as most illustrative of the juridico-ethical consequence of the theory:

> Before him (viz. Epikuros) one only admitted of atoms movement and heaviness, and reflection [. . .] Epikuros assumed that even in the midst of the void atoms swerved a little from the straight line, when came freedom . . . [115]

Bayle immediately seizes on the capacity for the atom to swerve of itself as the origin of freedom within the Epicurean doctrine, and it is not unreasonable to draw parallels between what Lucretius would term the clinamen (declination) and the smallest possible desires to motion that are the essence of the Hobbesian theory of the conatus. For his part Marx keenly stresses that it is fallacious to believe that any atom deviating from the straight line of its fall is either repulsed from and by the line, or in so doing submits itself to causal necessity as it collides with the next falling atom. Marx, illustrating clear Hegelian influence, writes:

> The relative existence which the atom opposes, the Being-there that it must negate, is the straight line. The unmediated negation of this movement is another movement therefore, itself presented spatially – the declination from the straight line . . . The movement of the case is the movement of dependence.[116]

Marx therefore relies on the contradictions inherent in the purported simultaneity of the universality of the line of fall and the need for the particular falling atom not to be subsumed within that universal line; to distinguish itself as individual by standing out from it – in ethical terms, by revolting against the order of universal linearity to affirm itself in the swerve. Accordingly:

> Lucretius maintained correctly therefore that the declination broke through the bonds of fate; and just as what maybe said of the atom can immediately also be said of consciousness, the declination is something in the breast which can contradict and resist.[117]

Thus Lucretius proceeds immediately from the rebellious atomic swerve to the consciousness of each atom of this desire to fight and contradict the bonds of fate.

It is questionable whether the *contradiction* of atomic subsumption within the line is sufficient to ground the rebellious swerve as Marx maintains. It seems to us that while the line of fall is the activity that binds the atom to itself and completely dominates it with its power (to constitute extension), one power remains with the dominated atom, which is integral to the Epicurean theory (and a much misunderstood part of the Stoic), and that is the void. It is tempting to consider the void as a space between falling atoms, but that is to say the void is extensive, and so another line. The void is precisely nothing, and the nothing ought to be considered (as with the Stoics) as a residual power. Every atom, so to speak, voids; that is, in voiding it creates the possibility of being received outside of its dominating line. We believe this reading actually comes closer to Hegel's own interpretation of *das Leere* in the *Logik* (1969: 184ff.) and we thank Anton Schütz for drawing our attention to a not dissimilar (and more insightful) reading of the Hegelian theory, advanced by Derrida in his essay 'Ousia et grammē' (1982: 40ff.).

Be this as it may, the Epicurean link between the declination of the atom and freedom is unmistakeable, not least because of the immediacy of the clinamen to individual consciousness itself. By comparison, the Stoic theory of transition, which we argue Spinoza builds on (or reinvents), advances a different explanation of how it is possible for a determined straight-line motion to describe a curve. *The geometric core is the debate over the 'explanation' for transition from a determinate line, dimension, or order.* The prime ethical consequence, if we accept that this leap may be made, is that for the Stoa in varying degrees, and absolutely for Spinoza, every such declination from the determinate straight-line is itself necessary and determinate. What for the Epicurean is the line of fall, for Spinoza is the causal series, and what for the Epicurean is rebellion from order to freedom, is for Spinoza 'liberation' from one order at the price of subjection to another, more powerful order.

In the examination of Spinoza's mechanics that follows, we should therefore bear in mind that on each wing of the physical investigation there are logico-geometric questions and juridico-ethical consequences for anyone who accepts the inheritance of this albeit cursory outline of the Hellene debate on transition we have given. As we shall see, statics, which greatly informs the Cartesian mechanics, may broadly be regarded as the line of fall or the straight-line motion. Through his infinite power theory of the attributes, Spinoza begins to ask the question, initially in a mechanical context, about the ground or explanation for *transitions* from the straight line: not change, but the change of change. His response, and its juridical consequences for his theory of natural right, is that every transition must have a determinate, efficient and immanent cause, but, save in the case of God or Nature, every such cause, and so freedom, must come from without. It is only by following this logic to the limit that we can return to *determinately* locate this without within.

Notes

1 Cottingham *et al.* trans. (1988: 163).
2 Descartes derives this from the 'common notion' that that which has no attributes, properties or qualities cannot be known by us (PPI[52]).
3 'Et quidem ex quolibet attributo substantia cognoscitur; sed una tamen est cujusque substantiae praecipua proprietas, quae ipsius naturam essentiamque constituit, & ad quam aliae omnes referuntur. Nempe extensio in longum, latum et profundum, substantiae corporeae naturam constituit; . . . & cogitatio constituit naturam substantiae cogitantis.'
4 It seems appropriate to insert an indefinite article here, as Spinoza only purports to establish that there is a unique substance in EIP14: 'Praeter Deum nulla dari, neque concipi potest substantia.'
5 Cf. Garber (1992: 68–69), where there is given the example of risibility. This is not part of the essence of man, but is a proper accident to man.
6 Cf. Gaukroger in Gaukroger *et al.* (2000: 69).
7 Ibid. Gaukroger is clear that the proposed split was far more complexly mixed on the ground, as can be seen with Descartes' minimalist retention of force in his kinematic model.
8 Newton (1999: 444–445).
9 This precision is again due to Garber (1992: 67–68).
10 'Per attributum intelligo id, quod intellectus de substantia percipit, tamquam ejusdem essentiam constituens.'
11 Cf. Macherey's discussion of Hegel's reading (1990: 97: ff.).
12 'That which is there to be spoken of and thought, must be' (Parmenides 2009: Fragment 6).
13 This is the sense of *potestas* that Spinoza rules out when he makes everything in God's *potestas* actual, and not simply potential.
14 'Cogitatio & extensio spectari possunt ut constituentes naturas substantiae intelligentis & corporae; tuncque *non aliter concipi debent*, quam ipsa substantia *cogitans* & substantia *extensa*, hoc est, quam mens & corpus.'
15 'rem *extensam*, & rem *cogitantem*, vel Dei attributa esse, vel . . . affectiones attributorum Dei'.
16 This discussion draws on the concise consideration by Wintgens (2012: 121).
17 PPII36.
18 Gueroult 'The metaphysics and physics of force in Descartes' in Gaukroger (1980: 196–229); Gabbey 'Force and inertia in the Seventeenth Century: Descartes and Newton' in Gaukroger (1980: 230–320); Garber (1992: 294ff.).
19 Garber (1992: 296), emphasis in original.
20 Garber (1992: 295–296).
21 Ibid.
22 For example, Duns Scotus conceives metaphysics as a *scientia transcendens*, a science concerned with *transcendentia* such as being, or unity: (1950) *Quaes. subt. s. Meta. Aristotelis* prol. n.18.

23 AT III: 161ff.
24 Ibid.: 167–168: 'Or cette transsubstantiation [i.e. digestion] se fait sans miracle.'
25 Ibid.: 163–165.
26 Cf. Discours V *De nues*, especially the last paragraphs [AT VI 290–291].
27 Cf. Ch. 3.
28 K. Schuhmann (1987) 'Methodenfragen bei Spinoza und Hobbes: zum Problem des Einflusses' 3 *Studia Spinozana* 62, quoted in Aldié (2007: 43).
29 'Spinoza [est] disciple de Hobbes quant à la nature de géométrie [et] s'accorde avec lui sur la méthode génétique qui en est issue' (1974: 486).
30 'la mathématique . . . [t]andis qu'elle est conçue par Descartes d'après l'analyse des anciens et l'algèbre des modernes, elle est conçue par Spinoza d'après la géometrie d'Euclide, réformée par Saville et par Hobbes' (1968: 37).
31 (1974: 482 n.59).
32 (2007: 52–53).
33 'Adiungit quoque Euclides, lineam extremam circuli [. . .] appellari peripheriam, seu ut Latini exponunt, circumferentiam. Potest circulus etiam hic ratione describi. Circulus est figura plana, quae describitur a linea recta finita circa alterum punctum extremum quiescens cicumducta, cum in eundem rursus locum restituta fuerit, unde moveri coeperat.' My trans. Quoted in Audié (2007: 52).
34 *Euclid Elements* Book I Def. 15 defines a circle as a *fait d'accompli*: 'a circle is a plane figure bounded by one line, which is called the circumference, and is such that all straight lines drawn from a certain point within the figure to the circumference are equal to one another: this point is called the centre of the circle'. It was Guéroult (1968) who clarified the importance of genetic construction within Spinoza's thought, which work has been greatly augmented by the mathematical historical investigations of Audié (2007).
35 *Euclid Elements* Book III Def. 2 'A chord of a circle is the straight line which joins any two points on the circumference.'
36 Op. cit., n. 33.
37 A.W. Grootendorst adopts this translation in De Witt (2000).
38 J. Lagrée, 'Clauberg et Spinoza. De la logique novantique à la puissance de l'idée vraie', in (1989) *Méthode et métaphysique.*
39 'dirigit eum vel ad seipsum, seu, ad ipse quidvis rite cognoscat'.
40 'verbis interdum affirmant, quod mente negant, saepe aliquid sciunt, sed efferre nesciunt'. *Efferre* also has an important sense of germinate (the producing forth of the soil), which may not have been lost on neo-Stoic thinkers in the seventeenth-century Low Countries. Lipsius (1640: 79) conveyed the Stoic idea of the tripartite farm: boundaries as logic; soil and trees as physics; fruit as ethics.
41 Ibid. '. . .alia respiciat alios, uti justitia, quae est caeterarum virtutum usus erga alios, dum suum cuique tribuit & rectè cum hominibus contrahit'.
42 'Denique ex causis suis interdum res ita describitur, ut genus nullum consideretur. Quae definitio causalis dicitur, & ab essentiali, quae genere & differentia constat, distinguitur.'
43 (1990: 17–24).
44 Gueroult (1968: 50ff.).
45 'il [Spinoza] retrouve alors le dualism cartésien' (Macherey 1990: 103).
46 Eisenburg, P. 'On the Attributes and their Alleged Independence of One Another: A Commentary on Spinoza's *Ethics* IP10', in Curley and Moreau (1990: 2).
47 Cf. de Muralt (2002: 19).
48 As Wolfson himself noted (1958: I: 238ff.). It seems remarkable that Wolfson should have pursued the subjectivist interpretation when he so forcefully argued that Spinoza's concept '*intellectus*' indeed was derived from Maimonides and the Schoolmen indebted to him.

49 As to which, see Gueroult (1968: 26–27).
50 Aristotle's definition of the straight line largely builds on Plato's definition in *Parmenides* [137E] that a line is a middle in front of its two ends (i.e. the continuum obscures the indivisible points), which indicates that Euclid's definition in the *Elements* was a later innovation. Cf. Heath (1956: 166).
51 Which Spinoza refers to as being written in his final Letter 84 to 'a friend' dated to 1676, the year of his death. Cf. Garrett (1996: 49).
52 TdIE §19 n.
53 Letter VI.
54 EIIIP7 'The conatus with which each thing endeavours to persist in its own being is nothing but the actual essence of the thing itself.'
55 'Quare definitio vel explicat rem, prout est extra intellectum, et tum vera debet esse et a propositione vel axiomate non differre, nisi quod illa tantum circa rerum rerumve affectionum essentias versatur, hoc vero latius, nempe ad aeternas veritates etiam se extendit; vel explicat rem, prout a nobis concipitur vel concipi potest . . .'
56 'Verum enimvero neque etiam opus est, ut earum seriem intelligamus; siquidem rerum singularium mutabilium essentiae non sunt depromendae ab earum serie sive ordine existentium, cum hic nihil aliud nobis praebeat praeter denominationes extrinsecas, relationes, aut ad summum circumstantias; quae omnia longe absunt ab intima essentia rerum.'
57 To be precise, Spinoza uses 'quicquid = whatever', which implies that the infinite *T* exceeds the infinite *I*. The reasons for this over-determination of power will be treated in Chapter 5.
58 Hence, we disagree with Gueroult and Negri, who quotes the former (1991: 191), in regarding the *potestas* as purely polemical and discarded with respect to God once the fullness of his *potentia* is realised. We also note the telling mistranslation by Parkinson (2000) of EIP34, where 'est' becomes 'exists' when Spinoza is saying precisely that what is in God's *potestas is* necessarily, not *existing* actually (i.e. that which is in God's *potestas* is necessary, not contingent).
59 Cf. *De Natura Deorum* (1933) 2.21, discussing God's thinking attribute.
60 See (1943) *Letter* CXVII.13. This seems more likely to have been Spinoza's source for the doctrine, for he owned Seneca's letters.
61 Cf. Bréhier (1970: 11).
62 In (2006) under that title.
63 E.g. Parkinson (2000); Garrett (1996); Wolfson (1958).
64 E.g. Parkinson's translation (2000) inexplicably translates 'sunt' with 'exists'.
65 Remember that Spinoza initially assumes an infinity of substances.
66 *Theodicy* (2010: 78). Cf. the discussion in *Serres* (1997: 472).
67 (1990: 107ff.).
68 (1992: 44).
69 Letter 12 to Meyer.
70 A point that Deleuze makes (1990: 202–203).
71 We owe this inspiration to Emile Bréhier's brilliant *Théorie des Incorporels* (1970: 7–8), which provides a brief but very suggestive interpretation of Chrysippos' theory of the cone.
72 Bréhier (1970: 7).
73 Berkeley (2002), para. XXXV.
74 *De comm. Not.* Ch. 39 (SVF II 159, 34).
75 For a conservative interpretation, which unsurprisingly ends up violating the text, see Hahm (1972).
76 Bréhier (1970: 8).
77 Plutarch, *De comm. Not.* Ch. 38 (SVF II 159, 1), as quoted by Bréhier (op. cit., n. 76).

78 '. . . quidam Stoicorum forte audiverunt nomen animae, et etiam quod sit immortalis, quae tantum confuse imaginabantur; imaginabantur etiam, et simul intelligebant corpora subtilissima cetera omnia penetrare, et a nullis penetrari. Cum haec omnia simul imaginabantur, concomitante certudine huius axiomatis, statim certi reddebantur, mentem esse subtilissima illa corpora, et subtilissima illa corpora non dividi etc.'

79 There is no space to pursue this here, but we believe a case can be made that Spinoza's criticism is in fact misattributed. The doctrine of porous matter filled with air is actually closer to that of the Peripatetic thinker Strato than the Early Stoa, who we interpret as regarding the circulating activity of the *pneuma* as formally incorporeal and thus having no need of pores into which to pass. Interestingly, Spinoza was obliquely accused of 'Stratonism' by, among others, Bayle, as J. Israel reports (2006: 454–457). Could it be that Spinoza thought he was improving what he mistook for a Stoic doctrine by actually developing the real Stoic doctrine independently?

80 Morfino, V. 'The misunderstanding of the mode. Spinoza in Hegel's *Science of Logic* (1812–16)', in Sharp and Smith (2012: 38).

81 'Definitio, ut dicatur perfecta, debebit intimam essentiam rei explicare, et cavere ne ejus loco propria quaedam usurpemus.'

82 AT I, 152, 22–25.

83 (1996: 261–267).

84 (1991: 171–171).

85 Cf. Kline (1972 vol. 1 'Projective Geometry').

86 Bréhier (1970: 8).

87 Determinate in the sense that the child has sufficient skill to craft a pot. Clearly, there is an indeterminate capacity in the average human child to eventually learn this technology.

88 Leibniz (1989: 214) *Principles of Nature and Grace* §6.

89 'Petrus ex. gr. est quid reale; vera autem idea Petri est essentia Petri obiectiva, et in se quid reale, et omnino diversum ab ipso Petro. Cum itaque idea Petri sit quid reale habens suam essentiam peculiarem, erit etiam quid intelligibile, id est, obiectum alterius ideae, quae idea habebit in se obiective omne id, quod idea Petri habet formaliter, et rursus idea, quae est ideae Petri, habet iterum suam essentiam, quae etiam potest esse obiectum alterius ideae, et sic indefinite. Quod quisque potest experiri, dum videt se scire, quid sit Petrus, et etiam scire se scire, et rursus scit se scire, quod scit etc.'

90 Suàrez and others also use this terminology, but there is no evidence that Spinoza directly read these works.

91 Cf. de Muralt (2002: 19ff.).

92 (1972).

93 Cf. e.g. Aquinas (1947) Ch. 10, 'Quod Deus est sua essentia', where Aquinas expressly states that the essence of a thing is that which 'signifies' the thing (excluding any accidents), and that formal essence stands over as potency from the actual thing in act, save in God, who has no potency but is pure act, and so formal and actual essence coincide in Him.

94 'Idea vera (habemus enim ideam veram) est diversum quid a suo ideato. Nam aliud est circulus, aliud idea circuli; idea enim circuli non est aliquid, habens peripheriam et centrum, uti circulus, nec idea corporis est ipsum corpus.'

95 'Et cum sit quid diversum a suo ideato, erit etiam per se aliquid intelligibile, hoc est, idea quoad suam essentiam formalem potest esse obiectum alterius essentiae obiectivae, et rursus haec altera essentia obiectiva erit etiam in se spectata quid reale et intelligibile, et sic indefinite.'

96 TdIE §31.

97 TTPIV on faith and works.

98 Negri makes the distinction (1991: 190ff.).

99 EIIIP18 Sch. 2.

100 See Deleuze's entry 'Sign' in Deleuze (1988), where the grounding of the sign in the affects is discussed.
101 Metaphysical Discourse §II; New Essays II, c.21 §42 in (1989).
102 (EIIP44 Corol.1 Sch.).
103 Cf. de Muralt (2002: 31).
104 Spinoza expressly considers the finite corollary in EIV Def. 6.
105 My emphasis. Compare Stobaeos' report of Chrysippos SVF I.26.11.
106 Ibid. Note the use of attribute is different from that in the *Ethics.*
107 I.4; Geb. I/244.
108 Ibid.
109 Cf. CM II.1 'On God's Eternity'.
110 Ibid.
111 'Series' is Spinoza's own terminology (TdIE §99ff.), and had already been used by Lipsius in *De Constantia* to refer to the chain of causation.
112 Evidently this would be an inexhaustible movement, save that Spinoza believes in an attainable limit of infinity as a moment of passage, as is shown in his belief in intuition and the beatific moment in this life, *pace* Leibniz.
113 (1841) 1971–1990: 256–308, hereafter *Differenz.*
114 *Differenz* Pt.II Ch. 1.
115 'Avant lui (c.-à-d. Epicure) on n'avait admis dans les atomes que le mouvement de pesanteur, et celui de réflexion [. . .] Epicure supposa que même au milieu du vide, les atomes déclinaient un peu de la ligne, et de là venait la liberté . . .' *Differenz* p. 279.
116 'Die *relative Existenz* aber, die dem Atom gegenübertritt, *das Dasein, das es zu negieren hat,* ist *die gerade Linie.* Die unmittelbare Negation dieser Bewegung ist *eine andere Bewegung,* also, selbst räumlich vorgestellt, die *Deklination von der geraden Linie . . . Die Bewegung des Falls ist die Bewegung der Unselbständigkeit.*' Differenz p. 281, emphasis in original.
117 Ibid. 'Lukrez behauptet daher mit Recht, daß die Deklination die fati foedera [the bonds of fate] durchbricht; und, wie er dies sogleich auf das Bewußtsein anwendet so kann vom Atom gesagt werden, die Deklination sei das Etwas in seiner Brust, was entgegenkämpfen und widerstehen kann.'

Bibliography

Aquinas, T. (1882) *Sancti Thomae Aquinatis (doctoris angelicae): Opera omni* (13 vols), Typographia Polyglotta, Rome.
—— (1947) *Compendium theologiae,* S.J. Cyril Vollert (trans.), B. Herder Book Co., St. Louis, MO and London.
Arnim, J. von (1979) *Stoicorum veterum fragmenta* (4 vols), BG Teubner, Stuttgart.
Audié, F. (2007) *Spinoza et les mathématiques,* PUPS, Paris.
Berkeley, G. (2002) *The Analyst,* D.R. Wilkins (ed.), Dublin.
Bove, L. (1996) *La stratégie du conatus,* VRIN, Paris.
Bréhier, E. (1951) *Chrysippe et l'ancien stoïcisme,* PUF, Paris.
—— (1970) *Théorie des Incorporels chez les stoïciens,* PUF, Paris.
Clauberg, J. (1968) *Opera omnia philosophica, postum hrsg. von Johann Thedoro Schalbruch,* orig. 1961, Nachdruck Olms, Hildesheim.
Cottingham, J. (ed.) (1992) *The Cambridge Companion to Descartes,* Cambridge University Press, Cambridge.
De Witt, J. (2000) *Elementa Curvarum Linearum Tome 1,* A.W. Grootendoorst (trans.), Springer, Berlin.
Deleuze, G. (1988) *Spinoza: Practical Philosophy,* R. Hurley (trans.), City Light Books, San Francisco, CA.

—— (1990a) *Expressionism in Philosophy: Spinoza*, M. Joughlin (trans.), Zone Books, New York.
—— (1990b) *The Logic of Sense*, C. Boundas (trans.), Continuum, London.
—— (1994) *Difference and Repetition*, P. Patton (trans.), Continuum, London.
—— (1998) *Essays Critical and Clinical*, D. Smith and M. Greco (trans.), Verso, London.
Derrida, J. (1982) *Margins of Philosophy*, University of Chicago Press, Chicago, IL.
Eisenberg, Paul D. (1971) 'How to Understand De Intellectus Emendatione' 9(2) *Journal of the History of Philosophy* 171–191.
Garber, D. (1992) *Descartes' Metaphysical Physics*, University of Chicago Press, Chicago, IL.
Garrett, D. (1996) *The Cambridge Companion to Spinoza*, Cambridge University Press, Cambridge.
Gaukroger, S. (ed.) (1980) *Descartes: Philosophy, Mathematics and Physics*, Harvester Press, Sussex and Totowa, NJ.
—— (ed.) (2000) *Descartes' Natural Philosophy*, Routledge, London.
—— (2002) *Descartes' System of Natural Philosophy*, Cambridge University Press, Cambridge.
Gueroult, M. (1968a) *Descartes selon l'ordre des raisons: II – L'âme et le corps*, Aubier, Éditions Montaigne, Paris.
—— (1968b) *Spinoza: I – Dieu*, Aubier, Éditions Montaigne, Paris.
—— (1974) *Spinoza: II – L'âme*, Aubier, Éditions Montaigne, Paris.
Hahm, D.E. (1972) 'Chrysippus' solution to the Democritean dilemma of the cone' 63(2) *Isis* 205–220.
Heath, T.L. (1956) *The 13 Books of Euclid's Elements*, Dover, New York.
Hegel, G.W.F. (1969) *Werke in zwanzig Bänden*, Suhrkamp Verlag, Frankfurt am Main. The Roman numeral following the year refers to the volume number.
Israel, J. I. (2001) *Radical Enlightenment: Philosophy and the Making of Modernity 1650–1750*, Oxford University Press, Oxford.
—— (2006) *Enlightenment Contested: Philosophy, Modernity and the Emancipation of Man 1670–1752*, Oxford University Press, Oxford.
Kline, M. (1972) *Mathematical Thought from Ancient to Modern Times* (3 vols.), Oxford University Press, Oxford.
Kretzmann, N. (1970) 'Medieval logicians on the meaning of the propositio' 67(20) *The Journal of Philosophy* 767–787.
Lagrée, J. (1989) 'Clauberg et Spinoza. De la logique novantique à la puissance de l'idée vraie', in *Méthode et métaphysique, Travaux et documents du groupe de recherches spinozistes*, no.2, PUP, Sorbonne.
Lebrun, G. (1972) *La patience du concept: Essai sur le discours hégélien*, Gallimard, Paris.
Leibniz, G.W. (1962) *G.W. Leibniz: Mathematische Schriften*, C.I. Gerhardt (ed.), Georg Olms Verlagsbuchhandlung, Hildesheim.
—— (1989) *Philosophical Essays*, Ariew and Garber (trans.), Hackett, Indianapolis.
Lipsius, J. (1604) *Manuductionis ad Stoicam philosophiam* (3 vols), Ioannem Moretum, Antwerp.
—— (1644) *Philosophia & Physiologia Stoicorum*, Ioannis Maire, Leiden. [Note: Held at the Bayerische Stadtsbibliothek München, the text contains a reprint of the *Manuductio* and the *Physiologia* bound as one, presumably at a later date, given the disorder of the frontispieces.]
—— (1998) *De Constantia/Von der Standhaftigkeit*, F. Neumann (trans.), Dieterich'sche Verlagsbuchhandlung, Mainz.
Macherey, P. (1990) *Hegel ou Spinoza*, Éditions. La Découverte, Paris.
Marx, K. and Engels, F. (1971–1990) *Marx-Engels Werke: Ergänzungsband*, Dietz Verlag, Berlin.

Muralt, A. de (2002) *L'unité de la philosophie politique: Duns Scot, Occam et Suarez, au libéralisme contemporain*, VRIN, Paris.
Negri, A. (1991) *The Savage Anomaly: The Power of Spinoza's Metaphysics and Politics*, University of Minnesota Press, Minneapolis, MN.
Newton, Sir I. (1999) *The Principia: Mathematical Principles of Natural Philosophy*, I. Bernard Cohen and A. Whitman (trans.), University of California Press, Berkeley, CA.
Parkinson, G.H.R. (2000) *Spinoza: Ethics*, Oxford University Press, Oxford.
Schuhmann, K. (1987) 'Methodenfragen bei Spinoza und Hobbes: zum Problem des Einflusses' 3 *Studia Spinozana* 61.
Serres, M. (1997) *Le système de Leibniz et ses modèles mathématiques*, Epimethée, PUF, Paris.
Sharp, H. and Smith, J.E. (2012) *Between Hegel and Spinoza*, Bloomsbury, London.
Wintgens, L.J. (2012) *Legisprudence: Practical Reason in Legislation*, Ashgate, Farnham.
Wolfson, A. (1958) *The Philosophy of Spinoza: Unfolding the Latent Processes of his Reasoning*, Meridian, New York.

Chapter 3

The physics of right

. . . and all reality belongs only to unities.

Leibniz to de Volder, 30 June 1704[1]

3.1 Introduction

At a recent Spinoza conference in Aberdeen, Filip Buyse reports[2] the revelation by Jonathan Israel, at a similar conference at the University of Sydney, of a letter by Spinoza's contemporary and Leiden alumnus, one Dr Cornelis Bontekoe (aka Dekker). The letter of the former student, it is reported, informs its recipient that many young students had often visited Spinoza when he lived at Rijnsburg, and there learned from a geometry tutor who was engaged in rewriting Descartes' *Principles of Philosophy* in geometrical form. It seems that rather than the hapless Caesarius being a singular case of a young man receiving tuition from Spinoza, the philosopher was giving tutorials in Cartesian natural philosophy to a much wider range of Leiden students in parallel to their courses under Heereboord, this latter attempting to assimilate the more acceptable aspects of Cartesian physics into the Scholastic framework. Furthermore, Buyse notes[3] the discovery by Pina Totaro of a letter from Nicolaus Steno dated 4 September 1677, in which we are told that Spinoza regularly attended Steno's anatomy lectures given at Leiden, but that the surreptitious attendee had changed under the influence of Descartes' works and *uno certo van Enden*,[4] the infamous Latin tutor whose role in Low Countries and French radicalism is recounted at length by Nadler (2001) and Israel (2001, 2006). Perhaps these biographical enhancements will allow Spinoza scholars to be more open about what they have always suspected: that Spinoza's *Ethics* implies a physics of depth and originality, and that there is more to the *Physical Interlude* after EIIP13 Sch. (hereafter the 'PI') than meets the eye. Indeed, perhaps now it is time to link Spinoza more clearly to the state of physics in the Low Countries, and to see him as someone well versed in the advances of the day, but concerned not with the results of these advances, but rather the reasons behind the principles that had been moving towards clarification through his century.

As we shall show, if one makes this link to contemporary physics to which he had access, and in particular the physical underpinnings of Descartes' laws of motion, much of his thinking becomes far clearer. In this, we will rely on the recent arguments by Gaukroger,[5] McLaughlin[6] and Schuster,[7] each of whom by various paths have revealed how Descartes' kinematics is really a statics, and a hydrostatics at that. Furthermore, we will add much to these routes to interpretation by drawing on another source of physical thinking available to Spinoza, with which his contemporaries had been battling since Jordanus at least: the *Mechanical Problems* of the Pseudo-Aristoteles, which Spinoza owned as part of his Basileus edition of the *Aristoteles Stagiritae Opera Omnia*.[8] Starting out from the extremes of the *Mechanical Problems* and Cartesian (hydro-)statics, as the third vertex of our physical triangle we draw on the work of Giordano Bruno to understand how Spinoza's position on limits and the infinite differs from the Italian heretic's Neo-Platonist ideas. It is in the *Mechanical Problems* and in Bruno that we find revealing discussions of that most troublesome idea 'motion and rest', though to link this conception to Spinoza's own, again we must look to Descartes, this time in his theory of light, to understand how motion and rest becomes ordered by infinite power.

This is all quite far from interpretations that see Spinoza as a Hobbesian in his doctrine of forces. There is no evidence whatsoever that Spinoza knew Hobbes' physical theory; it is simply a result of the widespread research into statics and kinematics, with a view to a theory of dynamics that overturned the Peripatetic dogma, that the two thinkers should have comparable ideas at a superficial level. They are dealing with the same theoretical object, but the methods they are using are quite different. Our aim in the second part of this work will be to construct and to show the great difference of Spinoza's theory of natural right from that of Hobbes. This chapter therefore serves to provide the context for that leap, and by moving from the simplest machines to a nascent theory of dynamics, to show how our exposition of the attributes in the foregoing chapter feeds into these physical theories to create a *sui generis* system of natural right. Consequently, we might summarise the broad aims of this chapter as follows:

(a) to establish Spinoza's competence as a 'physicist';
(b) to show the context of his material knowledge;
(c) to outline his understanding of machines as paradigms of things;
(d) to indicate the origins of his terminology of power, force and right;
(e) to explicate his theory of motion and rest, not only as a key component of his thought, but as a prime example of his method; and
(f) to prepare the ground for an understanding of the nature and limitations of the general equilibrium of power of machines.

3.2 Methodological note

As noted above, this chapter builds on the findings of Gaukroger, McLaughlin and Schuster (*opere citato*, respectively) with respect to the re-establishment of the principles of statics at the core of Descartes' theory of kinematics. In the seventeenth century, unbeknown to its participants, a battle was raging over the best route to providing a theory of dynamics *qua* theory of variations in motions. Galileo had overturned the Scholastic theory of motions with his mathematisation of kinematics, and initially felt a similar move using his method for kinematics could be made to achieve a dynamics, before abandoning these attempts and endeavouring to use the other branch of physics, the theory of static forces. At the other end of the century, Newton would resolve the problematic by showing how kinematics was indeed the route to understanding, by deduction from mathematically accounted variations, the forces acting on a body.

Gaukroger, McLaughlin and Schuster, very broadly speaking, place Descartes very much at the midpoint of this struggle. The critical finding that overturns much interpretation and mitigates criticism of Descartes' theory of kinematics, exemplified by his laws of collision, is that while Descartes *presents* his kinematics in the language of Galileo, his private thinking is almost entirely framed by the methods of statics, and in particular hydrostatics. The result, as these ingenious researchers amply demonstrate, is that the patent absurdities of some of Descartes' theories are indeed incorrect, but they do not result from an inexplicable lapse of thought on Descartes' behalf; there are perfectly rational grounds for a believer in the power of statics to have been so convinced his approach was the correct one that he would ignore empirical evidence in favour of theoretical coherence – rational grounds that can be reconstructed today to explain the absurdities. Descartes was wrong, but he was rigorously wrong.

Turning to Spinoza, the detail of the above results immediately suggested a simple interpretative move: as with Descartes, have we been reading Spinoza's physics through all-too-Newtonian spectacles. We have a thinker authoring a book on Cartesian physics, teaching the method, and openly adopting all but one of the Cartesian laws of collision (indeed accepting incorrect ones and actively denying a correct law). Do we have a thinker whose *Ethics* stands at least on one pillar – the kinematics of the PI – who, in fact, is erroneously using kinematic language to express an utterly different theory of static (and dynamic) forces, that subtends this language as the *logos* grants meaning to the letter? An aspect of this chapter will concern whether such an interpretation may be borne out. Clearly, we cannot assess the juridico-ethical meaning of *transitions* in the power of acting if *that which transits* is not itself correctly understood. We hope to establish by the end of this chapter that that which transits is not the atomic 'corpuscule' in plenum that appears on the face of Spinoza's physics, but that the language of simple bodies *expresses* a theory of forces even more tightly and coherently than hitherto guessed.

3.3 Statics – the first order of immutability

3.3.1 Nature as machine

Coming down to Spinoza's time, there are five simple machines listed by Heron of Alexandria: the lever, the pulley, the wedge, the wheel and the Archimedean screw. Renaissance mechanicians added a sixth machine: the inclined plane. The study of these machines we call statics, and the essence of this study is the equilibrium of forces; whatever force we put into our machine produces an equal force coming out. Each machine relies on this fact to its advantage, by *communicating* the impressed force in some new manner to produce a desired effect. Descartes, in his *Traité de la mécanique, explication des machines et engins par l'aide desquels on peut avec une petite force levier un fardeau fort pesant* (1637) (hereafter the TM), describes the following machines:

(a) The lever (*vectis*) is a balance that uses distance from the fulcrum to permit a new distribution of effects (a small weight far from the fulcrum can lift a heavy weight close to the fulcrum).
(b) The wheel (*axis in peritrochio*) is an infinite number of levers around an axle using the resistant force of its fixture.
(c) The pulley (*trochlea*) distributes weights around a wheel and axle.
(d) The wedge (*cunea*), used to split wood or stone, distributes an applied vertical force along its opposing sides as two levers.
(e) The inclined plane, used to load ships, is a right triangle ABC where the uppermost point is the angle θ between the hypotenuse AB and vertical BC, with a cord linking a smaller weight resting on AB to a greater weight hanging parallel to BC over angle θ – the oblique wedge of the hypotenuse serves to resist by a factor of that obliquity the downward force of the weight at BC.
(f) The screw (*cochlea*) is a combination of the above: it is a continuous wedge deployed obliquely, therefore also a continuous inclined plane, turned by use of a wheel.

These six simple machines may be understood in a manner most revealing to Spinozism by reference to the block and tackle (*polispaste*), which is a system of pulleys in common use in merchant shipping, and thus a sight Spinoza would have seen every day in his youth, as the block and tackle was found not only along the canals of Amsterdam, but also jutting from the gable of every tall merchant house. If the essence of the pulley is to distribute forces around a wheel and so invert an applied force, the block and tackle uses multiple pulley configurations to distribute those same forces across more and more wheels on the same block, each affixed in some manner (to a davit[9] for upward pull, and to the load to be lifted for downward pull). Now, if the rope, which cannot vary in length, is held tense and the lifted load does not move, then the system is in equilibrium. More importantly, however, the downward pull exerted by the load is being borne not just by the hauler, but by each part of the rope taken around the pulley wheel and upwards once again to the support of the system: the load is distributed equally. Thus, in a gun tackle, the weight is distributed once to the hauler and once to the davit holding up the block; that is, the load is distributed by a factor of two, and the hauler obtains an ideal mechanical advantage at each moment such that he need exert only half the force to lift the same weight (ignoring friction). For each new loop of the same rope we run around a wheel in the block, we add a new part to the tensed rope to which it distributes the load equally, dividing the weight by three, four and so on. This is how Descartes explains the pulley system in the TM.

The block and tackle is perhaps the most instructive machine because it highlights three principles that Descartes discusses in the TM, and reveals a fourth, that of moment, to which Descartes would return in correspondence with interested parties. The first principle is that of communicative tension: the rope must be tense to be useful, and once it is, it communicates all the applied forces equally through the system. The second is simply a new perspective on the first, composition of forces: the effects produced by the system are composed of all the forces applied to the system. Descartes would use the same argumentation in *Le monde* §14 when discussing his theory of composition of light rays. The third is the trade-off between force and distance common to all machines: by the number of times the rope is wrapped into parts, so the length of rope that must be drawn from the system to produce the same effect is multiplied. In short, a pulley rope must be pulled 10 ft to raise a load 10 ft, but a gun tackle of two parts requires that the rope be pulled 20 ft to raise the load 10 ft. The fourth principle is the grounding principle for the foregoing, that of moment. In a letter to Mersenne, Descartes makes clear that taking any machinic assemblage in equilibrium, the force needed to move it from equilibrium is the force applicable only at that instantaneous moment of initial motion. He writes: 'I say begins to descend and not just descend, because it is the beginning of the descent to which one must pay attention.'[10] Putting to one side the importance of this insight for the subsequent development of calculus (not least because Spinoza dismisses the examination of the applicates of curves that Descartes' analysis implies),[11] the significance of this principle is its understanding that given equilibrium under tension, any variation in that tension will produce instantaneous movement to a new equilibrium: (a) by the action and reaction of the composed forces; and (b) by the least possible such actions and reactions. Lagrange (in his *Mécanique analytique* of 1811) would later formulate this *Principle of Pulleys* in revealing analytic terms by naming the parts of the system (the parts of rope) exerting the static forces P, Q, R . . . etc. and calling the instantaneously applied infinitesimal differences of displacement p, q, r . . . The forces will be in equilibrium when the following holds:

$$Pp + Qq + Rr + \ldots = 0$$

We think this analytic anachronism is very important for understanding in more modern terms the intuitive understanding of simple machines of Spinoza's contemporaries in a manner revealing of Spinoza's own thought. The above expression asserts, in effect, that if some displacing force p is applied to P, then to maintain equilibrium reactive forces as q, r . . . must occur. For simple machines, by their nature their state is not supposed to be maintained and some 'work' will be produced from the system. If a sailor pulls the rope, the machine will do the minimum possible to find a new equilibrium and so rebalance like a lever. It works to maintain equilibrium; it is a by-product of resistance (in Spinoza's sense of 'endeavour', not the modern sense used in the physics of materials). It is our assertion that this equilibrium forms the first building block of Spinoza's conception of Nature. The above expression of static equilibrium is nothing other than the first building block, under the attribute of Extension, of the immutable order of finite things: whatever effect occurs in infinite mediate mode, the sum total of contemporaneous effects with that first effect will have a net effect equal to zero. We call this the '*general equilibrium*'.

Yet, can we be sure this was Spinoza's understanding at all? Descartes' TM formed part of his *Brieven*, which Spinoza owned, and furthermore it had been produced initially at the request of Constantin Huygens, the father of Christian, the latter acquainted in some manner with the 'Jew of Rijnsburg'. Indeed, in *Letter 30A* of 7 October 1665, we have the claim by Spinoza that he had discussed the younger Huygen's draft *Dioptrics* and *Parhelia* with the author, and had been related a problem concerning lens compensation. Now the same TM was passed between *savants*, coming also into the hands of Father Mersenne, for example. Also, the TM itself is not completely novel, despite Descartes' arrogant belief to the contrary. Flemish mathematician Simon Stevin's works had been edited by Snell, and would have been known at least in outline to Spinoza. Nor was research in the field of statics in any way alien to Leiden University or the Schoolmen; many of the basic ideas of statics, though incorrectly determined, could be found in natural philosophical textbooks and drew most obviously from Aristoteles' *Physics* and the *Mechanical Problems* of the Pseudo-Aristotle (both of which were owned by Spinoza). Given the ground-breaking work of Galileo and Roberval, the collecting endeavours of Mersenne, and the earlier efforts of Italian mechanicians such as Baldi, Tartaglia, Bruno and Ubaldo, it would be frankly amazing if Spinoza, passing himself off as capable of teaching the new philosophy of Cartesian mechanism, was at least broadly competent in his understanding of contemporary statics, if not innovative. That he was may be given by the following direct example of his deployment of this science, and by a wider discussion of statics' indirect relevance to Spinoza's acceptance of all but one of the Cartesian *Laws of Motion*, which is examined in the following section.

As to the direct example of some skill in statics, the much overlooked Letter 6 to Oldenburg, in which Spinoza critiques Boyles' experiments on nitre, contains in its last section *On Solidity* two experiments Spinoza devises for determining the absolute 'weight' (*pondus*) of an object, which combine pulleys and, in the first case, an interesting inversion of the idea of the inclined plane – a frictionless mirror. Spinoza writes:

> it comes very near the true weight. But I would consider it worthwhile to examine this, so as to obtain, so far as possible, the ratio between the lateral or horizontal pressure of air and the perpendicular pressure.
>
> (Letter 6)

Spinoza goes on to describe, with accompanying figures, two simple machines. The first is particularly interesting in that a weight *G* is suspended by a cord over a pulley wheel, the other end of the cord being attached to a piece of marble *B* resting on a thoroughly smoothed flat mirror. This piece of marble rests contiguous to a second piece of marble *A* attached by a cord to a hook *E* on the same plane. The downward force of *G* will pull *B* away from *A*, indicating the force exerted to achieve this work. Notice how Spinoza takes the principle of the inclined plane and inverts it so that the perpendicular plane now ensures 'no' oblique resisting force is applied. Additionally to this mechanical sublation of the wedge-like force of the inclined plane, Spinoza illustrates his understanding of the intervention of friction by using a mirror (possibly one he could himself grind smooth) and marble, presumably polished also as smooth as desired. Spinoza then briefly posits an experiment to test vertical weight by allowing the marble to hang free from the pulley-wheel and noticing how the force of *G* pulls this marble away from the now fixed lower piece of marble. Spinoza does not feel it necessary to insult Oldenburg's intelligence by going into this second experiment in detail, suggesting that the first experiment is, he feels, more novel and deserving of explication to his correspondent of the Royal Society.

While Spinoza is clear here that the potential difference in relative weight is due to the differential of horizontal and vertical air pressures pushing on the examined object, it is interesting to see in the experiment an intuition about possible difference in weight due to direction. This interest is possibly due to the intuition's possible source in Spinoza's library, in the *Mechanical Problems* or simply *Mechanica*.

We assume Spinoza knew, if not from his surreptitiously attended Leiden University lectures then from simply reading the text he had paid no small sum for, that the *Mechanica* was written by someone other than Aristoteles, possibly also a member of the Lyceum but earlier than Archimedes and Euclid. It is a remarkably practical treatise with its discussion of meathooks and galleys; it indicates a geometrical capacity and insight in excess of Aristoteles; yet its belief that the generation of the circle takes place without fixed proportion indicates that the author was not aware of trigonometry. Possible identities of authors have been suggested, such as Straton, Heron of Alexandria,[12] and Archytas of Terentum.[13] We shall refer to the author of the *Mechanica* as the *Pseudo-Aristoteles*.

Can we adduce any further evidence that Spinoza did actually read the *Mechanica*? Guido Ubaldo spent some time attacking the *Mechanica* in his own work,[14] and we shall see that Descartes also seems to have taken on board some of its arguments. In fact, the *Mechanica* offers quite a trove for the Spinoza scholar of coincidences, parallels and all-but-affirmative sources. It seems our problem is rather of determining whether Spinoza derived certain theses directly from those of the Pseudo-Aristoteles, or they were mediated to him via Descartes. By way of example, *Mechanica* Problem 15 (hereafter cited *Mech.* §[problem no.]) reads:

> Why are pebbles at the seashore rounded? At the start they were oblong stones and shells. Is it because the parts more distant from the middle are

> carried faster in any movement? . . . And whatever is carried faster gets hit harder itself.

Of course, we find not dissimilar arguments about force wearing away angular parts of corpuscles in both Descartes and, in his recapitulation of Descartes' position, in Spinoza (DPPIIIP2). In Spinoza's synthesising of Descartes, however, the erosion is immediate on the first motion of the corpuscles, for body and extension are equal and the corpuscles cannot occupy more extension in motion than at rest. The direct use of collision deriving from circular motion at least suggests a common heritage to this idea.

Returning to our thread, the Pseudo-Aristoteles appears to have intuited the difference between weight towards the centre of the earth and what we would now call inertia or mass operating along a line perpendicular to the earth. Thus, in *Mech.* §10 our unknown author writes:

> Why is an empty balance beam easier to move than a weighted one? In the same way also a wheel or any such thing; the heavier is harder and the smaller is lighter. This is true not only opposite the weight, but sideways. Opposite to its downward inclination it is harder to move anything, but there is no downward inclination sideways.

The downward inclination (*rhépō*) for this purpose is the Pseudo-Aristoteles' realisation in *Mech.* §8 that the circle must be raised on one side if it is to fall on the other, or, in more modern terms, the circle, like the lever (but with an infinity of arms), must have its centre of gravity shifted upwards in order to produce an effect, the downward inclination, which lowers the centre of gravity back to the equilibrium state. However, with remarkable honesty the Pseudo-Aristoteles admits that this inclining action, which derives from his foundational principle of the circle, only operates vertically, whereas experience tells him and us that a cylinder does not roll sideways of its own accord. The Pseudo-Aristoteles raises a question that he does not answer: what, ignoring friction, causes resistance to sideways motion? One can see from Spinoza's Letter 6, even if he is not directly drawing inspiration from the *Mechanica*, the same question about what we would call mass (resistance to acceleration) but Spinoza regards as relatively disposed *weight*, is being considered as a valid question – horizontal 'weight' is not necessarily the same as vertical 'weight' – and is being answered by using the Cartesian hypothesis that this weight is due to horizontal ambient pressure (i.e. the constant pushes of air corpuscles).

The *a priori* principles of the Pseudo-Aristoteles derive from the quasi-mystical powers of the circle, whereas Spinoza's concerns are expressly the result of thinking a plenum of motive corpuscles, yet the common thread is the practical intuition that forces in different directions might not compose in the same way, and thus could produce different relative weights. Even if the *Mechanica* is not the inspiration for Spinoza's experiments to determine absolute weight, it at least indicates a commonality of practical competence between the two thinkers of mechanics.

This, combined with Spinoza's attempt to use the simple machines in a combination that innovates on the inclined plane to produce a lack of friction, certainly does not suggest only a passing interest in statics. We suggest that Spinoza had at least a moderate degree of competence in the field, hampered though he may have been by his concerns regarding analytic approaches to the subject.

The most interesting coincidence of interests, however, in the *Mechanica* of the Pseudo-Aristoteles, is its discussion of the circle and the lever. It is to this critical relation we must now turn if we are to understand why Spinoza accepted Descartes' *Laws of Motion*. We shall see that it is because Descartes' kinematics is really a statics based on the lever rotating about a fulcrum that Spinoza's debt to statics is further entrenched by the weight of evidence.

3.3.2 From kinematics to statics; from statics to kinematics

The continued importance of the *Mechanica* for the teaching of mechanics in Spinoza's time should not be underestimated, even though its theories had been shown to rest on false premises even in Hellenic times. The Pseudo-Aristoteles seeks to explain simple machines[15] by reference to the circle and periphery[16] motions. What we aim to show in this section is how an author potentially known to Spinoza uses kinematic proportions to explicate an early theory of machines. It is this building up of a non-force-based theory of statics, and related motions as a theory of kinematics, from a single principle of circular motion, which is one of the more striking and lasting contributions of the *Mechanica*. In *nuce*, the Pseudo-Aristoteles notices that a radius around *A*, which runs *Af*, and is then extended out again to *AfF*, can be seen to describe two arcs, one through the inner point on the radius *f* called *bfc*, one through the outer point *F* called *BFC*. He further proves using elementary geometry that as *AfF* rotates the arc, *BFC* is always longer than arc *bfc* and in a certain proportion. If we now extend the radius from *A* in the opposite direction out to where it meets the circle described by *Af* rotated, one immediately sees that moving this foreshortened arm a small distance continues to produce the greater movement of radius *AfF*. In the first instance, the circle thus explains the link between lever and distance travelled.

The reason for this link is given by the Pseudo-Aristoteles in his introduction – the circle has the marvellous properties of being able to go in two directions at once, and to have different points on each radius going in different directions and describing motions of different length. This power is combined to what 'normally' happens: normally a thing only goes in one direction. An object on the circumference seeks to travel in a straight line, but the circle carries or displaces (*pherein*) this natural tendency according to downwards inclination. In Peripatetic fashion, the Pseudo-Aristoteles calls the straight-line tendency the *according-to-nature* or natural (*kata phusin*), and the circle's intervention or effect on the object the *contrary-to-nature* or unnatural (*para phusin*). If one considers *Mech.* §1, one can see that the arc lengths *BF* and *bf* are decomposed into their natural (*HF*, *hf*) and unnatural (*BH*, *bh*) tendencies (see further the translation of the *Mechanica* by T.N. Winter (2007)).[17]

The Pseudo-Aristoteles has been speaking of the determinate relation between the two contrary motions each point on a circle makes; he now attempts to determine the *certain proportion* of natural motion and unnatural motion. A technical note: the Euclidean definition of a ratio is a relation between two magnitudes; the proportion is defined as the relation of equivalence between two ratios.[18] Spinoza knew this perfectly well when he spoke of a certain proportion of movement and rest, and it appears that the Pseudo-Aristoteles uses proportion (*logos*) in the same sense, for he in effect writes:[19]

$$\frac{BH}{HF} : \frac{bh}{hf}$$

Or in words, the radius determines a proportion between every point along its length, such that every point describes a motion composed by a constant ratio of natural and unnatural motion. By simple algebraic manipulation of the proportion, we see:

$$\frac{HF}{hf} : \frac{BH}{bh}$$

or that the natural motions and unnatural motions in ratio all stand in proportion along the length of the radius, which is intuitively obvious. The Pseudo-Aristotle can thus correctly write that if a point is displaced by two motions in ratio, but *these have no constant proportion* (*logos*) and no fixed time, no straight line can be produced. He then concludes that if the same motion is in a fixed proportion, but not in a fixed time, a curve is produced. In simple terms, our author has realised that at the start of its journey describing an arc, our point starts to move more along its tangent than with respect to the unnatural constraint of the circle, but that over time its natural motion becomes smaller and the unnatural motion accounts for more of what the point actually does. It is an important intuition, but it also shows the primitive level of the Pseudo-Aristoteles' geometry; we immediately can, and indeed the Alexandrines could, see that what is described is a trigonometric function, namely the wave produced by the cosine in the unit circle.[20] This provides a further important lesson for understanding Spinoza – that just because he claims that the ratio of motion and rest is certain, he is not claiming it is static as some scholars are wont to believe; the ratio's terms may vary, and ratios might both diverge or converge, provided the proportion of the ratios remains the same.[21] A trigonometric function is a certain function, but the elements placed in ratio by it are varying. Thus, the great trouble people have attempting to explain how a thing may remain individuated if it gains motion or rest may be somewhat avoided if we first reject the consistent attempt to translate *eadem ratione* as 'a certain proportion' when in Lem. V Spinoza deliberately uses *proportione* to talk about the relation between different ratios of motion and rest. We shall return to this in due course.

Apart from these geometric limitations and the apparent appeal to the Aristotelian theory of time to account for the production of the circle, the *Mechanica*'s actual attempts to explain simple machines are where the problems of relying solely on kinematics (i.e. solely on the proportions of motions) start to appear. Despite clever explanations of the balance, wedge and lever, and of the role of radial distance from the fulcrum (centre) in assisting in lifting heavy weights, the Pseudo-Aristoteles goes too far in relying solely on these motions for explanation. When explaining[22] the ability to lift a heavy load by placing it on a lever close to the fulcrum, and using the arm at some distance from the fulcrum, our author only makes explanatory reference to distance travelled along the respective arc-lengths. Force is applied to raise the lever and weight, but it is the reciprocal distance from the fulcrum that alone is relied upon to explain the *cur ita sit* of the work performed. This is why the Pseudo-Aristoteles is confounded when he realises that the inclination of the circle in a vertical manner, which presumably he regards as the *fons et origo* of 'force', in no way helps him explain how things such as Zeno's arrow are 'inclined' sideways. More subtly, the arc-length motion is regarded as the relevant work performed by the lever, when Galileo and Descartes would reveal that the work performed only had reference to the straight-line motion in this case, and was augmented by the moment of force applied. Peripatetic physics would be hamstrung by this need to explain the complete motion by distances travelled, by natural and unnatural tendencies, and a refusal to accept the quantitative role forces such as weight/inertia and impetus had to play.

With these ideas of proportions of natural and unnatural motions (*kinesis*), which are explained by the supposedly paradoxical marvel that is the circle, we now have quite an interesting context with which to jump to the work of Descartes and Spinoza in kinematics and statics. It is as if Descartes, in his reaction against the Schoolmen, adopts the mirror-opposite position of the Pseudo-Aristoteles, for the Frenchman starts his early investigations on the basis that all motions are in fact explicable by forces, and that the science of forces – statics – teaches us all we need to know about kinematics. For these insights, gratitude is owed to McLaughlin, Gaukroger and Schuster,[23] who, with various papers, have explicated Descartes' debt to statics and hydrostatics, mediated through his mentor Beeckman. The reader is referred to these with strong recommendation, and we will only briefly summarise the relevant insights for Spinoza.

In the TM, Descartes leaves the lever to last because of the simple machines it 'is the most difficult of all to explain'. He continues:

> Let us consider that while the force which moves this lever describes the entire semi-circle *ABCDE* and acts along the arc *ABCDE*, although the weight also describes the semi-circle *FGHIK*, it does not move upward by the length of the straight line *FOK*. Thus the proportion between the force necessary to move this weight to its gravitational weight must not be measured by the ratio between the two diameters of these circles, or between their two

circumferences, but rather by the ratio between the semi-circle of the larger circle and diameter of the smaller circle.

But the above simply assumes the sum total of all the movements around the semicircles. Descartes realises this and, positing that the force required at each point *ABCDE* can easily be shown to differ, he continues:

> in order to measure precisely what this force must be at each point of the curved line *ABCDE*, we need to know that it acts everywhere the same as if it were pulling a weight on a circular inclined plane, and that the inclination of each of the points of this circular plane must be measured by the slope of the straight line which is tangent to the circle at this point.

This insight that each point on *ABCDE* can be treated as a force to rectilinear motion, which, however, is constrained, echoes but inverts the Pseudo-Aristoteles, who placed the power of constraint entirely in the circle and reduced all else to motions alone. The same Cartesian logic can also be found in Spinoza's proofs of the motion of a stone in a sling, in DPPIIP16; the stone endeavouring to move at a tangent to the circle of its constrained impulsion. The introduction of the inclined plane is designed to show, as we saw above, that as the inclination becomes steeper, so the motion sideways becomes more a motion upwards, and thus more contrary to the downward motion of the weight hanging free over the apex of the slope. With the circle, deployed as a lever, the inclination changes with respect to the constant downward force of 'gravitation'.

Notice how Descartes realises that it is only the instantaneous moment of disequilibrium on both ends of the lever that is relevant, not, as the Schoolmen thought, the full motion around the curve, or an infinite number of tangents to that same curve (see above). The instantaneous movement is composed immediately by the relevant forces, thus denying a hierarchy of natural and unnatural motions as with the Schoolmen, and the motion produced is determined by the immediate inequality of forces. As Gaukroger shows, Descartes thinks that this imbalance in the lever is what impels things to motion, or at least the motion of a weight on a lever due to disequilibrium of forces is explicable clearly and distinctly in the same way as one free weight is impelled to motion when another free weight collides with it. The damning quotation is given by Gaukroger,[24] from a letter to Hobbes:

> His assumption that what does not yield to the smallest force cannot be moved by any force at all has no semblance of truth. Does anyone think that a weight of 100 lbs in a balance would yield to a weight of one pound placed in the other pan of the scale simply because it yields to a weight of 200 lbs.
>
> (18 January 1641, AT III: 287)

The semicircles to which Descartes refers can be considered as a geometrical expression of the nature of motive force, which Descartes effectively defines as the product of scalar weight/bulk and a magnitude of determinate motion, or motive force = bulk · speed [*sic*].[25] The weight, being scalar, is simply applied as a point on the lever. The location of this point on the lever arm is determined by the speed, the speed being treated as proportionate distance from the fulcrum of the lever. Thus, distance is proportionate to the relative speed of the opposing bulk, subject presumably to the determinate directions of the motion (assessed by reference to inclined plane). McLaughlin ingeniously shows[26] how Descartes' *Rules of Impact* (the *Rules*, PPII[46–52]) can be very clearly explained using this lever/balance model:

> Rule 1: if the arms of a balance are of equal length and the weights are equal, the scale is in equilibrium, and the conflict is a draw.
>
> Rule 2: if the weights are equal, the longer arm (greater speed) determines the winner.
>
> Rule 3: if the lengths of the arms are equal, the heavier body wins.

By way of example, consider a balance (as illustrated in Figure 3.1). On the left-hand side, a bulk of 1 lb has four units of motion, while on the right-hand side, a bulk of 2 lb has two units of motion. Applying Descartes' rules, we obtain:

$$\frac{m_1 v_1 + m_2 v_2}{m_1 + m_2} = \frac{(1\cdot\vec{4}) + (2\cdot\vec{2})}{3} = 2^1\!/_3$$

The careful reader will immediately realise, however, that this case of unequal speeds and unequal weights is *not* included in the *Rules*. Our reason for choosing this example is that Spinoza spotted the glaring omission and remedies it by inserting the case as DPPIIP26, between his proofs of Rule 2 and Rule 3.[27] It thus again illustrates his intimate understanding of the static basis of Descartes' theory. For Spinoza realises not only that, in applying Descartes' arithmetic formula for calculating resultant momentum, the formula above produces a seemingly

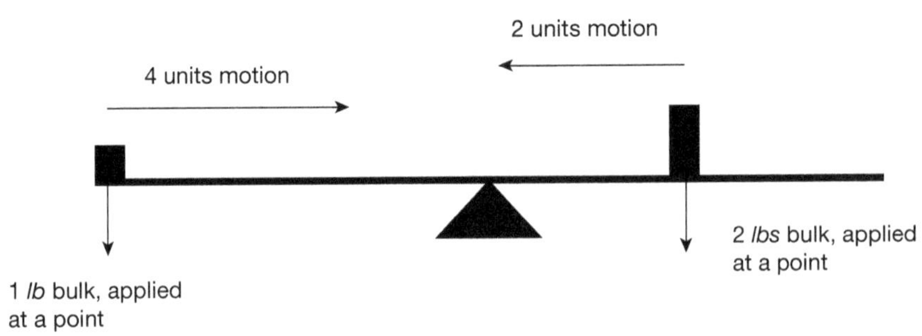

Figure 3.1 Static theory of impact

unhelpful result, but also that if the underlying static test of weights diversely opposed on a balance is applied, then equality results, thus $1 \cdot 4 - 2 \cdot 2 = 0$ (the little arrows sitting on top of the numbers tell us that the magnitudes are directed, in opposed directions in this case). Most interestingly, if this is indeed Spinoza's thought process, by opposing the weights to produce equilibrium, he perhaps sees the importance of the role of the negative (or opposite determination) in a way that Descartes did not. By seeing that equilibrium pertains, that is, that placing both weights on the lever simultaneously produces no effect, Spinoza is able on his premises to conclude:

> *A* and *B* will be reflected in opposite directions, retaining their own motion undiminished.
>
> (DPPIIP26 Proof)

In other words, equilibrium of motive force, irrespective of direction, means there is no *reason*, no cause, for any effect, and so there is no effect with respect to motive force. The relative opposition of the determinations, however, does produce an inequality, and this does produce an effect, an inversion of *relative* directions. This certainly appears to be Spinoza's thought process, for as Lécrivain has noted,[28] Spinoza recasts the *Rules* using three possible cases that must pertain, namely modification of direction only, modification of motion only, modification of direction and motion simultaneously. Spinoza repeatedly treats each case by searching for a reason for any variation from the existing state (equilibrium) of some thing. When this reason does not exist, so the relevant effect necessarily cannot occur; not simply, however, because there is an absence of any cause, but because no cause has been sufficient to disturb the *pre-existing causal equilibrium of the balance*, lever, pulley and so forth that holds it in its current state.

Similar thinking stands behind Descartes' *Rules*, the Fourth of which can be seen as an application of the above thinking. It reads:

> Fourthly, if body *C* were wholly at rest and were slightly larger than *B*, whatever the speed at which *B* were moved toward *C*, it would never move this *C*, but would repelled from it in the contrary direction; because a body at rest resists a great speed more than a small one, and this in proportion to the excess of the one over the other, and, therefore, there would always be a greater force in *C* to resist than in *B* to impel.
>
> (PPII[§49])

As Gaukroger notes, Descartes effectively ignores considerations of speed in favour of the relative bulk of the bodies. If we place *C* on a balance, and *C* is infinitesimally heavier than *B*, placing *B* on the other pan will not move *C*. But if *B* is infinitesimally heavier than *C*, the hypothesised immediate action, as McLaughlin notes, is grossly disproportionate: *B* descends as far as it can and raises *C* an equal and opposite amount. This is, in effect, the static interpretation of the Fifth Rule.[29]

That Spinoza understands that statics is driving Descartes' Laws of Motion and *Rules* is also quite evident from other parts of his synthetic reconstruction of the Frenchman's *Principles*. At DPPIIP13 and P14, Spinoza discusses in greater detail Descartes' claim that the 'immutability of the *work* of God' causes the conservation of motions in the world (PPII[42], my emphasis). Immutability is renamed 'constancy', though not so much to change the theological conception as, we conjecture, to acknowledge that Descartes' immutability and the Stoic concept of constancy (cf. Lipsius *De Constantia*; Seneca *De Constantia sapientis*) are doing similar things. Moreover, Spinoza speaks here not only of constancy of God's works, but of God's concurrence, which preserves not just motions, but *states*.[30] As such, the preservation of motion is demoted to a corollary of the wider claim that states are preserved by God's constancy of the 'highest degree'. Once we realise that this constancy, or tenor, of states is serving the role of the static equilibrium, we can see how DPPIIP23 ('when the modes of a body are compelled to undergo variation that variation will be the least that can be') indeed 'follows quite clearly' from DPPII14. We have, in effect, the Cartesian God as the rope in tension to the highest degree in a cosmic system of block and tackle. A variation in this equilibrium is communicated to all the parts and the entire system, in its absolute constancy, immediately and concurrently endeavours, successfully (EIP35), to attain a new equilibrium state. And because the system is under tension, the requisite compensatory motions and determinations will occur concurrently and as equally as possible with the 'new' variation, such that the reactive motions will be exactly equal and opposite, and the resulting motion of the parts of the system will be the least they can be. Indeed, summing the individual motions, the total motion under tension will be = 0. Hence, Spinoza correctly speaks of the difference between 'the least variation that can be' and 'the least absolutely' in the Proof to DPPIIP28 (Rule 4). In that case, he uses the difference to show how non-variation in disposed motion can be absolutely the least even as the variation in *relatively* disposed determination is perceived as a complete inversion.

If kinematics is taken as a statics, we can see how Descartes could come to these conclusions, especially if he believed that the correct experiments for deducing weight and motion were not the observation of masses in motion, but the observations of static weights in (dis)equilibrium. We can also understand how, if Spinoza could accept Descartes' laws of motion (save one), he, too, would wholeheartedly accept that statics explained the laws of kinematics. Thus, he writes to Oldenburg in Letter 32:

> I did not assert that any of the Rules were wrong except for the sixth, regarding which I said I thought that Mr Huygens too was in error.

But what of this Sixth Rule with which Spinoza disagrees? It is a difficult question to which we have read no answer in the scholarly papers. The Rule *per* Descartes reads:

> Sixthly, if body *C* at rest were most accurately equal to body *B* moved toward it, it would be partly impelled by *B* and would partly repel it in the contrary direction. That is, if *B* were to approach *C* with four degrees of speed, it would communicate to *C* one degree and with the three remaining would be reflected in the opposite direction.
>
> (PPII[51])

We cannot engage in a detailed analysis of Spinoza's reasons for disagreement here, but what will be instructive is to understand how the static basis of this model could have confounded both Descartes and Spinoza. Using the lever analysis, one is immediately confronted with the experimental problematic of accounting for absolute rest. It seems as if the resting bulk must be placed exactly at the fulcrum; the application of the motive bulk occurring at some distance away along the lever arm. The result: the motive bulk keeps moving; the resting bulk *twists* about the axis of the fulcrum. Applying Descartes' parallelogram of forces, the resting bulk has no vector, and so again it appears that the motive bulk simply continues on its merry way. Descartes realises this cannot be right, and it would be surprising if Spinoza disagreed with Descartes simply because the geometry of the lever told him the motive bulk would continue as before. Even in the abstraction of Cartesian thought experiments, as Spinoza makes clear, it is quite obvious that for the motive bulk to continue, it must pass through the locus of the resting bulk and thus propel it to motion with the same speed. It is worth noting here Huygens' correct solution to this rule of impact (which, as we have said, Spinoza also rejects): the motive bulk collides with the resting bulk and stops at rest, transferring its entire motion and determination to the resting bulk, taking on entirely the character of the previously motive bulk. One wonders what natural philosophers would have thought if Descartes or Spinoza had realised that this is what the lever and the parallelogram were really telling them: that everything continued the same as before, but the equal bulks had *inverted* places. It may be that Spinoza, in ignoring Descartes' arithmetic assertion that if the incoming equal bulk has four units of motion, one unit is transferred and three retained, and rather than speaking of 'a slight impulse' being given to the resting bulk, Spinoza is being more consistent with the lever hypothesis: *a bulk placed closest to the fulcrum will move least of all.* The disagreement may also follow from Spinoza's more consistent application of Descartes' relativity of motion and rest. After all, a body at rest is simply 'not separating from its contiguous surroundings', and so really is in motion to the same degree as the things around it.[31] Spinoza may therefore feel that Rule 6 should be treated as if the two bulks are in motion, and we should ignore some additional power of resting over and above weight itself, which Descartes sometimes implies. This may be seen if we notice that, of course, the more motive bulk, by definition, also has weight, and so exerts its own power of resting (inertia) in its endeavour to continue in rectilinear fashion.

With (a) this additional static context in mind, in which the forces are held by some tension in equilibrium, and whereby, on the introduction of momentary disequilibrium, the relevant system takes the least possible transformation to return to an equilibrium state; and (b) the idea of a kinematic expression of such rules in terms of variations within proportions of motive qualities ((un)natural, motive, resting, bulk), we are now in a position to treat of the physical concepts that have the most bearing on the theory of natural right. These are force, work, power, capacity for work, and the alternative nomenclature of right itself.

3.3.3 Force, work, power, capacity for work, right

This book was, to a great degree, inspired by our feeling that something did not quite fit with the common interpretations of Spinoza's theory of natural right. Repeated readings of the *Ethics* and TP added weight to the idea that the Hobbesian terminology of 'force' was operating in an entirely different manner in the work of Spinoza, who had clearly seen fit to reintroduce the idea of *potentia* not simply as a replacement for force (*vis*), but as a complement to it ('*vis*' is used as term of art in *The General Definition of the Affects* and EIVP6ff., for example). Once again, we must return to Descartes for an explanation of this deployment, an explanation at once illuminating and frustrating. We owe to Duhem (1905: 339–340) the insight, which seems to be continually overlooked even today among scholars of Descartes and indeed of Leibniz, who so famously skewered Descartes' theory of 'force', that *what Descartes meant by 'force' is entirely different from what everyone else meant and means today*.

We can see why this is frustrating; the decision to completely change the meaning of a word in common natural philosophical use should not be taken lightly, and the result was that Descartes' correspondents universally failed to understand what the Frenchman was trying to say. To be fair to Descartes, very early on he set out what he defined 'force' to be, and he came back on several occasions in correspondence to explain this definition and that it was different from the common meaning. Once again, apparently alone among seventeenth-century thinkers, it is Spinoza who immediately grasps what Descartes means by *vis*, just as he grasped the difference between motion and determination. Given the role force plays, with power and thus right, in the Spinozan political and juridical theory, it is thus of utmost importance that we understand this difference.

So how did Descartes define force? On 12 September 1638, Descartes wrote to Mersenne:

> One has above all to consider that I was talking about the force necessary to lift a weight to a given height, and such force always has two dimensions and is not the same as the one necessary to support the height at any point, since that force has only one dimension. These two forces differ as much from each other as a surface differs from the line.

We can perhaps see how this brilliant insight into the geometric difference between force in the common sense and force in Descartes' sense would have passed Mersenne by at the first reading. Hence, on 15 November 1638, Descartes must write to Mersenne, who had reported his and Desargues' miscomprehension of Descartes' letters:

> You have finally understood the meaning of the word force as I understand it when I say that the same force is needed to lift a weight of one hundred pounds to a height of one foot as fifty pounds to a height of two feet, that is to say, that the same *action* or effort is needed.
>
> (our emphasis)

Descartes' patience then characteristically expires:

> I would like to believe that I did not explain myself well enough on this point previously, since you did not understand me. But I was so far from thinking of the power [*puissance*] of a man when referring to someone who is stronger than someone else, that it did not occur to me that the word force could be understood in that sense. And when it is said that less force is needed for one effect than for another, that does not mean that less power [*puissance*] is needed – even if one had more power [*puissance*] it would have no bearing – but that less action is needed. And in this work I did not talk about force as equivalent to the power [*puissance*] of a man, but only as action and equivalent to the force by which a weight can be lifted.

Perhaps to the non-specialist, Descartes' meaning is still not apparent. In simplest terms, what Descartes means by *force* is what we now mean by *work*. Work, as we define it, is a quantity derived from multiplying what we call force by a distance travelled. Descartes, with admirable practicality, claims in the same letter that it is impossible to know *a priori* what a machine can do unless one measures the quantity of its effect. Or, in Spinozan terms, we do not yet know what the body can do. By way of example, clearly the power (*puissance*) of an adult is generally greater than that of a child, but if we ask both to lift a one-pound bag of flour, both will have the capacity so to do. All we have established is that a child can, in this respect, perform the same *work* as an adult. We still do not know with certainty how much more power (*puissance*) an adult has. Naturally, Descartes' definition of force in this manner is deeply confusing and we do not propose to adopt it. Hereafter, when we must refer to 'force' in the Cartesian sense of 'work', we will mark this with an asterisk thus: *force**. In this vain, it is worth specifying that what Spinoza means by power (*potentia*) is not to be confused with the modern meaning of power, which is the time derivative of work defined above; a conception completely unknown to his time.

Before we move to Spinoza's understanding of force*, let us now explicate the geometric insight Descartes had with respect to the production of actions or effects, for it is greatly informative of Spinoza's *Ethics*. The idea is a little complex, especially as Descartes perceives what must occur geometrically but unclearly, such that his geometry misses the mark. Let us try to describe what Descartes means when he claims that force* or work has two dimensions: the force applied and its projection onto the distance actually travelled (which Descartes regards as the motion, or speed, ignoring the time element). Take as an illustrative case the cannon ball, rather than the raising of a weight to a height, to indicate how the forces are composed to produce a distance travelled. The force applied horizontally by the cannonball is easy to understand. The vertical force must take into account the downward ambient pressure of corpuscles that causes things to fall – the vertical upward push is thus netted-off against this downward pressure, and if our cannonball still rises, there is net upward motion. In the first instants of launch, the cannonball can be treated as travelling the rectilinear distance onto which the vertical and horizontal forces are projected. This is the work, or force*, performed by each of the forces. To decompose the work due to the respective forces, we simply work backwards. We take the distance travelled and project it onto the horizontal or vertical, which are now treated as scalar components of the distance. We immediately see that the upward work performed is less than the upward force exerted due to the action of the downward force exerted. Formal *potentia*/force exceeds actual work/force*. Evidently, this model does not account for acceleration under the conservative field of gravity and is erroneous.

We now consider Descartes' actual example of raising a weight to a height. This ignores direction, and takes the composed force applied as one side, and perpendicular to this the distance travelled as another. The resultant rectangle has an area that Descartes regards as a scalar; a scalar that may be compared with other scalar products of force/power and distance, so that he can conclude that raising 50 lbs 2 ft is the same force* as raising 100 lbs 1 ft. If force* is understood as force (i.e. not as work), Descartes' theory appears to result in the madness that indeed a child's strength is exactly the same as that of an adult or a spring or whatever, solely because it appears *force only ever equals what actually happened*. In Spinozan language, it appears as if the power of a thing is equal only to what actually occurs, and in no way discloses or denies a greater unactualised or formal power.

The realisation that work reduces to a scalar quantity that is capable of comparison does not arise fortuitously. There is a kernel of the geometric intuition, derived from the logic of composition of forces that although the events *caused* in the world are composed of forces operating in several dimensions, the *effects* reduce in the last analysis to the 0-dimension of the scalars. It is the vague realisation that higher dimensional causes *contract* into lower dimensional effects; that for an effect to occur, there must be an in-tension understood as a reduction in dimension. This is why Descartes speaks of the resulting *action* of the application of *puissance* over distance, and why Spinoza would immediately adopt action as the sign of God or Nature, which is considered as infinite activity. There is thus an eternal movement of production of power from God or Nature in the generation of the dimensional complexity of forces at work, which always returns to God or Nature in the simplicity of the actual, of the present instant, of work being performed.

Now let us examine evidence that Spinoza appreciated Descartes' terminological somersaults. To do this, we refer to EIVP5 (and the Demonstration of EIVP6), which states quite clearly:

> The force* [*vis*], and the increase, of some passion, and indeed its perseverance in existing, is not due simply to our own power, but is defined by comparing our conative power with the power of the passion's external cause.[32]

We say that here Spinoza fully accepts Descartes' meaning of force* as the action of some cause (i.e. its work) precisely because he realises it must be defined and so generated by a comparison between powers. This is the law of composition of forces in action, for Spinoza is describing the production of real effects, but it takes into account, with the use of force rather that (composed or resultant) power, that composed forces may produce no effect if they are insufficient to alter an equilibrium. Only a power that produces an effect defines for us the actuality of that power as force*. *Vis* appears already in EIVP3, which reads:

> The force* by which a man perseveres in existence is limited, and is infinitely surpassed by the power of external causes.[33]

Here, Spinoza opposes the work (force*) of actually existing with power of external causes. Why? *In nuce*, Spinoza is claiming that the power of ever-finite thing, considered as it were in abstraction from the universe, is indefinite. Each finite thing endeavours to do the most it can do, and in abstraction it will succeed indefinitely. It is because, in the universe, each such power is comparatively finite, that the work of existing is likewise finite. Being, as work, is the product of a finite thing's power and the power of all other things. For Spinoza, it would be absurd to suggest that the *work* or force* of a human in existing would be infinite, because then this human would be a God in actuality, and not formally. And Spinoza believes that his proof of the uniqueness of substance rules this out. Thus, he presents the finitude of the force* of being as axiomatic (we are finite: EIV Ax., P3).

This leads us directly back to EIP34–36 and allows us, as Negri notes,[34] to fully engage with the concepts of *potentia* and *potestas* that ground Spinoza's thinking. These propositions deal with the unique case of God or Nature, and in that sense they appear to dissolve into each other as negations of the falsehood that God could do more than He actually does (free will). Yet they also ground the principles for consideration of finite things. God,[35] we are told, has the ability (*potestas*) to produce anything we may conceive.[36] Gueroult tantalisingly calls this the 'circle of the *potestas*'.[37] Yet God is the sole substance, and self-caused. There is no other power that could restrain God's activity. When God's power is considered infinite, we see Spinoza means by infinite 'necessarily without external determination', such that no matter how small God's power might actually be, the lack of any determination renders it infinite nonetheless. In such circumstances of unrestraint, Spinoza's God's power to produce (*potentia*) immediately fulfils his capacity to produce (*potestas*); *potentia* and *potestas* are equal. In the case of finite things, no such equality pertains. Let us imagine that a human also has the ability (*potestas*) to produce anything we may conceive. It is not, however, the ability (*potestas*), but the power (*potentia*) of the finite thing that enters into the determination.[38] Like the upward push that the cannon gives to the cannonball, we can imagine this *potestas* as notionally extending out from the finite thing. Yet it is mitigated by the power of external causes (the downward pressure of the air corpuscles), and the result is the force* or work actually produced. The *potestas* stands in this case as the shadow cast by a *potentia* that has been determined by external *potentiae*. If we relate that *potentia* to the effect produced, we discover the work, or force*. Spinoza does not deploy this 'theological' terminology to finite things, however. Rather, he prefers to regard the difference between attempt and realisation as that between formal and actual being.

Does the terminology of work play any role for Spinoza, given its usurpation by force*? Indeed, work continues to be a major feature of the Latin text of the *Ethics Part 1*, where Spinoza speaks of God determining singular things to work (*operor*) in a certain and determinate way. Parkinson (2000) translates this as 'operate in some way', but we respectfully suggest this understates the clear mechanical meaning that Spinoza is trying to convey: that the subsidiary effects of God or Nature are the respective determinations of finite things by comparisons of the respective powers of acting (*agendi potentiae*, see EIII Post.1). Why, then, does Spinoza use *operor* in EI but *vis** in EIV and the *General Definition of the Affects*? This might result from the problem of conveying the mechanical idea of extended work into the field on intensive passions. To work conveys the general idea that a force is projected along a distance; this makes little sense in the case of the passions. It seems that as a consequence, Spinoza deploys force* to describe the work of actually existing passions in order to convey differences of intensity rather than extensity. As such, force* for Spinoza may have the more specific definition of a power of existing projected along a notional line of quantified intensity, to produce the work of the passions.

It is well worth comparing the stress Spinoza places on the extension of power along a line within the fuller conception of the verb *operor* with the meaning Marx assigns to work (labour). *Operor* means to work, to labour, but also to be occupied and to take pains. Marx, for his part, is careful to reintegrate occupation and the taking of pains into the labour concept because it is this that marks out man from machine:

> Apart from the exertion of the working organs, a purposeful will is required for the entire duration of the work. This means close attention. The less he is attracted by the nature of the work . . . the less, therefore, he enjoys it . . . [and] the closer his attention is forced to be.[39]

Understanding the way we do the transition from substance to attribute in Spinoza, we may view this statement as Marx's deployment of his own transition from Spinoza's mechanical apparatus to that 'metabolic' process he attributes to capitalism. Indeed, we would argue that it is this change of dimension that divides the 'civil' Spinozan sphere of the finite *c-m-c* circuit from the capitalist sphere of the *m-c-m* circuit, while at the same time ensuring that the two circuits can coexist; the civil sphere being blind to the capitalist sphere, just as individual *in statu naturali* actually within the Spinozan city 'is bound by no law to obey anyone but himself' (EIVP37 Sch. 1). In Chapter 5, we will return to the question of whether this dimensional chasm between the Spinozan and Marxist meanings of *work* is bridgeable.

We hope to have provided a variety of evidence of Spinoza's competence as a Cartesian 'physicist' who was continuing not only to interrogate the work of Descartes, but to perhaps do so with the aim of following the Pseudo-Aristoteles in trying to derive these principles from some primary notions. In particular, we believe this evidence supports rereading Spinoza's theory of natural right with due attention to its mechanical background and Spinoza's expertise. With the *static* toolkit of concepts of force*, work, power and *potestas*, we are now in a position to begin to understand the physical underpinnings of natural right. We give the final definition of right in TPII in order to see how we might initially interpret it:

> By the right of Nature then I understand the laws or rules of Nature in accordance with which all things come to be; that is, the very power of Nature. So the natural right of Nature as a whole, and consequently the natural right of every individual, is coextensive with its power. Consequently, whatever each man does from the laws of his own nature, he does by the highest right of Nature, and he has as much right as his power extends.[40]

A human has certain laws of its nature that determine its *potestas*, its ability to do. Its *potestas* is formally indefinite, but is determined to finitude and non-fulfilment by external causes. This *potestas* varies in its fulfilment as the *potentia* of this human varies. In respect of extension, the clash of two or more *potentiae* produces some body-effect, which is the work of these causes. In respect of thought, we conjecture, the comparison of two or more *potentiae* produces some idea-effect, which, at least in terms of the passions, is the force* of these causes. In each case, the current *potentia* of each individual is projected onto a line that is either distance or intensity, thus giving a clear explanation to the words *quantum potentia valet* (as far as its power extends).[41] This we call the *static interpretation of natural right*. We believe in our explication that the idea that *potentia* has conceptual space to, and indeed must, vary is quite evident. Indeed, immediately following the above quotation (TPII[5]), Spinoza informs us that it is the cognitive variations from imagination to reason that determine how *potentia* is to vary natural right. To achieve this leap, Spinoza must move from statics, and static kinematics, to dynamics. This leap is achieved by passing through hydrostatics considered as a celestial science.

3.3.4 Hydrostatics – fluid immutability and the celestial vortices

The commonest way of approaching the question of hydrostatics is to think about the action of various solids in fluid media. Thus, a classic experiment is to consider the action of cork, which falls in air, but rises in water. Well known are the Peripatetic arguments about natural tendencies. The Cartesian reduction of all corporeal questions to ones of corpuscles transmitting turbulence demands a different approach, for, as Spinoza writes to Oldenburg regarding Boyle's definition of fluidity, a distinction of bodies into solid and fluid generates an absurdity:

> if large bodies move in such a way that the ratio of motion to their bulk [*mole*] is that of minute bodies to their particular bulk, then they too would have to be termed fluid.
>
> (Letter 6)

On this model, what is relevant is the motive action of the corpuscles among themselves, both in terms of lack of friction and in terms of ability to transfer motion to larger bodies, and of course the relative bulk, motion and solidity of the body immersed in this relative fluid. As Shuster has shown,[42] Descartes' model of hydrostatics is a response, at the request of his mentor Beeckman, to the work of Flemish engineer Simon Stevin on the so-called hydrostatic paradoxes (paradoxes also treated by Boyle, his work of that name being sent to Spinoza by Oldenburg). To illustrate a significant feature of this model, Shuster draws our attention to Descartes' comparison of two vessels, one marked *B* whose mouth is narrower than the base and stepped at the sides. The question is to explain how the fewer water corpuscles at the surface are able to exert pressure across the entire face of the base. Descartes' conjectural solution can be found in a slightly different but far more suggestive form when explaining light corpuscles in his *Le monde* Chapter 14 (Figure 3.2).

Here, the downward pressure of the corpuscles may *really* by expressed in all directions, but the law of composition of forces allows Descartes to decompose these actions into vertical and horizontal moments across all the corpuscles of water, thus connecting the corpuscles in the mouth of the stepped vessel with every corpuscle across the base. The related diagram of light corpuscles in *Le monde* shows how these compositions can be broken down, to determine how the force of the upper corpuscles is distributed equally under tension to the lower, how it can be reconstituted, and how, in effect, it can be redirected.

Our discussion of statics immediately suggests Descartes' background thinking here: fluid-corpuscles can be treated like a block and tackle under tension, with each of the motions of the corpuscles acting like parts of rope communicating a global equilibrium to the whole. This thesis relies both on containment of the fluid and, just as importantly, the incompressibility of the fluid. If the tendencies

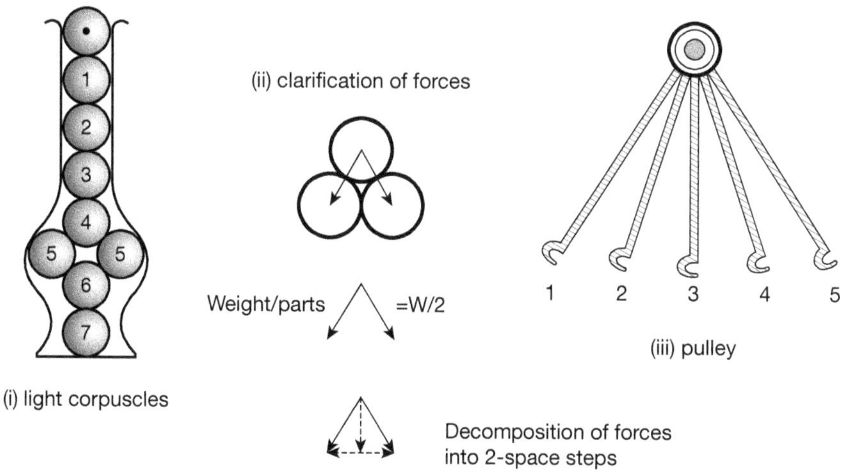

Figure 3.2 Figures from Descartes' *Le monde*, Chapter 14, with clarificatory diagram

to motion of a fluid under these conditions can be broken down into their constituent parts per corpuscle, provided the above conditions hold, any variation in one corpuscle's tendency to motion creates an instantaneous disequilibrium of forces that must be compensated by all other corpuscles in the fluid. In other words, we immediately recover what amounts to Lagrange's *Principle of the Pulley* expressed in analytic form: $Pp + Qq + Rr + \ldots = 0$. If this still appears a surprising leap to make, we allow Descartes to speak for himself:

> You can also easily conceive how several of these rays, coming from diverse points, come together at the same point (or, coming from the same point, go out toward different points) without impeding or depending on one another ... In just the same way, the diverse forces with which one pulls the cords 1, 2, 3, 4, 5 *all come together in the pulley*, and the resistance of this pulley extends to all the diverse hands that are pulling those cords.
>
> (*Le monde*, Ch. 14 §§5–6, our emphasis)

In fact, the application of a Cartesian coordinate system further clarifies the case of incompressible fluids, by decomposing these tendencies to motion into motions along the x, y and z axis. In this case, Lagrange's *Principle* can be loosely related to Euler's formula for hydrostatics given in his *Principia motus fluidorum* (1756–1757; §36):

$$\partial u/\partial x + \partial v/\partial y + \partial w/\partial z = 0$$

where u, v, w are the decomposed[43] velocities of the notional points of fluid with respect the three axes of Cartesian space. As Euler writes: 'this condition expresses that through the motion no part of the fluid is carried into a greater or lesser space, but perpetually the continuity of the fluid as well as the identical density is conserved'. Note in particular how the variations in impulsions are related to the Cartesian plane, not Cartesian time. We hope the reader can see from this that if we take an arbitrary cube of incompressible fluid corpuscles under tension, any motion by one, say in the x direction, must be compensated by all the others as they endeavour to fill the space left by this corpuscle with as little effort as possible, thus instantaneously resuming equilibrium. Of course, both these analytical principles are anachronistic, but the concept *behind* them, that of the conservation of equilibrium of a fluid plenum through the least possible action, is clearly present in the Cartesian fluid-corpuscular hypothesis. Where this latter falls down is its struggle to account for compressible fluids.

We do not know if Spinoza read of Descartes' experiment above, or if he had read *Le monde*, but Letters 6 and 32 indicate a not insignificant theoretical interest in hydrostatics, and importantly the much overlooked Letter 41 of 5 September 1669 to Jarig Jelles details hydrostatic experiments involving bent vessels. So Spinoza is also interested in analysing the relation between vertical and horizontal moments of force across water corpuscles. If we look at the diagram he provides of his first experiment, for example, we can see that Spinoza has constructed nothing other than a *simple machine*.

It is a simple machine because the restriction provided by the vessel sides, as they do in the case of blood (Letter 32), allows downward force to be *transformed* into horizontal force, and again into upward force at exit *D*. The rigidity of the vessel sides is of paramount importance; like the wheels of the block and tackle, it allows for the communicating medium, there the rope, here the water, to be

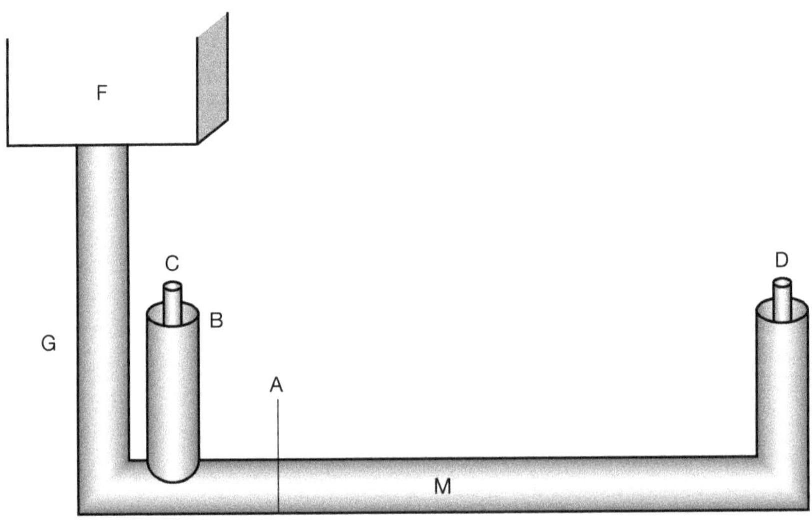

Figure 3.3 Figure from Letter 41

held in sufficient tension that the force from tank *F* is communicated almost perfectly to exit *D*. And, given what we have established with relation to the geometrical nature of work (or force*) above, Spinoza's conclusion that 'this led me to believe that the length of the tube was no hindrance, or very little' gains particular significance. Spinoza has confirmed that in certain cases of hydrostatic tension (just as in rigid machines), the distance across which a force or power is projected makes little or no difference. But Spinoza also faces a fundamental problem common with the experiment proposed by Descartes, and indeed with any theory that seeks to reduce explanations to ambient pressure of transporting corpuscles. This problem is that explaining a body's motion by the motion of more fluid corpuscles is not really an explanation at all, just a deferral. Why are these corpuscles in motion, and why the ones pushing against them? What causes things to push more downward than sideways? What, ultimately, causes tensions in fluid corpuscles such that they are moved to travel on mass in a certain direction? The route to an answer to this conundrum too derives from Descartes' celestial mechanics.

We can only briefly set out the pertinent aspects of Descartes' celestial theory here, which builds upon his hydrostatic theory explicitly in *Le monde*, and more implicitly in the Third Part of his *Principles*, which Spinoza had begun to recast in synthetic form as DPPIII. In brief,[44] Descartes seeks to explain what he initially thought to be circular, then elliptical, transits of the planets about the sun or other stars as appropriate. His Laws of Motion have established the fundamental rectilinearity of all motion, so he needs to explain in a metaphysically sound manner what takes the place of the sling in restraining rectilinear tendencies to circular motions. By metaphysically sound, we mean he wishes to avoid immaterial forces or divine pushes that characterised the celestial models of Kepler, Tycho and later Newton. His solution is the hydrostatic vortex. Descartes posits three kinds of matter in the universe, fire, air and earth in *Le monde* Chapter 15, which become, in effect, light corpuscles and the corpuscles that, in their varying degrees of motility, constitute the celestial fluid or celestial 'bodies' proper.[45] It is light, the matter that constitutes the stars, that generates each vortex. This theory is explained in the *Principles* broadly by claiming that sunspots are indicative of the rough face of the sun, and that as the sun spins with great speed through its natural circular motion (deriving from luminescence), these sunspots (not the light itself) perturb the celestial fluid around it, by friction, dragging the fluid around it. As Shuster has shown, the speed of this derivative motion is so great it extends out to a point just beyond Saturn (the 'last' planet around our sun), which Descartes marks *K*, and Shuster terms the 'K-point' (Figure 3.4). Between the sun and the K-point, the vortical speed of rotation is such that bodies are 'locked' into orbit; beyond the K-point, any body of planetary size will be able to break free of the sun's constraint and pursue its rectilinear tendency to motion as a stone leaves a sling. The locking is a result of the celestial fluid being dragged round the sun at such speed that this speed up to the K-point makes up for the fluid corpuscles' relative lack of mass insofar as in combination they can push each planet away from its

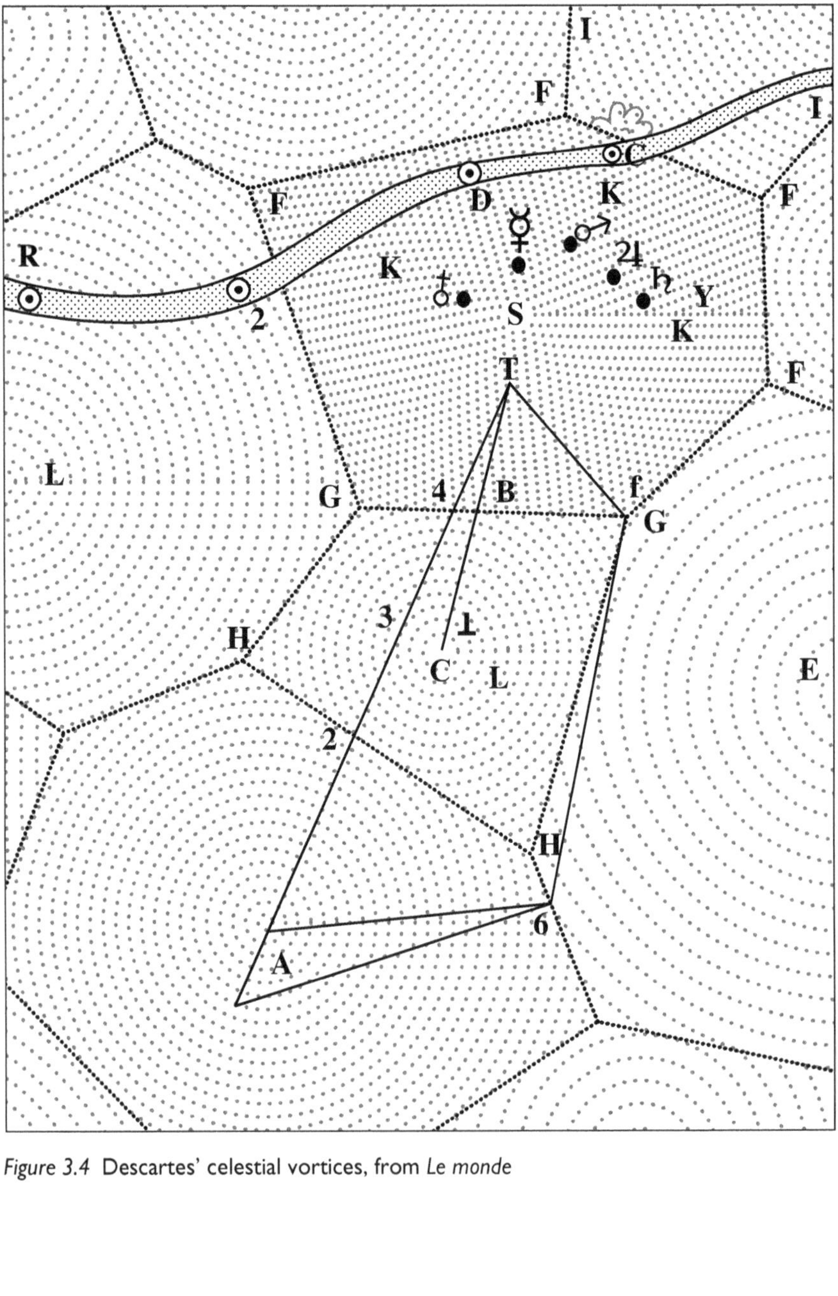

Figure 3.4 Descartes' celestial vortices, from *Le monde*

tendency to rectilinear motion. Planets, being dead stars, have a residual circular motion that creates an envelope within each celestial lock in which smaller bodies are drawn into moon-orbits of these planets.[46]

The general effect, therefore, is akin to the stone in the sling in that the planet or stone has a tendency to rectilinear motion that is composed into a circular motion, this latter capable of being decomposed into: (a) assistance to the rectilinear motion by virtue of the greater speed of light to matter of the third kind; and (b) an instantaneous divergence from the straight-line towards the sun, caused by the drag of the outer celestial fluid inwards. The relevant question for us is the difficult one of what is causing the sun to rotate in the first place, which reduces to: what causes light corpuscles to spin? If this is the sole reason why the celestial fluid is held in a state of tension, so that it can communicate rotational motion to planets and comets, then there must be a sufficient reason for it. This takes us very deep into Descartes and Spinoza's theories. Gaukroger notes[47] that the reason for this eternal circular motion is unclear, and so implicit is it in the work of Spinoza that it seems to have gone almost universally unnoticed. Descartes' *Météores* argues that the rotation of light corpuscles explains differences in colour, while *Le monde*, as we have seen, seems to argue for a link between light and flame. The link partly turns on Descartes' belief that not only does the spin of these luminescent spheres drag celestial matter around itself, but at the same time this most subtle and agitated matter escapes in all directions, causing modal disturbances in the celestial vortices, whence stars' visibility. It seems that the strange properties of the circle noted by the Pseudo-Aristoteles have not been completely abandoned by the Cartesians, but return as a fundamental physical principle. The route to the answer is metaphysically clearer with Spinoza's thought, and it is to him that we must now return.

3.4 The second order of immutability – towards a dynamics

The troublesome conception of motion and rest is perhaps due to the sheer concentration of physical ideas within those two words. In this section, we will argue that motion and rest must be related to circular motion: the incidence of opposites in one place that so beguiled the Pseudo-Aristoteles. Yet this is not merely a Peripatetic theory – the Cartesian reference to fire and light already points us to Stoic conceptions of the element of prime motivation. Furthermore, there seems to be no little Brunian influence in this conception of motion and rest, for the introduction of infinite motion and rest, understood as an infinitely powerful circular motion, provides a limit case for universal activity. In this section, we will attempt to advance as far as possible as we can with Spinoza's physics and its antecedents, in order to complete the physical context within which we will interpret his theory of natural right. As part of this, we will move to suggest the generative relation between the attributes and bodies approaching infinite power.

3.4.1 Motion to rest

The Pseudo-Aristoteles' doctrine of the circle, which combines opposite motions, had become to the Schoolmen a doctrine (broadly speaking) of motion that culminates itself in rest. Aquinas, for example, deploys this idea in his theory of the passions:

> Now since being at rest is the end of a movement [*quies est finis motus*], it is prior in intention and posterior in execution. Therefore, if the passions of the irascible power are compared to those passions of the concupiscible power that signify resting in the good, then the passions of the irascible power are clearly prior in the order of execution to passions of this sort that belong to the concupiscible power, in the way that hope [*spes*] is prior to joy [*gaudium*] and is thus a cause of joy—this according to the Apostle in Romans 12.12 ('Rejoicing in hope' [*spe gaudentes*]). On the other hand, a passion of the concupiscible power that signifies resting in the bad, e.g., sadness [*tristitia*], stands midway between two passions of the irascible power.
>
> (Aquinas, ST 1–2 Q.25 r.)

Descartes' responses to Scholastic web-weaving are well known, calling the theory of the terminus incomprehensible, and writing in *Le monde*:

> They attribute to the least of their motions a being much more solid and true than they do to rest, which they call only a privation. But me, I conceive of rest as also a quality, which ought to be attributed to matter while it remains in one place, just as motion ought to be attributed to it when it changes place.
>
> (AT XI 40)[48]

For Descartes' part, however, as Gabbey (1996: 167) has argued, he is happy to adopt the terminology of motion and rest without publicly providing any clear and distinct explanation of what rest is supposed to be. In PPII[36], he claims that God created matter together with motion and rest, and while his Rules of Collision are shown by Gabbey (1980: 265–272) to utilise rest as a quantity, nowhere in the Cartesian works in Spinoza's possession does this conception of a (conserved) quantum of motion *and* rest receive complete clarification. As if to confirm the point, Spinoza's DPP, though it fills certain other gaps in Cartesian mechanics, provides no explanation either. This is not to say that Descartes had no idea of what rest meant, or that at the least he had a vulgar conception of the term. Garber (1992: 160ff.) provides ample evidence from *Le monde* and Descartes' letters to Henry More that 'rest' was understood by the ex-soldier to be a body's activity of not separating from bodies contiguous to it; activity because even in his PPII[26, 24], Descartes decries the prejudice that 'in all motion there is action, while in rest there is cessation of action'.[49] Now it may be that Descartes felt what may relatively appear to be rest for a body *A*, in its active refusal to separate from contiguous body *B*, is in fact *A* and *B* moving together such as a man's standing aboard a ship may be decomposed into his rest relative to the moving ship, and recomposed as his moving relative to the coast. Yet apart from the problems this hyper-relativism causes in granting every body in a plenum a frame of reference, Garber (ibid.: 280) also notes that Descartes begins to think that resistance to separation/motion results if and only if a collision occurs, such that rest in this sense is caused and opposes itself to any incoming action. Here, rest seems to be a (re)active quality of a body, but not one that is continuous with the duration of the body, such that it could ground an individuating proportion of motion and rest. In other words, in the general equilibrium, every rest is already reactive.

Nevertheless, as Lécrivain[50] has remarked, even in writing the DPP Spinoza felt it necessary to replace motion and rest on the same plane by speaking of motion *and* rest. Furthermore, by Letter 91 (1676), Spinoza is openly attacking the Cartesian idea of rest:

> from Extension conceived by Descartes, to whit an inert mass [*molem*], it is not only difficult . . . but quite impossible to demonstrate the existence of bodies. For matter at rest [*Materia enim quiescens*], as far as in it lies, will continue to be at rest, and will not be set in motion except by a more powerful cause.

What may have initiated this departure from the perceived equivalence in Descartes of inert mass and matter at rest? We are not aware of anyone having completed the triad of conceptions regarding motion and rest, which would have completed Spinoza's intellectual milieu, perhaps because whereas with widespread Scholasticism and Spinoza's clear intimacy with Descartes' physics, there is at best only circumstantial evidence that Spinoza knew of the theses of Giordano Bruno, theses drawing in part on Nicolaus Cusanus. Garrett[51] has undertaken some work to show the broad similarities with certain of Bruno's conceptions of the active divinity, but we are unaware of his making any link between Bruno's theory of motion and rest and Spinoza. Perhaps closest has come Deleuze, who in an off-the-cuff remark in his *Expressionism in Philosophy*, states[52] that Spinoza's theory of motion and rest has an aspect of an old Platonism about it. We suspect at least that Deleuze, who certainly knew Cusanus through his tutor and renaissance specialist De Gandillac, may well have seen some similarity with the thinking of the Rhenish thinker, if not also Bruno.

What, then, is this possible similarity? We rely here on Védrine's *La conception de la Nature chez Giordano Bruno*, which, in a short excursus, links the quies-motus couplet to the Cusan logic of infinity, and interestingly also through Cusanus to a possible similarity with Duns Scotus. This is not so much the idea that 'to move in an instant and to not move are one and the same thing',[53] but rather, from a basis of the perpetual animation of minimal elements, rest is constructed not by the slowness of motions, but counter-intuitively by their speed. Consider the following way of comprehending this from Bruno's *De minimo*:[54]

> Eighthly, [the coincidence of opposites is shown] in the maximum and quickest movement and also in absolutely slow movement, namely maximum rest, which for all intents and purposes are the same thing. In fact, something [mobile] moved absolutely from *A* to *B* and from *B* to *A*, is at one and the same time at *A* and at *B* and at every point along the route between. For this reason it remains at rest. That is why the divine wisdom, which attains everything and is in everything, is called the most mobile of all because He remains everywhere and is immobile. He is also called the most mobile because He extends himself the most rapidly from one end [*fine*] to another and disposes all things in every place between appropriate limits. We attribute to Him movement because He is the growth [*vegetatio*] and the life by virtue of which all is put in motion; we attribute to him rest because He is eternity and substance itself in which and for which all things remain.
>
> (our translation)

As Védrine notes,[55] this text is practically a direct quotation from Cusanus' *Wisdom According to the Idiot*.[56] Apart from the proto-Spinozan overtones of Bruno's ideas of God's substantiality and extension, which look not simply to where God is but what He is *doing* there, the conception of rest particularly as moving in two or more places at once offers an interesting interpretative conjecture for Spinoza's thinking on movement and rest. We might say that given the priority of motive substance, or substance properly considered as flux, rest is any motion that approaches the limit. Védrine informs us that Bruno was unsure about fulfilling the consequences of this idea, and that he oscillates between considering rest as an aspect of movement and as the inverse resistance to movement; that through a passage at the limit, the finite world of movement becomes opposed in a fatal dualism to the immobility of infinite eternity. Yet it is this idea that rest actively *resists* determination to passive motion that we wish to draw from Bruno. For this latter thinker, the problem seems to centre on his only regarding the absolute as the limit, such that the beautiful continuity of Bruno's world of minimal coincidences reintroduces the discrete at, and as, its boundaries. The question is whether, rather than only regarding rest as an absolute limit, we understand it as a relative limit. In such a way, resistance to motion arises as a continuous spectrum of ponderousness relative to other motions. Could we then propose an interpretation of Spinoza in which proportions of motion and rest stand for proportions of what we would consider motion in the common sense and motions that are so relatively fast that they constitute resistance to motion in the common sense? On this model, it would seem possible for motions and rests to be posited as singular things, each circulating according to the logic of the Pseudo-Aristoteles, but now with the Brunian nuance of coincidence and passage at the limit. Let us consider if Spinoza's texts bear such an interpretation.

From the above, it should be quite apparent that we must take care when Spinoza states the Axiom: *omnia corpora vel moventur, vel quiescunt* – Latin that is quite difficult to translate. Every body, we are told, is either being-moved or [being] at rest. The temptation is to turn this into the statement that every body is either moving or at rest, but this sublates the twisted language that attempts grammatically to indicate that motion is properly passive, whereas being at rest is properly something active. Yet, more than this, we must ask what it is that is being-moved or being-at-rest; a question that has caused some debate in Spinoza scholarship.

Klever (1988: 176) has noted a forerunner of the phrase 'proportion of motion and/to rest' in Letter 6 to Oldenburg. Here, in remarks *On fluidity*, Spinoza speaks of the proportion of motion to 'mass':

> So if large bodies move in such a way that the ratio of their motion to the mass [*molem*] is that of minute bodies to their particular mass, then they too would have to be termed a fluid . . .[57]

Klever regards this passage as a *reductio ad absurdum* of Boyle's position by a thinker of 'matter in motion'. Is this really Spinoza's intention? He makes the point that if f_1 is the proportion of motion to mass of some commonly recognised fluid F, then if one considers some so-called solids, which, collected together as S, have a proportion of motion to mass $= f_2$, and $f_1 = f_2$, then S is as much a fluid as F. We may say that Spinoza shows the distinction fluid/solid to be absurd, but *only* the linguistic distinction, for he accepts that the linguistic absurdity rests on the nature of underlying motion; he does not attempt to find a better justification for the 'truth' of really existing fluidity or solidity. It is critical to distinguish the premise shown false by absurdity, and the auxiliary premise that remains intact. The false premise is the assertion that large bodies cannot form fluids, quoted from Boyle. The auxiliary premise that clarifies the absurdity only shows the commission of a primary error: that names are taken for things, not things for names, and does not in its own right constitute a hypothesis shown false by the absurdity of its consequent (the essence of the *reductio*). It is quite possible that Spinoza regarded the essence of this auxiliary premise, the proportion of two terms, as perfectly correct, but as for his contemporaries in several areas of statics and kinematics, he was still considering whether the *moles* term was the best candidate for pairing with motion. As is well known, he quickly preferred '*quietus*'.

How do we explain the Scholastic echo of Spinoza's use of '*ratione motûs ad quietem*' in Letter 32 to Oldenburg? A suggestion that Spinoza, even briefly, considered that motion terminated in rest seems quite far from the mark. It is much more likely that here the *ad* is indicating the ratio of motion *to* rest (*m*:*r*), both to emphasise the importance of the ratio, not its constituents, but also perhaps again because the concept Spinoza has in mind is closer to circular motion conceived in the manner of the Pseudo-Aristoteles and/or Descartes. In many respects, as Manzini (2008) has shown, Spinoza was closer to Aristoteles' intent when he felt Aristoteles was more correct, than the Schoolmen were.[58]

There is a more general reason, however, for considering our conjecture that Spinoza regards rest as something akin to a relativised resistance to motion engendered by speed approaching the limit. This is the simple observation that the Cartesian conception for what we would now call momentum – the motive inertia of some object – is the product of what we would now call mass and velocity (*mv*), but which is something closer to the product of 'bulk' and determined speed. Is it not surprising that Spinoza should accept all but the sixth of Descartes' *Laws of Motion*, and yet construct a system that dissolves Descartes' key kinematic insight about the relation of bulk and speed into a consideration only of speed? Yet if we consider that when Spinoza is talking of rest, he is talking indeed about relative resistance to motion as: (a) constitutive of relative heaviness; and (b) constituted by relatively very great speed, then we not only recover Descartes' central thesis of a kind of momentum, but this thesis remains consistent with the easily overlooked categorical intent that motion and rest are both aspects of body; bodies ultimately defined in the same manner: as expressions of Nature's power (EII Def. 1). Spinoza avoids having to posit without reason two fundamentally different types of corporeal – motion and rest – by accepting only motion as a body and expression of power, but by classifying motions at the limit as rest (ponderousness). There is no place here for some additional 'body' possessing motion or at rest; the body *is* the motion and rest – body is a mode of substance. In this way, the troublesome phrase 'ratio of motion and rest' finds a literal meaning that fits the defining, individuating activity of a disposed body that is its 'momentum' understood as the relation between its resting component (ponderousness) and its motive component (speed). And there is a further important consequence: this sense of 'momentum' as a product or proportion of heaviness and speed gives us a single quantum that is the name and the mode that individuates a disposed body. It does not individuate things (*rei*); Spinoza clearly states bodies (*corpora*: PI Lem. 1). It is constructed from 'real' expressions of Nature's power, but the calculation itself that results in this 'momentum' is simply the modal appearance of this power. 'Momentum' is not of itself something, rather a physical quantity, and as such the certain and determinate proportion of motion and rest grants us the appearance of substance as its own effect – as substance in act.

This relation to a conception of momentum has one significant flaw, however. Momentum is described as a product ($m \cdot r$), but Spinoza in fact takes the inverse relation (m/r). He speaks both of ratios of motion and rest *and* proportions, and we know proportions are ratios of ratios. While the Demonstration to PI Lem. 3, dealing with the simplest bodies, speaks of the ratio of motion and rest, this is augmented in Lem. 5 concerning composite bodies to a proportion that determines the conservation of reciprocal ratios of motion and rest (i.e. $m{:}r :: m{:}r$) must be maintained. Proportion here has to be understood as a view from the whole, whereby the role of the part-ratios in constituting the whole does not vary even as they do. As Lem. 6 continues, the individual ratios of motion to rest of corpuscles can vary provided the whole proportion, or form, as Spinoza suggestively terms it, is maintained. Rather than approaching this matter from purely Euclidean considerations, as Matheron, Rivaud and others have done, if we approach Spinoza's ideas here from static considerations (but putting briefly aside our hypothesis regarding circular motion), we very quickly see what Spinoza is *trying* to do. Looking first at Lemmata 5, 6, and in particular 7, we see discussions of this proportionality or 'form' being maintained 'as a whole . . . whether it moves in this or that direction [*versus*], provided that each part retains its motion and communicates it to all the others'.[59] The inclusion of 'direction' here informs us that Spinoza is now talking about determinate *magnitudes*, not absolute motion, and the Cartesian distinction holds for Spinoza also. When we speak of a composed body, therefore, we must be careful to distinguish the proportionate ratios of motion and rest from the total or partial motions in certain directions of all or parts of that body. Our belief is that this Lemma 7 is a statement of a static principle: any variation to the directed motion of some element of composed body *U*, say *P*, varied by some very small *p*, will, by virtue of the tension of that composed body, be communicated to the remainder of *U*'s parts, and these parts will vary reciprocally such that the composed body will retain its form, or proportionality. In other words, Spinoza is vaguely grasping at:

$$U = Pp + Qq + Rr = 0$$

which can be read as a statement that the proportion of motion to rest of *U* remains the same despite compensatory variations among partial proportions of motion to rest *P*, *Q*, *R*. The zero on the right-hand side, as we know, provides the condition for the block and tackle and other pulleys; that it is under tension if one variation of a part is counteracted by the others such that the whole equilibrium is maintained. Spinoza, though, relies on the nature of proportionality as Euclid defines it (i.e. that if one antecedent changes with respect to its consequent, all antecedents of the proportion *must* reflect this change, by genetic definition). Euclid calls this property being homologous (*lit.* same expression or reason) (i.e. any change in motion of one must be reflected across all parts according to a constant of proportionality).

Part of the problem is that Spinoza's use of proportion in the PI is confusing; it more strongly implies that any positive change in one motive force compels the same positive proportionate change in the other(s), whereas the balance, lever, fluid and other object of statics indicates that both additively positive and negative actions occur to ensure that the whole object retains its state. Furthermore, if Spinoza is claiming that something like the momentum is being conserved, and not the relative determinate magnitudes of motion, then he is quite wrong about statics. Yet in the broad outline of physical reality that Spinoza is struggling to render geometrically, we firmly believe that the static physical theories of Spinoza's time, discussed at length above, support such an interpretation. Let us see if we can push Spinoza's ideas a little further to illustrate how they might be developed. We do not doubt that a line can be drawn from the definitions of proportion in *Elements* Bk. V, the means of finding the fourth proportional in Bk. VIP12, through Descartes' *Géometrie I*, where he deploys the same example, and Spinoza's persistent use of the example in TdIE, EIP15, PI and EIIP40. The best way to comprehend Spinoza's thinking is to see it. The most obvious geometric interpretation of the proportionality is that which reveals the role of the constant (Figure 3.5).

Motions are shown on the vertical axis; rests on the horizontal, and by constructing quadrants of the two, we can locate an infinity of ratios proportionate to $m_1{:}r_1$. One can see this proportionality as determined by diagonal line K; any quadrant that begins at vertex O and has its opposite vertex along K is proportionate. Algebraically, we take $m_1{:}r_1 = m_2{:}r_2$ with $K = r_2{:}r_1$ and $1/K = r_1{:}r_2$. Evidently, if a body characterised by a certain proportion of motion and rest according to this model undergoes an increase in its power of acting, for the proportion to be maintained, both m and r must increase in accordance with K, such that any change Δm is accompanied by a proportionate change Δr across the ratios in proportion:[60]

$$m_1{:}r_1 + \Delta m_1{:}\Delta r_1 = m_2{:}r_2 + \Delta m_2{:}\Delta r_2$$

which immediately tells us that the variations are in proportion, such that:

$$\Delta m_1{:}\Delta r_1 = \Delta m_2{:}\Delta r_2$$

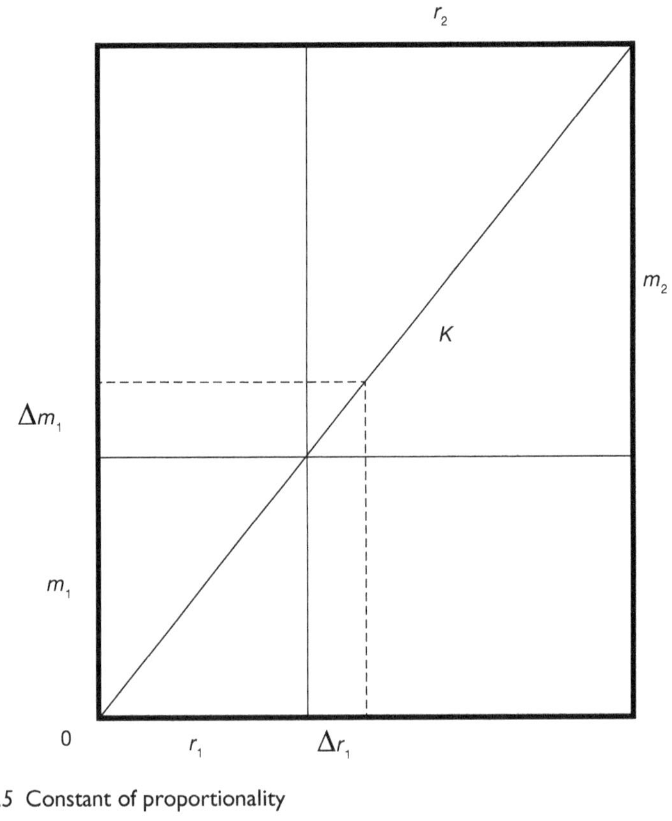

Figure 3.5 Constant of proportionality

which still expresses the constant K, and shows us just how static-kinematic (rather than dynamic) this notion from the PI of bodies in motion is.[61] We are just seeing that the motions vary as the rests vary, just as parts of a tilting lever move more or less to retain equilibrium. If you doubt this, just rearrange the proportion into a more familiar form:

$$\frac{\Delta m_1}{\Delta r_1} - \frac{\Delta m_2}{\Delta r_2} = 0$$

We can swallow the negative operator up into the second term, and take into account each 'body' $n = 1, 2, 3, \ldots$ as a part of the machine in question:

$$\frac{\Delta m_1}{\Delta r_1} + \frac{\Delta m_2}{\Delta r_2} + \frac{\Delta m_3}{\Delta r_3} = 0$$

This, to us, expresses the structure of what Spinoza is driving at, even if the components of the equation are problematic, and that it appears he wants to talk about some erroneous quotient of momentum. It seems that Spinoza's error is that of Descartes': a vote for a kind of *momentum* theory of statics, when what Bernouilli finally discovered was a static theory of virtual '*moments*' (the genetic link of these two terms is not accidental). If one thinks about it further, however, one can see that Spinoza's rejection of Descartes in Letter 81 is actually incomplete, because the above conjecture about the proportion of motion to rest makes more sense if he had continued to accept the Cartesian equation of inert mass with Extension and ignored Descartes' underlying statics. If we replace the rest elements with extension along the three Cartesian axes, consider the aggregate of the motions m along each of these respective axes, and make the changes as small as required, we are very close to a workable formula, but at an expense too terrible to bear for Spinoza; the loss of insight into the inmost nature of things.

So it is indeed the case that Spinoza conceives rest in inverse proportion to motion. What, over and above the geometric formulation, is the metaphysical meaning of describing rest as a reciprocal $1r$? Here, we can only speculate, but we feel that the reciprocal nature of rest *in se* must implicate an inversion in our thinking about rest. It has been natural to regard rest as resisting motion, and this antagonism producing momentum, but in a reciprocal relation we are not opposing terms, but treating the numerator (motion) as being made up of, constituted by, the denominator (rest). In this case, is it not more appropriate to speak of rest in terms of the *permittivity* to motion of substance rather than corporeal resistance? On this interpretation, we see that a motion (mode) passes through the world according to the degree it is welcomed by that world, and so when we distinguish a body also by its degree of rest, we are asking a local question about permittivity to motion for all and any mode that may be placed in the given environment. It is perhaps a fine point, but such a model of rest is more in keeping with the incorporeal nature of the attributes that subtend it.

3.4.2 An increase in finite power: from motion to inclination to motion

We can link the above interpretation to the corpuscular fluid hypothesis: given an arbitrary group of corpuscules under a tension appropriate to relative fluidity, any directed motion (as small as required) by one corpuscule will be communicated to the rest such that the overall directed motions $\partial u / \partial x + \partial v / \partial y + \partial w / \partial z = 0$. But what is this tension that ensures the communication relied upon by Lem. 7?

Now we reintroduce our hypothesis concerning circular motion. First, we remember that the ratio of motion to rest constitutes a motive force P', Q', R', . . . which can be considered the ratio of ('absolute') speed to bulk, and is not a directed motion, as above, but is an instantaneous tendency to motion expressed as a certain ration of motion and rest (EII Def. 1). With this in mind, consider Spinoza's Definition after PI Ax. 2:

> When a number of bodies of the same of different magnitudes are constrained by others in such a way that they are in reciprocal contact with each other, or if they are moved with the same or different degrees of speed in such a way that they communicate their motions to other in some fixed ratio, we shall say the bodies are reciprocally united with each other, and all are simultaneously one *body*, or compose an individual, which is distinguished from others by this union of bodies.
>
> (emphasis in original)[62]

The union of bodies is derived from all manner of motions of the constituent parts such that there is reciprocal communication. In other words, for a rigid spherical body all the parts are pushing inwards, and they can only be still pushing inwards in the case of a rigid body because we are not talking about the directed motion of Lem. 7, but of tendency to motion – the expression of Nature's power. We suggest, therefore, that for Spinoza, motion and rest, considered absolutely, is the as yet undirected circular motion that inclines the parts of a united body towards each other, thereby ensuring reciprocal communication. This is the more primary proportion of motion and rest that must be maintained – we are speaking here of an equilibrium not of directed motions, but *an equilibrium of tendencies to motion* as constitutive of the individual. This means that if the individual is to persist through time on Spinoza's model, not only must the directed motions maintain equilibrium, but the tendencies to motion must remain in equilibrium. The condition of individuality appears to be this; if an individual undergoes a small variation to its motive force (tendency to endure), which Spinoza will term a 'transition', it will persist through these variations or transitions. If we take the equilibrium condition for statics as the expression that a machine communicates motion and rest to its parts in a constant proportion, then variations in the power of acting must be able to occur while the proportion K remains the same. As we saw above, the logic of proportionality allows for the variation of ratios along an infinite constant. The additional problematic, as it were, is that this constant must be maintained over against every other machine in the general equilibrium. Here, the critical importance of power returns to inform our interpretation of the PI and suggest why Spinoza felt it so important to abandon a rest = Extension equation. Alone, in the abstract, every machine can be taken as an isolated system and only its motions considered to explain what it will do, but Spinoza is very much interested in what more helps a machine 'isolate' or distinguish itself in the general equilibrium, and his response is *within* this general equilibrium, it is the finite power imparted to each thing by every other. Consequently, what a thing does is not its static *potestas*, but its *potestas* forced into a determinate form by its degree of finite *potentia*, and to see this, each machine must be placed in its material context.

Again, we believe it most instructive to see Spinoza's grasping at a concept in the light of later developments, which shed light on a tendency rather than a fulfilment. We can see, as Lagrange did,[63] how *d'Alembert's Principle* would follow *subject to the Spinoza's erroneous wish to roll up the mass term into the forces as 'weight'*. The essence of the principle from Spinoza's perspective is that where a local equilibrium pertains, any disequilibrium introduced will be met with compensatory motions in order to maintain equilibrium of the forces. In other words: things only change to maintain equilibrium. For example, if *S* is a simple body, then, if the forces in its location change, it 'resists' that change or is annihilated. Now, a simple body cannot be annihilated (its rest is minimal), so the only other candidate for change is its motion; hence, the simple body will transit away from its current position. This is *more* than the conatus doctrine of being, which essentially expresses the endeavour to persist in one's being – to continue indefinitely. This is the additional thesis that a conative thing that transits to a greater power of acting is still that unity. This is therefore still an equilibrium theory, but raised a power, so that there is both equilibrium of motions and rest in each machine considered alone, and equilibrium of transitions – Spinoza states that a thing's parts are able to move *more* quickly or slowly (*iam tardius, iam celerius*) without any change of nature (PI Sch.) – due to the impulsion of finite powers across the whole face of the universe (ibid.). To our mind, if this is an approximation of Spinoza's view of the world system, then it shows him at his most 'classical', in the sense that it is a theory of general equilibrium. Yet in observing that *S* simply 'resists' some application of external power, we immediately ask: (a) what externality means in a world with no outside? and (b) have we adequately accounted for the transition that occurs as *S* changes to remain the same? As to (a), we observe that God or Nature's substantiality may be reflected in the transiting conatus, but alone this tensed global system has no reason to alter. It is only by realising that the attributes must eternally work in the world, and so 'super add' infinite power to the system to keep it moving, that we are driven to look for a source of this power, and that modal source, being immanent, we locate again in that body which has passed to the infinite, namely rest *qua* infinite motion. All duration, as Bove notes,[64] is resistance and is defined by finite power; but eternity is free act and is defined by infinite power. We sense that we are eternal, and so we maintain that insofar as things of Extension are constituted by infinite rest, they are the sources of this infinite, inexhaustible power. It is this power that is the origin of the possibility of not just mute existence, but also working, and of liberated intuition, not just bounded reason, as we shall see in Chapter 5.

As to (b), we will now attempt to outline how the intensification that accompanies positive variations in motion to rest is the source of attributes' variations, or changes in the perception of substance. We must note that Bennett (1984) has argued that we can regard Spinoza as thinker of gradient as part of a field theory, though this seems premised on the idea that the attribute of Extension means substance is extended like a fluid *surface*, which we deny.[65] It seems to us that his broad thrust is correct in that we also feel that power in the world constantly modulates the tendencies to motion of the world, over and above simple mechanism, though we have sought to build up from principles of statics known to Spinoza and do not accept his contention that the attribute of Extension simply constitutes a Cartesian coordinate system in which every event takes place. Most importantly, once it is understood that motion is itself a body, just as rest is, not something possessed by a neutral body-thing, and therefore an expression of power, we can begin to conceive that the Hobbist notion of neutral atoms as conveyers of accidental motions is quite alien to this theory. A motion is already a body, though it combines with other motions, and rests, to constitute a body in the common sense of that word. Here, we have the ultimate division in juridical-physics: (a) the Hobbist-Newtonian view that any application of force on a thing is entirely negative, nay an interference with some possible liberty; (b) the Cartesian-Spinozan view that the application of some force is constitutive of the thing itself, the very ground of its liberty. In physical terms, this manifests itself in the loosely expressed Cartesian hydrostatic model in which fluid conveys planets around the Sun; a model Newton proves is false because the conveying fluid must through collisions retard the motion of the planet, such that it will come to a halt. Once we understand that Spinoza is moving beyond the fluid model to a model of infinite power expressed by Extension as incorporeal tendencies to motion, we perceive what is at stake in Spinoza's political theory of circulation of natural right (cf. *infra.*) and just how fundamentally different the points of departure are between Hobbes and Spinoza.

We must return to these matters in the following chapters, for we are as yet unfinished with the nature of motion and rest. We have moved from the equilibrium of motion to the equilibrium of tendencies to motion, and located this latter in the expression of Nature's power per EI Def. 1. Yet what precisely is the nature of this expression? How do we arrive at tendencies to motion from the attribute of Extension? The answer is attained by a direct and an indirect route. The direct route is Spinoza's explanation of Creation in EI; the indirect route is the completion of our understanding of Letter 12 on infinity and its critique of Cartesian mathematics.

The direct route is the simpler, provided we realise that in the creation of the attributes, the three orders of the modes map relatively well onto the phases of matter (also called elements)[66] described by Descartes. This can be tabulated (Table 3.1).

Table 3.1 Typology of bodies in Descartes and Spinoza

Rotation	*Descartes*	*Spinoza*
Infinite	Light (formerly fire)	Infinite immediate motion and rest – inexhaustible power
Relatively slow (motion)	Celestial fluid	*In toto*, the infinite mediate mode; separately, the finite modes with relative conative power
Approaching infinite (rest)	Celestial bodies proper (formerly earth)	Finite modes with relatively greater conative power, and commensurate degree of infinite power

As we state above, what distinguishes the three modal orders is their respective power of circulation, or degree of motion and rest (PI Ax. 1). Light corpuscules are, for Spinoza, an infinite power of motion and rest; that is, infinite rotation understood as motion so fast that it passes to the limit and becomes rest (i.e. the ability to be everywhere at once). Between the remaining modes, there is a notional division determined by whether the motion approaches rest more or less. As motion approaches rest, we have bulk or weight, which is able to express itself as a motive force capable of resisting other motions. Where motion recedes from rest, the relative body is not capable of expressing itself as having place in the world that resists other bodies, but must pass across or be communicated through resting bodies. To be clear, by 'body', Spinoza does not mean a lump of matter; he means motion is a body or rest is a body. It is a categorical claim – motion and rest are *not* incorporeal, and so a wide swathe of ontological furniture is brought within corporeality, including motion as such, and, in line with Stoic doctrine, the passions. Following Seneca, fury becomes a body. Now, because bodies that recede from rest as motion play a derivative role in the universe, they may be seen as transporting bodies: they grant to bulks their directional motion. Composed bodies are compositions of bulks as motion:rest and directed motions as motion:rest. We thus have a transporting fluid of motive power, and so the infinite mediate mode can be rightly called the entire face of the universe if one considers that such corpuscules constitute the greater part of the celestial vortices illustrated by Descartes. This is, however, as with Descartes, a continuum. Light corpuscules can slow rotation to become 'dead stars' or planets; solids and fluids can be considered their supposed opposites depending on their own absolute changes or the context in which they are viewed. On this model, the attributes create by positing and synthesising motion and rest into expressions of power that fall into the three modal categories.

The indirect route is to take the extensive nature of the attributes to the limit to discover why they cause tendencies to motion that unite bodies. In Chapter 2, we saw that what was an incorporeal attribute that simply allowed the world to be viewed with a 3D grid is transformed by Spinoza when he makes the attributes the infinitely powerful actions of God or Nature. In Chapter 2, we endeavoured to describe how causal series contracted under the influence of the attributes, but it is perhaps difficult to grasp (especially as Spinoza does not always account for direction), and so we will proceed using a more intuitive (and cruder) model below. If we imagine Cartesian 3-space, we may conceive how, if this space is an incorporeal attribute understood as an act of Nature, the act of Nature in imputing tendencies to motion into the very fabric of Extension operates as a kind of contraction of that incorporeal space. This is not quite what happens, though. Rather, the infinite circular motions must take priority, and so in the limit case what we have as the attributes feed into the world; there is not simply a contraction, but a contraction and a *twist*. Spinoza thus refounds the Cartesian celestial vortex not on motions, but on tendencies to motion, which are caused immanently by the attributes themselves. And every point on this attributive framework exerts that tendency as an essence, expressed as actual power, intended as formal power. It is the attributes themselves that ground the universal dynamic equilibrium. Spinoza's attributes indeed create the surface described in Chapter 2, but unlike Descartes, whose vortical model he began to render geometrically in DPPIII, this surface is actively involved in shaping the perception of substance itself.

If we can agree that this organic development did indeed occur in Spinoza's mind, we can understand his misgivings about the mathematical in Letter 12. For it is easily shown in Chapter 2 how the nonconcentric circles (torus) example of that letter derives from a thought experiment in hydrodynamics in DPPIIP9. Now we can understand why the inequalities are of such critical importance. They indicate that in the given example, static Cartesian 3-space is simply not up to describing what Nature can create. We are not claiming, however, that Spinoza believed in some new non-Euclidean geometry, as the above sketch suggests. Rather, his belief that mathematics can only approximate reality must surely be understood as deriving from a view that even if Nature's Extension was as geometrical as Descartes claimed, it would instantaneously become unintelligible to the Euclidean geometer as it twisted, contracted and relaxed. His dismissal of Tschirnhaus' interest in the applicates to curves, and his failure to engage in any obvious way with the analytical insights of his acquaintances Huygens and Hudde, seems to suggest that he felt mathematics could not produce an adequate geometry to fit the metaphysics he envisaged. Yet to Spinoza's credit, he understood perhaps more than anyone the difference between concepts and the signs that represent them. Rather than pursuing fruitless researches into equations of the fifth order as Tschirnhaus did, he aimed always to understand the concept first, and to express himself as best he could afterwards.

There is a lot going on here, indicative of the swirl of ideas in late seventeenth-century science. It is our contention that primary circular motion, imbued into substance to produce its affects, is the origin of Creation, as Spinoza defines it. There results a very clear geometric conception of a spin or rotation that, depending on the speed of that rotation, transfers motion and rest to surrounding bodies. But not only does this rotating singular thing transfer, and thus alter, the motion and rest of surrounding bodies, but it also 'drags' them towards it. This is not an attractive force in the Newtonian sense; rather, the bodies travel in straight lines but the rotation causes the straight lines to become contracted towards and around the source of spin. This is the tensional aspect of the attributes that grounds the essences of particular things, provided we never divorce these essences from their determination to exist by finite modes. If we combine this rotating action with the 'natural' rectilinear motion of a given simple body, we thus come upon the essence of dynamics. For dynamics is nothing other than the relation of a *variation* in motion to the action of some force (*potentia*), and not, as the Peripatetics thought, the relation of natural motions to these forces. We can therefore decompose any simple physical event into three elements: given natural motion; variation of the 'speed' of that motion; variation of the direction of that motion due to a 'twist'.

The actual motion of the corpuscle is consequently a composition of forces: the addition of: (a) the corpuscle's initial motion:rest; (b) the additional motion:rest due to its coming into the sphere of acting of the spinning corpuscle (think the sun) and so being impelled along in the current; and (c) the inward drag of this current, which is due to the attribute of Extension itself being 'wound up' in its act of expressing the spinning corpuscle. Thus, the deviation inwards appears to be a pull, but is neither due to an attractive force, or the non-explanation afforded by other corpuscles pushing inwards, but is entirely due to the straight lines of the surface of the attributes being twisted inwards.[67] It is this deviational tendency to motion that is the ultimate ground of composed bodies holding themselves together. We agree with Klever that Spinoza's example of churning milk, in Letter 6 'On Fluidity', is most revealing of his physical commitments. Klever (1988: 177–178) draws our attention to the way that the heavier parts of the milk are forced upwards in the vortex, but on reaching the surface cannot combine with the air, which also forces these parts downwards. Where we respectfully depart from Klever's analysis is that whereas he puts the greater emphasis on the *gravitas* of the parts (butter) relative to the media (milk/air), we say that it is not for nothing that Spinoza introduces this example with: 'but when milk is stirred and so acquires a new motion to which all the parts cannot equally accommodate themselves'. Had Spinoza merely written 'if the milk is stirred', then it would be correct to focus on the explanatory role of relative *gravitas*, but he does not. We suggest that the key initiator of the *change of equilibrium* is the stirring so that new motion is acquired. Spinoza is quite specific on this, and we find it difficult to believe that he suffers from Nelsonian blindness with respect to the causative primacy of the introduction of intensive circular motion. On the contrary, this text is a confirmation that circular motion is the point at which Nature's acts move from attribute to mode with immanent power. We are thus taken back to the primary flux of the smallest corpuscles, the minimal, original case of this 'stirring', when, in his next comment in Letter 6, Spinoza maintains that particles of water 'are always moving ceaselessly'.

Coming back, briefly, to the idea of an immutability of tendencies to motion, we now explicate why we found Gueroult's phrase ('cercle de la *potestas*') so tantalising. One can see from the above diagram that while the spinning corpuscle is acting on the smaller corpuscle, and, it appears, dragging it towards itself at greater speed, the initial motion of the smaller corpuscle ensures that it will not simply 'forget' its own conatus, and will always endeavour to proceed away along its rectilinear path. The endeavour of our spinning corpuscle thus fails, this failure being the difference between the work our spinning corpuscle performs, and its desire that the smaller corpuscle act entirely in accordance with its intention (simply ignore the smaller corpuscle's motion above to see how the same corpuscle would move at a steeper angle inwards). If we accept for a moment an abstract Cartesian space as shown above, then the circle of capacity inscribes in that space, at every point, a *power*, a degree of disequilibrium in addition to the general equilibrium that whatever body finds itself 'there' expresses to the extent not otherwise restrained. This power is infinite and eternal; that is, it is irresistible for the bodies in it and inexhaustible for the bodies exercising it.

Finally, we need to consider how the above considerations relate to natural right. We have seen that there are three physical levels to Spinoza's theory, the static equilibrium (formal being), the dynamic equilibrium (actual essence), and then a dynamic disequilibrium (formal essence). In Chapter 4, we will show how Spinoza is careful to couple existence and act within power, and we interpret him as assigning the doctrine of capacity to maintain equilibrium to existence. As to working, this takes place across the two dynamic concepts. The dynamic equilibrium theory shows that when a power is impressed into a system, some effect is produced that involves the system being destroyed or moving, and in the plenum performing work as it forces obstacles out of its way. This work is natural right as resistance or effort, and given the nature of the equilibrium (even if that equilibrium affords a delay between inputs and outputs), we can see how Spinoza's theory of will operates like a mirror: every impressed power is symmetrically expressed. But in addition to this work, Spinoza posits a second dynamism that flows immanently from the attributes (contractions). This power of working evidenced by natural right is nothing other than the power of God or Nature, and being infinite in the world, is work that is free (in Spinoza's sense) and inexhaustible. In Chapter 5, we will explicate this 'work' aspect of natural right for itself and with reference to its modal effects, which we believe is either ignored or subsumed into a limited reading of the conatus doctrine. Our aim in Chapter 6 will be to raise these elements of natural right to the social level to explain Spinoza's doctrine of the city of greatest natural right.

Notes

1 Leibniz (1989: 179).
2 Buyse (2011: 1).
3 Ibid., p. 4.
4 Ibid., p. 5.

5 'The foundational role of hydrostatics and statics in Descartes' natural philosophy' in Gaukroger (ed.) (2000: 60ff.).
6 'Force, determination and impact' in Gaukroger (ed.) (2000: 84ff.).
7 '"Waterworld": Descartes' Vortical Celestial Mechanics – A gambit in the Natural Philosophical Contest of the Early Seventeenth Century', Anstey and Schuster (2010: 35ff.).
8 Cf. Manzini's thorough study of this book's influence (2009).
9 A crane-like arm used for lowering items to or from a quay.
10 AT (II: 233).
11 Consider, in the case of the inclined plane that the load at *D* is to be raised rather upon an arc *EDG*. It is then irrelevant at every moment what the rest of the arc *DG* will actually do; the only relevant motion is the instantaneous motion that, at the instant, is equivalent to moving along a tangent *ADC* to the arc, or an inclined plane.
12 Heron drew on several predecessors. In particular, he reports what some believe to be Straton's doctrines. Cf. n. *supra*.
13 Cf. Winter (2007). However, the style of Archytas' known work on the mathematics of music and proportion seems at odds with the more functional use of proportions in the *Mechanica*.
14 Cf. Palmieri (2007).
15 The wedge, lever, pulley and wheel (*Mech.* §9). The screw was invented, as we all know, by Archimedes.
16 The author uses *peri-pherein* – *lit.* to be carried or displaced about something.
17 Adapted from the translation by T.N. Winter (2007).
18 *Elements* Bk. V Def. 6.
19 Following Winter's translation (2007).
20 If one looks at the natural motion in the diagram. Clearly the unnatural motion would produce a sine wave.
21 Rivaud (1924), Gabbey in Garrett (1996).
22 *Mech.* §3.
23 Cf. the references at the beginning of this chapter.
24 Gaukroger (2000: 73).
25 This is something like momentum ($p = mv$), but all the components are incorrect. Mass is required (not relative weight) and it must be multiplied by velocity. Descartes uses absolute speed, and even then he wishes to ignore the temporal element of the distance/time quotient, so that he speaks of absolute motion.
26 In Gaukroger (2000: 100).
27 Lécrivain ('Spinoza and Cartesian Mechanics', in Grene and Nails (1986: 15–60 at 53) also notes this appearance.
28 Ibid., at 54.
29 PPII[50].
30 Cf. also EVP20 Sch.
31 See the detailed discussion in Garber (1992: 156ff.).
32 'Vis et incrementum cuiuscumque passionis, eiusque in existendo perseverantia non definitur potentia, qua nos in existendo perseverare conamur, sed causae externae potentia cum nostra comparata.'
33 'Vis, qua homo in existendo perseverat, limitata est et a potentia causarum externarum infinite superatur.'
34 (1991: 191ff.).
35 Spinoza abandons the *sive Natura* here.
36 Conceive in the strict sense (i.e. clearly and distinctly). God cannot produce formal contradictions.
37 Gueroult (1968: 389).
38 Following Negri (1991: 191).

39 *Capital*, I (1976: 284).
40 'Per ius itaque naturae intelligo ipsas naturae leges seu regulas, secundum quas omnia fiunt, hoc est, ipsam naturae potentiam . . . consequenter quicquid unusquisque homo ex legibus suae naturae agit, id summo naturae iure agit, tantumque in naturam habet iuris, quantum potentia valet.'
41 The geometrical meaning of Spinoza's words becomes obvious.
42 Anstey and Shuster (2010: 35ff.).
43 Hence, the small delta: ∂, which Euler adopted from Alexis Fontaine. It is the partial differential notation and broadly it tells us to look only at the variable that follows, and set any other variables to constant. Here, for example, it tells us to look only at how the point changes with respect to x, and to ignore y and z. We then take the case of y, ignoring x and z, and likewise z, *mutatis mutandis*. We then recompose the results. There should be zero change if the conditions of equilibrium and incompressibility can be said to hold. We *strongly* recommend the reader refer to Euler's seminal paper.
44 Here, we rely on Anstey and Shuster (2010) (op. cit., n. 42) and Gaukroger (2000) (op. cit., n. 5) for helpful analyses.
45 *i*PPIII[21, 24].
46 Except in the case of Saturn, which, as Spinoza notes, is a claim of rashness on Descartes' part (Letter 26).
47 (2001: 61).
48 Trans. due to Garber (1992: 279).
49 Quoted in Garber (1992: 279).
50 In Grene and Nails (1986: 45).
51 As an introduction to the White and Stirling translation (2001).
52 (1992: 235).
53 Védrine (1967: II-iii, B.), quoting *De l'infinito*.
54 Ibid.
55 Ibid., n. 17.
56 (2009, Ch. VII).
57 'Quare si corpora magna tali proportione moveantur, ut eorum motus ad eorum molem sit, ut motus minutorum corporum ad eorundem molem, fluida etiam essent dicenda . . .'
58 'Aristoteles' here covering pseudo-Aristotelian authors in the *Corpus*.
59 'Retinet praeterea individuum sic compositum suam naturam, sive id secundum totum moveatur, sive quiescat, sive versus hanc, sive versus illam partem moveatur, dummodo unaquaeque pars motum suum retineat, eumque, uti antea, reliquis communicet.'
60 We can also observe that any transition in $m_1{:}r_1$ is accompanied by a transition of that ratio's hypoteneuse along K, which we will call k_1, such that $(k_1 + \Delta k)^2 = (m_1 + \Delta m)^2 + (r_1 + \Delta r)^2$. If k_1' is the solution, then $k_1' = 2m(\Delta m) + \Delta m^2 + 2r(\Delta r) + \Delta r^2$.
61 The PI is not the whole physical theory, but effectively the static-kinematic part, built on and implying further critical elements.
62 'Cum corpora aliquot eiusdem aut diversae magnitudinis a reliquis ita coercentur, ut invicem incumbant, vel si eodem aut diversis celeritatis gradibus moventur, ut motus suos invicem certa quadam ratione communicent, illa corpora invicem unita dicemus, et omnia simul unum corpus, sive individuum componere, quod a reliquis per hanc corporum unionem distinguitur.'
63 (1811, II, II.4).
64 (1996: 130).
65 Cf. also Bennett's defence in Garrett (1996: 64ff.).
66 Cf. PPIII[52].
67 This sounds a lot like general relativity, but the notion of twisting attributes does not appear to generate the curved time-space of Einstein. The model of twisting is a

consequence of the Cartesian celestial model, combined with our suggestion of spinning corpuscles.

Bibliography

Anstey, P.R. and Schuster, J.A. (eds) (2010) *The Science of Nature in the Seventeenth Century: Patterns of Change in Early Modern Natural Philosophy*, Springer, Dordrecht.

Aristoteles (1961) *Aristoteles Latinus*, L. Minio-Paluello (ed.), Desclée de Brouwer, Paris-Bruges.

—— (1972) Aristoteles Latinus XXVI 1–3 Fasc.Sec. Ethica Nicomachea – Trans. Antiquissima Libr.II–III sive 'Ethica Vetus', R.A. Gauthier (ed.), E.J. Brill, Leiden.

Bennett, J. (1984) *A Study in Spinoza's Ethics*, Hackett, Indianapolis, IN.

Bruno, G. (2004) *Cause, Principle, and Unity, and Essays on Magic*, Cambridge University Press, Cambridge. Includes a translation of *De vinculis in genere.*

Buyse, F. (2011) 'On how Spinoza unmasks Descartes' physics in his Principles of Cartesian Philosophy', archived at: www.benedictusdespinoza.nl/lit/Filip_Buyse_Scottish_Seminar_Aberdeen_March_2011.pdf.

Cues, N. de (2009) *La sagesse selon l'idiot: Idiota de sapienta*, Hermann, Paris.

Garber, D. (1992) *Descartes' Metaphysical Physics*, University of Chicago Press, Chicago, IL.

Garrett, D. (1996) *The Cambridge Companion to Spinoza*, Cambridge University Press, Cambridge.

Gaukroger, S. (1980) *Descartes: Philosophy, Mathematics and Physics*, Harvester Press, Sussex & Totowa, NJ.

—— (ed.) (2000) *Descartes' Natural Philosophy*, Routledge, London.

—— (2002) *Descartes' System of Natural Philosophy*, Cambridge University Press, Cambridge.

Grene, M. and Nails, D. (eds) (1986) *Spinoza and the Sciences*, D. Reidel Publishing Co., Dordrecht.

Gueroult, M. (1968a) *Descartes selon l'ordre des raisons: II – L'âme et le corps*, Aubier, Éditions Montaigne, Paris.

—— (1968b) *Spinoza: I – Dieu*, Aubier, Éditions Montaigne, Paris.

—— (1974a) *Spinoza: II – L'âme*, Aubier, Éditions Montaigne, Paris.

Israel, J.I. (2001) *Radical Enlightenment: Philosophy and the Making of Modernity 1650–1750*, Oxford University Press, Oxford.

Klever, W. (1987) 'The Helvetius affair or Spinoza and the Philosopher's Stone: a document on the background of Letter 40' 3 *Studia Spinozana* 439.

—— (2006) *Enlightenment Contested: Philosophy, Modernity and the Emancipation of Man 1670–1752*, Oxford University Press, Oxford.

Lagrange, J.L. (1811) *Mécanique analytique*, 2nd edn, Ve Courcier, Paris.

Leibniz, G.W. (1989) *Philosophical Essays*, Ariew and Garber (trans.), Hackett, Indianapolis, IN.

Manzini, F. (2009) *Spinoza: une lecture d'Aristote*, Epimethée, PUF, Paris.

Marx, K. (1976) *Capital* (3 vols), Penguin & New Left Review, London.

Matheron, A. (1985) '"Le droit du plus fort": Hobbes contre Spinoza' 110 *Revue Philosophique* 149–176.

—— (1988) *Individu et Communauté chez Spinoza*, Editions de Minuit, Paris.

Nadler, S. (2001) *Spinoza: A Life*, Cambridge University Press, Cambridge.

—— (2004) 'Les vérités éternelles et l'autre monde: les raciness juives de Spinoza' 4 *Les Études Philosophiques* 507–522.

Negri, A. (1991) *The Savage Anomaly: The Power of Spinoza's Metaphysics and Politics*, University of Minnesota Press, Minneapolis, MN.

Newton, Sir I. (1999) *The* Principia*: Mathematical Principles of Natural Philosophy*, I. Bernard Cohen and A. Whitman (trans.), University of California Press, Berkeley, CA.

Palmieri, P. (2007) 'Breaking the circle: the emergence of Archimedean mechanics in the late Renaissance' 62 *Arch. Hist. Exact Sci.* 301–346.

Pappus (1660) *Mathematicae collectiones a Federico Commandino Urbinate in Latinum conversae, et commentarijs illustratae*, Ex typographia HH. de Duccijs, Bologna.

Parkinson, G.H.R. (2000) *Spinoza: Ethics*, Oxford University Press, Oxford.

Rivaud, A. (1924) 'La physique de Spinoza' 4 *Chronicon Spinozanum* 24–57.

Védrine, H. (1967) *La conception de la nature chez Giordano Bruno*, Vrin, Paris.

White, W.H. and Stirling, A.H. (trans.) (2001) *Spinoza: Ethics.* Used for Garrett's intriguing *Introduction*, Wordsworth Editions, Ware, Herts.

Winter, T.N. (2007) *The Mechanical Problems in the Corpus of Aristotle*, Faculty Publications, University of Nebraska-Lincoln.

Chapter 4

Natural right I

The logic of existential consciousness

> Ac praetera, ut saepe in aquarum vorticibus vidi contingere, in majori illo coelestis materiae vortices sint alii minores vortices.[1]
>
> Descartes PPIII[33]

4.1 Introduction

With the 'event' theory of the attributes and a detailed understanding of bodies as machines tending to and locked within immutability, we are now in a position to elaborate on Spinoza's theory of natural right; a theory whose short definition combines a wealth of technical aspects that would otherwise be easily overlooked. As we shall show in the first section, natural right properly divides into two elements – existential and essential power, insofar as these prevail. This chapter will focus on the former, which necessarily prevails for every given machine because it is determination to exist; the following will concern itself with the somewhat overlooked 'essential' element of natural right.

4.2 Consciousness of natural right

Let us immediately move to establish the relation between natural right and consciousness and the synthetic 'properties' of consciousness as such.

4.2.1 Preliminary remarks on the synthetic nature of natural right

4.2.1.1 EI Def. 4 revisited – understanding the perception of substance

Chapter 16 of Deleuze's *Expressionism in Philosophy: Spinoza* is entitled 'The ethical vision of the world'. The title is pregnant in its implication of Spinoza's thinking about how ethics can even occur for the one substance. We might crudely unpack the title as: *the ethical is the perceptive – it is because substance perceives itself that ethics becomes possible*. The point is not to become too bogged down in the sense of perception as an all-too-human inadequacy despite this being a major feature of the doctrine. At first instance it is substance that perceives itself. Remember again the categorical differences that determine the process of substance's coming to be: in the first 'act' of substance, by virtue of its very properties, that is, its very power, substance exists as having properties (a divine nature) and in particular capable of differentiating what it does infinitely. In the second abstract moment God or Nature acts in the proper sense by Thinking or Extending etc., which events express solutions to the divine nature, which substance differentiates according to the logic of each of the infinitely many attribute-solutions. It is due to this second action upon itself that what simply exists is brought under what we can only describe as a further domination by the essences of the attributes. God or Nature tirelessly *labours* upon itself in the act of creation; a trinitological event the creation of which is the '*general Natura naturata*' being the 'Son, Product or immediate Creation of God' (KV, I Ch. IX). For Spinoza it is not enough that God or Nature determine a state of being that is perfect (the creation of the infinite immediate mode) but that infinite things follow from It in infinitely many ways; that is, God or Nature strives to create as much as Its infinite power permits. Is this, therefore, a good creation? It is perfect according to the divine intellect, which understands everything *sub specie aeternitatis*, but the creation is *not* good. There is nothing in anything that in itself renders it good or bad. Rather, that which is good is the labour of creation itself, and it is good in a naturalistic sense: it is good because and only because it gives God intellectual pleasure to labour upon its creation. Here, therefore, we would clarify the statement 'it is because substance perceives itself that ethics becomes possible' as follows: it is not perception that is the ethical act, rather, it is the perception through the attributes that opens up the possibility of ethics, it is the labour of substance to create this difference between the actual and the formal. To repeat there is not an ethics yet. There is a difference between a physics and a logic that is opened up by the labour of God or Nature. God or Nature creates ethics as such almost as a groundwork of the future. So at this level, in this synthesis, we already have a kind of exemplar of a labour-towards-ethics for the finite thing grounded likewise in its consciousness of both its existence and its essence. The Spinozan doctrine of natural right is centred on this labour.

As Spinoza defines it, God intellectually loves Himself (EVP35), not as external object but as resolved in the action of that intellectual love; He loves Himself as cause of self (ibid.: Dem.). Here there is already an important divide: the singularity of this love and its origin in the labour of the *causa sui*. We focus on the latter aspect here. Note how Spinoza's God could not be described as a worker in Marx's sense: for Marx work is occupation, a bending of the will to the task that pains the worker, and the more so the less the worker loves the task.[2] Thereby a breach appears between the image of the puritan labourer expressing God's work, and Marx's generative labour of the worker, who, in her pain – her very hate of the task (or obsession with it)[3] – provides a basis of surplus value (growth).[4] Spinoza's

God is incapable of bending His will, it is set always to its task and takes excessive pleasure in it. And this pleasure is not drawn off by any other substance. In other words, God is unprofitable.[5]

The Spinozan worker continues within Marx's system, but only as part of a sphere in which the *living* worker that hates is constrained within a species of understanding that dictates (as self-evident) that her labour *power* is loving as God's work. We find Spinoza's doctrine of *finite* love and hate sublated into an exponential process which instantiates the first part of EIIIP43 – 'hatred is increased by reciprocal hatred' – in the accumulation of labours by the system, and sets each layer of that accumulation into a complete unity of self-evident substance through the second part – '*et amore contra deleri potest*'. But note the asymmetry of the relation: hates[6] are reciprocally augmentative, but finite love only subtracts hate rather than operates, as Parkinson incorrectly translates, as its converse.[7] Hence, the Spinozan worker destroys in such a manner: 'I love this present accumulation of hates; this present accumulation of hates is nothing but love.' Nietzsche would claim[8] that 'we can destroy only as creators', but the emphasis surely turns on the worker's ability lovingly to destroy the *hatefulness* of creation at every instant – a most 'valuable' triumph of the will.

Ethics for Spinoza's part resides in the attributes insofar as they conceive substance; insofar as they strive to labour upon it. Immanence combined with the eternity of the creative act means, however, that this striving is unevenly distributed across substance, such that finite modes have more or less ethical power to labour upon creation. The empty difference between substance's infinite power of being and infinite power of working[9] becomes a real difference between a finite mode's power of existing and its power of working (*potentia operandi*). We can now perhaps understand the difference acutely remarked upon by Gueroult, when Spinoza in the DPP reworks the Cartesian *cogito* as *ego sum cogitans* (Gueroult 1972: 76–77). Being and thinking are no longer assigned to the 'I', but rather the 'I' is generated by the eternal 'act' of substance causing itself to be, and the attributive event of substance in immanently causing some determinate modes to think together (literally *con-science*). As we shall see as we now examine natural right, this categorical difference is integral to its definition.

4.2.1.2 Spinoza's definition of natural right

Spinoza's prose definition of the right of nature remains consistent in its core metaphysical construction through the TTP, *Ethics* and the *Tractatus politicus*. Here is the relevant quotation from the former:

> By the right and established laws of Nature I mean nothing other than the rules governing the nature of every individual thing, according to which we conceive it as naturally determined to exist and work in a certain manner.
> (Geb III/188)[10]

Here from EIVP37 Sch. 2:

> Each person exists by the highest right of Nature, and consequently, each person by the highest right of nature acts necessarily according to his own nature.[11]

And here from TPII[3–4]:

> Since God has right over all things, and God's right is nothing other than God's power insofar as that is considered absolutely free, it follows that every natural thing has as much right from Nature as it has power to act, for the power of every natural thing by which it exists and works is nothing other than the power of God, which is absolutely free.[12]
>
> . . . and consequently whatever each man does from the laws of his own nature, he does by the highest right of Nature, and he has as much right over Nature as his power extends.[13]

It is trite to point out the role of power in the definition; the key qualifiers on which we wish to focus are the following:

(a) the power of existing;
(b) the power of working (*potentia operandum*);
(c) according to the laws of a thing's nature; and
(d) as far as this power avails it (or extends).

We believe that the work completed in the foregoing chapters place us in a strong position to understand each of these qualifiers. We will provide a preliminary summation of their meaning.

To understand the difference between the power of existing and of working, we must relate the definition to its physical and causal inspirations. When we speak of existence, everything is constantly determined to existence in some way (*certo modo*). Here we are speaking of some body *B* as an effect of the great causal chain. When we are asking about its natural right in this respect, we must engage with *B*'s complete definition, such that we assess its continued genesis. What is it to generate *B*. If *B* is to be considered as a machine, then we are first looking for the conditions that generate its static order of immutability = 0. In Spinozist terms, what causes it to maintain a constant global proportion of motion and rest as it endures. The second thing we are looking for are the conditions that determine the certain mode of existing. A thing does not exist unless it is also in act, and so we must determine what a thing's current motion and rest is, which it is endeavouring to maintain (even if relatively speaking the machine appears to stand still).

Later in this chapter we will also describe how variations in the power of acting feed into what I term existential consciousness: the consciousness of duration.

It is vitally important to distinguish the motions involved in constituting *B*'s existence in some way from the motions that B itself brings about. This is the critical division between EPIII (existence), and EPIV (bonded work) and V (free work), and it is most easily understood as the difference between *B* as effect (existing) and *B* as also cause (working). We have called this causal power 'essential' and insofar as it constitutes our active consciousness, our essential consciousness. If God or Nature's power is to be properly considered as immanent, then the creative power must also be immanent to each thing as cause, and further, as we will show, each thing endeavours in a simulacrum of God or Nature to act indefinitely. We will show in the next chapter that this endeavour relates to the second dynamic order of immutability and that it is the creative desire to determine transitions in the universe towards some equality = 0.

The laws of *B*'s nature describe the common notions we develop about how *B* transforms incoming determinations into expressions of *B*'s own nature. An instructive Stoic example would be the cylinder of Chrysippos, which when impelled while lying will roll. Nothing in the impulsion need have a 'rolling' property to give to the cylinder; the impulsion is converted into a rolling motion that expresses the cylindrical nature of the thing's existence. This is a key condition of Spinoza's natural right theory that many overlook in their ascription of 'anarchic licence': if *A* is some simple impulsion and *B* is a cylinder, it is by *B*'s natural right that it rolls, *not* by *A*'s, for *A* does not satisfy the criterion of acting by its natural laws (it is an indistinct impulsion). Conversely, if our rolling cylinder picks up some dirt particles *C* on its way, this dirt is not only impelled by the converted power of *B*, but is constrained (lit. *coäctus*)[14] to roll and express the laws and so act by the sovereign right of *B*. The mechanical examples Spinoza could provide are many, including the action of the lever around a fulcrum, or, inversely, the determination (*coäction*) to rotate that a fixed sling imparts to a stone.

Finally, our understanding of the unusual use of 'force*' by Descartes, we believe, reveals to us the import of 'as far as it extends [or avails]'. This is a Cartesian determination of the quantum of extended right by reference to the motion a thing makes along a line; literally the work done in modern parlance. Yet, as we showed in Chapter 3, we must learn to distinguish between the power a thing possesses and the work it actually does. Both a child and an army in unison can each lift 1 lb 1 ft, and they *de facto* have the natural right to do it, but anyone who concludes from this that both have equal power in every circumstance is frankly a fool. We do not yet know what a body can do means precisely that the current instances of extension of *B*'s natural right do not exhaust it. And this becomes more so the case as *B* increases its power of acting by availing itself of the tools of Nature and of the mind (concepts), of which the city is a leading example (cf. Chapter 6).

With this summary complete, we now pass to consider the power of existing and its intimate relation to existential consciousness in greater detail. First, we will formalise the division between existential and essential consciousness according to the cause/effect asymmetry. We will then explain at length the genealogical linkage between Spinoza's theory of the conscious stone and Seneca's example of the bridge constituted by transition. It is this transition that founds the first immutability of a given thing (its conative desire). Finally, we will examine how once constituted the machine can undergo transitions and how this is linked to the passions of pleasure and pain.

4.2.1.3 Natural right as consciousness – methodological division

With our definitions in place we now turn to the direct relation between consciousness and natural right. It would perhaps suffice to proceed to the construction of such a consciousness synthetically, as Spinoza does, but in order to be fairer to the reader we propose to initiate a methodological distinction of consciousness that follows directly from the double nature of natural right.

That such a distinction is possible has been shown by Balibar,[15] who conjectures that there is 'differential' between appetite and desire in consciousness. In due course we will proffer our own view, which accepts the division of consciousness but places the division prior even to the first kind of cognition. In the interim, we define:

> *Existential consciousness* is the natural right of a singular thing insofar as we consider its power of existing.
>
> *Essential consciousness* is the natural right of a singular thing insofar as we consider its power of working, where working is taken in both its passive (bonded) and active (free) sense here.

These interim definitions are posited so as to assist presentation of the peculiarities of each in what follows. Now, if we consider that existential consciousness pertains to the affective right of a thing, that is its psychological substructure, whereas essential consciousness is the realm of thing's ethical activity in the world, we are struck though not surprised by the discernible genetic similarity of these two conceptions to Hegel's science of subjective spirit and philosophy of objective right. The relation, however, is not the object of study here.

4.2.2 Pre-consciousness – the actual essence of things

In order to understand consciousness we must understand the conatus, which is the primary endeavour of consciousness. To understand the conatus, EIIIP7 instructs us to consider its actual essence. We must therefore look at the problematic of determination to existence of particular things – a problematic that draws on the rather dense Corollary to EIP25:

> Particular things are nothing other than the affections i.e. modes of the attributes of God, by which the attributes of God are expressed in a certain and determinate way.[16]

What is at issue here is how particular things can suddenly *pass* from being a random multitude of modes to suddenly constituting a new particular thing that immediately endeavours to persevere in its existence. First and foremost this requires us to bracket out until the end of Chapter 5 the nature of the divine affection in question and regard only what this affection has revealed about the attributes when it particularises a thing. We must hold in our minds the *logical* interrelated and inter-determining structure of the essences and their degrees of power, on the one hand (including the role of God or Nature in acting to constitute these essences), and, on the other, actively ignore for the time being the *ethical* role of the divine modes in particularisation. As ever with Spinoza we will find it best obtain a 'whole' picture by limiting ourselves to the logico-physical aspects, and only then will we be able to pass to the next whole, the physico-ethical picture.

We focus then on things and related essences. It is at this point that the 'grid' interpretation of the attributes, which we saw in Chapter 2, is at its most dangerous; the formal essences are regarded as eternal qualitative intensities just waiting to be actualised by some reconfiguration of modes in existence. Deleuze, in *Expressionism in Philosophy*, warns against this:

> A modal essence expresses itself eternally in a relation, but we should not confuse the essence and the relation in which it expresses itself.
>
> (1990: 209)

But there remains a desire to retain something qualitative with Deleuze, which is not, we say, in Spinoza (ibid.: 208). This debate is more fully analysed in the work of Duffy (2008) so we move to apply our own interpretation, which stresses the finite 'horizontal' character of determination to exist. This turns on the following claims:

(a) that Spinoza is clear each existing thing is perfect in its being;
(b) that the formal being of a thing is the act of some other thing *U* (or things) as it endeavours to reorder the modes of God or Nature;
(c) that the actual essence of a thing *A* is the success of *U* in so reordering the modes of God or Nature, which success is determined by every other existing thing;
(d) that it is the finite actual essence that is expressed by *A* via the existential conatus, not the infinite formal essence; and
(e) that it is only once determined to exist that *A* can begin to express a formal essence in God or Nature.

The problem with the Hegelian and Deleuzian interpretations, from our perspective, is that they set too high a bar on the power of creation. They appear to equate the formal essences with seminal principals. On this view it seems that particular things only come to be if the creative agent *U* is absolutely successful in its endeavour. But only God or Nature is thus competent, and indeed, having such natural right we find that God or Nature's immediate creation, the infinite immediate mode, is perfect in its kind and, better, 'extensive'; it has come to earth as *the Son, Product and Effect.* If this is the manner in which Spinoza treats the Messiah, we should not hold out hope for the rest of us. Now, it may be argued that even if *U* is necessarily less successful than God or Nature in exercising a power of working, the formal essence of this attempt is nevertheless expressed by *A*. Apart from directly contradicting the text (EIIIP7), such a claim puts another incredible onus on *U*. *U* is either expected to have a true idea of what it is creating, which confers power on *A* (a requirement that Spinoza would point out excludes all 'beasts' and the majority of humanity), or *U* just had any idea of what it wanted to do, and *A* is supposed to express to this idea, however mutilated and confused it may be. Absurdly, if Borelli sets out to draw a square circle, the figure he actually draws expresses square circularity with its utmost endeavour. It might be objected that Hegel and Deleuze fully comprehend the immanence of the attributes in the world, but Spinoza is making a subtle yet critical distinction between the work performed through the attributes on modes and the indirect redistribution of the attributes by the modes. The attributes are not a *table* on which the world occurs – this still implies transcendence because the table is other than that which it supports – nor is the table a fluid upon which the world is tossed like a ship. On the contrary, the consequent motions of things are that which can only lead to the morphology of the table itself if the principle of immanence is to be satisfied. The power of the attributes must be sited inside the system; the causal power of God or Nature must not be really distinguishable from the power of finite things save in terms of quantum. This perhaps provides one reason why Spinoza refuses an Aristotelean but also Stoic path of distinguishing classes of causes and instead speaks only of immanent causation, reluctantly admitting one could only erroneously speak about God as a '*remote*' cause of particular things in the general equilibrium in comparison to His being a '*proximate*' cause of that which follows absolutely from the divine nature (EIP28 Sch.).

It follows that the attributes must be 'dropped down' into finite machines and Spinoza's distinction between the formal being of ideas and formal essences must be observed. As we have stated, we take the view that formal ideas are indeed the will of *U* to reorder the modes in such and such a way, but this will need not be accompanied by an intuitive cognition (of a formal essence) that *U* is exercising God or Nature's derivative power of creation. What *U* actually achieves is nothing other than the causal nexus as *U*'s attempts meet the actions of every other thing. This causal nexus is the actual essence of a thing: that which brought about that it be at all. What then determines that a determinate collection of modes transits from being this thing (or group of thing) to the new, created thing *A*? The answer is why Spinoza proves EIP25 Corol. by reference to EIP15 and EI Def. 5. No new being is created; rather we have the one being endeavouring to be and affections of that power of being through the attributes. Once again the infinite power of God or Nature is used to drive being. We realise that *any arbitrary group of modes endeavours to be as a particular thing*; the question is not whether they should be allowed to be, but whether, to be vulgar, they are able to 'get away with being'. Thus a pile of sand endeavours to be as much as a rock and indeed this pile has the perfect right to be, it is just that the pile of sand has such a tiny finite power of existence that almost anything could affect it and most likely decompose it. Likewise a multitude of people has as much being as the Leviathan, and has a perfect right to be, it is just that a multitude of people is extremely easy to decompose. This is the lesson of the *Tractatus politicus*. Clearly, the power of existing and power driving a certain proportion of motion and rest are not enough – we have also to consider a power existing that determines a thing's ability to endure. We thus consider there to be three elements individuating a thing in unison: the power of existing, which is absolute and variable only in reason, the characteristic proportion motion: rest, and the power conferred by being in the presence of other things. Three layers of individuation: simple, relatively directional, transitional.

Accordingly, we cannot accept Deleuze's interpretation, with its need to grant a seminal quality to single essences, in particular. Multiple formal ideas strive to fulfil acts of creation, but the more proximate to God in the modal structure one moves the less individuated one must become. Deleuze looks to characteristic relations and the forms discussed in the physical *Lemmata* in support of his thesis, but as we have argued the form of a particular thing constitutes a superficial normalcy for its constituent parts, but the conditions in which this surface has the desired conative effect are due not just to the attributes as such, but to the finite powers acting in any relative locality. Deleuze might also argue that the eternal attributes, being constitutive of the essences, are the proper intensive loci for the formal essences that wait their turn in duration, but this may only be admitted at the greatest degree of abstraction. To improvise on an analogy we made in Chapter 2, there is nothing vegetational in a rock crevice as such, yet algaes and lichens find a home there just the same. The power of the crevice is expressed by the lichen, but is not the cause of life. One wonders, therefore, whether Spinoza continues to believe life nevertheless follows from the Extended world, or whether, following the Stoics, he in fact ranks what he calls attributes such that the highest attribute – Thought – is alone the cause of the unity (*hexis*) of living minds (*psuche*).[17] It is arguable that Leibniz intuited this very problem when he developed the idea of living force (*vis viva*) over above the implicit Cartesian forces.

Returning to the formal essences, we observe with Spinoza in EIIP7 Sch. (which EIIP8 seeks to repeat as proof) that all individual ideas, like bodies, derive from their proximate causes. Spinoza's point, in our view, is that each cause is endeavouring like God or Nature to bring about the full actualisation of itself, but that its finite degree of power will result in other causes at least restraining if not overpowering these causes. Yet Spinoza does not see here a clash of causes in the same way as a clash of bodies, but a superimposition of finite powers that produce an actual effect or, in certain cases, no effect at all. Yet God knows all these endeavours to act and their appetitive determinations, so he need not know the formal being of ideas abstractly; rather he simply needs to know that finite things have been thwarted in their appetites. In the white spaces, however, God is infinitely implicating formal essences. This is a point that, when allied with Spinoza's physical theory, means the diagram in EIIP8 Sch. needs to be viewed as one of great importance in the history of natural philosophy. We are presented by actual modes, chords D and E, in a circle that is otherwise empty. The circle constitutes a proximate cause of these chords and an infinite number of rectangles that could be described therein. Spinoza ingeniously in our opinion is not saying that the non-existent rectangles are formal essences because they do not exist, but because the circle *qua* cause is trying with all its power to create those triangles, yet it is being restrained in its act by the other powers working upon that circle. To put it differently and somewhat absurdly, if our circle were somehow abstracted from the universe and allowed to be a second substance, it would itself create every single rectangle in that circle by virtue of relative lack of restraint. One might argue that this forced geometrical example relies on a physical inconsistency about what circles can do, even if unrestrained, but actually Spinoza is illustrating our point made with respect to Deleuze: that as one moves up the metaphysical order individuation becomes increasingly difficult in favour of simple concepts and natural laws. Therefore note also the danger Deleuze has run – by prioritising anterior formal essences before existing things he has inadvertently judged them as less than perfect. Spinoza is consistent in his view that only the actually existent is perfect, though its power of acting and thus realising posterior formal essences, which power follows from its existence in the world, may vary. Now approaching from a different angle, one might argue that the white spaces are open to all kinds of interpretation, and we could draw flowers or write the *Ethics* there and all these express the formal essences in God's mind. This would not be incorrect – everything is permitted – but it misses Spinoza's critical focus on the multiplicity of rectangles constituted in this very circle. Our conjecture is that the describing of this circle here turns the blank space into a space upon which something may be *constructed* that uses the pre-existing circle. The circle has as it were arranged the formal essences by its presence such that the next step in our geometric construction, the drawing the chords, has become possible. Consider this: we would be doing very well to draw the chords first and have the endpoints falling on the subsequently described circle. It is almost as if the Euclidean method is being treated as the kneading together of bodies of increasing complexity and ideational power, such that the formal essences are being called forth with increasing accuracy and concentration of their power. There is no need for these formal essences to be seminal or ideal forms of a dodecahedron; they just need to be *inflected points* expressed more and more perfectly by constructed machines; expressing the wider affections of the attributes, and thus apparently *reflecting* the points around them. Failed finite attempts to build this or that dodecahedron; God thinks these formal ideas *qua* modes, but this is a wholly separate matter from the formal essences in attributes (EIIP8). We thus need to be very clear about the distinction between infinite and finite causes of things, and the finite causes of things coming to exist.

4.2.3 Existential consciousness

4.2.3.1 Existing interpretations of the unity of consciousness

We first assume that unity of consciousness is solely a matter for existential consciousness, or natural right insofar as we consider that which constitutes an individual thing. By this we simply wish to signify that we do not regard essential consciousness as a priori unified, but rather as formally open-ended, the unity one experiences being derived not from the self but from the determination of essential effect by the natural right of other things. Before we explicate our thinking concerning unity of existential consciousness, it is worth noting some of the attempts to explain this theory by reference solely to effects, and not to causes.[18]

Jarrett has recently addressed this issue in his *Spinoza on Teleology, Value, and the Unity of the Mind* in Miller (2009: 131ff.). As we shall see in due course the title itself suggests a methodological flaw in this approach for it avers that Spinoza asserts unity of mind rather than unity of consciousness. This is not mere picking at words, but is precisely to point at the problem, for Jarrett diligently draws on Della Rocca, Carriero and others to carry out a survey of the *idea* of the mind. Yet we say that the idea of the mind is an effect of consciousness, not its cause. In the same collection (Miller 2009: 151–169) Koistinen comes closer to the truth in positing Spinozan 'subjects' as bundles of modes that express in some part an eternal power – that is God as thinking force. The use of physical notions is to be applauded but the interpretation, we respectfully suggest, does not follow Spinoza's order of reasons but is rather too twenty-first century in its talk of bundles. He needs to think in terms of compositions of modes. This, we believe, causes Koistinen to err in drawing a direct link between God and the thought of a 'subject' as if a finite thing's thought in duration is that which 'bundles' ideas is equivalent to the eternity of God's thought. That we think is due to God's eternal thinking, but what we think is the effect of our finitude. In other words, we need to make the important distinction developed by Balibar (1992) between appetite of an existing thing and desire, which is consciousness of that appetite. In similar vein, but with Scotist overtones, Deleuze (1990a: 181) attempts to locate univocal consciousnesses in the eternal Thought of God, which forms are expressed as our power of thinking as such. Over and above the concerns we have already expressed both in terms of the categorical nature of the attributes and the primary importance of determinate causes, again we have a problem of immediacy of cause of finite modes, which Spinoza expressly rejects. We repeat that if each consciousness is to be named as this unity, it must be determined by its coming to existence, which coming to existence expresses God's power of thinking 'locally'. *Contra* Deleuze, there can *be* no names in substance but *Deus sive Natura*. If we are properly to establish what unifies consciousness, we must also be prepared for that which cannot be unified by virtue of the order of Nature.

These critiques suggest that explaining the unity of a mind by a certain degree of force seems somewhat *a posteriori*. From the physical point of view, there seems to be implied a certain jump from the *potentia* at work in individual parts, which may vary, and the consistency of the concept 'a mind' as an effect of communications of these parts. Force or speed once again, as with power in the political sphere, seems to explain matters once they have occurred, but not their aetiology. Yet it is as an effect that we may better comprehend Spinoza's meaning, for what is it that determines and distinguishes cause (the communication of a certain proportion of motion and rest across a subregion of space) from effect (the idea that passes across these 'consistent' communications)? Indeed, what is it that determines any effect to be an idea as such, or marks it out as an affect worth having an idea about? Here we must turn to the physicalist notion of what more generally might be termed synthesis in Spinoza's thinking. Spinoza does not use this word as such, but it is a useful way of describing actualisation of effects. Note that synthesis is not something one thing does to two other things; rather, it is the imparting of a quantum of motion from one thing to another thing. Thus a stone is the necessary cause of its motion and the person who throws this stone is the determinate cause of the stone's motion. The effect (stone in motion) is the synthesis of these two causes. The effect involves these two causes, to use Spinoza's terminology, and expresses them in a certain and determinate way. The interesting move Spinoza makes is to explain ideas of bodies in parallel, such that this stone and the idea of this stone are both syntheses of the same causality that brought this stone to be here. But surely then Spinoza makes a grave anti-realist error in inferring ideas of ideas and ideas of ideas of ideas, which are likewise products of the chain of cause and effect. The criticism claims that Spinoza infers more syntheses on the mental side than actually occur on the corporeal side, for surely nowhere can be found the effects of the effects that are co-present with an actual body in the same way that ideas (affects) of ideas (affects) are co-present with ideas of that body. There appears to be more mind in the world than body. This suggests that the proportion of motion and rest a body has is not sufficient at all to explain the unity of consciousness.

4.2.3.2 Unity of existential consciousness – the example of the stone

The clue to a possible solution may possibly be derived from Spinoza's Letter 58 to Schuller, which discusses such a stone in motion and its mind. Spinoza writes: 'Now this stone, since it is conscious of its conatus and is not at all indifferent, will surely think it is free.' This attribution of 'consciousness' (a treacherous term in seventeenth-century philosophy) immediately follows a claim that the stone also is conscious – that its motion is taking place (i.e. the stone is conscious that it is moving and is free). The additional 'consciousness' of endeavour thus seems to be adding something, namely that not only does the stone know that it is moving at time t_1, but that the stone knows that it wants to continue moving through time $t_2 \ldots t_n$. Here we distinguish the effect/synthesis of stone at t_1 (stone and impulsion has done enough to do this amount of work), which constitutes the idea of the body $I(x)$ at that point, and the force, or power of acting, which remains involved in the stone at t_1 as the as-yet-unfolded motion of the stone through $t_2 \ldots t_n$. 'Conatus' or 'endeavour' super-adds a certain tension in the stone wherein is bound the formal future of the stone, that is, its passage through $t_2 \ldots t_n$ unless determined by external causes to do otherwise. This tautness or force is an effect in the stone at t_1 that, however, is not manifest as the bodily locus and completed movement that constitutes for the stone the being at t_1. It seems to be the case that Spinoza wishes to mark this non-manifested force as an effect that is conceptually separate from the effect of being at t_1, but that must be considered as entirely implicated in the effect of being at t_1 as the limit point about which manifest effect and non-manifest effect turn. By marking the separability of two bodily effects in each action, Spinoza feels able to thereby declare, within Thought, that that which is manifest effect is the idea of the body and, at its boundary, we find that which is beyond and apparently unites this idea. The nature of the conatus suggests that we ought to understand this additional element as the conative endeavour or power, which is expressed at each moment. Certainly this interpretation is suggested when Spinoza says we are conscious of endeavour, properly interpreted as an equality: consciousness *is* that endeavour (EIIIP9). Yet we still do not have a reason why conatus and consciousness are linked.

Perhaps a reason can be found in nominal distinction Spinoza employs. Whereas *individuation* seems reserved for the so-called 'Short Physics' with its relativistic arguments, *singular* or *particular thing* is a term used at various points, including in the discussion of intuitive knowledge in Part V *Ethics*. For example, the demonstration to EIIP24 is actually quite revealing when set out in the Latin, for it continues to rely on Spinoza's terminological distinction between ideas/bodies, on the one hand, and singular things, on the other:

> The parts that make up the human Body belong to the essence of the human Body only insofar as they communicate their motions to each other in some fixed ratio, and not insofar as they can be considered individuals without relation to the human Body. For the parts of the human Body are highly composite individuals, whose parts can be separated from the human Body whilst its nature and form are preserved, and can communicate their motions to other bodies in another ratio . . .[19]

At this point in the demonstration, Spinoza clearly changes register (or level):

> So the idea i.e. the knowledge of each part will be in God, and indeed will be in God insofar as he is considered as affected by another idea of a singular thing, which singular thing is prior in the order of Nature to the part itself.[20]

Let us propose the following interpretation: individuals are constituted of parts, individuals being simply a certain proportion of motion and rest communicated across the parts. Thus the parts of the human body are also individuals, and the hierarchy of composition to the whole of the universe is maintained. As such, parts and individuals are synonymous, which should not surprise anyone because Spinoza is clear that even the *corpora simplicissima* are individuated by movement and rest. But, in addition, Spinoza posits singular things (*rei singularis*) that are 'prior' to the parts 'in the order of nature'. One might object that Spinoza, given the final reference to EIIP7, is using the word *res* in the sense used there (i.e. in 'parallel' to the ideas across the attributes of Thought and Extension), but it should be noted that even so both individual and part are physical notions and that if anything Spinoza is using *res* to indicate precisely thing-hood (however imprecise the signified of that term may be) in Extension and/or in Thought – hence, its introduction with reference to God's cognition in EIIP24, and its use opposed to *ideas* in EIIP7. Thing-hood appears to cut across the attributes (and indeed the types of cognition).

Now we are not proposing that the singular things alone and without explication will somehow solve the apparent conundrum for Spinoza's philosophy of the regulative principle of composite bodies, because they will not. We do conjecture, however, that these singular things are specific concepts on which Spinoza seeks to rely to explain his world. In order to clarify the work this concept of singular thing is doing, we suggest that Spinoza's views benefit from a comparative review of Stoic conceptions of unity (*hexis*) and constancy (*diathesis*).

The impetus for making such a hypothesis comes, once more, from Spinoza's Stoic hinterland, mediated through authors such as Lipsius, Seneca and Epictetus, though, as previously cautioned, we have the benefit of expanded research on Stoic doctrines whereas Spinoza had the benefit of proceeding alone. The Stoic doctrine of unity[21] is, unsurprisingly, tripartite, both in terms of there being three levels of unification, and in there being a typology of unification for three types of things: inanimate objects, animate objects, and mind. The first level of structure – *diestota* – may be termed as 'discrete', though in fact it is divided into two aspects: (a) a complete disorder of elements that does not permit numeration; and (b) an order of elements that permits counting (*arithmo leptos*). Contiguous structures are constructed from conjoined discrete elements, such as chain links. In the case of each of discrete and contiguous units, their most notable feature is that the parts will continue to exist even if their relation in the whole is destroyed. As Sambursky notes,[22] while larger contiguous bodies may indeed combine and even generate sufficient 'force' to withstand great shocks, once overcome the elements of such a body are dispersed without any care for the destruction of their mutuality. This, the Stoics wonderfully term it, is due to a lack of 'communication' (*diadosis*) between the parts. Thus, if Hercules throws a javelin, it is not just the part he holds that is launched, but the tension in his body is communicated through this part to the whole javelin, which at that moment itself becomes globally 'tense' with force. We find the most fascinating form of communication at the third level of unity, which is that of *sumpatheia*, manifesting itself in inorganic matter, animate matter, and the mind, as respectively *hexis*, *phusis*, and *psyche*.

The Stoic view, then, seems to offer Spinoza an excellent way of solving the problem of unity by immanent means.

We hypothesised in Chapter 2 that the doctrine of the attributes could be developed from the Stoic theory of action to provide a 'surface' across notionally discrete points. Our understanding of Spinoza's example of the stone likewise answers the requirement that something more constitutes the limit of modes of extension or thought in order to offer a prior synthetic unity within which these ideas can be said to occur. It is this *surface of power* that then operates, as it is affected by exterior forces, as the united ground and primary cause of consciousness. The Scholastic transcendental of 'unity' is thus replaced by an immanent unity grounded in what Spinoza regarded as a real physical process. Likewise, a second transcendental, that of temporal flux, is now located as duration of the real. Duration is not an object for us because it is an operation by power on the modes – an activity that, as Spinoza writes, distributes events into past and future and the central axis of present act. Once again Spinoza indicates a profound understanding of Stoic theory, here insinuating the incorporeal of time into the activity of each attribute. Yet an additional twist is granted by the tying of this theory of duration to the physical doctrines we have discussed in Chapter 3. The indefinite nature of act, in the form of conatus that endeavours to persist in its being, suggests not only that immanent duration 'grounds' the order of the modes, but that it offers an additional dimension to the activities of motion and rest. In other words, the conatus has a direction operating over and above the spatial motions of a stone, a direction that forces itself into the world of the modes.

We turn to Seneca's bridge example of transition, for it is in our view far more illustrative of Spinoza's thinking. We quote the relevant passage:

> There are others, however, which, after many increments, are altered by the last addition; there is stamped upon them a new character, different from that of yore. One stone makes an archway – the stone which wedges the leaning sides and holds the arch together by its position in the middle. And why does the last addition, although very slight, make a great deal of difference? Because it does not increase; it fills up.
>
> (*Letters to Lucilius* CXVIII[16])

It is fascinating that the early Stoics had the genius to suggest that in the cases of architectural construction, among others, when the construction is completed something additional, a *metabasis*, 'sets' the construction fast. All the more fascinating that it was the Romans who invented the arch and that Seneca, presumably via a later Stoic teacher, is able to see that the arch of a bridge is a quite beautiful illustration of this transition. What we have is a concatenation of causal series in which blocks are placed into a certain relation, which determines both a quantum of body and of relative rest. With insertion of the keystone, something converts the collection of blocks on either pillar of the arch from determined to fall down to determined to support greater bodies. Somehow, Seneca thinks, the blocks 'fill up' (*implet*). The common translation as 'fills up' is not entirely wrong, but it disguises the etymological link to *implexus*, that is the state of being entwined or involved. Symbolic games are not of interest to us, however; rather the nature of what has occurred here, and which in the Stoic philosophy is an exercise of the divine *pneuma* through the bridge's constituent parts. How is Spinoza to have interpreted this physical event? We have already seen Spinoza's interest in weight and gravitation, his reading of the work of Borelli on such subjects, and his own hydrostatic experiments involving the concept. It thus seems quite apparent to us that he has at the very least a strong inkling that such a transition is explicable only by the conjoint exercise of finite powers and some great power, of which gravitation is but the primary example.

To understand this example, it is critical to realise that all power for Spinoza is exercised absolutely formally, but only determinately actually. As part of this, every effort of work requires determinate actual conditions open to its exercise in a given way; in other words, the formal essence at work over a given portion of enduring extension can only be actualised for finite things by the like exercise of power by the things then in that region. Thus the simple bodies subject to this power will constantly tend downwards, and indeed the constituent blocks will operate in like fashion. Yet placed in the 'arch' relation, this already operating formal power is actualised in a specific way as new 'individual thing'. Nothing has changed in the formal exercise of the power of course; what has changed is the relation between the blocks whereby they communicate their individual motions through each other in mutual determination towards a global proportion of motion and rest. Sitting atop these finite powers is the transitional but still determinate power that initiates downward motion.

It could be argued that given the action of this constitutive power at every moment, and its necessary constancy, nothing has changed and there is no formal essence in the earth (or celestial fluid if we follow Spinoza) that suggests to itself 'bridge'. Remember we are talking of a finite thing, and that the determination to existence of any other finite thing is a concatenation of the formal essences exerted by the sum of powers acting upon it. But equally important is to observe that if Seneca constructed his bridge in mid-air, the desired relation would not persist – it is necessary that the power of gravitation is supplemented by the conative resistance of the earth as the bridge endeavours downwards at every instant.

One can hopefully see why regarding natural right as exclusive of dynamic variation is nonsense. If this downward force and complementary resistance were not taken into account, an individual thing would just be a collection of simpler bodies that just happen to be sitting together at a given moment. If this were Seneca's bridge, the first gust of wind would blow it over.

This is the interpretation of unity of consciousness or natural right in Spinoza: that there is a requirement not just a certain proportion *m:r*, but the additional requirements of: (a) finite things in forcing bodies into a certain relation; and (b) an infinite power amounting to a sub-tension for that relation. To suggest that consciousness unifies itself completely runs against the Axioms of Spinozism by suggesting that there is something the cause of which is without reason. The unity of our existential consciousness, rather, is fundamentally reliant and grounded causally upon the activity of other powers as they grasp or bind together our constituent elements as something which together not only exerts resistance against destruction (conatus) but which, as so constituted, *works*. This places Spinoza completely at odds with Malebranche, who, as Simmons writes,[23] regards consciousness as immediate awareness of one's mental states. Malebranche perhaps is the first in a long line of thinkers in the wake of the *Ethics* who can only continue pre-Spinozan philosophies in perceiving effects, and think that to define consciousness as the ideas that we know is in any way satisfactory. Is this not the reason that Malebranche is left with an infinite desire to be happy, one that can never be satiated, and one that lacks sufficient reason? An infinite desire to be happy, and yet, though such desire be in concord with God's plan for us, be also the ground of our own confusion.[24]

Now, the communicative action from the keystone to the base of the pillars is resolved as a single act, a unity in its resistance, which is absolutely simple, that is, which must limit the unity of our consciousness to simple endeavour to persevere in our being, and the transitions in this endeavour as duration. As a bare minimum, this indefinite existing grounds natural right *qua* this persistence in time, not because existence is temporally extended *in se*, but because for itself it remains present. As between Peter and Paul it is relatively extended as time, and so can be quantified as the first element of natural right – the power to exist as far as one prevails.

It is in this transition from part to united whole that also provides the key to the nature of Spinoza's 'real' geometry, a geometry that also feeds through into the work of Leibniz. By 'real' geometry we mean that the ensemble of points that are put into motion to constitute lines, planes, and so forth are each united wholes in the above sense. For Spinoza there is no abstract Cartesian plane upon which we can inscribe an infinite variety of forms; the plane itself must be constituted as an actually existing surface upon which new modes may be described. The surface of Chrysippos' cone, like the surface of the bridge, enters into being as a new *situs* of further activity and therefore the immanent condition of corporeal causality. Through duration the surface of the whole face of the universe changes as 'points' are constituted or seemingly destroyed; a dynamic geometry. We say 'seemingly destroyed' because by virtue of the very event of a surface intervening in the great series of causation, those transitions that occur are affirmed in eternity down the chain. It follows that while the characteristic corporeal relations that signal our real geometric 'point' may be destroyed, the attribute's intervention as transition remains present *sub specie aeternitatis* and it may rightly be said that the world that follows is inscribed upon a geometry inflected by this 'point'. It would be very fertile (but far beyond the confines of this work) to compare this doctrine, in which Nature as the one substance constitutes the sole existing point from which all real geometry, considered as the elaboration and destruction of countless real points, issues, with that of Leibniz who argues[25] that composite substances as magnitudes are constituted from many simple substances that 'must be everywhere'.

Bracketing Leibniz's objection, Spinoza, we maintain, sees consciousness as such a 'real point'; it is the *situs* upon which corporeal ideas and passions swarm, like a Spinozan multitude crossing a city's bridge. Just as our corporeal relation finds a habitable zone in formal essence enacted for us in the world, so our affects find a habitable zone in and through us. How foolish we must be to name this multitude of bodies such as hate or fury 'mine'. They are like worms in the blood of consciousness, nourished by the flow of ideas, hungering after their own desires, whispering counsel like Iago. Was not Seneca's Hercules driven before *Fury*?

> Fiery Erinys[26] cracks her brandished scourge, and closer, closer yet, holds out before my face brands burnt on funeral pyres.
>
> (*Hercules furens*, §976)

How Lockean to declare ownership of these fruits of the field of consciousness because we poured our labour into them – what bitter harvest! It is in this sense alone that constituent power of existential consciousness stands in relation to the multitude: it is the real geometric condition of the multitude's swarming at all, and has nothing to say about who, what, or wherefore. To turn Kant, synthetic unity is the condition of possibility of all and of only *Schwärmerei*. Everything that fills our consciousness is a fruit of work, that is, of essential consciousness as the expression of the power of existing that generates existential consciousness. The elaboration of this conception will be a matter of the next chapter, but let us first construct a bridge between Spinoza's conception of consciousness as grounding natural right, and that other leading thinker of what he terms '*das Naturrecht oder das philosophische Recht*', namely Hegel.

4.2.3.3 Unity of existential consciousness – relation to the Hegelian philosophy

By drawing in Hegel here, our intent is to demonstrate not so much certain similarities, but a very specific difference in how both thinkers come to the idea of a conscious unity that grounds natural right. Our interest is the character of this unity, whether it has (a) texture, or is (b) simple or devoid of distinguishing aspects. Such a question is one of *transcendental empiricism*. In a sense, both respond in terms of (b) (though Hegel might be said to adopt a superabundant 'frothy' indistinction),[27] but we will argue that Spinoza's concept at least remains open to the possibility of (a).

In what in some respects may be considered a sister work of this book, P. Ziche has sought to establish the mechanical inspirations of the thought of Hegel and Schelling ('Mathemathische und naturwissenschaftliche Modelle in der Philosophie Schellings und Hegels' (1996)), though Ziche is clear to warn us that for the latter thinkers, these mechanical sources are used '*als Metaphor*',[28] whereas we advance the stronger claim that in line with Cartesian trends, Spinoza believes dynamised mechanical explanations are sufficient for all phenomena. In a way that is almost impossible with Spinoza, Ziche has been able to follow Hegel and Schelling's university experiences and isolate the courses on natural philosophy that can be shown to have influenced Hegel's critique of what he believed to be Newton's views. For Hegel, significant interest in the operation of the lever and its philosophical import appears already in the *Jenaer Schriften* and is a relatively constant theme through to the *Wissenschaft der Logik*, where Hegel returns to the lever and the *moment* of force that impels it to lift in order to explain the passage from *Sein* and *Nichts* to *Werden*:[29]

> Something is sublated [*aufgehoben*] only insofar as it has entered into unity with its opposite; in this more particular signification as something reflected, it may fittingly be called a moment. In the case of the lever [*Hebel*], weight and distance from a point are called its mechanical moments on account of the sameness of their effect, in spite of the contrast otherwise between something real, such as a weight, and something ideal, such as a mere spatial determination, a line.[30]

With this linkage the problematic translation of the Hegelian concept of *Aufhebung* becomes almost dangerously trite: Hebel = lever, heben = to heave, aufheben = to lever up, *Aufhebung des Werdens* = *the leverage of Becoming*. It should be noted that Hegel clearly takes on board this language, but only to add that 'levering up' does not do *Aufhebung* sufficient justice (1969: 113–114). Approaching from Spinoza's perspective, we are, however, very much alive to what Hegel is driving at here, and it is not some Archimedean claim to be able to lift the world with fixed point and lever (though the philosophical joke seems to be there). Rather, Hegel is interested here in the communication and connection that is instituted between different masses as soon as they are placed on the unity of the lever and put into motion (the moment). He is not so much interested in the corporeal action of the lever, as the condition of its leverage, its incorporeal unity via which the different masses are united as differences. For our part we would thus roughly interpret *Sein* as the body of the lever that is 'shot through' with an indistinguishable unity that makes it all *Sein*, this indistinction immediately revealing itself as *Nichts*. Hegel's next move, and that which now distinguishes his *Aufhebung* from the mechanical concept is to argue (ibid.) that this indistinguishability of the *Nichts* from itself but also from *Sein*, and vice versa, institutes an unquiet passage from one to the other as incessant activity, this disappearance of each into the other in which the logical unity of the $A = A$ and $A = B$ occurs, is becoming, and grants each a new significance; a promotion and a relief of duty.[31] Our reading is that the event of *Sein*, the *Nichts*, lacks a distinction in the body of *Sein* upon which it can work, and therefore its unspent power is left incessantly to search for activity. The *Nichts* is not itself a lack; it is the tragedy of lacking activity, because of the *Gleichberechtigtheit des Seins* – the right-equality of Being – that propels Becoming. It is this movement that Hegel raises up into the will, which is '*the definite place and origin*' of right, but which is likewise characterised by its indeterminateness in universal equality and its constant need to pass over into practical application and give voice to Reason in which content produces form from self.[32]

Our interest here is not, however, this unrest of 'indifferentiation', which it seems the Stoic doctrine of requiring a body about which some event may be predicated precludes,[33] but the nature of the Nothing that unites Being and thereby indifferently brings together qualitative differences in some third constituted out of itself. *Nichts, das reine Nichts*, though of extreme interest insofar as its event is tragically unrealised, is pure and simple equality itself. Think again about the lever or the bridge: in one sense the unity itself of both machines is for itself simply the case of the unity and indifference of the corporeal parts. For Spinoza likewise, advancing Descartes' move to empty out substance, grounds the source of unity alone in immanent power. Yet, in the case of actually existing things, as we have seen, Spinoza's doctrines of efficient cause and determination to exist in act by some other finite thing require that every united thing – and thus consciousness as the event of that unity – have determinate finite causes. First, at this level, God or Nature does not have any choice about which thing exists; He is as indifferent as the Epicurean gods. But if the constitution of each finite thing is the effect of the power of other finite things, it is *proximately* the effect of finite power and must obey the law of natural right: each thing has as much natural right as its power extends. Insofar, therefore, as a given finite consciousness is caused to exist in act, it exists thus far, as far as its constituent power *extends*. There is a definite geometric aspect to Spinoza's concept (and that of the Stoa), which is intentionally lacking for Hegel. If we imagine bridge or lever, the geometric interpretation sees the unifying power as a magnitude, that is, a surface spread through the bridge or lever and completely *intermixed* with each. When we are considering the constitution of an existing consciousness, we are also already considering its extension, and hence already the question of natural right.

Second, with respect to infinite formal essence there is also an absolute power of differentiation and qualitative character. We have already seen the basis of this geometric interpretation of the attributes with Descartes in Chapter 2, where he saw the host as having a specific surface, and clouds as having a kind of 'crust'. It is this geometric surface, dynamised by *potentia*, which opens the possibility for asking the question, *pace* Hegel, of whether the condition of unity of consciousness may be subjected to a kind of empiricism (in our view a full *scientia intuitiva*). Perhaps this is the first questioning for a theory of natural right: a thoroughgoing analysis of the texture of consciousnesses to determine the *variable* conditions of any possible bodies of law. Of course, one might question whether Spinoza's geometry was a method appropriate to the task, and given Spinoza's inability to pursue an *analysis* of natural right we might agree, for it was the success of 'the science of discovery, in other words the science of Analysis'[34] that perhaps inspired Leibniz to begin sketching an *analysis situs* as a new 'geometry' capable of discovering the essential in forms.[35] We have nowhere near the space to pursue this here, but one could begin by turning the Achimedean joke back on Hegel by stating that a lever is useless without a fixed point, and then establishing the *a priori* necessity of a fixed point in a dynamic consciousness. Not the fixed point of its cause, which is uninteresting for this purpose, but rather by positing a magnitude of consciousness, which is deemed a collection of indistinct and indistinguishable points (or substances) but proving that nevertheless, without reference to any 'third' point, that at least one of these points *must* be distinguishable as fixed by virtue of its *not* being in act.

This is certainly one point of departure from Spinozism, one that Deleuze pursued by other means, but as noted we cannot trace this line here. Our object has rather been to illustrate what is at stake in Spinoza's Cartesian-inspired conception of natural right, how the notion of extension cannot be overlooked when considering the full concept of existing consciousness, and how and to what degree this mechanical model reads through to Hegel's philosophy of right and indeed his whole 'science'.

Now the realisation of an undifferentiable consciousness – one in which every 'way' is open to our machine – also leads us to another difference with Hegel and an interesting debate with Wittgenstein.[36] Let us work back from Wittgenstein's idea of rules-as-machines or symbolic machines. In his *Philosophical Investigations* he writes:

> The machine as symbolizing its action: the action of a machine . . . If we know the machine, everything else, that is its movement, seems to be already completely determined. We talk as if these parts could only move in this way, as if they could not do anything else. How is this—do we forget the possibility of their bending, breaking off, melting, and so on?[37]

And then the philosopher engineer continues:

> But we do not say this kind of thing when we are concerned with predicting the actual behaviour of a machine. Then we do not in general forget the possibility of a distortion of the parts and so on.[38]

We do not propose to delve into the fundamental distinction in interpretation of what logic and so rule-making is that lies between Spinoza's (albeit antique) materialist style of philosophy and that of Wittgenstein and his colleagues. Apart from such a discussion meriting a book in itself, it really would only be clear if the Stoa and Hegel were brought in to support Spinoza's cause, for this latter's fascination with mechanism does perhaps bear to greatly on the implicit logic in his work, which differentiates the three epistemic orders. In this regard Wittgenstein's thought, insofar as it is more generally considered as an assault on the Enlightenment subtext of sublime machines or automata stuffed with their God-given codes, does cause Spinoza trouble. Some machines go wrong, and even more critically, every machine fails in some degree – there are simply no ideal mechanical forms and Spinoza in any event does not seem intent on positing them.

There is actually a brace of problems here: (a) are we sure Spinoza is not positing ideal machines; and (b) in the case of finite machines, how does he account for mechanical failure? These are both aspects of the question of mechanical *efficiency*. As to (a) we will actually discover in Chapter 5 that Spinoza will posit one machine that *is* perfectly efficient, but as we will see, this efficiency is achieved by right, not by transcendental ideality. We will delay discussion of this special case until then. As to (b) there are two aspects we would like to examine. *First*, also presaging what will be discussed in the following chapter, we must understand Spinoza's machines as bound up in the relation between the geometry of their formal essences and how that geometry affects and effects the finite modes that express them. The modes themselves will take on a determinate nature, but it will be due to the power of the mode whether and to what degree it will be recomposed by another mode, and in any event it will be subject to recomposition on encountering a formal essence. This is the resistance or conatus of a given existing thing. Spinoza understands that if machines did not resist – try to pursue their determinate series – then there could be no inefficiency. All machines try to be perfect but save in one case they all fail. This is not the same as positing ideal machines, which actual machines fail to 'remember', for the whole machine has to be 'there' (a) resisting insofar as its commonality is engaged, but (b) differentiating itself by virtue of that which is uncommon.

We stress in the context of Wittgenstein that the rules of these machines are not information in the sense of codes, but properly physico-mathematical, in the sense that $x_2 + y_2 = a_2$ is the 'rule' of a circle in the Cartesian plane. This is the sort of example Wittgenstein might give to discuss rule-making, but the point Spinoza evidently grasps is that the formula is not the source and origin of the rule; rather, it is the structure of the geometry – the normed space – which in this instance can be encapsulated in a rule. It is we claim the normed space *qua* attribute which is that which is 'mysteriously present', to use Wittgenstein's phrase; that which is immanent to the empirical determinations of each machine.[39] For Spinoza, Wittgenstein's rule is as much a machine as the machine about which it makes predictions.

So indeed there is a notion of 'inefficiencies' in Spinoza understood within the mechanics of composition of modes, but this inefficiency is embodied in the phrase '*omnis determinatio est negatio*' and so does not exactly satisfy the fullest meaning of 'inefficiency'. This is the *second* aspect of our discussion. To see this we bring Hegel back in. On our interpretation Hegel agrees with Spinoza that inefficiencies occur as 'things' encounter each other and so struggle to assert their being. The difference is that Spinoza cashes out the consequences of this struggle in terms of determinate compositions manifested (if we remain in Extension) in terms of motion and rest and variations of these. Considered this way the system of such machinic encounters – which is itself a machine and so this runs from top to bottom – is still actually perfectly efficient in this sense: everything that goes into the encounter is mechanically useful and everything that comes out is mechanically useful, even if one or more machines is decomposed in the process. Determination is negation, and that is all. Hegel, on the other hand, believes that even if it were conceivable that only mechanically useful work could be deployed in such an encounter, the ensuing struggle will also negate some of the determination/negation itself and convert what was useful into what is useless from the point of view of the encounter's constituents. And furthermore Hegel sees this analysis as applicable even to Being itself, where ontological inefficiency drives the dialectic to that point in which inefficiency is raised to a principle and we understand that the very structure of inefficiency is germinally none other than that of the dialectic. Hegel's conception still retains a kind of efficiency in the sense that what is termed inefficient still must be cut from the machine's input and is not created *ex nihilo*. Hegel's point, building we believe on Leibniz, is that inefficiency is only such because of the normative order (read attribute) from which it was through struggle born. However, inefficiency triumphs because it is the means by which that order is overthrown – inefficiency has utility for what is not recognised by an order. It is the internalisation of this realisation whereby a machine also recycles its inefficiencies to reorder itself that moves us from machine to system properly said and from study of nature to logic. *Per* Hegel:

> This *negative self-conscious* moment, the movement of knowledge . . . *is, however, certainly lacking to the content of Spinoza's philosophy*, or at least is only externally associated with it, since it falls within [external, mathematical] self-consciousness.[40]

To end this subsection we should, however, remark that the manner in which we have divided Hegel from Spinoza, while necessary to elucidate the material issue concerning mechanical inefficiency, is open to detailed refinement and debate of interpretation.[41] There is a key argument to be made that Spinoza actually incorporates something akin to the Hegelian idea of excessive inefficiency and implicates this into his notions of pleasure and pain, whereas we will understand them as primarily indicative of actual variations of bodies, in line with the Cartesian milieu. This approach would then feed into a logical analysis of the affects, which would explain Spinozan creativity. Our problem again would be that while EIII could be read this way, drawing as it seems to do on Stoic theories, the way in which the affects are constructed, even '*per accidens*' suggests that precise modal composition is at work and that complete changes of *order*, as opposed to modal representations of order, are excluded.

4.2.3.4 Unity of existential consciousness – continuity of this unity

It is to be noted that one would not be alone if one still failed to see in what unity consists in constituting consciousness. Marx, that excellent reader of Spinoza, does not seem to have grasped every facet of the theory of the unity of consciousness when he writes in *Capital*:

> the labour-time socially necessary for [the products'] production forcibly asserts itself like an over-riding law of nature. The law of gravity thus asserts itself when a house falls about our ears.
>
> (Bk. I, Ch. 1, s. 4)

It is also because the law of gravity asserts itself that the house does not fall down. It is simply that we do not perceive this overriding law until collapse. What determines the delay in the point of destruction is the ability of the house, like the system of exchange relations, not just to defy gravity, but use it to its advantage. The work performed in each case is not absolute, but must be work towards sustaining an appropriate relation that proceeds with the grain of power and entrenches it. Thus the labour-time socially necessary determines also what labour must be performed, or, the workers must produce what the market itself demands, though with the additional problematic that the market is variable. We digress, however.

One will worry that Spinoza's theory of consciousness is a *fascist* theory of consciousness in that the parts are constrained in order that a stronger free being be generated. This is to confuse a tool or instrument with a constituent of consciousness. In Chapter 6 we will discuss the importance of tools for Spinoza's *Ethics*, and so we note here only that a tool may be defined as that which can be used to express our determinate nature in an augmentative way (i.e. it adds not absolutely to consciousness but actualises what was only formally there). There is no reason to assume that Spinoza did not distinguish between the spider and the web, and regard the web as an extension of consciousness, rather than considering spider-web a new consciousness. The constituent elements of existential consciousness, however, are placed into a relation in which each best exerts its own power of working with respect to each other without any domination of one over the other. We speak with Seneca of a keystone, but each part is key in the constitution of the bridge, as Seneca himself makes clear. As we have already asserted, the Stoic *hegemon* is not any part of the bridge, but is the power of some third thing over against which the now-created bridge exerts its endeavour to persevere in its being. The bridge is thus equal for itself, but subjugated for another as the condition of its finite existence. This may suggest to us that there remains a Spinozan *hegemon*, to which all else must be passive. Apart from missing the point that this mechanical *hegemon* is entirely indifferent to finite things, as we shall see at the end of the next chapter, it is by passing through the idea of God that we come to understand the true nature of our existential consciousness in its absolute relation. Here Spinoza and the later Malebranche approach each other in their view of the generality of the divine will. Riley (in Hochstrasser and Schröder 2003: 62) has shown how Malebranche maintains a view that the most just way in which God can govern His creation is through the initiation of eternal laws that are applicable to all equally, though in particular instantiations the productions of the interactions of law-like *volontés* may be deemed, as Boursier claims, generative of 'monsters'. Ignoring the subtending of Spinoza's schema with power, one can likewise understand that the general event of creation of the infinite mediate mode in act determines an infinite range of possible outcomes, which amount to the exercise of the divine power for and against all equally. It is not the case, however, that Spinoza accepts in any way the Malebranchian view that this 'general will' of creation is good and just because it is what God determined it was just to do, but nor does Spinoza occupy the space Malebranche ascribes to Hobbes (and Locke) of determining the choice as being good because it is exercised by the powerful. Rather Spinoza's position is that God or Nature's free, necessary creation is neither good nor evil, for it simply is. The power to 'sanctify' or assent to one's acts only exists where the agent is finite, for in reason one can imagine that some greater power could delegitimise that act at any moment. God or Nature's power of working is utterly unrestrained and it is necessarily wrong to even consider the goodness of such an act.

Having elaborated the positive theory of existential consciousness, which consciousness is generated by a power, that is, a transition to existence, we now turn to consciousness of the transitions that the existing unity may undergo.

4.3 Existential consciousness and the affects

4.3.1 Distinguishing between the affects and conative modulations

It would be wrong to confuse the affects with the changes in a body or mind. That which is constituted as a body, its 'parts' in the sense of Letter 38, are something other than that which binds them as we have seen. Thus changes in the arrangement and composition of these parts are not-conscious[42] to essential consciousness and stand in relation to it as cause to effect. Here we note the important idea that causation does not stop at the edge of the body, but continues within it. Nor should it be assumed that the binding surface of existential consciousness somehow excludes all determination *ab initio*. That is to posit absolute self-determinative domination, which is impossible in particular things. Lest we forget, a thing comes to be unified and remain so only because the necessary conditions are created, and Spinoza feels that if one could instantly remove those conditions an existing thing would almost immediately cease to exist. The essence of existential consciousness was not hiding in some transcendent attribute until called upon by God – it was there formally *in situ* at the relevant time by reason of the arrangement of the machines and composition of their modes. There being determination (i.e. causation) within the body so unified by existential consciousness, Spinoza rightly considers that when any bodily part acts by some external cause, it stands asymmetrically as cause in respect of existential consciousness and produces some effect upon it. Note, we say *upon it*, for existential consciousness is not for itself a thinking thing insofar as we consider it cause of essential consciousness. There is no affect in existential consciousness, but rather only determination to existence in a certain direction (appetite) and, if not indifferent, some transition, each of which feeds through proportionately to the primary affects of essential consciousness. Consciousness occurs at the level of attribute. The 'of what' of consciousness, including affect, occurs at the modal level. The logical order 'of what' is given by the attributes; the revelation of this 'what' in the present is granted by the infinite immediate mode of God or Nature. It is for this reason that Spinoza specifies in the revealing EIIIP59 Sch. that satiation of hunger alters desire not because some ideational sign appears in essential consciousness registering this satiation, but because composite elements of the body determine existential consciousness to some new act (appetite), which essential consciousness affirms as a change in the *ideatum* of desire. We now move to consider the critical import in changes in appetite in relation to positive and negative transition.

4.3.2 The principles of positive and negative transition

Here we meet a pressing question: how can pleasure alone lead us to God? Surely pleasure leads us to what we desire, and what we desire changes like the winds over the ocean. The answer to this conundrum involves tying together many of the most exciting and difficult aspects of Spinoza's concept of natural right. We shall attempt an explanation.

First, we need to explicate the nature of pleasure and understand what it is to increase the power of working. By way of hermeneutic observation we note that Spinoza decides to use the verb '*transire*', which means 'to pass over, through or in front of'. Spinoza would no doubt have been aware that 'transit' suggestively refers to a passage of the celestial body across the sun, but it is with a more philosophical sense in which it is used by Seneca in his Letter CXVIII to Lucilius to describe an ethical passage in one's pursuits from the indifferent class to that of the Good:

> 11. I mean something like this: there are certain things which are neither good nor bad – as military or diplomatic service, or the pronouncing of legal decisions. When such pursuits have been honourably conducted, they begin to be good, and they change over from the 'indifferent' class into the Good.[43]

He then also uses the term in respect to alteration of 'form':

> 16. . . . One stone makes an archway – the stone which wedges the leaning sides and holds the arch together by its position in the middle. And why does the last addition, although very slight, make a great deal of difference? Because it does not increase; it fills up. 17. Some things, through development, put off their old form and pass [transeunt] into a new form.[44]

This is of course a reference to the Stoic doctrine of metabasis though it is unclear whether Spinoza knew of the deeper aspects of that theory. What we can draw from the usage of '*transire*' here and in celestial mechanics in Spinoza's time, however, is that a transition or passage appears to operate in respect of and towards or about something else, either the Sun or the Good, that it results in a state incommensurable with the precedent state, and that transition therefore is as much about a person's virtue as her relation to the *pneuma* and the Good. All this puts us on notice when we see Spinoza deploy '*transire*', but the direct physical relation to the conatus doctrine should not divert us from working from physical principles up and then seeing how the Stoic doctrine itself undergoes transition to the Spinozan.

To do this we must again remember what Euclid taught: that numbers and magnitudes are fundamentally different.[45] If we say that pleasure is simply an increase in relative capacity to work, we have *not* increased by a power but increased *simpliciter*. Geometrically, we have extended a directed line segment, we have not turned a directed line segment into plane, and only increasing a power turns a line segment into a plane. Readers of Duns Scotus here will no doubt hear the ringing of alarm bells, but the relation of power to geometry is actually critical in the development of early dynamics. In what, then, does an increase in power of working, or pleasure, consist? A geometrical interpretation renders two elements clear:

(a) an increase in the directed line segment; and
(b) a change of direction.

This is nothing other than a description of Descartes' own parallelogram rule for composition of forces, which, Spinoza must have realised, is an incredibly useful way of thinking about how forces superimpose on each other. Now, for the purposes of ethics, the above elements may be rendered:

(a) an increase in desire; and
(b) a change in what one desires.

So it seems that Spinoza has not only refounded the doctrine of the transition on a physical footing, but he has managed to bring along the sense that transition causes a change in a being's relation to reason and the Good. And we see that just as one's volitional compass closes in on the Good, one's desire for this Good increases; a moment of connection in principle between Spinoza and the Stoa once again.

Let us not overlook just what an increase in appetite means, because it draws on the change in appetite also. Here, the theory of contractions in the attributes, manifested as the physical stresses of pleasure and pain in the Cartesian and Spinozist philosophies, come to the fore. Reverting to the physical situation of the simplest bodies, the lack of an arbitrary coordinate system leaves us unable to view acceleration as an 'extension' of space travelled in equal time. A proportion of motion:rest, as a simple body perceives it, is actually a flow of extensive modes relative to the apparent flow of other things: literally the surface of a simple body open to encounters (EIIP14). Thus if simple bodies *A* and *B* are travelling with the same proportion motion:rest in the same direction, then the flow of finite modes (affections) they encounter is the same with one exception. There is no perceived flow of *B* for *A* and vice versa; each appears to the other not to be moving, in full application of the Spinozan principle that one experiences a mode until determined not to. As we have said before, the physical notions at work here were well known to seventeenth-century natural philosophers. The Spinozan twist is the idea of duration, or the attributively ordered flux of finite modes.

The conception that transition includes both increase in desire and change in what one desires is in fact quite hidden away in the *Ethics*, almost as if Spinoza himself either noticed it later, or thought it so obvious he overlooked its specification. This principle appears as a clarificatory scholium to EIIIP59. Here Spinoza writes:

> It remains to remark concerning love, that it very often happens that while we are enjoying a thing which we longed for, the body, from the act of enjoyment, acquires a new disposition, whereby it is determined in another way, other images of things are aroused in it, and the mind begins to conceive and desire something fresh. For example, when we conceive something which generally delights us with its flavour, we desire to enjoy, that is, to eat it. But whilst we are thus enjoying it, the stomach is filled and the body is otherwise disposed. If, therefore, when the body is thus otherwise disposed, the image of the food which is present be stimulated, and consequently the endeavour or desire to eat it be stimulated also, the new disposition of the body will feel repugnance to the desire or attempt, and consequently the presence of the food which we formerly longed for will become odious. This revulsion of feeling is called *satiety* or *weariness*.
>
> (emphasis in original)[46]

The passage opens as if only love was being considered, but the examples given about satiation of hunger suggest that it applies in every case of a transition. We take the view that this wider understanding of transition is Spinoza's view, but that he wishes to focus on love because the transitions due to it lead us to the specific goal of ethics, the *summum bonum*. This we will show from the simplest case.

We now consider in the simple case acceleration of *A* with respect also to *B*. This is perceived by *A* as an increase in the flow of duration: more extensive modes are experienced relative to those by *B*. This difference in 'power' is perceived as *B*'s apparent decrease in power, although *B* has retained a constant proportion motion:rest. Yet if *B*'s deceleration is only a perceived loss of power, we can understand why arbitrary reference frames will only lead us away from the comprehension *objective* of what has happened. No things have changed, no being has altered, and no bits of substance have traded place: God or Nature is immutable. Rather, it is the incorporeal attributes as acts of God or Nature that have locally varied in their work. The variation partially involves the reordering of the experience of all things so that one thing, *A*, is capable of encountering more things, and so experiencing more modes, than before. Thus if *A* attains twice the proportion of motion:rest than *B*, *A* will in principle have twice as many modes flowing through its consciousness as B (noting that while this makes more sense if we set time as an arbitrary constant, *A*'s perception of increased flow has nothing *in se* which grants an experience of change: *we feel and think we are eternal*). The notion of attributive contraction and de-contraction readily suggests Spinoza's thought process here: acceleration is partially a function of the degree of contraction of flow. This is not contraction meant in the sense of restricting flow transversally, but nor is it meant in the Bergsonian sense of the intensity of the transition of the virtual over motion.[47] Rather, a contraction of the causal series in the sense given in Ch. 2.4.

This is what the geometric conception of acceleration helps to reveal to us, provided we understand that the operation of acceleration comprises an element of simple multiplication *and* an element of directional mutation (nil being a special case, as we shall see). By these two elements a line becomes a plane and thus, if we care to consider *A*'s traversal of a line as explicating the experience of a certain number of modal encounters, then the plane figure explicates the experience by *A* increased both by augmenting the line length *and* sweeping out a plane in the direction and to the degree required by the acting power. The modal encounters of *A* are increased by the magnitude proportionate to the plane on that transversal.[48] Understanding this is itself a moment of transition: it *is* the case that at each moment *A* is travelling in two different directions, but it is doing this double movement at a higher degree of power, a movement which at the lower degree of power results in a single linear effect, which may be considered the *linear flux of existential consciousness*.

Geometrically the operation of transition produces the existing magnitude of motion:rest *and* it 'curls' that motion:rest according to the directionality of *the transition's* magnitude. This is a relation of powers that is explicated through duration, and is easily shown for the *corpora simplicissima* as a genetic geometrical relation in Figure 4.1.

Importantly, we specify that this elucidation is stated only for the simplest case, that is, they only make sense for the *corpora simplicissima*, and not for bodies with a greater surface open to encounters (EIIP14). The reasons for this require only a little reflection, but we will postpone this consideration of complex cases to the next chapter so that we may continue insofar as possible Spinoza's theory of right in its clearest limit cases in order to establish boundary cases. Notice that the simple body's existing appetite is completely determinative, as in Cartesian physics,[49] of whether a transition is to be deemed positive or negative. Does this

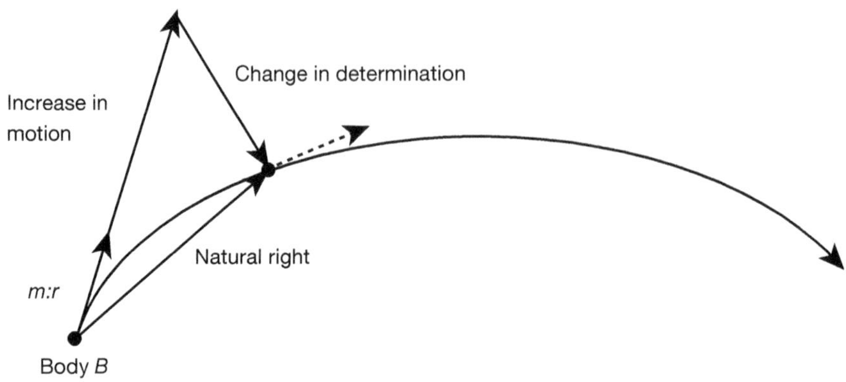

Figure 4.1 Components of natural right, geometrically

mean one can 'turn away from the idea of God'? Absolutely speaking, the total power of this idea means no idea in its presence can turn away, and, if we speak of the substance of which it is the thing, only another substance could achieve such an act. Resistance to the idea of God, for Spinoza, comes rather from the failure of a thing's power of working to allow it to conceive (rather than perceive) of the idea *of* this first idea and to mistake its appetite for desire after some confused imagining. In other words, each thing must first be the essence of the idea of God for itself.[50]

So, in the case of positive transition, what is this direction and what is this degree that determines the second element of the transition? In the absolute case the direction is God or Nature and the degree is infinite. However, we are never in the presence of God or Nature in the sense that we are bound to perceive substance through and by the order of the attributes. Thus we must first look to some mode of Thought which best directs us to God, that is, because such a mode necessarily involves God's infinite power of being, a mode that explicates God to the greatest degree. This is the idea of God.

To clarify how this all works together, we posit a 'notional' thinking simple body *A* capable of having knowledge of only one idea of God or Nature. *A*'s power of acting is varied continuously from the minimum of death to the maximum of beatitude. We then consider two moments when *A*'s power of working is increased, indicating how desire is increased and is increased towards the supreme good. We could present this diagrammatically indicating the power of thinking the idea of God as a continuous variation, and then observing the transitions in this power. One would then see that in absolute terms to think God is to think the infinite and that this is the transition from the world of ideas to the world of intuition. Yet were such a diagram produced it would of course be absurd: principally because *A* will be determined to beatitude because nothing else can intervene to prevent this, and because *A* is granted immediate access to the true idea of God even if from the beginning A does not comprehend this idea. Such a diagram thus would describe only an ideal (quasi-transcendent) case, and should be treated with utmost caution.

It seems that Spinoza has not only refounded the Stoic doctrine of the transition on a physical footing, but he has managed to bring along the sense that transition causes a change in a thing's relation to reason and the Good by reference to the flow of experiences. And we see that just as one's volitional compass closes in on the Good, one's desire for this Good increases; a moment of connection in principle between Spinoza and the Stoa once again.

4.4 Conclusion

We have now determined the characteristics of how natural right constitutes existential consciousness. As the existence of finite things is nothing other than determination to exist, guaranteed by God or Nature's power of being, we have shown how existential consciousness is natural right considered as being-effect – as concatenation of God or Nature, body, motion and rest, and the variations induced by transition. In short, to be determined to exist as a relation of parts – as character – is first to express the natural right of other things, immanently subtended by the infinite attributes, this latter expressed as degree of reality. In this way we hope to have clarified how natural right is inseparable from its transitions, is inherently dynamic, and that in this dynamism of the existential transition we can locate solutions to several apparent paradoxes of the Spinozan system: notably that of thinking unity, extensive unity, the nature of time, causation, and eternity, and the relation of simple things to God and the idea of God. We now pass immediately to consideration of natural right experienced as being-cause, that is, as essential consciousness.

Notes

1 'And as I have often seen occur in the vortices fo water, in the larger vortices of the celestial matter are other smaller vortices.'
2 Cf. *supra*. Ch. 3.3.3.
3 It seems evident that the converse of pain should also be relevant, not only because it is a surplus, but because it is well known that an excessive labour on a task is just as useless to the industrialist as the 'go slow'. The point is completion of a task within a socially necessary labour time.
4 *Capital* (1976: 284).
5 Though God is the necessary but not sufficient condition of profitability; there must be power extended along a line for any work to occur (cf. Ch. 3.3).
6 The use of the noun is intentional; hates are bodies and the verbal use of 'to hate' confuses the event of pain with the body it accompanies. In this sense the worker's labour is twofold: she must create a body of hate as the principal instrument for her work on the raw material before her.
7 Parkinson (2000: 197). A greater degree of symmetry would be obtained by treating love as the involute of evolutive hate, but Spinoza might respond that love remains a passion lacking the reason necessary to attain the status of an integral of hate. EIIIP44

seems to state that hate is carried over into love when entirely conquered, but the Dem. makes clear that the increased love is due to the causes of: (a) loving; and (b) the pleasure of *relieving* a certain quantum of hatred. For more on relief in general, see our discussion of *Aufhebung* in Ch. 4.2.

8 *Die fröhliche Wissenschaft* (2000: §58).

9 We will return to God or Nature's power of working at the end of this chapter, for it seems to us easier to comprehend Spinoza's thinking about substance once we have examined the finite case of consciousness.

10 'Per ius et institutum naturae nihil aliud intelligo quam regulas naturae uniuscujusque individui, secundum quas unumquodque naturaliter determinatum concipimus ad certo modo existendum et operandum.'

11 'Existit unusquisque summo naturae iure, et consequenter summo naturae iure unusquisque ea agit, quae ex suae naturae necessitate sequuntur . . .'

12 'Nam quoniam Deus ius ad omnia habet et ius Dei nihil aliud est, quam ipsa Dei potentia, quatenus haec absolute libera consideratur, hinc sequitur, unamquamque rem naturalem tantum iuris ex natura habere, quantum potentiae habet ad existendum et operandum . . .'

13 '. . . et consequenter quicquid unusquisque homo ex legibus suae naturae agit, id summo naturae iure agit, tantumque in naturam habet iuris, quantum potentia valet'.

14 Letter 58, §2.

15 'A Note on "consciousness/conscience" in the *Ethics*' (1992) *Studia Spinozana* 37–53.

16 'Res particulares nihil sunt, nisi Dei attributorum affectiones, sive modi, quibus Dei attributa certo, & determinato modo exprimuntur.'

17 We will pursue these concepts in the next section (cf. Cicero 1933: 2.23–5; SVF 2.988).

18 It would be unfair to include Bove (1996) in this discussion because he builds up from the conatus to construct a conscious world, and does not address the issue of constructing consciousness in itself.

19 'Partes, Corpus humanum components, ad estiam ipsius Corporis non pertinent, nisi quatenus motus suos certa quadam ratione invicem communicant . . . & non quatenus, Individua, absque relatione ad humanum Corpus considerari possunt. Sunt enim partes humani Corporis . . . valde composite Individua, quorum partes a Corpore humano, servata omnino eiusdem natura, & forma segregari possunt, motusque suos . . . aliis corporibus alia ratione communicare . . .'

20 '. . . adeoque (per EIIP3) cujusque partis idea, sive cognitio in Deo erit, & quidem (per EIIP9), quatenus affectus consideratur alia idea rei singularis, quae res singularis ipsa parte, ordine naturae, prior est (per EIIP7)'.

21 We rely strongly on Sambursky (1959: 8) and Christensen's concise *Essay* (1962) for this analysis.

22 Sambursky (1959: 84) refers to the quotations that follow.

23 Simmons, A., 'Sensation in the Malebranchean Mind', in Miller (2009: 118).

24 Ibid., p. 119.

25 *Principles of Nature and Grace* §1 (1989: 207).

26 I.e. one of the Furies, which Amphitryon urges Hercules to 'repress' (ibid.: §973).

27 *Die Unruhe des Nichts*. Cf. also the final quotation to the *Phänomenologie des Geistes* (1969: 3, 447):
'aus dem Kelche dieses Geisterreiches
schäumt ihm seine Unendlichkeit'.

28 (1996: 243).

29 Ibid., including quotation.

30 'Etwas ist nur insofern aufgehoben, als es in die Einheit mit seinem Entgegengesetzten getreten ist; in dieser nähern Bestimmung als ein reflectiertes kann es passend *Moment* genannt werden. *Gewicht* und Entfernung von einem Punkt heissen beym Hebel, dessen mechanische *Momente*, um der *Dieselbigkeit* ihrer Wirkung willen bey aller sonstigen

Verschiedenheit eines Reellen, wie das ein Gewicht ist, und einen Ideellen, der blossen räumlichen Bestimmung, der Linie.' (*W.d.Logik* Ch. 1(c), rem. *Aufheben des Werdens* (1969: 114), emphasis in original.)

31 Derrida focuses his critique on this additional sense of *Aufhebung*, which he translates as as *relèver*, in his '*The Pit and the Pyramid*' (1982: 69–108 at 88, 92), though one might ask if he should also have pursued his insights ('*Ousia et Grammē*') (1982: 42) to consider the geometric case of the product of two negations of negation (which is exactly the geometric case of present natural right). Ziche pursues the Hebel into Hegel's distinction between quantitative difference and qualitative difference (i.e. indifference) and makes links to Hegel's explanation of infinitesimal calculus (1996: 251ff.).

32 Phil. des Rechts §§4–7 (1969: 46–56); Enzyklopädie II §466–467 (1969: 438).

33 Stoic categories are built from reality up; that which is not immediately apparent, such as the incorporeal, may only be justified through metabasis to the concept, Chrysippos' cone being the prime example. Hegel might say his doctrine of *Sein-Nichts-Werden* satisfies this criterion.

34 'The String Whose Curve Is Described by Bending Under Its Own Weight, and the Remarkable Resources That Can Be Discovered from It by However Many Proportional Means and Logarithms', *Acta Eruditorum*, marked 'Leipzig, June 1691', in Leibniz (1962).

35 '. . . tout se peut expliquer dans la Géométrie par le calcul des nombres et aussi par l'analyse de la situation . . .' (Leibniz 1903: 329).

36 The input of Wittgenstein's thinking on rules-as-machines was suggested by an anonymous reviewer and is gratefully welcomed.

37 (1958) at §193.

38 Ibid.

39 (1958) at §193.

40 *Lectures on the History of Philosophy*, quoted by Maxwell in Sharp and Smith (2012: 109).

41 Cf. e.g. Sharp and Smith (2012) for a discussion of Hegel's reading of Spinozan negation by various contributors.

42 We say not-conscious because there is no possibility of the unconscious becoming conscious for essential consciousness, as we shall see.

43 '11. Quod dico talest: sunt quaedam neque bona neque mala, tamquam militia, legatio, iurisdictio. Haec cum honeste administrata sunt, bona esse incipiunt et ex dubio in bonum transeunt.'

44 '16. . . . Unus lapis facit fornicem, ille qui latera inclinata cuneavit et interventu suo vinxit. Summa adiectio quare plurimum facit vel exigua? quia non auget sed implet. 17. Quaedam processu priorem exuunt formam et in novam transeunt.'

45 Euclid's *Elements* strangely repeats its proofs for numbers and then for magnitudes. The reason seems simple: numbers are considered wholly distinct from magnitudes, the former having no magnitude (they are scalars). The importance of this appears in the manner in which they combine.

46 'Attamen de amore hoc notandum restat, quod scilicet saepissime contingit, dum re, quam appetebamus, fruimur, ut corpus ex ea fruitione novam acquirat constitutionem, a qua aliter determinatur, et aliae rerum imagines in eo excitantur, et simul mens alia imaginari aliaque cupere incipit. Ex. gr. cum aliquid, quod nos sapore delectare solet, imaginamur, eodem frui, nempe comedere cupimus. At quamdiu eodem sic fruimur, stomachus adimpletur corpusque aliter constituitur. Si igitur corpore iam aliter disposito eiusdem cibi imago, quia ipse praesens adest, fomentetur, et consequenter conatus etiam sive cupiditas eundem comedendi huic cupiditati seu conatui nova illa constitutio repugnabit, et consequenter cibi, quem appetebamus, praesentia odiosa erit, et hoc est quod fastidium et taedium vocamus.'

47 Cf. e.g. *Time and Free Will* (1960: 106–110).

48 One wonders whether some alteration in the power of being also occurs as *A* contracts encounters towards it, at least as *A* approaches the limit. This seems to be ruled out by Spinoza's decision that all variations of a thing's power of acting occur entirely in the attributes.

49 Cf. DPPIIP27, Rule 3. It seems Spinoza only accepted rigid interactions according to the hydrostatic 'balance' model, as Gaukroger has shown (Ch. 3).

50 Otherwise there must be some thing in the universe that has mental presence for us as the idea of God. Clearly no such thing can be because it is the idea of something that lacks particularity. We are required therefore to express this idea in actual Thought.

Bibliography

Balibar, E. (1992) 'A note on "consciousness/conscience" in the Ethics' 8 *Studia Spinozana* 37–53.

—— (1997) 'Spinoza: from Individuality to Transindividuality' *Mededelingen vanwege het Spinozahuis*, Vol. 71, Eburon, Netherlands.

—— (2007) *Spinoza and Politics*, Verso, London.

Bergson, H. (1960) *Time and Free Will*, Harper, London.

Bove, L. (1996) *La stratégie du conatus*, VRIN, Paris.

Christensen, J. (1962) *An Essay on the Unity of Stoic Philosophy*, Munksgaard, Copenhagen.

Cicero, Marcus Tullius (1931) *De finibus bonorum et malorum*, Harvard University Press, Cambridge, MA.

—— (1933) *De natura deorum/Academica*, Harvard University Press, Cambridge, MA.

—— (1956) *Letters to Atticus* (3 vols), Harvard University Press, Cambridge, MA.

—— (1958) *Epistulae ad familiares, Quintum fratrem, Brutum* (3 vols), Harvard University Press, Cambridge, MA.

Deleuze, G. (1981a) *Confrontation avec le commentaire de Gueroult*, lecture dated 10 March 1981, archived at: www.webdeleuze.com/php/texte.php?cle=40&groupe=Spinoza&langue=1.

—— (1981b) *L'éternité; récapitulation; les trois genres de connaissance; éternité; experimentation; immortalité et éternité; le rapport entre Ontologie et Ethique*, lecture dated 17 March 1981, archived at: www.webdeleuze.com/php/texte.php?cle=43&groupe=Spinoza&langue=1.

—— (1981c) *Untitled lecture of 24 March 1981*, archived at: www.webdeleuze.com/php/texte.php?cle=45&groupe=Spinoza&langue=1.

—— (1988) *Spinoza: Practical Philosophy*, R. Hurley (trans.), City Light Books, San Francisco, CA.

—— (1990a) *Expressionism in Philosophy: Spinoza*, M. Joughlin (trans.), New York, Zone Books.

Derrida, J. (1982) *Margins of Philosophy*, University of Chicago Press, Chicago, IL.

Duffy, S. (2006) *The Logic of Expression: Quality, Quantity and Intensity in Spinoza, Hegel and Deleuze*, Ashgate, Aldershot.

Gueroult, M. (1968b) *Spinoza: I – Dieu*, Aubier, Éditions Montaigne, Paris.

—— (1974a) *Spinoza: II – L'âme*, Aubier, Éditions Montaigne, Paris.

Hegel, G.W.F. (1969) *Werke in zwanzig Bänden*, Suhrkamp Verlag, Frankfurt am Main.

Höchstrasser, T. and Schröder, P. (eds) (2003) *Early Modern Natural Law Theories: Contexts and Strategies in the Early Enlightenment*, Kluwer, Netherlands.

Leibniz, G.W. (1903) *Opuscules et fragments inédits de Leibniz*, Couturat (ed.), Félix Alcan, Paris.

—— (1962) *G.W. Leibniz: Mathematische Schriften*, C.I. Gerhardt (ed.), Georg Olms Verlagsbuchhandlung, Hildesheim.

—— (1989) *Philosophical Essays*, Ariew and Garber (trans.), Hackett, Indianapolis, IN.

—— (2010) *Theodicy*, A. Farrer and E.M. Huggard (trans.), Cosimo, New York.
Marx, K. (1968) *Texte zu Methode und Praxis II: Pariser Manuskripte 1844*, Rowohlt, Reinbek bei Hamburg.
—— (1970) *A Contribution to the Critique of Political Economy*, Progress Publishers, Moscow.
—— (1976) *Capital* (3 vols.), Penguin & New Left Review, London.
Marx, K. and Engels, F. (1971–1990) *Marx-Engels Werke: Ergänzungsband*, Dietz Verlag, Berlin.
Miller, J. (ed.) (2009) *Topics in Early Modern Philosophy of Mind*, Springer, Netherlands.
Nietzsche, F. (2000) *Die fröhliche Wissenschaft*, Reclam, Ditzingen, Germany.
Parkinson, G.H.R. (2000) *Spinoza: Ethics*, Oxford University Press, Oxford.
Sambursky, S. (1959) *Physics of the Stoics*, Greenwood Press, Westport, CT.
Sharp, H. and Smith, J.E. (2012) *Between Hegel and Spinoza*, Bloomsbury, London.
Wittgenstein, L. (1958) *Philosophical Investigations*, G.E.M. Anscombe (trans.), Basil Blackwell, Oxford.

Chapter 5

Natural right II

Ethics of essential consciousness

> I know . . . that I will . . . but I do not know all . . . what my desire and my pain are.
>
> (Malebranche 1958 VI, p. 161)

5.1 Introduction

We now consider not the cause of the machine's existence, but this machine as cause of work. We call this for convenience its 'essential consciousness', which may be decomposed into two types: (a) formal being of work; and (b) formal essence of work. The first is the realm of intellect or will, and is bounded; an expression of our finite struggle in the general equilibrium. The latter is 'free' – an expression of God or Nature's infinite power.

5.2 Finite essential consciousness

5.2.1 The general equilibrium

Our first task will be to concretise the distinction between essential consciousness and existential consciousness and explicate what it means to endeavour to work in the world. This will allow us to clarify the origins of the affects and the foundation of the norm of the present in the endeavour to work. Let us begin with an intuitive[1] motivation for our understanding of the difference of essential consciousness drawn from our physical work in Chapter 3. The stone and the bridge helped us grasp the nature of existential consciousness, but Spinoza as we saw was just as interested in fluids and indeed regarded solids and fluids as relative conceptions, and we think it is the fluid that helps us make progress here. Again in Chapter 3 we saw how if we took some free amount of incompressible fluid and pushed some part of it, the rest of the fluid would change shape in whole or part to accommodate this push. If the fluid is held in a tube, a push at one end will be instantaneously communicated to the other, as Spinoza demonstrated by experiment. This rather loose unity of the fluid (it is easily separated) might be considered its existential consciousness, though it be quite an abstraction from the reality of its existence, for, even to be at relative rest in the Cartesian sense, the fluid's power is being subjected to a multitude of powers, which are cancelling each other out (the definition of relatively disposed rest). Conversely, it is clearly seen that if our fluid is disposed to relative motion, it does so under the efficient cause of some other thing. Its appetite (which for Spinoza equals will) has come from somewhere (EIIP49 Sch.).

Let us now (without explanation) give our fluid an appetite: we take up the fluid in a jug (state S_i) and proceed to pour it slowly onto the centre of a wide, rimmed dish. In this simple example we can see precisely what will happen, the water, under what Spinoza believes to be the action of the downward impressing power of air corpuscles, will be forced out of the jug down onto the centre of the dish. The falling corpuscles and the air pressure will cause the fluid to meet the resting 'body' that is the dish, and spread across its surface almost uniformly, before the fluid meets the rim that restrains it. Finally the dish will fill and, if big enough, the fluid will occupy the lowest distributed volume it can in the dish and attain a flat upper surface due to the combined air pressure above across that surface (state S_j).

With existence we considered how some thing in extended 'space' was constituted and remained the same; now with formal being we are considering how some thing in extended space *and duration* is constituted and, and this is the key, *remains the same*. This fluid has not remained the same, you may exclaim. Yet it has not remained the same only *in* duration, just as a spatial magnitude does not remain the same as one moves through the space of that magnitude. Indeed, has our incompressible fluid taken on a greater or lesser of volume? By definition, no. The space and duration have changed from the perspective of extension, but Spinoza is considering such matters *sub quadem specie aeternitatis*, and from this conception they have not changed at all. Strictly speaking it appears Spinoza grants a direct relation between a relatively spatially varying activity and a durationally varying series of volitions. All else being abstracted, when the power implicated in state S_i obtains, state S_j already determinately and necessarily obtains, and it is only the restraint of some third power that ensures the passage between states is not instantaneous (and so for Spinoza eternal).[2] This is the double meaning of existing *in act*, it is not enough simply to abide, but each thing must also express a power. Every thing from this finite perspective is as water being poured onto the surface of the world; a *fons vitae* to use the title of ibn Gabirol's work. It can hopefully be seen that state S_j stands as the horizon of the appetite and will of the fluid in question and the difference between S_j and S_i and every moment between is felt as that actualisation of will and satisfaction of appetite over against this horizon. The idea of the dish and its rim is used to give an intuitive sense of this as it stands over against the pouring fluid. As we shall see below, the attribute of extension enclosed within this horizon constitutes the *formal being* of the fluid's essential consciousness. It is finite power as it endeavours to work in the world in order to achieve the actualisation of that power. When Spinoza describes natural right as equal to power *quantum potentia valet*, this 'as far as power extends or prevails' must be understood also within this context of relative duration.

As our thing traverses the duration from S_i to S_j, it does so determinately, satisfying all restraints, before arriving at the expression of this power in the effect. We have what we would now call a linear system, and thus the limitations inherent in applying this analysis to the real world (i.e. a system of three bodies already becomes unpredictable though just as necessary).

This all follows from the idea of the dynamic machine we attributed to Spinoza in 3.4.1, and the bridge of Seneca. If we take our fluid as a system F of parts expressing a determinate proportion of motion and rest, its constituent power of thinghood is for Spinoza the case where all the transitions of the parts (their accelerations here) cancel each other out (= 0) and create a surface across which any additional power is immediately communicated. When the additional thing G is applied to F, and it applies a transition to F, either F or G are decomposed as things, or F and/or G will accommodate this new power by a change in its motion.

We now extrapolate this to the world of the plenum and see that every part of the universe must accommodate every change in every other part; that is, there must reign a general equilibrium such that the sum of the transitions in the parts of the whole face of the universe = 0. One might rightly ask how this equilibrium ever was or ever will be disturbed. Is it true that God or Nature pours motion into the universe? We will see how shortly.

First, however, we want to briefly consider the results for the natural right theory, and this reduces to a consideration of the will (=intellect), which we argue is experienced as the norms of the enduring present.

5.2.2 The norms of the enduring present

We believe we have sufficient tools to consider a question that pertains to understanding Spinoza's theory of natural right *viz.* is Spinoza a thinker of the norm? In a very technical sense derived from the foregoing, it is indeed the case that Spinoza has a theory of the norm grounded within essential consciousness and determined as the difference between formal being and actual essence. One should not be surprised by this, given that the Roman Stoics handed down the idea of the first law, the imperative of the present which will be obeyed and must be seized rather than erroneously and unsuccessfully resisted. Goldschmidt (1969: 169) informs us that:

> there is only one moral fault and it is understood that the Stoics attributed to it an equal gravity whatever the form it took: it is to disobey the imperative of the present.[3]

Working from within an albeit Hegelian methodology with respect to Spinoza, Matheron too has realised that Spinoza adopts a version of the Stoic theory, which e call the 'norm of the present'. In a passing remark (1969: 296) Matheron indicates his sensitivity to the fundamental difference Spinoza draws between the power individuals desire to exercise and their failure to achieve it. While Matheron seems to locate difference in 'pride' as the overestimation (imagination) of one's domination of the world, and indeed draws on TPII[15] to support this, he continues to claim that the natural right to desire and pursue some object is a right in itself, separate from the natural right determined by the composition counteracting forces in the actual failure to acquire the desired object. Without justifying his phrasing, Matheron writes:

> This right to try our look and to undertake is called *formal right* in opposition to real right; it rests on a most illusory opinion, but, from the moment this illusion exists, the dynamism it creates is natural and legitimate.
>
> (1969: 296–297, emphasis in original)[4]

By alternative means Matheron arrives at a similar conclusion to our own as to natural right in the finite case, with a critical division between formal and actual right, but as Matheron's continuation clarifies, he regards formal right as a separate 'illusory' thing from actual right, and not, as we do, a continuum of power that grounds a dynamism worthy of that name.

Our conjecture is that natural right is first divided into existing and essential natural right. The former pertains to that which constitutes the thing in act, and is the composition of the rights that caused it. Insofar as the formal right of each cause is restrained from acting alone in constituting this new individual, we see that the actual essence of the individual – the surface that is its consciousness – is attributable to the created thing as the 'forma' of its own being. Being complete in its present existence, the *res cogitans*' first moment is the experience of willing its being to endure indefinitely, the so-called experience of eternity. The natural right of existing is thus unique in its simple actuality as being the equation of what is desired in the present and what is granted by the universe – to exist. This is a separate issue from the transitions that the existing thing experiences, which remain changes that nevertheless affirm this continued existence. This part of consciousness we term: *the norm of being present.*

With essential right we experience the limits of our finite power as the site in which incoming transitions are resisted and reflected out into the universe. 'The actual intellect . . . must . . . just like the will . . . be related to passive and not to active Nature' (EIP31), that is, the will is experienced as a present idea insofar only as it is passive to some incoming transition, and it is only regarded as will with respect to something as the reflection or communication of the translation onwards, in the form of some complex motion. Hence, will is a necessary, not a free cause; the volitions we aggregate as will cannot exist or be determined to work unless determined by another cause, and again by another (EIP32 and Dem.). Here we see that the conatus, insofar as it is related to existence only, can at once be seen as resistance and as that resistance appearing to us as will, or *to will is to resist.*

Now this will is the immediate reflection of an incoming transition, but there is no guarantee that we will make good our habitual mechanism of resistance; our usual volition may be thwarted and its power dissipated in a manner unintended, like water crashing against rocks. Our finitude *and the infinite extent of the universe in equilibrium* necessitate that we be restrained from without, and experience our will *formaliter* as the 'form of the world as it should have been'. It is this second 'ought to be' that is the power driving the cognition of rational normativity, such as civil conceptions of justice. For while it is evident that Spinoza regards this right as consisting '*magis opinion quam re*', this does not rule out that the second kind of knowledge continues to experience what we term *the norm of becoming present* with respect to the complexity of civic life. It is this difference between what we believe we will, our finite power, and the extent to which that power prevails, our natural right – this norm of becoming present – which is used even in dynamic interpretations of his theory to damn Spinoza and to claim that a theory of natural right in such equilibrium conditions is of no value to humanity (despite its explanatory merits even at this stage). Our argument, however, is that Spinoza's theory of natural right goes much further than this.

5.3 The infinite machine

5.3.1 The transition from finite to infinite mechanism

We now return to the key question of Spinozism: if we posit the general equilibrium of enduring existence, how do we account for the variations in this equilibrium? If the universe is like a lever, what moment impels it to tip into action? If the universe is fluid, what pressure or pull draws it forth to flow to a determinate end? If Spinoza rejects the idea that God initiated change in the universe at some notional beginning, how does he account for God or Nature's immanence in the world without either breaking the equilibrium or subsuming God or Nature in it? Spinoza has clearly noticed this problematic already at the finite level:

> I say that I entirely grant that if a man were placed in such a state of equilibrium [aequilibrio] he would perish of hunger and thirst, supposing he perceived the food and drink which were equidistant from him.
>
> (EIIP49 Sch.)

These questions are highly relevant for Spinoza, but we do not believe their asking traces the route by which Spinoza came to his solution of them. In fact, we have been tracing what we regard as Spinoza's theoretical route in this research. In Chapter 2 we marked the transition from corporeality (formal being) to the necessity of the incorporeal attributes (formal essences) as power; in Chapter 3 we used this power to pass from motion to rest as the limit of motion and site of the simple bodies; in Chapter 4 we again deployed power to discover the transition from simple bodies to the constitution of the machine; now in Chapter 5 we deploy this same dialectic method and raise up the machine. For what, it seems to us, Spinoza arrives at, is the possibility of raising the power of a machine to the limit, and to consider a machine that in its capacity for infinite production of work, stands as to the other machines as rest stands to motion, and thus becomes the site and possibility of their operation.

Again we want intuitively to first consider what such a machine would be like, before we seek textual justification. Here we consider a machine with an infinite power, and so we suppose that such a machine (a) cannot be restrained from producing any of its effects by any other machine, and consequently but also by right (b) cannot exhaust itself or be exhausted, such that however tortuously it may bring about its result, it is deemed to have succeeded as if it had taken the most direct route (homology of power). Such a machine, producing its effects unbound thus suffers no duration, but works eternally, and so from the finite perspective it completes it, works at every moment. And insofar as this machine produces its effects, we must consider that nothing in the machine can alter, but only the things upon which it works, which are brought to it like gold to the furnace, the character of which latter determines what effect is to be produced for that thing. Such a machine sounds quite incredible and at odds with Spinoza's determinism, and yet Spinoza confronted an example of it every day; indeed he had mastered the art of crafting instruments for examining this machine more carefully. This machine is of course what we now call gravity and which Spinoza never called weight (*pondus*), which was always a function of motion, but which at least we may consider as the prime example of the Spinozan transition as a variation in the power of acting.[5] Here an important note of caution: we are deploying certain metaphysical interpretations of gravitation as a hermeneutic tool, which we show helps us understand key aspects of Spinoza's texts. A direct connection from the abundance of his physical insights to a theory of gravity, which Harris shows Schelling also proposed,[6] cannot be found explicitly in texts, and indeed we have noted a number of points where his physical theory of motion is erroneous, but what we are trying to pursue is an indirect connection between the problems that his physical theory has presented us with (principally an immobile equilibrium of finite power), and his solutions to parallel problems of the relation between finite humans and an infinite God within the ethical sphere. In fact, the Spinozan theory allows us to offer up any hermeneutic machine[7] for the interrogation of infinite power, provided we remember our focus is not on what is revealed about the machine, but what it has combined with – that infinite machine. We believe it severely restricts Spinoza's thinking to regard this infinite power as limited to a gravity-like power, or even a duality of attraction and repulsion (again Schelling).[8] So at the point of comprehension the finite hermeneutic machine can be abandoned or modified (TdIE §31). Now, the initial benefits for deploying this hermeneutic tool of gravitation principally derive from considering how gravity is considered to operate (here for ease we give a non-relativistic rendering):

- it is perceived as having spatial and eternal, not durational, extension; if it appears to change it is because finite machines have moved in it;
- at every point where it acts, it acts without question or restraint with respect to any finite machine;
- one can place an almost infinite number of finite machines in a given locus and no weakening or delay in the application of gravity will be observed; and
- if a finite machine is placed at point *A* and transits to point *B*, this line can be straight, or massively curved, or deformed into any variety of bizarre shape, and all the work gravity can be said to produce is that which accelerated the finite machine directly from *A* to *B* (i.e. the work done is path independent).

In describing in EI a fundamental difference between the infinite machine and the finite machines, Spinoza is actually proffering an explanation for a tricky physical problem of reconciling the differences between conservative and non-conservative forces. It is this difference that provides a wonderful framework for understanding Spinoza's enterprise. Non-conservative forces are forces that are not retained and arise from resistance and the like. Spinoza's proximate synonym, finite power, refers to the *potentia* constituting the world of duration and the struggle to persist in being, the prime example being the conatus, but he is also aware of structural resistance as 3.3.1 showed. Finite power is passed into each thing by some external cause and is directly passed onwards down the great chain, being experienced as will. Conservative forces never dissipate, and the proximate Spinozan synonym of infinite power marks these above properties.

How does this infinite machine solve the problems mentioned in the first paragraph of this section? It is easier to defy Spinoza first and posit an absolute spatial extension to explain this. Once posited, the infinite machine is assumed for now to exert its power at every point in that space without restraint and eternally, such that we can ignore whatever bodies are filling it for the time being. The lack of restraint means that whatever quantum of power so distributed, at that point in space it is possible for us to assign that quantum of power *as a fundamental disequilibrium* affecting whatever bodies might occupy that space *over and above the general equilibrium pertaining between finite machines*. It is in this specific sense that such an infinite machine can be considered superabundant; to the general equilibrium it super-adds a determinate degree of disequilibrium. The practical result is that a machine in equilibrium at that point is affected *as if* a new machine had suddenly appeared and determined it, with the consequence that the first finite machine is either destroyed, or changes its motion to compensate (it falls). In Spinoza's real relativistic geometry, however, as we saw in Chapter 3, it is not that a quantum of power is distributed across absolute space, but that extension itself is contracted; it is the attribute of extension that is the working of the infinite machine.

Does Spinoza in fact posit such an infinite machine? The *Ethics* provides plentiful proof, with EIP17 forming the axial point. God [as machine] acts from the laws of its nature and is compelled [*coactus*] by no one, to which is added as Corollaries that (1) there is no cause that, either extrinsically or intrinsically, incites God to action apart from the power of his own nature; and (2) God uniquely is a free cause. There is a polemic aspect here that seeks to show how a God that chooses or wills has less power, but we are interested in the meaning of this infinite power, which determines but is not determined save by that which inheres in every machine (its nature or determinate structure as machine). The Scholium to EIP17 pursues the polemic, but then returns to the positive aspects when it informs us that truth and the formal essence of things are in the intellect of God *objective*, with this intellect being the essence and thus power of God (per EIP34–35). This leads Spinoza to note that while we should not ascribe will or intellect to God, this prohibition derives from the manner in which they differ from the finite intellect or will, which we say is a difference of limit. One manner of reading this is to argue that because God's power encounters neither cause nor restraint, there lacks the struggle inherent in finite willing or intellection that produces volitions or ideas. Thus God is a machine that, were its power reduced, would then engage in struggle and restraint and suddenly discover the world as will and representation (to turn a phrase). EIP31–33 reinforce these points while also ensuring that we consider God's power as necessary, and not operating by freedom of the will.

The thus constituted free cause is then placed into the dual structure of machines, already outlined, in EIP27 and P28. EIP27 states that 'a thing which was determined by God to operate in some way cannot render itself undetermined', which both emphasises the one-directionality – the immanent 'verticality' – of God as cause and, on our interpretation, confirms the specificity of the God-machine's infinite power over against the general equilibrium. This is clear from the manner in which this Proposition is immediately followed in EIP28 by consideration of 'horizontal' causality between particular, finite things. The Scholium serves to remind us not to misrecognise completion of God's work in exercising his infinite power as somehow temporally prior to the present, for eternity is the present in which God is immanent cause, and it is in the present that we must seek the operations of this infinite machine. With this we hope to have shown how our interpretation of the infinite machine-finite machines relation elucidates Spinoza's theory.

Two further important questions have arisen: (a) how can it be that this infinite power acts everywhere, rather than from a beginning, and if everywhere, being infinite how can it be everywhere determinate (rather than homogenous or causing everything to clump together)? (b) how can we say that this power is eternal and yet also that it can appear to change its determinations? Both questions take us to the deepest heart of the *Ethics*. To explain this let us first continue our use of 'gravitation' as a special analogous case of Spinoza's theory of infinite power.

It will be easier to adopt an arbitrary two-dimensional spatial frame of reference. Conceive that this space expresses infinite power by reference to a (as yet unexplained) central point *A*, such that at every point of this space there is some transition waiting as it were to be impressed on any body that finds itself there. Now even Descartes realised in PPIII that if the central element is the source of some transition in the space around it, the transitions will vary as we move out. The reasoning is simple: place a small square around A and consider that all the power expressed by A lies along its perimeter. Now dilate the square; the perimeter will increase but the same amount of power must be distributed along it. As the square increases, so the power is reduced at each point. The proportionate deduction necessary as we move out, as Newton made famous, is the inverse square of the absolute distance $|r|$ from A (inverse cube for 3-space). This small step reminds us of the physical specificity of Spinoza's meaning of infinite (i.e. it is simply the limit case of finitude, not the mathematical infinite).

Now let us interrogate the natural right of this infinite power, proposing that the general tendency is instigating a transition towards A. We draw a line from arbitrary point P_0 to P_1 to show the path of some simple body in motion, and then draw a line straight out from A intersecting P_0 P_1. Keeping it simple, if P_0 P_1 is a directed motion towards A, and the simple body that travelled it was, in equilibrium, stationary at P_0, then (by Spinoza's definition of natural right) in this case the power on the simple body exerted extended along a line is equal to P_0 P_1 in the time we are looking at. We stress again aspects of what a real, physical 'infinite' power means here: it means the power exerted is not alienated and is always available for further work at P_0. It does not mean the simple body attains A instantaneously; the simple body transits to a greater power of acting, but the eternal act remains at every point of the space, this latter does not change and succeeds every time anything moves to its locus.

We are forced to cheat a little because for ease we are adopting an absolute space rather than the Spinozan conception we encountered in Chapter 3 of an Extension, which itself is modulated. In the case of this modulated Extension, the power consists in the actual tensions of Extension at every point, but these are experienced in the relatively disposed world of time and space as mysterious tendencies to motion at every point. To smooth this problem out we deploy the trick of differential calculus and take our line P_0 P_1 and reduce our interest to the limit of instantaneous power exerted at every point. At this limit we can then assign to every point a specific degree of causality, which instils a further transition on the simple body, but is not alienated in that body, it remains at the spatial point. It is in this sense that one might want to think of formal essences as intensions of infinite power, that is, by tensions that appear to super-add a determinate quantum of *potentia* or disequilibrium to every simple body in space $= -1/r$ (subject to the common nature of the body) (cf. *infra*.).

Now if we return to interpreting Spinoza's own concept of the machine, what we need to think of is not a linkage of points to *potentia*, but rather that each attribute is itself formally affected in determinate places, which are expressed by bodies, according to their composition, as modal sources of power such as A. These modulations, to expand on J. Bennett's insight, grant incorporeal 'gradients' that appear as disequilibria of power in space as we *perceive* it of substance. This should tell us that disequilibrium is not how we should conceive substance, but we must admit it is somewhat difficult to ascertain whether we should regard the infinite power of this substantial machine as entailing: (a) a 'higher' equilibrium, due to the necessity of the divine nature, in which the modulated activity of substance is in fact conserved, with apparent disequilibria being resolved globally through corporeal effects; or (b) a higher disequilibrium in which always some more *potentia* flows into the world, perhaps evidencing similarity to the doctrine of Anaximander (1991), who founded the law-like cosmos in indefiniteness. We would, however, disagree with Bennett's elision of formal essences. Yes indeed the attributes are affected, and these affects of the modes, but the attributes already contain within themselves the formal essences. Thus when Bennett speaks of things as modes affecting attributes, we supplement this analysis by stating that the attributes are already contributing to this picture at every point with the 'gradients' that flag for us formal essences. The modes are not gradients; they are what give gradients a purpose. For what is the point of a gradient if nothing will be determined by it, and there are only modes left in the schema to be determined by gradients. With respect Bennett has confused effect with cause – just because a mode expresses the power of a formal essence this does not mean that the formal essence is a mute construct, and not the active power it actually must be.

We can see how the possibility of some machines being sources for God or Nature's infinite power helps to determine this infinite power in the attributes, but a second determination is also important. The *potentia* at a point might be described as hungry for something to do, because it is entirely formal; it needs a body to subject to a transition. But which transition occurs depends on the nature of this body, and the easiest way to see this is to imagine that our simple body is already moving in another direction than $P_0\,P_1$. What happens geometrically as the body is accelerated is that it changes speed and/or direction. The interrelation between the motion (C) due to a thing's conatus and the infinite *potentia* ($-1/r$) can be considered like the inclined plane of Chapter 3, with the conative motion resisting the infinite *potentia* only in that degree to which it is inclined away from the direction of the infinite *potentia*. Following Descartes, the two powers are composed and we see that indeed the determine power due to the point in space does not exhaust what occurs there, but is itself determined by the nature of the body that encounters it. *Every body in transition presents a solution both to the nature of its body and the divine nature.* It seems to us that this is the physical corollary of the Spinozan hermeneutics, in which our mind with its variable conative power does not read the world, because there is no content other than God or Nature to read, but forces a reading of itself in which the potentia at a given moment is called forth and interpreted according to the idea-body presented to it. The simple body's acceleration is a solution to a formal essence, but so is the completion of the Senecan bridge. Of course, in the Spinozan plenum there is always a body of some kind being acted upon, and this plenum attracts the criticism that the finite general equilibrium would actually counteract any purported transition.[9] A further open issue, which may be integral to the theory, is whether it is the bridge that expresses the formal essence or the natural right expended in its construction, and which consequently brings the infinite mediate mode closer to the infinite immediate mode. With this we hope to have explained how a formal essence in an attribute is not like a picture or a seed of some finite occurrence or thing, but is actually a wider tendency to action, which in a sense needs to be realised or *called* forth by appropriate compositions of finite bodies.[10]

Is this an appropriate physical analogy for discussing Spinoza's theory of infinite power? It might be tempting to regard those infinite motions that pass into rest as the modes of Extension introduced in EIP21–23 (cf. Ch. 3.4.1) as the 'sources' expressing God or Nature's infinite power in the world. Certainly, by definition, rest is expressing infinite power, follows necessarily from Extension, and is consequently eternal and indestructible. Surely something as perfect and virtuous as an indestructible 'mass term' may readily be considered a cog in the infinite machine that expresses this power into the world of duration? Our work in Chapter 3, however, suggests that following Descartes, Spinoza may have preferred to regard what began as celestial fire and became light for Descartes, as the infinitely powerful Nexus[11] between attribute and mode. We shall return to this idea shortly. In the interim, the gravitational hermeneutic tool readily assists us to understand its equivalent in Thought, which Spinoza predictably introduces in EV on human freedom. Here we find the enigmatic Propositions 22 and 23:

> In God however there necessarily exists an idea which expresses the essence of this or that human body under a species of eternity.[12]
>
> The human mind cannot be absolutely destroyed with the human body but there remains something of it which is eternal.[13]

Spinoza's Scholium clearly demarcates this something ('*aliquid*') from the world of finite duration, including the possibility of any memory. There is a dual aspect to this '*aliquid*', one aspect pertaining to the attributes, the other to the modes. In this section we will consider the attributes, leaving the modal perspective to the next. So, beginning with the attributes, the implication is that this something is incorporeal, not corporeal. We regard it as important to carry this logic through and not interpret EVP23 Dem's references to God's conception of an idea of our mind as a reference to this eternal thing being limited to an idea (a corporeal). Chapter 2 stressed that we are dealing with a God in act, and when Spinoza says God conceives of the idea of our mind 'which expresses the essence of the human body' he is referring to that very moment in duration for us in which the corporeal multitude of things compose a mind-body, or we are determined to exist and to act in the general equilibrium. We underscore that God is the immanent cause of this, but only 'remotely' in Spinoza's sense that it is a matter of the finite world of modes, not necessary modes, and as such He is said to have the idea only because nothing else conceived or could conceive this idea in its totality (i.e. guaranteed the efficient law-like causality). This corporeal discussion is categorically a different issue from that of the eternal essences, which this idea expresses. The eternal essences stand like points in a powerful, highly tensed attribute waiting for the right composition of bodies to occur upon them, which will express most fully this infinite power. The mind on this reading of EVP23 is the condition of transition to thinghood of a mind that has ideas of a body. It is such eternal formal essences that are 'things' that remain after the idea-body has passed.

It is possibly quite insulting to Spinoza to deploy here Hegel's phrase 'spiritual masses' but on a crude level it does help us think about that which Spinoza is driving at: namely that in the mind there *is* something that meets the above-mentioned criteria parallel to those of 'rest'. The next step, however, is to determine whether this 'something' is simply passive, or whether it actually expresses God or Nature's infinite power in the world. Several Propositions establish precisely this. From EVP25 Spinoza establishes how the mind develops in understanding God and so increases its power (EVP25) and contentment (EVP28) so passing over into exercising the third kind of cognition, from our desire to understand clearly and distinctly the second kind (EVP28). We now come to the *crux* in EVP29–32. First, EVP29 reads:

> Whatever the mind understands under a species of eternity, it understands not from the fact that it conceives the present actual existence of the body, but from the fact that it conceives the essence of the body under a species of eternity.[14]

The Demonstration makes clear that the mind conceives its body in two ways, first with relation to finitude, second under a species of eternity. This Proposition confirms that it is under the species of eternity that the mind conceives not of the actual body, but from the actual body back to the essence of that body. In other words, although Spinoza privileges the third kind of knowledge, he is not excluding bodies from being cognisable in this way because there are bodies that perceive not only with respect to duration, but also conceive with respect to their immanent cause (i.e. their ideas 'involve the eternal and infinite essence of God') (EVP29 Sch.). From this linkage back to God or Nature, EVP30 returns to our mind by concluding it is necessary that our mind know this linkage – the *idea Dei* – even if it is not aware that it knows this, and with EVP31 Spinoza resolves this motion by saying that 'cognition of the third kind depends on the mind as its formal cause, insofar as the mind is itself eternal'. Combined with EVP32, which notes that exercise of the third kind of cognition brings pleasure and is accompanied by the 'idea of God as its cause' and we see that indeed the mind, insofar as it is blessed (but always blessed to some degree), has the qualities we are seeking, that is, such a mind is the source of God's infinite power in the general equilibrium.

Now it is EVP40 and its Corollary that specifies not only that each thing containing this eternal something may vary in its perfection, but tellingly that 'partem mentis, quae remanet, quantacumque ea sit, perfectiorem esse reliqua'. We emphasise the fascinating insertion of the subclause 'whatever size [the eternal part] may be' for it would seem strange for Spinoza to simultaneously be regarding the eternal part as an unchanging feature of individual mentality, which is simply a gateway to divine contemplation, when at the same time he speaks of quanta of size with respect to it. Yet our mechanical interpretation has led us to expect precisely this, namely that as with simple bodies expressing infinite motion and rest, we can start accumulating them in one place in order to vary their eternal activity. We cannot change their infinite power, but we can rearrange it in concentrations to focus its affects and so 'draw down' the infinite into the finite. We can build machines and by building them we Love them, we reveal their formal essences. Here in the context of EVP40, however, Spinoza's focus is on conceptual construction. Given EVP30 already discussed, we surmise that Spinoza is inviting us to take the innate source of infinite power that we possess and to begin assigning to it concepts *qua* bodies, which, if possessing the requisite mechanical unity, express power approaching the infinite also. We must extend the surface of this machine such that a greater flow of power passes through it, multiplying transitions in the world. Here the best concept is explicitly stated to be the idea of God, but it seems to us that the accrual of concepts of the third kind of knowledge amounts to the construction of a complex machine 'more perfect than the rest'. The task of the sage thus becomes the construction of these 'right-producing machines'.

Indeed we regard this as the moment where Spinoza's conception of the *potentia absoluta* in the individual lifts up away in no small amount from similar theses, say in Descartes or Pufendorf, which remain wedded to a nascent modern liberal political subject. For, by means of this accrual and construction of infinite powers, Spinoza seems not only to be giving content to an infinite power of acting, but actually beginning a process whereby the masses out of which natural right is expressed, themselves become a decentred locus on which the philosophy of right is notionally grounded. In other words, it is machines built directly upon the attributes and expressing absolute power that now disclose the 'subjects' of natural right, the pre-individuals rather than a given individual. It is not so great a step to cut right loose from the individual altogether, and to begin the examination of these machines as varied incorporeal automata that drive 'blind fury' in our world.

Stepping back from such considerations, if our interpretation has grasped the essence of Spinoza's teaching, then we would be wrong to assign to Spinoza the nascent liberal idea of each individual's simple, inalienable power; the source of free activity in the world. On the contrary, the individual thing is determined to will the accumulation of infinite ideas, of concepts, in order to increase one's eternal perfection, and in duration to increase one's reality and engender disequilibriating effects, or transitions, in the finite world. This inalienable power can, indeed must, combine with other sources to transform the world. We hold this to be one of the most profound implications of EIP36 – that nothing exists from which some effect does not follow, for each thing always expresses at least a 'point' source of infinite power. This results in each singular thing always already being conscious of an endeavour to determine some other thing, partially to be the formal essence of that thing. And when we speak of some other thing, this includes all things that constitute the actual individual right up to the composed mode, which is the body of that individual. Thus the essential consciousness of the singular thing is aware of the inevitable difference between: (a) the active flux of the attribute that bears its formal essence; (b) the modal world that expresses that essence; and (c) the expression in that modal world of the need to make up this difference that is driven by the singular, absolute power immanent to it. Remember from the *Letter on Infinity* that the matter in motion in the torus struggles to satisfy the inequalities of space inexpressible by nay number. There is thus to be found another striving, another conatus in the *Ethics*, about which more shortly.

It is the difference between the finite world of duration and the formal power of acting conferred by infinite essences (in every attribute) that creates also an immediate ethical difference between the norms of the enduring present and this albeit contented working of the sage for the third kind of knowledge whereby eternal infinite power will be expressed into the finite world. It is a difference first insofar as the sage comprehends this very difference in the operation of the world (this was the *manuduction* effected by the *Ethics*),[15] and second insofar as the exemplary role of the virtuous[16] derives not simply from being able to struggle and resist a little more than others, but that this exemplar pursues uncommon and radical tasks with limitless, not simply unlimited, activity. Yet the exercise is in essence only logical, or logico-physical in that the logical power stands over against physical actuality of the general equilibrium and impels it. There is a difference here between, on one side, the finite and the actual and, on the other, the infinite and potential; a coupling that encloses natural right in the self-determination of the substance-attribute. Each right-producing machine can be led to the sources of its power and can determine that this power is a fostering or nourishing one, a source of power for the multitude. This is as far, it would seem, as the concept of natural right extends, but we cannot pass on without completing the ethical vision, which just as much derives from the physics in Chapter 3. This is the ethics of the modes.

5.3.2 *The affects of the infinite machine – a modal ethics*

Let us consider again the transitions of a body. This time we will not consider each transition separately such that we would be restricted only to consideration of the simplest cases of variations in motion and rest. Rather, we will consider the very great number of transitions undergone by a body, both pleasurable and painful. When pleasure and pain occur simultaneously and in the same degree, Spinoza calls this a *fluctuation of the mind* (EIIIP17 Sch.). We suffer at any present moment determinations, which are helpful – in accordance with the laws of our nature – and deleterious – against the laws of our nature. These variations are mixed with ideas into an affective confusion that appears as our finite, modal duration. The composition, however, is at least abstractly analytical: every encounter is not entirely in common with us for something differentiates the machines that encounter each other. Thus in each encounter, *sub quadem specie aeternitatis* there is one abstract part that is in common and in accordance with the laws of our nature, which has a certain degree of intensity to procure a certain and determinate transition (*force**), and one abstract part that is uncommon and against the laws of our nature, having itself a certain degree of intensity to procure a certain and determinate transition (*force**). Composing the two elements and considering the abstract flow of time from the first moment of this encounter to the last, we have nothing other than a mode. But let us be slightly more analytic with what is going on here, for pleasure and pain are not as simple as they seem. We need once more to pay heed to Spinoza's distinction between:

(a) *potestas*, understood as capacities to do, and so the laws of a thing's nature that can be assessed as 'in common' or otherwise through encountering some other thing; and
(b) *potentia*, which we have been looking at in some detail and which relates to the transitions of the thing (and so variations of the temporal series).

In fact we are looking from yet another angle at something we have already dealt with: the difference between disposition and relative disposition. We have focused up to now principally on the latter, for we wanted to impress the role of the attributes in relation to transitions. We underline the fundamental link between the relativity of transitions due to *potentia* and variations in the experience of time. We claim that for Spinoza the temporal aspect has nothing to do with the *potestas* of a thing considered in the infinite understanding (ignoring whether capacities may be lost or acquired). The result of this analysis is this: for a given mode we must consider:

(a) its variations with respect to duration (application of *potentia*); and
(b) its variations with respect to its nature (agreement of *potestates*).

Taken together these elements of a mode are none other than the means for assessing the perfection of thing the mode expresses. Hence, Spinoza writes:

> For the perfection of things is to be estimated from their nature and power alone.
>
> (EI Appendix)

Now, as Spinoza writes, these encounters are many and varied and so we must consider that we have a sum of affects in accordance with nature, each of various degrees of intensity, and a sum of affects against nature, each also of varying degrees of intensity. The composition of all these likewise reveals itself as a mode, albeit of presumably ragged outline. If we examine only *potestas*, holding *potentia* constant, these encounters as we have said occur according to commonality of nature. Here also there is potential for confusion between essences and modes. The essences underwrite the *potestas* of a mode (as form) but do not engage themselves in the encounters of durations – only the modes encounter each other in relations of composition. Now the modes, as modes, are in themselves all in common. Thus all modes may encounter each other, though they express different *potestates*. This is the reason why it is possible to undergo painful experiences from things that are against nature. The modes open us to the possibility of experiencing otherness, and so perfection, at the price of pain. But what the mode undergoes in its complete commonality with another mode is not what each thing can recognise through its own inner nature (EIIIP5). Hence, the difference in cognition: one can experience the decomposition of a mode m_1, which expresses one's formal essence, but not the nature of the thing that caused the mode m_2 that decomposed m_1. This is conjectural but it seems that Spinoza regards the measure of commonality as a spectrum of difference at the modal level such that any two modes' difference can be found by comparison of their natures p_i. In an encounter of m_1 and m_2, then, we can compare the scalars p_1 and p_2 in the geometric manner for intensive quanta, simply: $p_1 - p_2 = x$. In this case we may posit a limit as x tends to 0, which is the maximal commonality between modes. We will return to this special case shortly.

We can see from this why Deleuze was led to 'posit' the modal essence as a category of Spinoza's thought, despite no such term being used by Spinoza. Deleuze argues[17] that the EIIP8 Corol.'s statement:

> when singular things are said to exist, not only insofar as they are included in the attributes of God, but also insofar as they are said to endure

justifies his claim, repeated as Duffy notes[18] in his lectures, that there are two types of essences deployed by Spinoza, one eternal and pertaining to the attributes, the other modal and existing in duration. Our reading of Deleuze is that he sees the intensive *natures* of things as being modal corollaries of the intensive essences of those same things, each of which determine the form of a modal existence, with particular emphasis on the role of natures as mutable, material 'essences' over against the eternal ideality of their Thinking and Extending counterparts. We feel that the thrust of this argument is correct, but the willing abuse of terminology hides important aspects of Spinoza's claims, perhaps to favour the qualitative language of essences over any deployment of *potestas*, nature, and law. If this is indeed the move Deleuze makes, in our opinion it actually reduces the radical power of Spinoza's insight, namely that the law of the singular thing is: (a) expressible in terms of its quanta; and (b) a mutable law. Furthermore, it actually argues for a break between the attributes and modes that is arbitrary and denies the causality (and so explanatory roles) between the two, and, at the same time, occludes the actual difference between formal essences as causes and modes as effects that make ethics possible.[19]

Ethics – there is no universal harmony in Nature, only discord (EI Appendix). Yet from discord comes a specific social concord, from below. The composition is not determined in advance according to divine ethical-aesthetical considerations; the composition occurs by comparison of powers – by right – and emerges from the many. Yet we must be careful not to confuse the attributes and the modes. Deleuze argues strongly for the idea of a modal essence but in so doing conflates attribute and modes. The advantage is indeed also to render eternal attributes, with their infinite reason, susceptible also to the multitude, but this deals Spinoza a low blow. It is an attempt to liberate the multitude from the apparent hierarchy of substance-attribute, but in each of these latter what has most reality also comes from the depths. For we have seen that the infinite machine is not given but constructed from below, from infinitely many substances each with an attribute. By keeping the structure of the attributes and their essences separate, and by holding apart the dynamical laws by which the formal and actual essences are composed, we in fact grant to them the independent materiality that is due to the essences, oppose this to the physicality of the substance, and so open the possibility of ethics as the *positive* difference of the two that stands alone as the modes, being neither substance nor attribute. To underline this claim, we reiterate the move above in which the dynamic laws of transitions permitted us and Spinoza to pass to the idea of the mode as a multitude of these transitions undergone in duration. And for this to take place at all the formal essence cannot be a finite mode but must be in the attribute, it must be the situs of modal composition. This is not the same thing as claiming that there is a vessel (formal essence) into which pours very many finite modes, instantiating an inverted Augustine duality. The formal essence is indeed composed with the modes; this is existence:[20] the modes determine to exist and so express the formal essence as actual, subject to a condition. This is the condition that the given composition of 'incoming' modes is not such that it overwhelms the pre-existing composition expressing the formal essence in question. This is decomposition. It is, as Deleuze terms it, a bad encounter. Our point as that the modal composition and the attributive essence must be considered according to the species of power they express and not run together. Consider, for example, the intension brought about by a stone falling in water: the stone is the source of a motion that travels simultaneously through the water in every direction at a certain speed, but the stone (and indeed the water corpuscules) do not themselves travel in these directions. Rather, a disturbance of the water having its source with the stone and determined by its power travels outwards. It is as if a 'shadow' of the stone's presence passes through the corporeal. Now consider this stone's implication of power is of the order of the infinite machine and thus has its source in a formal essence (i.e. the source of infinite power is incorporeal). We claim that Spinoza's categorical distinction of the mode reflects the proposition that while the source itself does not travel, and indeed cannot be exhausted in its implication of power, the mode does travel and reflects the power of the source while being other than it. This is why Spinoza defines the mode not just as *affection of substance*, but also as that *which in something else and conceived through [i.e. by means of] it* (EI Def. 5). This otherness it seems to us has its reason in each finite mode's almost instantaneous separation from the source that determines the necessary transition to affect, as is clear from the constant speed of the resulting mode and thus its capacity for diffusion and dispersion. The infinite immediate mode proves to be the special case of this, not an exception, for the order of reasons proceeds from the finite to the infinite in the shortest possible time. Any affection that necessarily follows from the nature of the infinite machine not only has infinite power at the source, but, Spinoza argues, continues to be determined as infinite as it leaves the source and so on to infinity without any diminution:

> Whatever follows from some attribute of God insofar as it is modified by a modification which, through that same attribute, exists both necessarily and as infinite must also exist both necessarily and infinite.
>
> (EIP22)

Fascinatingly, perhaps also worryingly, Spinoza relies on the preceding demonstration about the necessity of essences that follow from the nature of God to establish this Proposition. He avoids trying to explain it by arguments to the effect that such infinite modes are extremely subtle and pass through other modes at great speed.[21] In other words, it is our view that he actively sidesteps the Cartesian corpuscular explanation of infinite modes, which corpuscules are somehow unimpeded. But at the same time Spinoza wishes to retain the distinction between cause and effect; between essence and mode. The movement of thought appears to be that as this mode can neither be corporeal nor confused with its cause (i.e. incorporeal), it must therefore be neither, which is termed affect. And 'affect' in this infinite or exemplary case is perhaps most instructive, for we see that it is manifested as a kind of formed 'simulacrum' of the formal essence it expresses. This is to say, and here we incorporate aspects of the Deleuzian theory,[22] by definition the formal essence implicates its power in a certain form, this form affects the surrounding bodies in such a many that this affection simulates the form of the given essence *qua* mode no matter how far it travels from its source. It quite literally looks as if the source is everywhere almost at once. Note well, however, that the source is not necessarily the machine that produced it. We have to be careful about the nature of the Spinozan simulacrum, for what is being expressed is operating at a different level from the individual that initiates the mode. Take Spinoza's example of the architect: is the house he builds a simulacrum of the human or of the formal essence around which the composed idea of a house has formed, itself composed with the human? Of course take the *idea Dei*: when the human expresses this idea in the world its infinite power is assignable to the formal essence of the infinite machine, not the human *qua* finite machine. And then also, insofar as the modes propagate in the world and come to settle in actualisations of this house, this human life, this imperium, do these modal sinks not also in their actualisation at the model level express a formal essence. Every mode, every affective composition, leaves a machine bearing with it the mark of very many essences not to die a ragged death but rather in search of life, in search of an actualisation of a further formal essence. This is to maintain always its defining (generative) role as *affection of substance*, for every actualisation implicates at that very point yet another formal essence of substance. The mode, then, is not simply the slave of replication, for when it is defined as being conceivable only through an other, the other in question includes also the formal essence that it actualises.[23]

In the finite case we see that by the relative powers of finite modes the form that each expresses is composed in varying degrees with other forms, thus confusing their respective sources and generating the confused and mutilated ideas in our consciousness (affects in the sense of human passions). Yet it would be unduly limiting to consider the modes as composed according to simultaneity. The concatenation of series is indeed expressed by the composition of modes in the present, but just as each series determines the logic of a life, so ought the modes to be considered as having a certain 'seriality': the arc of a life determined according to its varying pitch or *potestas*. Consequently when we consider again what Spinoza writes about the endeavour to change:

> In this life we endeavour above all that the body of infancy . . . shall be changed into another body which is capable of very many things, and which is related to a mind very much aware of itself, of God, and of things.

we are invited also to consider the modality of this life as it were coming towards us along a temporal axis – the present at every point varying with the mode – such that life indeed has its arc, a loving *fold* under which are organised all the bodies that may be admitted within a mode of that given intensity at the appointed time. The bodies (modes) affected by that mode, that mode which expresses the formal essence of some thing in an attribute, that formal essence being a singularity expressing the power, that is the essence, of substance.

Substance expresses its power as immutable unity (a will against separation); attributes express their power according to a dyad of motive or ideational intensities (a will to emendation); the modes express their power according to a triad of composing, decomposing, and recomposing (a will to creation).[24] This is the intention. However, the incompressibility of Spinoza's world only allows for modes in the form of impulsions, to which is superadded the excessive force of the infinite machine that we express. It does not seem that it could be possible for a modal life so described to occur even in the topos of consciousness. At the very least there seems to be something missing at once marking the boundary between attribute and mode and at the same time permitting a mode-specific reality to be described. To isolate this element, we turn first to the notion of fostering and its role in the Ethics V.

So now, as promised, a point of clarification on the nature of this '*aliquid*' as lacking content. We simply repeat our contention that essences must be conceived as degrees of power that stand as to ideas as the constitutive power stands to the bridge. It is that constitutive power that enables the bridge to attain thinghood, but the very same power could have been 'tapped' to do infinitely many other things in that subspace of Extension. Or another example: the ideas are solutions to a differential equation that includes in itself both essences and 'nature' as determined by the other bodies occupying the subspace. Remember also that here once again we are speaking of formal essences as proximate powers of God or Nature, and not the formal being of ideas that amount to our endeavours to think in the finite world – modal compositions. Thus the '*aliquid*' must be seen not as a 'seed' of a mind but as a nourishing contraction actually encompassing an infinitely wide set of solutions, of which this mind ('hic amor . . . quibus omnibus fovetur') (EVP16 Dem.). It is the form of the modal composition that is our existence, this latter expressing that form as a mode defined by its degree of intensity, or pitch, and severally reciprocal rest and distinctness in Extension and Thought. Does this mean Spinoza marks a transition from fertility to rational mind? If this something is the eternal part of the mind, it is the eternal part of all its trans-human possibilities, to borrow Balibar's term (1997). As Spinoza writes:

> From [the foregoing] it is apparent that the power of the mind over the affects consists . . . fourthly in the multitude of causes by which the affections, which are related to the common properties of things or to God, are fostered [*foventur*] . . .
>
> (EV20)[25]

This statement is only intelligible if formal essences and modal compositions are considered separately in their own right. The infinite power of the mind consists also in its being not only the situs of the multitude, but that by which the multitude of affects are fostered. It is not the mind as idea, even in God, which is critical; rather, it is the fostering power that opens one to the multitude, and thus the path to the common notions and then God, which plays the key role.

What is this fostering? This is to return to the suspended question about the nature of this infinite power that fosters, here in the very heart of Spinozism, and the nature of the Spinozan revelation. God Loves Himself (EVP35). It is not enough to separate God from finite things by separating the *amor intellectualis Dei* (hereafter 'Love'), the love by which God affects Himself, from love as defined in EIII Def. Em. 6. This is to disregard the ethical demand of positing the infinite machine. Rather, we must consider Love as love affecting the infinite machine. But we are told that the affections of God or Nature are specifically the affections of God or Nature's attributes, and are named *modes* (EIP25 Corol.):

> Particular things are nothing other than the affections i.e. modes of the attributes of God, by which the attributes of God are expressed in a certain and determinate way.

The temptation is to interpret this Proposition as claim that it is the mode that is the thing, ignoring the specification of particularity or confusing it with a claim to individuality. Once we consider that from the perspective of EV Love is *the* affection of the infinite machine, we are on guard against such a reading. We have to explain the apparent coincidence between Love as God acting to affect

Himself[26] and the derivation of particular things as affects of God's attributes. For this reason already the first suggestion of a conciliation, where we are to regard individuals as parts of God's love, fails. Love insofar as it is expressed by the third kind of knowledge and has no evident parallel in Extension is very much a rare and excellent subset of the world – it cannot possibly by deployed to account for all the machines in it in a general way. This is easier to see, however, if we approach the matter from the perspective of the infinite machine, with a question: *if God undergoes the affect of Love, why can we not perceive this affect here with us as we perceive all finite things?* Because:

(1) Love, as infinite affect of God, is eternal affect; it cannot be endured like other emotions (EVP33); and
(2) being eternally present to the mind *sub specie aeternitatis*, that is being essential consciousness as such, it is the immanent condition of perceiving all things.

In other words, we interpret EIP25 Corol. as the claim that it is God's affections (Love) that particularise things understood as picking out or actualising their essences (EIP25 God as cause of essence as well as existence). Consequently, the modes are no individual things; the modes are the picking out or actualisation of the formal essences constituted in the infinite understanding (EIP22), this picking out at any one moment in perceived duration constituting a 'particular thing'. In this sense, the Love of God is the certain and determinate *selection* by God of an essence for actualisation. This is the physico-ethical aspect of EIP25 that we determined to ignore at the beginning of Chapter 4. Until now, we have pursued the synthesis of a dynamic system of finite machines set constantly into machine by a singular machine that pours its power into the world; substance and its attributes; physics and logic. Yet in addition, this infinite machine undergoes a very remarkable and specific form of affect – Love – which passes through this system and picks out aspects of the essences and constitutes them as particular things. This is the ethics in the *Ethics*, and its form is that of a modality at the highest pitch and motive power.

This is not all that can be said, however. This idea of Love as selection implies too great a passivity for that which is selected, as if Love 'passes' over the finite machines like a shadow. It is here that the nexus between Cartesian celestial mechanics and the sources of power in the celestial fire intercedes once again to explain why Spinoza speaks not merely of a perception, selection, or mute cognising of a machine, but of fostering. As we know, God is the only possible cause of the operations of finite machines (EIP26), and this causality operates by God's infinite power, which is His essence. Does this power, however, also operate through Love? Well, this Love is God's self-affection. If we take the nature of love as passage to a greater power of acting combined with idea of the object loved (EIIIP13 Sch.), then for the infinite machine we make the same transition as we did for that machine's power in general and ask what is the nature of such a reflexive affection? The answer seems to be that it is the constant determination of God's self to positive transition, to ever more Love. Following our earlier analysis, it seems that for God or Nature there is nothing that can be conceived that is against the laws of its nature, and as such any affection must be composed entirely of intensities in accordance with the laws of that nature. In *nuce*, Love is the passage to limit of all affects. *Cupiditas, quae ex ratione oritur, excessum habere nequit* (EIVP61). We thus have a mode of the highest intensity, which is nothing other than the modal form of the infinite machine (its immutability), transiting through the world of Thought and Extension according to their laws with ever-increasing speed, in infinitely many directions from infinitely many sources.[27] Now, once we understand the intimate link between Love and the limit case of transition that it carries with itself as it passes across and actualises the formal essences, we believe that it follows that this passage is not mute, but that it combines within itself the diffusion of this excessive power as it passes. It is this that makes Love fostering and not a mere cognition understood as a finding out what was there. It is Love because it is accompanied by pleasure and the highest contentment of mind (EVP32 and Corol.). The intuiting observer does not simply perceive, but conceives (i.e. affects what is perceived and produces additional effects). We have a Spinozan theory of revelation.

How might we consider this affection? This is a difficult question. It seems that insofar as Love actualises the infinite understanding by particularising it, there is no determination as negation, but rather only particularisation in a certain and determinate manner. We believe this is the first part of the story insofar as we consider absolute nature or *potestas* alone. Remember the limit case of commonality between modal intensities. This is none other than the relation of potestates between God or Nature and finite thing at that moment when the latter's modes encounter the infinite immediate mode. It seems that for Spinoza, this encounter of maximal commonality is to be conceived of as a composition of the modes in question into a new mode of the greatest reality or perfection (E1 Appendix for perfection of all that is).

Turning to the second part of the story, *potentia*, the mode is Love passing across the multitude of finite machines locked in their general equilibrium. Yet insofar as Love also fosters, that is always determining to a greater power of acting, there must be some determination as negation even if this determination does increase a machine's power. And if this is indeed a determination, however positive, then the finite machine must resist it by virtue of the conatus doctrine. In physical terms, the machine must resist in order to be accelerated, otherwise it is destroyed. The question is interesting for two reasons:

(a) *First*, because it goes to the issue of whether Spinoza's world remains determinately vicious even in the case of the revelation that is divine Love, or whether this infinite love escapes the State of Nature. Compare this with both the Hegelian struggle for recognition, itself a kind of brutal revelation of the higher synthesis made possible by the struggle itself, and also Hegel's idea of truly divine love as being a formative force that is non-violent. The inability to finally decide on Spinoza's position regarding Love must be one of the moments of any appraisal of Hegel's relation to him.

(b) *Second*, and more technically, because there is a real question about whether Love conceived as a mode is coherent because:
    (i) Insofar as Love has most in common with each thing, the commonality of Love and a given second mode augments each to infinity: the resulting composed mode explodes (i.e. its absolute intensity or degree of affect goes to positive infinity and becomes rather an abyss or Khaos, which may or may not be intended).
    (ii) We can ask how can a mode interact with simple bodies, for example, when these are determinable only by other simple bodies. Either the entire mode determines this single body or it is parcelled out between several in some unknown degree. It would seem that the mode thus must simultaneously be globally an affection of the attributes and locally a finite body so that it can implicate its power into the natural order.

We do not have space to answer these questions, and (b) goes far beyond what Spinozism can offer. We would rather seek to summarise the points we have made thus far about Love:

(1) The intellectual love of God ('Love') is an infinite affection of the attribute of God transiting positively through that attribute according to God's natural laws.
(2) Intuition is the clear and distinct conception of a thing accompanied by Love such that that which is intuited (i.e. conceived and Loved) is particularised.
(3) Insofar as a thing is affected by this Love, its power of acting is augmented and this increase in perfection is called fostering.

Love, then, as infinite immediate mode, is the revelatory moment that particularises things and constitutes the present. As such, it is the bridge between attribute and mode, for now we see that the finite modes do not categorically affect the attributes, but are determinations of the infinite immediate mode, with the result being the infinite mediate mode. This is why confusion reigns: the finite modes disturb the divine Love according to its own laws and so cloud our view (Letter 64).

Now we do not believe we have stated anything novel for Spinoza in these conjectures, but have rather rearranged and brought together certain Propositions of the *Ethics*. This work allows us to return to the ethical role of Love and its relation to natural right.

We have already discussed the textual evidence for the notion of fostering. Just as we have seen an affective parallel between love and Love, and have argued for a parallel between existential and essential consciousness, now we claim there is a parallel between conatus as existential striving and fostering as essential striving. This conception can be found in EVP39:

> In this life, therefore, we endeavour [*conamur*] above all that the body of infancy be changed [*mutetur*] into another body which is capable [*apta*] of a great many things, and which is related to a mind which is very much conscious [*conscia*] of itself, of God, and of things.

The conatus to persevere in one's being is augmented by a conatus to change: (a) into another body of greater aptitude; and (b) another, related, mind of greater consciousness. The duality of the conatus is absolutely core to any true appraisal of Spinoza's thinking, and we feel that the implicit assumption that there must be another side to the existential conatus, a sort of conatus to 'live well', is that which Judith Butler[28] is searching unsuccessfully for in her reading of the *Ethics*, to pick just one example. Butler, possibly in the swell of the Deleuzian 'joyful' reading of Spinoza, falls back onto a Spinoza in which the affects are celebrated in a sense because that is what the present has needed (a joyful Spinoza to oppose to the death-obsessed Hegel), but by short-circuiting Spinoza, by making the affects of Part III operate under finite conditions and not considering the limit case, we miss Spinoza's notion of Love as fostering and the correct relation between existence and essence, between perseverance in being and mutation. We must ask of Butler whether it is necessary to reconsider the Spinozan assault on suicide if this is only an existential doctrine and if we can ask whether mutation at every stage is not also a continuous suicide of a particular thing in order to achieve the actualisation of the flux of formal essences. The formal essence issues forth a modal affect that composes with other modes and organises lesser modes (bodies). The bodies do not die; only the principal mode can 'die' by being decomposed (e.g. by losing the ability to organise its bodies). So Spinoza counsels against destroying one's bodies, which is to destroy one's mode, but that is all. It is not the same thing as arguing that this mode expresses the formal essence, but only imperfectly, and that one should seek to emend this mode to improve its expression, and to do so by varying one's mode's perfection. And when we consider that the formal essence itself is part of the continuous activity of God, we also have determination at this level. So there is much of the self to be relinquished in order to recover ever-greater joy through conative mutation. Such a reading is at odds with the prevailing tenor of Spinozan interpretations in which suicide is taken as outwith Spinozism. Take, for example, Žižek:

> What is unthinkable for [Spinoza] is what Freud terms 'death-drive': the idea that conatus is based on fundamental act of self-sabotaging.
>
> (Žižek 2003: 34)

Evidently, it depends about which conatus one speaks, that pertaining to existence or to essence. If the latter, then change becomes that for which we strive, a change in which it is possible for the Spanish poet to become other than himself by means of the power of particularisation (Love) (EIVP39 Sch.).

A reading in which we fall back on the finite affects also then risks interpreting 'living well' as an excess of these finite affects. This misses Love and so misses how this affect alone is not selfish pleasure, save insofar as it is pleasure for God's self and so pleasure in common. Love is pleasure for self that produces pleasure in what is actualised. It is not enough to multiply encounters; one must tend to the field of the mind so that it becomes a habitat for generation of bodies. Now it is also worth underlining that Spinoza only uses this verb *fovere* with human minds, and while he links it through to infinite power, he does not speak of formal essences fostering finite things.[29] It is unclear whether this thus marks off human from divine, the former as an advancement of nourishing power on the divine due to the complexity of the relation that expresses the raw infinite power, or whether Spinoza situates life in the attribute of Thought alone. If the latter, then one might perceive another reason for parallelism being an inadequate appellation for Spinoza's attributes; for he may have taken on board the Stoic tripartite distinction of *hexis* into inanimate, vegetative and soul,[30] and determined to place inanimate and vegetative together as mechanical body, following Descartes, while continuing to regard *mens* as being the highest form of *hexis*. The knowledge of things passes up from the physical God through mind to an *amor Dei* that is life.[31]

5.3.3 Further speculations concerning the infinite machine from the modal perspective

This section is entirely conjectural, offering only the author's current conception of Spinoza's infinite machine in the hope of providing further guidance for the interested. We note the coincidence between the conception of Love as infinitely intense as to nature and so capable of the greatest number of things (EIP35), and Spinoza's insight that 'One' ought not to be said of God (Letter 50). We propose that at the level of substance, this coincidence is best understood by considering that the infinitely many substances that are united in God or Nature are indistinct but as a *complexum*, not a traditional unity. At the core of this is the idea that insofar as each substance is complete in itself, it cannot appear as existent, not because it is absolutely not, but because it exists absolutely as complete (and so relatively before us). A mechanical analogy helps a lot here: think of a series of gears, each representing such a substance and spinning in the classical fashion about its axis. Each and every gear that completes a revolution returns to itself; because its power extends nowhere, its natural right is zero. Each element of this great system of gears is thus constituted according to its nature, but also against its nature in the manner discussed in Chapter 3. That is, if we read EI in the light of Aristoteles' *Meta.Z*, each is synthesised from essence, existence, and we would add from our reading of Spinoza, from an excess of the two. We might call these not possible worlds, but bare worlds – worlds of raw matter.

This idea becomes decidedly material when we consider how we could find out how any given mode is composed. The method is simple enough in conception:

just as we find how many x's are in y by y/x,[32] and over a time period summing all the contributions of each y/x at each point in time, so when given a mode we just divide it by the simplest modes and determine their relative contributions through the duration of that mode. In other words, we divide a composed mode by the pleasure (with nature) and pain (against nature) constituting it and determine the respective intensities of each and every sub-mode of pleasure and pain.

Now this has an obvious mechanical analogy. We have taken on faith that our composed mode is actually a system of gears and applied the case of the most fundamental gear to that system, but applied it inversely (division). This is comparison by natural right – every gear that matches the applied gear jams and is factored out of the system. Only when a difference of right pertains does the right of a given gear stand forth, and it does so out of the substantial level at the level of the modes. Due to the nature of pleasure and pain, this process has to be applied twice; applied once to determine the right with nature, and once literally against nature to determine the corresponding right against nature. This is a kind of transcendental empiricism for Spinozism, one that, in the result, *collapses* down into the modal world of immanence. And it is not merely an academic exercise for Spinozism we claim, for it is this interrogation of substance that is internal to the system itself. An interrogation carried out by the infinite immediate mode.

So it is somewhat in this manner that we envisage the infinite machine: a substantial system of whirring cogs determined to collapse into modal actuality as the fostering power of the infinite immediate mode passing across the attributes.

5.3.4 *Potestas, potentia finita rei, potentia absoluta Dei*

The foregoing interpretation, if correct, helps us interrogate the *potestas-potentia* distinction noted by Gueroult (1968: 388) and famously elaborated by Negri (1991: 191ff.). Negri emends Gueroult in the sense that the former underscores the critical difference between the polemical use of the *potestas-potentia* distinction in EI and its redeployment later in the *Ethics*, and particularly the *Tractatus politicus*, where the *potestas* is no longer hypothesised to be negated, but actually plays a constitutive role. The thrust of this distinction seems broadly correct in that it mirrors other redeployments of terms by Spinoza depending on whether they apply to God or Nature, or as between finite things, and the example we have explicated is that between formal essences in God and the formal beings of ideas that finite minds endeavour to think. Here is how Negri characterises the new meaning of *potestas* with respect to *potentia*:

> Power (potestas) . . . must be employed with the opposite sense, as a basis that makes the real, concrete, and determinate contours of *potentia* stand out more clearly, with respect to any order of possibility or intellectual construction.
>
> (1991:192)

The interpretation we advanced in 4.3.1 above immediately suggests that Negri's reading can be further differentiated into a characteristic tripartite structure, as follows:

- *Potestas*: As the finite endeavour to produce effects, to formally express one's nature (TPII[7–9]), one's habits, one's civil laws and 'sense' of justice, one's obligations and rights in a social contract (TPII[12]). It is capacity to do what we imagine ought to be, and it always falls short, because our will is always determined and not free (cf. TPII[6], where Spinoza critiques the common belief that man '*absolutam habeat potestatem*' from God). This appears modally as the intensity of the mode.
- *Potentia rei sive finita*: The actual finite power a thing has in the *well-ordered* general equilibrium; that power which constitutes the action of things and resolves on each thing's natural right; its actual power of expressing its nature insofar as it prevails. It is the condition of the actually existing order of a sovereign multitude (TPII[17]); the world of struggle, desire and resistance in duration. This appears modally as the extensity of the mode.
- *Potentia absoluta Dei sive potentia infinita*: The intervention of infinite power in the order of the general equilibrium, which is sourced in each individual's mind, but may be augmented both by variations in the general equilibrium but also by the sage who accrues infinite concepts and seeks the company of others for this purpose. This power achieves no more natural right than the *potentia finita*, but its paths are myriad, thus generating new concepts, and its work is tireless. This appears modally as the affect of Love – a constant revelation and nourishment of the other modes insofar as they express particular essences.

To stress this latter point, the distinction between finite and infinite powers does not, however, change how natural right is assessed; it remains the amount of work actually done, or power extended along a line. What has changed, as we intimated at the start of this section, is that: (a) producing the said effect, insofar as the production derives from infinite power, is effortless and brings 'contentment of mind'; and (b) the passage from the beginning to the end of the line may be effected by whichever route possible through the world of duration (homology of right). It is this latter capacity of infinite power that assists the feasibility of exercising natural right across the city, as we shall see in Chapter 6.

We believe this tripartite structure duly clarifies Spinoza's ethical thinking's relation to that of his political theory, but nor should it be seen as imputing to Spinoza a deeply novel methodological structure, both internally (the division now corresponds to the types of cognition) and externally. By the latter, we refer the reader to de Muralt's examination (2002)[33] of the division by Duns Scotus within *potentia* itself between the *potentia absoluta Dei* and *potentia ordinata*, and how this feeds through Occam and others to provide a framework for Descartes, and hence Spinoza, for dealing with questions of will. The precise relations to Spinoza are extremely complex, as de Muralt shows by examining the divisions between successors of the Most Subtle Doctor and the Cartesian 'breakaway', and must be the subject of separate investigation in light of the advances we hope to have made, but we believe it important to mark the possibilities for establishing a more precise relation within this constellation.

5.4 Against a Hobbes-inspired interpretation of Spinoza's theory

This interpretation puts us at odds with authors who advance a 'possession' theory of natural right. Den Uyl[34] is a prime example, when he writes:

> Spinoza's doctrine of natural right is not a statement about degrees of power nor advice about how to obtain power, but rather a statement about the possession of power *per se*. The dynamics of human interaction may be a function of degrees of power; but the conditions for that interaction – that is, the *possession* of a given degree of power – is a separate matter and is signified by the term 'natural right'.

We interpret this as a claim that Spinoza believes that natural right is the unquestionable ground upon which the 'dynamics' of social interaction are based. It is a statement that natural right is properly natural, extends from the state of nature into the city, and consequently is an immanent problematic around which society must operate, whether it likes it or not. We cannot help but sense a certain kind of fear in Den Uyl's interpretation, which is not so much his own, but part of that fear of the state of nature that inheres in the Hobbesian doctrine. Whereas for Hobbes, however, power can be 'domesticated' by the state, Den Uyl at once acknowledges Spinoza's claim to the contrary, but nevertheless, by taking natural right as 'given', fences it off from the possibility for ethical life. And this fencing operates in its legal sense as enclosure, and its political sense as constitution of a finite, atomic, liberal subject: this given natural right is a possession of each that is turned on itself such that the individual is defined by the (finite) natural right that it has. It amounts in our humble opinion to a sublimation of power per se, a sublimation that is cast in the Hobbesian doctrine as liberty within the bounds of the individual, but, according to Spinoza, is a chimaera. Why? For the primary physical reason that whereas Hobbes locates the deviation of atom from the line of fall in the very conatus of the atom itself, Spinoza locates all transitions in power in some third thing. The 'garden' of Hobbist liberty, grounded on physical static forces plus a magical conative impulsion, is erroneous in its physical premises; the liberty that is permitted as the price of submission to Leviathan is empty. Den Uyl is arguing that with Spinoza's theory of natural right, this magical conatus is tied down into the finite, determinate world, which, while coherent from a physical perspective, removes the possibility of law, politics and ethics from the theory. Yet it is Hobbes' doctrine that is the cul-de-sac because we pursue power into the atom and locate a free will that, however, has no reason and as such precludes itself from the activities of the new science, which is asking what it is that a body can do. For Spinoza, what is at stake here is the very possibility of ethics as the emendation of the human condition, an emendation predicated on the belief that we may only determinate what happens by right if we can be certain that only what happens will happen. To the extent that Spinoza takes on Hobbes' theory of natural right, he does not merely remove free will from that theory and reinforce the deterministic aspects, but also, as we have seen in this chapter, thereby establishes the necessity of an infinite power that implicates transitions into this determinate and finite order, and infinite power that is the mind and is variable as to greatness.

Let us phrase this in terms of the alienability of rights. Finite power is alienable because it is communicated to us by finite causes and we immediately communicate it onwards as our volitions: our natural right within duration is alienable. Even though the crux of this finite but indefinite power is the existential conatus, even this must be regarded as alienable because it is determined to exist and to act, and can be determined to destruction. There is no inalienable finite right called conatus in this sense. There is, however, the infinite power of God or Nature immanent to mind which we express and which, by definition, is inexhaustible. This essential, mutative conatus is inalienable. By reason that it always implicates power into the world but never loses any amount of itself, this right may be described as inalienable, and even so with the inflection that while body may be decomposed and ideas likewise, this eternal part remains inalienable in God or Nature; an inflection that switches the emphasis over from the 'possession' of a right to be retained to the right only being known insofar as it is called forth into the world. Hence, it is inalienable only because it is a limitless good that is being shared into finitude. It is a right as an inalienable commons. This is completely at odds with the current juridical interpretations, such as Goyard-Fabre (2002: 102), which, despite Spinoza's words, see the finite, indefinite conatus of EIIIP7 as the *primum movens* and, with Hobbes, as the only causality of natural right.

Yet even if we are unable to grasp the differentiation of *potentia* and must remain in finitude, Spinoza's requirement of an efficient causal relation between power and what actually happens also instantiates equivalence between power *and* some interesting and useful information. This useful information is a concept, but it is easier to think of it as a machine or system, such as a lever or hydrodynamic structure. We have already disclosed the character of this equivalence in Chapter 4: power signifies something, and in the simplest case it signifies a transition in the proportion of motion and rest that constitutes some thing. And further, because we have shown that motion and rest themselves are transitions of the infinite immediate mode, in Spinoza's view we fall back onto substance in act. To state that something possesses power is also to signify that it possesses all these determinate parts, and by so doing, by initiating the process by which we discover the common and particular nature of things, it invites us to see, *pace* Den Uyl, how this concept (or machine) could operate under a different degree of power and about how we, even in our finitude, must *will* to emend it with the knowledge of its nature that we have obtained. And this, at the end of such great labour, is the path to liberation that Spinoza's theory of natural right promises.

Accordingly, a number of criticisms may be adduced that overturn the traditional juridical reading of Spinoza's theory of natural right:

- Methodologically, Spinoza defines a complete definition as knowledge *per causa.* If we assess natural right by the effects it has at any given moment, we have only looked at half the equation. We must describe the cause, and this Spinoza does when, in the definition of natural right, he moves from the free and necessary power of God or Nature to the power of things.
- Den Uyl's statement that Spinoza's theory of natural right is a statement about power one possesses first confuses power and power extended along a line. Only the latter is natural right, and it is only be treating of *all* components of right that we come to understand the breadth of its meaning
- Den Uyl's claim about the equivalence right = 'property' is too limited, in that it reduces down right to the mechanics of the general equilibrium of finite things. That is, all natural right, and particularly that which indefinitely inheres in thinghood as conatus, is alienable and always alienated in the end. Such a system would be ultimately immobile; it requires an inalienable right as a disequilibriating factor, which Spinoza also locates in and around the individual. If anything, this infinite power possesses or 'grasps' a body, not the other way round, but with respect to natural right this power is only grasped as inalienable, as infinite, insofar as it brings about transitions in the world. The statement is thus about community of goods: 'the highest good of those who follow virtue is common to all, and all can enjoy it equally' (EIVP36).
- Furthermore, Spinoza is always clear to specify that if anything *possesses* power, it is God or Nature.[35] It is all too Hobbesian to imagine atoms *owning and controlling* their own quanta of power, with rights of *usus*, *fructus* and *abusus*. Any dynamical power (except that which caused substance EIP34) is located in the formal essences of the attributes and these are the acts of God or Nature. To deny this would be to say either that at every moment a stone falls to the ground, the stone wills to exercise its power to accelerate, or that at the beginning of its descent it wills, in its finitude, to fall all the way to the ground as fast as it can. Spinoza, of course, calls this willing 'appetite', but he would also have it that: (a) the force that initiates descent is not the same force that acts halfway down (no potential);[36] and (b) possessing a new right at each instant is not real possession at all – one has been forced to explicate the right at that instant and that is the end of the matter.
- The 'dynamical' distinction between the power one has now and the possibility of variation is false. Let us take the raw case of a body continuing at uniform speed. This is *still* dynamical because there is still a sum of powers acting upon it, namely the power that constitutes it as a thing and the powers

that cause or permit this continued motion as satisfaction of the general equilibrium of all powers.

- It follows from this power that if one wished to imagine a being that was not being subjected to some dynamic force, this being would not be acting. But a being that is not acting has ceased to exist, so apparently only the dead have natural right.
- As we shown above, we can observe that if natural right was determined solely by motion:rest, then the smallest insect could topple a bridge. Indeed, on this argument, miracles could happen, for the sound waves from Joshua's horn could have toppled the Walls of Jericho. With such miraculous power was it that the Synagogue of Amsterdam excommunicated Baruch Spinoza on 27 July 1656, 'cursing him with the excommunication with which Joshua banned Jericho'.[37]
- Spinoza clearly defines natural right in terms of the power of existing and acting. Our division of consciousness into existential and essential aspects has attempted to elaborate how allegations of simple possession of natural right can close in an individual on a brutal struggle to persist, and in a sense to stop reading the *Ethics* at EIIIP7, taking the conatus straight into the political works. We regard Spinoza as according work equal status not only because work is about expressing one's common and particular nature, but because the doctrine of human freedom, inserting an infinite power at the point of the mind, ensures there is the potential for a transitive augmentation of power that differentiates existence from working, with working being the site of the experience of freedom, existence being reduced to a transitory state over against infinite labour.
- As Spinoza states in Letter 81, if the capacity to rest (even with motion) was the sole factor determining individuality, nothing would be distinguishable within the general equilibrium. It follows that we could not even assign natural right to any thing other than the general equilibrium as such. Simply 'having' power negates itself and we disappear in the divine order; dynamics negates this negation and liberates us as individuals, but only because of the nexus of finite and infinite power.
- A subtler argument that dynamic variation is permissible, but it comes from outside and is only reflected by an 'inertial' reaction of the conatus of EIIIP7, and consequently this conatus is just the site of some other 'donated' right, begs the question of whence this *external* power. It seems strange that someone who already actively abandoned 'transeunt' causality in the KVI[3] for immanence should not have noticed this infinite causal regress. On the contrary, immanence is Spinoza's solution to that very problem – namely, it places God or Nature's infinite power *in* the world at all times as the source of these motions, as the source of a conative endeavour to mutation. But where does he put them other than in the constituted 'machines' in degree according to their perfection? Not only does the argument from inertia alone fail to respond to this problem, but this immanence provides the explanation for the

differences between infinite and finite power, between duration and eternity, between existing and working, and indeed between struggle and peace.

- The application of the above insights has allowed us to explicate the *scientia intuitiva* and so Spinoza's recommendations on accessing this infinite power and organising its effects through infinite concepts and communion with others. It is thus wholly incorrect to claim that Spinoza's theory of natural right does not hold within itself advice on the obtaining of power. At best, it is a claim applicable only to finite power.
- All these metaphysical arguments place Spinoza's theory of natural rights at a fundamentally different level to that of Hobbes, and not simply because of their different foci, on physics/ethics and law/politics, respectively. Spinoza has gone beyond eccentric Hobbism and the fullest exploration of its mechanism, and has resolved through (meta-)physical reasoning on a kind of power (EIP34) that constitutes a limit case of all others and thereby attains new powers that it returns in full into the world (EIP35) at those points where its infinite formal essences are actualised (EIP36).
- All this benefits from even further textual examples:
  - First, from TTPXVI, 'each individual thing has a perfect right to do everything it can, in other words, its right extends to the limit of its power'. Why concern oneself speaking of capacity and limit unless a thing was, be it so determined, capable of operating at the 'highest pitch' of human freedom? Spinoza's is a natural right of the limit.
  - Second, in TPII[5], Spinoza goes on to admit that while his definition of natural right is all well and good, it requires everyone to follow reason in order to exercise it, which sadly most never attain. Accepting this, his political theory must deal with the ignorant and not ideals. To make this statement in his transition to practice makes little sense unless Spinoza envisages natural right as capable of reaching to its limit as part of the formal theory.
  - Third, in TPII[3] Spinoza states: 'God's right is simply *God's power* considered as completely free' (*ius Dei nihil aliud est quam ipsa Dei potentia quatenus haec absolute libera consideratur*). It makes no sense to specify that natural right is (a) God's power (b) insofar as He is considered as completely free, if natural right was defined as simply the power God has. Spinoza seems to believe that in theory, God could have infinite power but be in a position not to exercise it. This would be a God that did not act, which is equivalent to not being at all in Spinoza's view. Rather, Spinoza is claiming God has infinitely more power than could ever be actualised at one moment, but that He must necessarily implicate this power as the formal essences in the attributes according to the divine nature.

For these reasons, we claim that Spinoza's theory of natural right is founded on a definition that looks to the causes of right and, by the analysis of these causes, returns to natural right with an augmented theory of power, of the power of the unfolding whole and then with super-added power folded into it. This has only been possible because, unlike everyone else, Spinoza asked himself what is the nature of the first cause, what the first machine was, as limit case of all machines. Yet we might also approach from the reverse direction, the zenith of Spinoza's philosophy, to see a more decisive difference. This is that while both Hobbes and Spinoza genetically begin from some form of vital motion (circulation of the blood/circulation of substance into attribute), the Spinozan vital motion is just a means of attaining an intuition of the infinite machine in which circulating substance is taken up, but is a concept that now reveals itself as the primary content of the cosmos, helping us to shift our focus from the initial categories to the singular things and their causal series. It is these things that overpopulate Spinozism behind the geometric order. It is these that possess freedom in some degree, not this or that body expressing substance. The freedom of Spinoza is revealed at a different level of cognition, beyond the transition to and as intuition.

The Epicurean idea of a self-liberating atom, by virtue of its material action as vital circulation of motive force, of blood, of city, may well continue to inform Hobbes and, in a sense, Spinoza, but that which proceeds as free is produced by this cosmos and so becomes its freedom materially and not by reference to direct metaphysical suppositions. The logical necessity of God or Nature's freedom pales before this physical necessity of the freedom of the world-machine. Consequently, the Hobbist natural right or liberty of each is revealed likewise in its logico-juridical pallor before the materially constituted freedom of machines that determine themselves as machines (i.e. that call forth the power of the infinite machine). So is the triumphant beast of the atomic liberal subject expelled by the total intermixture in this 'subject' of the excessive condition of its freedom.

We hope, therefore, to have liberated Spinoza's theory of natural right from its hitherto designated Hobbesian sphere. We do not propose to engage in a critique that argues that by virtue of this difference, Spinoza's theory is not really a natural right theory, and that what we have here is indeed the distinction Hegel makes between philosophical right (i.e. Spinoza, which is really about ethics) and positive right (i.e. Hobbes, which is properly juridical). The critique is internal, and derives from the question of whether God or Nature's necessity means that the appearance of disequilibrium is resolved at the level of substance in a higher equilibrium, or whether such a God or Nature must have a certain indefiniteness in its own kind that permits nevertheless an excess of power. If the former case, then as the act of raising a weight 10 ft shows, in order to actualise such infinite power we must expend an equal and opposite amount of finite power. If the latter, is such indefiniteness tolerable (workable even) within Spinozism, or must the *nothing* remain banished?

Moving out from these distinctions from the Hobbist theory of the conatus, let us also compare this theory to those doctrines that see transitions as inherent acts of freedom. Now, when we arrive via the mechanical process at natural right, at work done, it is all too easy to miss something of geometric significance that throws a new light on the Hegelian, Marxist and Derridean reading of Epikuros' doctrine of the swerve (see Ch. 2.5). If we take the passage from line to plane as the negation of the negation, as the point reasserting its freedom against the line by voiding itself into the plane, then how, if we assume this Epicurean freedom, does this construction feed into natural right? Well, on the one hand, we have a negation of a negation as the transition of a point in a line into the plane, but, on the other hand, we are required to consider not just this abstract power, but the power of the rest of the world (or at least the local determinate conditions) as itself transitioning to remain the same (*constantia*). Natural right is not power, it is power to the extent it produces some effect and if we wish to consider it at a moment, we do not revert to power, but take the instantaneous natural right exhibited (also a magnitude). What then geometrically occurs; has a negation of a negation itself *negated* a negation of a negation? The answer is negative: this is the difference of the geometric perspective that is so easily ignored, for the combination, the *product*, of these two powers collapses back into a point, and the world *returns* into simplicity. The Derridean soldier is neither promoted nor relieved, but sent to war against other soldiers, or, to use Pierre Bayle's witticism, 'Dieu modifié en Allemans a tué Dieu modifié en dix milles Turcs'.[38] *Per* Spinoza: 'Quo plures res secundo et tertio cognitionis genere mens intelligit . . . mortem minus timet' (EVP38). For work or natural right at any given moment are not magnitudes, but scalars. As point, natural right forms the ground again upon which this process of negation builds, the real geometry of finite existence within the boundaries of one substance. On this basis, we might imagine Spinoza as regarding (neo-)Epicureanism as a freedom too easily won, which is sublated, in its own success, in the affirmation of substance's own necessarily determined liberty. Perhaps it is this Spinoza to whom Hegel speaks of work and the unfulfilled point:

> Therefore the only labour . . . of general freedom is death, and indeed a death that has no inner circumference or fulfilment, for what is negated is the unfulfilled point of the absolutely free self; it is therefore the coldest, flattest death.
>
> (*Phänomenologie* 1969(III): 331, §591, emphasis in original)[39]

Can Spinoza respond to these criticisms? We would say he fully accepts the eternal return to substance, but has more to add on the mutual self-destruction argument of Bayle. The missing distinction he would point to is once again the difference between finite and infinite power, which appears as the difference of duration (effort) and eternity (liberty). Having shown how the fluid system in act can be used as an intuitive example of dynamic equilibrium, whereby work is seen as intention to some definite end, we now endeavour to explain the meaning of infinite power in the world. Imagine a point particle P travelling at constant speed from A to B. U is a thing that acts on P. If we consider U as constituting a dynamic equilibrium for P (it is the blood stream to P's worm), then U must exert its finite power if it is to force P to accelerate or decelerate. Notice that there is a full range of transitions that *U* could perform, requiring more or less effort, and which results in the expression of natural right. Notice also that *U*'s power to produce a change cannot come from its equilibrium (which only resists) but from outside – *U* must itself have been determined to act to produce one of the determinate possible accelerations, and it expends itself in so doing. With infinite power, Spinoza signifies a power that is inexhaustible; one that institutes a transition of its own accord, does not tire in producing this effect, and indeed not only can produce a dynamic envelope of possible accelerations, but, by inexhaustibility, includes paths and accelerations of any form. Spinoza passes to the limit: *any operation whatsoever may be performed*, though this power endeavours to produce them all, and so resolves into a determinate surface, contoured by degrees of power relative to the locus of its source. The simplest example is the *P* that falls from *A* to *B*, but in between is lifted back a bit to *A*, then sent sideways by some particle *Q*, then back again by *R*, before arriving via this tortuous at *B*. Was what we now call gravity restrained from acting? Did *U* tire in any way? Absolutely *any* path could have been taken thanks to the intervention of bodies, and the same amount of natural right of *U* would have been expressed (*power between B and A*). We claim that it is such a power that Spinoza identifies with all 'things' in some degree and which is exercised as the *scientia intuitiva* as the science and exercise of this infinite, super-added power. It is a power of producing work that never tires in its exercise, no matter what variety of paths are demanded for that exercise, and it is because he believes the human as 'mind' can realise a mode of cognition that is nothing other than this power (at least in reasoning) that the sage is free (i.e. unfettered in this respect by the burden of the dynamic equilibrium). When we pass to consider a city of the wise in the next chapter, we ask the reader to bear in mind that such a city is operating also at this third level of consciousness in which the efforts of the sage operate without limit or exhaustion. Hegel continues to be correct that right resolves on a point and *P must endeavour to arrive at B*, but while Spinoza holds to the view that substantially this is inevitable, this definite natural right contains within it now three modes by which it may be perceived (or conceived) in which, in this third case, conception runs free and untrammelled in its ability to consider possible paths and to rearrange the machinery of the world to take them into account.

5.5 Conclusion – from the individual to the social

In the last two chapters, we have analysed Spinoza's theory of natural right and laid bare the basic structure of that natural right and its interrelation with consciousness. Following a conceptual division of consciousness into simple existential right and extensive or thinking essential right, we have determined that each is but natural right considered now as effect, now as cause. Our method of analysing right by limit cases has allowed us to see *first* that in the simple case natural right is constructed from the existential simplicity of God or Nature, a degree of body, defined by its common and particular nature, a certain proportion of motion and rest, transitions in this proportion, all extended along a line. *Second*, we uncovered the nature of the divine machine and the source of its power in the finite world of duration. The fact that this source pours forth from the individual, but is also capable of variation in size according to a logic of construction using infinite concepts and communion with others already indicates to us that having attained the third kind of knowledge, for it is the very product of labour to create this difference between the physical and the logical, the difference that creates the situs for ethics. Hence, *third*, we believe we have correctly determined the difference between the sphere of natural right, which makes ethics possible, and the sphere of Spinozan Love, which is the ethical mode for the multitudes of the world. The mode has its apex around the singularity of the labourer. Each labourer by natural right expresses the power of God or Nature by building out the situs from this apex as that place in which the multitude of bodies may congregate and be empowered by Love. This is, first and foremost, why the *sui iuris* human finds in the city the home of her freedom (EIVP73): the city is a building site of this mode. We must always return to into the city to discover the social operation of natural right.

Notes

1 In the modern, not Spinozan, sense.
2 One suspects Spinoza would locate this restraining power in the angle of pouring (it is an inclined plane) and the sideways pressure of the air corpuscules, which the fluid must force out of the way.
3 '. . . n'y a-t-il une seule faute morale, et l'on comprend que les stoïciens lui attribuent une égale gravité, quelle que soit la forme qu'elle revête: c'est de ne pas obéir à l'impératif du présent'.
4 'Ce droit de tenter notre chance et d'entreprendre, appelons-le droit formel par opposition au droit réel; il repose sur une opinion bien illusoire, mais, du moment que cette illusion existe, le dynamisme qu'elle engendre est naturel et légitime.'
5 It is very important to see that gravity, if Spinoza is thinking of it, is just a special case of his theory of transitions (and it is true that gravity is a special case of a wider theory, which we cannot broach here).
6 Harris, E. 'Schelling's Spinozism', in Curley and Moreau (1990: 368).
7 Compare the Cartesian hermeneutics advanced by Clauberg (Appendix 1, Spinoza's Library Bk. 127) and Lagrée (1989).
8 Cf. n. 4 *supra*. At the very least, such powers must be regarded *themselves as solutions* to the divine nature.
9 Cf. Part II of Newton's *Principia* for how such a model cannot work, although as we have already stated, motions as such are also bodies and it is not inconceivable that Spinoza regarded celestial fluid as ethereal motions (bodies) rather than as massive corpuscules (bodies).
10 Compare Hegel (1969: 6, 167–179).
11 A term deployed by Cusanus to describe the human link between body and the eternal Night. Cf. De Gandillac (1941: 446ff.).
12 'In Deo tamen datur necessario idea, quae huius et illius corporis humani essentiam sub aeternitatis specie exprimit.'
13 'Mens humana non potest cum corpore absolute destrui, sed eius aliquid remanet quod aeternum est.'

14 'Quicquid mens sub specie aeternitatis intelligit, id ex eo non intelligit, quod corporis praesentem actualem existentiam concipit; sed ex eo, quod corporis essentiam concipit sub specie aeternitatis.'
15 EII Pref.
16 EIV Pref.
17 Deleuze (1990a: 192).
18 Duffy (2006: 110).
19 For an excellent discussion of 'modal essences', we cannot recommend Duffy (2006) highly enough.
20 In fact, not quite – without the infinite mode's intervention, there remains no existence.
21 Cf. Descartes' *Optics, First Discourse* esp. (1965: 69–70), and PPIII[64], and, by way of background, his *Le monde*, Ch. 13.
22 Deleuze (1994: 69, 299).
23 This is the ethical aspect of the infinite immediate mode considered first as revelation, for despite its infinite power this mode is a simulacrum of its formal essence, Love as affection of God, which presents to us Being in no way as copy or representation of Love (or God). We simply do not see the ideality of the form that moulds this mode; *we see because of it.* Hence, Hegel is correct to argue that Being in this manner is pure Nothing, but for Spinoza the purported emptiness of the simulacrum of Love, deriving from the inexhaustible power of its source, is full, full of all the world that it particularises – the whole face of the universe. The simulacrum of God or Nature is not a mute copy of God or Nature, the simulacrum *is* the multiplicity, namely infinitely many things in infinitely many ways (EIP16). And if we realise this, we understand that the claimed 'purity' of Being was false all along; the simple and elegant form of the infinite immediate mode was itself composed of a multiplicity of modes deriving from one source. This, in some degree, is the result achieved by Hegel by means of the dialectic. The law of Being is unfolded in its plenitude and we discover on return that the law of Being (in relation to Nothing) is given by this very unfolding. No matter how deep we delve into the forms of the world, no matter what concatenation of causes determines the actualisation of some thing, that thing expresses exactly the same law of unfolding as did pure Being (in relation to Nothing). Spinoza, for his part, proceeds straight to infinite multiplicity, exploding in that direction for want of restraint.
24 It is a structure that evidently lacks void as a will to death (see Žižek below), which has a number of problematic consequences.
25 'Ex quibus apparet, mentis in affectus potentiam consistere . . . 4. In multitudine causarum, a quibus affectiones, quae ad rerum communes proprietates vel ad Deum referuntur, foventur.'
26 To emphasise, from Ch. 2 we know that the attributes are the acts of God or Nature, so the mode of the action is its affect and there is coincidence with the definition of mode in EIP25 Corol.
27 It is a question of considering the dynamic immutability of God or Nature distributed as essence according to the attributes of Thought and Extension, accelerating in proportion to the principles of rest and ideational distinctness. Again, this is simply what EIP25 Corol. states.
28 Cf. the discussion of Butler's encounter with Spinoza by Hull in Sharp and Smith (2012: 154).
29 EV20 links the *amor Dei* with 'fostering'.
30 SVF2.988.
31 'Dei natura gaudet infinita perfectione, idque concomitante idea sui, hoc est idea suae causae, et hoc est, quod in coroll. prop. 32. huius amorem intellectualem esse diximus' (EVP35 Dem.).
32 I.e. how many 2s are in 10 is given by 10/2.

33 Cf. also Boulnois, O., 'From divine omnipotence to operative power', in Schütz and Traversino (2012).
34 (1983: 8), emphasis in original.
35 Den Uyl himself quotes Spinoza two pages before stating: '[because] the power of things to exist and act is really the power of God, we can really see what the right of nature is' (TPII[3–4]).
36 If this is not clear, consider the absurd position of a point-like motive force acting on a body in what is otherwise a vacuum. By EIIIP4 it will, with that one moment of force, proceed in a determinate direction without the need for any further application of motive force. When a stone falls to earth, however, at each locus of its moment some derivative force is acting, which propels the stone up to the maximum power of acting of which that power of being is capable.
37 Cf. Nadler (2006: 5–6).
38 (1740: 262).
39 'Das einzige Werk . . . der allgemeinen Freiheit ist daher der Tod, und zwar ein Tod, der keinen innern Umfang und Erfüllung hat, den was negiert wird, ist der unerfüllte Punkt des absolutfreien Selbsts; es ist also der kälteste, platteste Tod . . .' Cf. also Derrida (1982: 83) and Badiou on Spinoza and death (2009: 198, 268–270).

Bibliography

Anaximander (1991) *Fragments et Témoignages*, M. Conche (ed.), Epimethée, PUF, Paris.

Badiou, A. (2009) *Logics of Worlds*, Continuum, London.

Bayle, P. (1740) *Dictionaire historique et critique* (4 vols), 5th edn, Des Maizeaux (ed.), Brunel *et al.*, Amsterdam, La Haye, Rotterdam, Utrecht.

Clauberg, J. (1968) *Opera omnia philosophica, postum hrsg. von Johann Thedoro Schalbruch*, orig. 1691, Nachdruck Olms, Hildesheim.

Curley, E. and Moreau, P. (1990) *Spinoza: Issues and Directions – the Proceedings of the Chicago Spinoza Conference*, E.J. Brill, Leiden.

Deleuze, G. (1988) *Spinoza: Practical Philosophy*, R. Hurley (trans.), City Light Books, San Francisco, CA.

—— (1990a) *Expressionism in Philosophy: Spinoza*, M. Joughlin (trans.), Zone Books, New York.

—— (1990b) *The Logic of Sense*, C. Boundas (trans.), Continuum, London.

—— (1994) *Difference and Repetition*, P. Patton (trans.), Continuum, London.

—— (2006) *Two Regimes of Madness: Gilles Deleuze – Texts and Interviews 1975–1995*, Semiotext(e), New York.

Den Uyl, D.J. (1983) *Power, State and Freedom: An Interpretation of Spinoza's Political Philosophy*, Van Gorcum, Assen, The Netherlands.

Derrida, J. (1982) *Margins of Philosophy*, University of Chicago Press, Chicago, IL.

Duffy, S. (2006) *The Logic of Expression: Quality, Quantity and Intensity in Spinoza, Hegel and Deleuze*, Ashgate, Aldershot.

Gandillac, M. de (1941) *La philosophie de Nicolas de Cues*, Aubier, Montaigne, Paris.

Goldschmidt, V. (1969) *Le système Stoïcien et l'idée de temps*, VRIN, Paris.

Goyard-Fabre, S. (1997) 'Hobbes et Spinoza ou La Différence des concepts – L'ampleur d'une litôte' 3 *Studia Spinozana* 229.

—— (2002) *Les embarras philosophiques du droit naturel*, VRIN, Paris.

Gueroult, M. (1968a) *Descartes selon l'ordre des raisons: II – L'âme et le corps*, Aubier, Éditions Montaigne, Paris.

—— (1968b) *Spinoza: I – Dieu*, Aubier, Éditions Montaigne, Paris.

—— (1974a) *Spinoza: II – L'âme*, Aubier, Éditions Montaigne, Paris.
Hegel, G.W.F. (1969) *Werke in zwanzig Bänden*, Suhrkamp Verlag, Frankfurt am Main. The Roman numeral following the year refers to the volume number.
Lagrée, J. (1989) 'Clauberg et Spinoza. De la logique novantique à la puissance de l'idée vraie', in *Méthode et métaphysique, Travaux et documents du groupe de recherches spinozistes*, no.2, PUP, Sorbonne.
Malebranche, N. (1992) *Œuvres*, Rodis-Lewis (ed.), Gallimard, Paris.
Matheron, A. (1969) *Individu et Communauté chez Spinoza*, Éditions de Minuit, Paris.
Molesworth, Sir Wm. (ed.) (1839–1845) *The English Works of Thomas Hobbes of Malmesbury* (11 vols.), London.
Muralt, A. de (2002) *L'unité de la philosophie politique: Duns Scot, Occam et Suarez, au libéralisme contemporain*, VRIN, Paris.
Nadler, S. (2001) *Spinoza: A Life*, Cambridge University Press, Cambridge.
—— (2004) 'Les vérités éternelles et l'autre monde: les racines juives de Spinoza' 4 *Les Études Philosophiques* 507–522.
Negri, A. (1991) *The Savage Anomaly: The Power of Spinoza's Metaphysics and Politics*, University of Minnesota Press, Minneapolis, MN.
Newton, Sir I. (1999) *The Principia – Mathematical Principles of Natural Philosophy*, I. Bernard Cohen and A. Whitman (trans.), University of California Press, Berkeley, CA.
Schütz, A. and Traversino, M. (eds) (2012) *The Theology of 'Potential Dei' and the History of European Normativity*, Divus Thomas, Bologna.
Sharp, H. and Smith, J.E. (eds) (2012) *Between Spinoza and Hegel*, Bloomsbury, London.
Žižek , S. (2003) *Organs Without Bodies*, Routledge, London.

6

Juridical physics

> certis est vinculis complicata, quibus vita nostra veluti religata coercetur.[1]
>
> (Pierius, *Hieroglyphica*, Bk. XIV)

6.1 Introduction

We have considered the following types of natural right:

(a) natural right as determination of another to exist and pursue the linear flow of that existence;
(b) natural right as determination to work, insofar as it expresses finite power as formal being and actual essence; and
(c) natural right as free work, insofar as it expresses the infinite power of formal essence.

We are now in a position to actively consider the dynamics of Spinoza's legal theory. Moving from a brief consideration of the composition of bodies, we will attempt to show how our understanding of natural right allows us to posit the city as a tool (or concept), which Spinoza hopes he can design to be a right augmenting machine. The inspiration for this model, we believe, has its physical origins in the Cartesian celestial hydrodynamics. As will be seen, our reconstruction of the Spinozan theory of natural right, in the light of Spinoza's categorical and physical premises, grants us a prospect over a juridical physics of astonishing grandeur.

6.2 The construction of the finite imperial mode

6.2.1 Complex bodies

If composite bodies are constructed along the lines of Seneca's bridge (thus having a degree of modal endurance due to expressing an essence), complex bodies permit composite parts to act according to their natures, such that the complex body β loses nothing of its 'form' or ability to communicate its characteristic movement and rest. To understand this, it is instructive to draw on the Cartesian celestial mechanics, for the model of the vortex, which we claim takes on the characteristic dynamic-system structure in Spinoza's physics,[2] operates what Schuster calls a kind of 'enveloping'.[3] DPPIIP16 suggests that Spinoza differs from Descartes in that the latter regards the action of the vortex as a combination of tangential and circular motions, whereas Spinoza believes the action results from a combination of tangential endeavour and *coäction* towards the axis of the greater power. It is to be observed, however, that the *ecliptic* of any such transitional work need not be set as simply the surface of β, but rather at the point at which the simple bodies in the region around β cross a threshold from being generally and particularly determined by the greater power to being generally determined by the greater power but particularly determined by the particular power. The stone in the sling is ultimately determined by David's power, but its motion around the sling's axis is particularly due to the nature of the sling; David, as the greater power, becomes 'David-sling' for the stone, indicating thorough intermixture. This, of course, is as far as β's natural right extends (its essential consciousness). Descartes infamously explains this region as akin to the eddies and little vortices one find in a river, whereby the vortices have a particular local movement due the vagaries of the current, and a general movement in that the whole vortex moves down stream. In Spinoza, it seems that the general thrust is rotated by a right angle, but that the basic principle remains the same.[4] Such a region is already possible in the case of transiting composites, by virtue of the enveloping action not only forcing the simple bodies together, but also in a direction, such that they elongate along that axis and affect the simple bodies ahead of that motion. In the case of complex bodies also, we can see that it is precisely because every act of β is equally subject to the general work of some greater power ω, that we are to a certain degree able to ignore ω in cases where the natural right of any b subjected to β becomes sufficiently small in relation to β. From the perspective of β, the work of ω disappears because β's perspective is the work of ω. From ω's perspective, as its power becomes sufficiently great $b = \beta$, such that the work of β does little to impede the general endeavour to force b around the source of ω. We shall call this the *vortical model* of natural right. This follows, Spinoza believes, from the general equilibrium of the celestial plenum, but it occludes something that 'shines' through to explain why this envelopment should occur here rather than there. This, we suggest, is the nexus of attribute and modes in the spinning action of the infinitely powerful thing, expressing formal essence. Here at this point in the general equilibrium, there is an additional recurrent disequilibrium as a free component derived from the attribute of Extension, which drags other bodies around it and towards it. As Spinoza realised, this disequilibrium must be super-added *and* sited at a specific source in 'β', on condition that previously bodies have been related by the general equilibrium in such a manner to express this formal essence in this way.

This structure becomes infinitely more problematic, however, when we aim to consider three or more bodies constituted by relatively equal power, each of which

his own solutions
ıng human relations
.n analysis may lead

relations. Just because
.ot entail that the same
und offers augmentation
ɹut not insofar as they fall
considering the transition
the civil relations can only
Spinoza's term, and may be
al civil conditions.

perium

formally for multiple interactions,
ne assumption hereafter that every
:ly great powers that determine for
ɜr, we move from considering how
ɹowers, to considering only how they
:ss. This is to say that we now consider
other *and* the ideas that pass between

ʒ β endeavours to cause each mode of its
thing β's own nature as a thinking thing.
:ans that this endeavour already expresses
ıatural right. Such cases are quite limited in
ty there will be a great number of equal rights
ıe ideas to express their own nature. One can
ˌition of powers that what results[5] is not in fact
ʒle to dominate ideas, but rather an instantaneous
a single ideational circulation and intensity. At
.he general equilibrium, but then we must add the
ısequilibrium, which implicates formal essential
he question thus arises: what is the structure of this
t can be seen from the nature of the right exerted by
ʌers are superposed a vector sum is created[6] for every
ıch, it is more correct that we continue to consider the
ɹy each thing on these small bodies. We are therefore
ıgnitude of the power exerted at a point, but rather the
ılong which the smaller bodies circulate, which, according
ɹstatic model, form a series of ecliptics around a given pole.
also provides the idea for considering what happens when
:ther at a given point. For:

avier bodies (with greater
a 'col', a point at which
two river currents flowing
ches of a hyperbola) in

ɔlds that given a relative
nasses are born around
decreases as one moves
ɜr bodies will be born

y will, all things being
n extension. In other
power at any point
ɜr, though Descartes

ation of powers to
schema of natural
owers, such that,
surfaces appear
ɜ a dynamic sur-
l *actualiter* by the
ıtural right and
nstantaneously
finite powers.
interpretation,
ody on which
rtional to the
:s will form a
ıtion around
se distances
ecause it is
runs quite
ɾe see that
ɜtermined
ɾdy in the
he other.
gularity,
or ideas

f equal
other
right
flows

(a) According to Descartes, at this point only the h
momentum) can pass over what we would term
circulatory flow of the powers meets, as the figure of
towards and away from each other (like to bra
Le monde illustrates.[7]

(b) Likewise, as we have seen in Chapter 3, Descartes h
extension of these small bodies in which the greater
spheres of primary matter, the impulsion of these stars
away from them to a threshold, at which point larg
away, like the comets, to other circulatory systems.[8]

(c) Accordingly, an ecliptic swept out by a given simple bo
equal, coincide with the equal degree of power exerted
words, the distance r from the pole to equal degrees o
will be the same (and inversely proportional to that pow
does not take this step in his formulation).

In case (a), the turbulence of forces equals out in the sumn create what we can term a 'col', another singular point in the right. In case (b), the rule holds subject to the summation of whereas in the Cartesian diagram of celestial vortices arbitrar between areas of circulation, Spinoza more correctly determin face at the point where a thing's nature is more or less expresse activity at that point. All this follows from our discussion of n the incorporeality of the attributes, which proceed 'everywhere' to determine actual modes as constituted by multiple instances c If we dare to venture much further than Spinoza in our physical we may observe that in extremely simplistic cases, the power on a two poles or bodies exert their natural right will be inversely prop respective distances from each body, and that the sum of these righ single transitive magnitude that is equal on a combined line of circul both bodies, and which is at every point equal to the product of th $(r \cdot r)$. The reason we choose to venture forward in this manner is quite revealing about the nature of the combination of powers, which contrary to the isolationist atomic model preferred by Hobbes. For while immediately about two bodies the flow of simple bodes or ideas is to be circular (or ecliptic), as we move out and the right of the other b dipole relation becomes relevant, the flow of each tends a little towards As we move further out, a point in the flow is reached that is a *col* si where the two flows run against each other, and in principle larger bodies can pass between smaller spheres of right.

Most importantly, as we proceed inwards from now on, the points c power can no longer be found between the bodies, for at these points th body overwhelms the right of the first, but outside of these regions th combines as if the two bodies were acting as one extended body, with the of simple bodies passing around both of them in a great ecliptic. The flow at every stage is deemed possible by a Cartesian conclusion stated by Spinoza in DPPII Def. 9 that a 'circle of bodies' is brought about by continuous impulsion between the bodies 'even though the figure formed by all the bodies together . . . may be very contorted', a conclusion enhanced by Spinoza's own hydrostatic investigations. We pick out this definition because of the remarkable similarity of the figure that accompanies it and the form of the flow of right around two poles in the regions outside that flow, which forms the just-discussed *col*. Though it may be objected the DPP figure presupposes a fixed tube, Spinoza's Letters 6 and 32, and the fundamental role of *motus ad quietus*, should have by now disabused us of any temptation of admitting a dualism of solid and fluid as prior to motion and its dynamic variations.

In this way, we can understand the kind of model that inspires Spinoza to declare: 'if two humans come together and join forces, they have more power over Nature, and consequently more right, than either one alone . . .'[9] Compare Descartes' pulley theory of light in Chapter 3. The summation of powers thus takes place, but in addition we see that formally three things occur:

(a) the power of being affected is likewise increased communally by the great ecliptics described;
(b) the greater force exerted in the outer ecliptics acts to cushion and protect the remaining inner ecliptics of each body in its immediate vicinity; and
(c) it is possible to consider that the power formally exerted derives from a unique pole determined as the common power of two or more bodies.

As to this latter point, which presages the issue of the common notion, Deleuze is thus perspicacious in his declaration that:

> should two individuals completely combine their relations, they would naturally form an individual twice as great, having twice as great a natural right. The state of reason in no way either does away with or limits natural rights, *but raises them to a power* without which such rights would be unreal and abstract. (1990a: 264, our emphasis)

Deleuze seems to have intuited that a conceptual distinction between the state of nature and the state of reason is indeed determined by the raising of a power, not simply in the additive sense, but also, with respect to the pseudo-individual thus combined, properly as a transition from one order of power to another. One can see that as we move around our two poles along lines of equivalent right, these directed *lines* of magnitude, when produced, will, by definition, always express the same power though constituted in different proportions. Once again, we recover the surface of Chrysippos, this time as the binding together of flows of *corpora simplicissima* along these contours of right. And each surface of right appears, in the equality of its power, to be projected from a source unchanging in that power but varying in its locus between the two actual origins. It *appears* as if the combined force has its origin elsewhere than in the individuals.

Returning to the circulation that now operates around two or more bodies, we can perceive why Spinoza is keen to adopt the language of lifeblood to describe the community of right within the city, and not merely as an abstract vital circulation, but as hydrostatic determinant. He states in an oft overlooked paragraph in TPV[5]:

> So when I say the best imperium is one where men pass their lives in harmony, I am speaking of human life, which is defined not just be the circulation of the blood and other features common to all animals, but especially by reason, the true virtue and life of the mind.[10]

Here it may be conjectured that Spinoza follows Hobbes in dividing vital motions such as blood circulation, which occur even when sleeping, from endeavour, pleasure and pain as the starting point of 'thought',[11] but while there is a division, Spinoza opposes the true life of the mind to vital motions within the social context. The language of reason is linked to power and life, and thus to the circulation of that reason that occurs between individuals of most like nature. Thus, also, if we turn to the key political propositions in EIV, we find a similar language of flows, harmony and increase in the power of being affected that derives from the above-described model of natural right. Turning to Propositions 39 and 40 of the Fourth Part, we see that these are among those that constitute suspended propositions that appear to lead nowhere in the flow of the *Ethics*. Indeed, EIVP39 is not even referred to by EIVP40, and it is quite possible to assume, given their respective subject matters, that the two are only indirectly linked, for they state broadly:

- *(P39)* Those things which bring about the conservation of the ratio of motion and rest that the parts of the human body have to one another are good (and the contrary are bad).[12]
- *(P40)* Those things which contribute to a common society of men, or, which bring it about that men live in concord, are useful (and the contrary introduce discord).[13]

Yet in light of the social *imperium* we are constructing from the principles of natural right, we are now able to interpret these passages also in reference to the flows of essential consciousness that pass about a multipolar world. As regards EIVP39, at the extremely abstract level of a dipole construction using two bodies, we can see (from the Scholium thereto) how 'the body needs many other bodies for its conservation', though these do not form a constituent of the body, which is preserved. These variable bodies pass in and out of essential consciousness, providing sustenance not simply by a transfer of power to that body, but by constituting its very world as a sort of 'cushion' or 'envelop' in which the very acts of willing may take place. This is easier to see if the circular flows are placed is generally subject to ω. Though Spinoza attempts to provide his own solutions to this issue of bodies acting equally on each other by simply taking human relations as a given, we will suggest that this failure to pursue such an analysis may lead his political theory entirely astray.

A related issue is that of the relative basis of augmentative relations. Just because one relation is augmentative in certain conditions does not entail that the same relation works to augment in any condition. Thus the ground offers augmentation of power to animals insofar as they occupy its surface, but not insofar as they fall towards it. We should therefore bear in mind when considering the transition from the state of nature to the civil state that many of the civil relations can only be augmentative in the wider city or *imperium*, to use Spinoza's term, and may be useless or positively harmful without those additional civil conditions.

6.2.2 Circulation: the lifeblood of the imperium

Assuming that the above vortical model holds *formally* for multiple interactions, we now move into the social realm proper, on the assumption hereafter that every body is already subject to infinite and relatively great powers that determine for every body relative motion and rest. Further, we move from considering how bodies may be composed by these greater powers, to considering only how they interact at the level of essential consciousness. This is to say that we now consider the natural right exerted by each on the other *and* the ideas that pass between them.

As we noted in Chapter 5, each thing β endeavours to cause each mode of its essential consciousness to express that thing β's own nature as a thinking thing. However, the general equilibrium means that this endeavour already expresses the whole face of the universe in its natural right. Such cases are quite limited in relation to human right, and in society there will be a great number of equal rights being exerted that determine simple ideas to express their own nature. One can see from the principle of superposition of powers that what results[5] is not in fact a frothy turbulence as rights struggle to dominate ideas, but rather an instantaneous summation of rights to produce a single ideational circulation and intensity. At the finite level, natural right is the general equilibrium, but then we must add the essential consciousness of disequilibrium, which implicates formal essential tendencies into this world. The question thus arises: what is the structure of this superposed consciousness? It can be seen from the nature of the right exerted by each thing that as these powers are superposed a vector sum is created[6] for every body in the plenum. As such, it is more correct that we continue to consider the potency *in actu* exerted by each thing on these small bodies. We are therefore interested not in the magnitude of the power exerted at a point, but rather the contorted lines of flow along which the smaller bodies circulate, which, according to the Cartesian hydrostatic model, form a series of ecliptics around a given pole. It is this model that also provides the idea for considering what happens when two flows come together at a given point. For:

(a) According to Descartes, at this point only the heavier bodies (with greater momentum) can pass over what we would term a 'col', a point at which circulatory flow of the powers meets, as the figure of two river currents flowing towards and away from each other (like to branches of a hyperbola) in *Le monde* illustrates.[7]

(b) Likewise, as we have seen in Chapter 3, Descartes holds that given a relative extension of these small bodies in which the greater masses are born around spheres of primary matter, the impulsion of these stars decreases as one moves away from them to a threshold, at which point larger bodies will be born away, like the comets, to other circulatory systems.[8]

(c) Accordingly, an ecliptic swept out by a given simple body will, all things being equal, coincide with the equal degree of power exerted in extension. In other words, the distance r from the pole to equal degrees of power at any point will be the same (and inversely proportional to that power, though Descartes does not take this step in his formulation).

In case (a), the turbulence of forces equals out in the summation of powers to create what we can term a 'col', another singular point in the schema of natural right. In case (b), the rule holds subject to the summation of powers, such that, whereas in the Cartesian diagram of celestial vortices arbitrary surfaces appear between areas of circulation, Spinoza more correctly determines a dynamic surface at the point where a thing's nature is more or less expressed *actualiter* by the activity at that point. All this follows from our discussion of natural right and the incorporeality of the attributes, which proceed 'everywhere' instantaneously to determine actual modes as constituted by multiple instances of finite powers. If we dare to venture much further than Spinoza in our physical interpretation, we may observe that in extremely simplistic cases, the power on a body on which two poles or bodies exert their natural right will be inversely proportional to the respective distances from each body, and that the sum of these rights will form a single transitive magnitude that is equal on a combined line of circulation around both bodies, and which is at every point equal to the product of those distances ($r \cdot r$). The reason we choose to venture forward in this manner is because it is quite revealing about the nature of the combination of powers, which runs quite contrary to the isolationist atomic model preferred by Hobbes. For we see that while immediately about two bodies the flow of simple bodes or ideas is determined to be circular (or ecliptic), as we move out and the right of the other body in the dipole relation becomes relevant, the flow of each tends a little towards the other. As we move further out, a point in the flow is reached that is a *col* singularity, where the two flows run against each other, and in principle larger bodies or ideas can pass between smaller spheres of right.

Most importantly, as we proceed inwards from now on, the points of equal power can no longer be found between the bodies, for at these points the other body overwhelms the right of the first, but outside of these regions the right combines as if the two bodies were acting as one extended body, with the flows of simple bodies passing around both of them in a great ecliptic. The flow at every stage is deemed possible by a Cartesian conclusion stated by Spinoza in DPPII Def. 9 that a 'circle of bodies' is brought about by continuous impulsion between the bodies 'even though the figure formed by all the bodies together . . . may be very contorted', a conclusion enhanced by Spinoza's own hydrostatic investigations. We pick out this definition because of the remarkable similarity of the figure that accompanies it and the form of the flow of right around two poles in the regions outside that flow, which forms the just-discussed *col.* Though it may be objected the DPP figure presupposes a fixed tube, Spinoza's Letters 6 and 32, and the fundamental role of *motus ad quietus*, should have by now disabused us of any temptation of admitting a dualism of solid and fluid as prior to motion and its dynamic variations.

In this way, we can understand the kind of model that inspires Spinoza to declare: 'if two humans come together and join forces, they have more power over Nature, and consequently more right, than either one alone . . .'[9] Compare Descartes' pulley theory of light in Chapter 3. The summation of powers thus takes place, but in addition we see that formally three things occur:

(a) the power of being affected is likewise increased communally by the great ecliptics described;
(b) the greater force exerted in the outer ecliptics acts to cushion and protect the remaining inner ecliptics of each body in its immediate vicinity; and
(c) it is possible to consider that the power formally exerted derives from a unique pole determined as the common power of two or more bodies.

As to this latter point, which presages the issue of the common notion, Deleuze is thus perspicacious in his declaration that:

> should two individuals completely combine their relations, they would naturally form an individual twice as great, having twice as great a natural right. The state of reason in no way either does away with or limits natural rights, *but raises them to a power* without which such rights would be unreal and abstract.
> (1990a: 264, our emphasis)

Deleuze seems to have intuited that a conceptual distinction between the state of nature and the state of reason is indeed determined by the raising of a power, not simply in the additive sense, but also, with respect to the pseudo-individual thus combined, properly as a transition from one order of power to another. One can see that as we move around our two poles along lines of equivalent right, these directed *lines* of magnitude, when produced, will, by definition, always express the same power though constituted in different proportions. Once again, we recover the surface of Chrysippos, this time as the binding together of flows of *corpora simplicissima* along these contours of right. And each surface of right appears, in the equality of its power, to be projected from a source unchanging in that power but varying in its locus between the two actual origins. It *appears* as if the combined force has its origin elsewhere than in the individuals.

Returning to the circulation that now operates around two or more bodies, we can perceive why Spinoza is keen to adopt the language of lifeblood to describe the community of right within the city, and not merely as an abstract vital circulation, but as hydrostatic determinant. He states in an oft overlooked paragraph in TPV[5]:

> So when I say the best imperium is one where men pass their lives in harmony, I am speaking of human life, which is defined not just be the circulation of the blood and other features common to all animals, but especially by reason, the true virtue and life of the mind.[10]

Here it may be conjectured that Spinoza follows Hobbes in dividing vital motions such as blood circulation, which occur even when sleeping, from endeavour, pleasure and pain as the starting point of 'thought',[11] but while there is a division, Spinoza opposes the true life of the mind to vital motions within the social context. The language of reason is linked to power and life, and thus to the circulation of that reason that occurs between individuals of most like nature. Thus, also, if we turn to the key political propositions in EIV, we find a similar language of flows, harmony and increase in the power of being affected that derives from the above-described model of natural right. Turning to Propositions 39 and 40 of the Fourth Part, we see that these are among those that constitute suspended propositions that appear to lead nowhere in the flow of the *Ethics*. Indeed, EIVP39 is not even referred to by EIVP40, and it is quite possible to assume, given their respective subject matters, that the two are only indirectly linked, for they state broadly:

- *(P39)* Those things which bring about the conservation of the ratio of motion and rest that the parts of the human body have to one another are good (and the contrary are bad).[12]
- *(P40)* Those things which contribute to a common society of men, or, which bring it about that men live in concord, are useful (and the contrary introduce discord).[13]

Yet in light of the social *imperium* we are constructing from the principles of natural right, we are now able to interpret these passages also in reference to the flows of essential consciousness that pass about a multipolar world. As regards EIVP39, at the extremely abstract level of a dipole construction using two bodies, we can see (from the Scholium thereto) how 'the body needs many other bodies for its conservation', though these do not form a constituent of the body, which is preserved. These variable bodies pass in and out of essential consciousness, providing sustenance not simply by a transfer of power to that body, but by constituting its very world as a sort of 'cushion' or 'envelop' in which the very acts of willing may take place. This is easier to see if the circular flows are placed in a larger general field of flow. The enveloping is always subject to a general norm that impels the entire circulatory apparatus around itself, but within and for that envelop there is a degree of protection as the greater impulsive power at a given point is, as we approach the smaller bodies that constitute poles, overcome by local power. As we build up an *imperium*, therefore, the question turns to the nature of the wider power, which bears along smaller bodies in a fashion that maintains their ratio of motion and rest (their 'form'). This is the purpose of EIVP40, where Spinoza posits the possibility of this more essential power, one that is considered harmonic with respect to society. It arises insofar as there is a coincidence of natures between humans and the general essential power in question, and Spinoza ultimately will locate this power in God. This coincidence of natures is rationality, as the Demonstration to EIVP40 declares. As such, it is not the individual acts, however rational in Spinoza's terms, of a given set of humans that *ex machina* constitutes a power over itself, but the very existence of an infinitely rational power that provides the sanction for certain types of willing. For Spinoza, the existential guarantee of the first idea that constitutes our act of existing, that which necessarily involves the idea of God, places what could be an outer force within the mind though it be clouded by confusion. People may, in their choices, see the better, but they will the worse.

Returning to our analysis of circulation, the variable bodies that sustain the form of the human body – 'bring it about that the human body is affected in many ways' – precisely because their flow extends about that body but also extends about other bodies and may return to us having been worked upon by others. Natural right is, in its circulation, inherently economic. As such, natural right in its guise as essential consciousness, which Spinoza states engages in 'works' (*operas*), is connected with other consciousnesses by a stream of these works as they pass around the great ecliptic. Clearly in the right of more and more humans, these ecliptics may be seen as only abstract representations of general circulatory movements, but always with this characteristic: that as some works are impelled away, so they are replaced by others. This model of trade circulation, which Spinoza briefly discusses in §28 of EIV Appendix, is facilitated by money ('a short way to all these [works]'), which thus comes 'to occupy the mind of the vulgar very much'. We can, of course, read many discussions of economic circulation that refer to or are inspired by Spinoza, in Marx, Balibar,[14] and Deleuze and Guattari,[15] for example. As this is a work primarily interested in the juridical aspects of natural right, we shall not pursue this avenue here, save insofar as we have endeavoured concretely to reconstruct the theoretical system of right Spinoza has in mind. In this regard, we underline these few points:

(a) The circulatory model at work in Spinoza's thinking operates by a flow of less powerful bodies around one or more poles taken as acting in the same manner. In their *Anti-Oedipus*, Deleuze and Guattari seem to advance[16] a model that involves poles of opposite character, their clinical objects oscillating between the two.

(b) Spinoza's model of work and works makes no distinction between trivial acts and labour. Any act is work and its effect is a work. Whether it passes into the circulation of right as a valuable thing is irrelevant.
(c) Spinoza, as no one will doubt, makes no claim that money is to be raised to a level any higher than any other object, though it be a general shortcut to these. There is no general equivalence conception in Spinoza, save in the sense that God or Nature could be said to occupy this role.[17]
(d) Spinoza does, however, understand that money, in occupying the mind of the vulgar, can play a role in generating a false general power, that is, the combined actions of many appear to project a norm onto an imagined origin of power, which in fact is inexistent. This is a modal issue and we might reason as follows: money form as mode is composed by the affections of society (i.e. it is composed of very many modes), but at least in the economy of Spinoza's vision, this composed mode finds no formal essence in the attribute of Thought as it passes across it. It finds no place to settle and take on any relative permanence; it has nothing to express other than the variety of wills that caused its component modes. Thus money appears a powerful phenomenon, but as soon as the wills that sustain it disappear – the citizens lose faith in the coin – so the money form collapses into worthless lumps of metal.
(e) Normativity, in the very specific senses of the norm of the present and of the general power at work, is involved immanently in every economic act as the condition of all essential consciousness. The Hebrew state discussed by Spinoza[18] works by using legal signs to attract and distract, thereby leading the populace in a desired direction. Such legal signs are useless if, before they even apply, the norms of the present and general will have acted in essential consciousness as the conditions of possibility of all work.

The concept of circulation with respect to a given simple body is intimately related to the strength of consciousness of EV, which is the endeavour to perform work on that simple body. In this regard, EIVP39 and P40 cannot be understood without regard also to strength of consciousness. Just as natural right takes on new and interesting characteristics when considered over multiple bodies with regard to circulation, so it offers insights when one considers the issue of augmentations and diminutions of power. The question, however, is how Spinoza proposes to explain such variations in right. His response is to advance a powerful theory of tool-making.

6.2.3 Augmentation of the power of acting I: homo faber

We have already seen in Chapter 2 the manner in which Spinoza's methodological treatise places great store with the concept of the tool. The key quotation is TdIE §31:

> But the fact is that at first, with the tools they were born with, men succeeded, however laboriously and imperfectly, in making some very simple things; and when these were made they made other more complex things with less labour and greater perfection; and thus advancing gradually from the simplest works to the making of tools to other works and tools, they have reached a point where they can make very many complex things with little labour.[19]

He continues:

> In just the same way the intellect by its inborn power makes intellectual tools for itself by which it acquires other powers for other intellectual works, and from these works still other tools – or capacity for further investigation – and thus progresses gradually until it reaches the very summit of wisdom.[20]

Now we are able to consider why the tool occupies this central position in his thought. It is necessary to think of a tool as a means by which one nature 'couples' with another nature *in some common respect* and thereby transforms the actualised power of the primary right N_p into an actualised secondary right N_s, which is in proportion as the virtue of the first thing (its constitutive transition T_p) is to the second thing (T_s). Thus N_p:N_s = T_p:T_s. One can see that as the contraction of the tool in question is greater, so a transition occurs in the right exerted through it to a greater degree. The opposite transition follows when $T_p > T_s$. Note that there is no suggestion from Spinoza that as a result of tool use some third quantum of power is super-added; it lacks a sufficient reason. Rather, we have to understand that the power that a user impresses through a tool is not as greatly dissipated as it would otherwise have been and is further augmented by the power and nature of the tool.[21] Accordingly, when a hammer hammers, it expresses the right of its holder insofar as that right is understood solely through its partial hammer-nature and insofar as the hammer thus used causes an augmentative transition in that partial right: there is intermixture. The hammer assists the hammerer better to express her hammering nature. Compare this with the Heideggerian *Dasein* of using a hammer, whereby *Dasein* is merely extended into the hammer, which becomes part of one's *Dasein* and extends it.[22] Spinoza already goes further than this by realising that simple extension of affectivity is accompanied by a transformation of power that renders tool use at once useful and instrumentalising. By instrumentalising, we mean that it clearly follows from the partiality of the tool's expression that the gain of power is always at the expense of a limitation of the formal essence of the self, and it is quite possible that one can be led astray by chimaeras and beings of reason. Hence, Spinoza proposes the *Idea Dei* as the tool par excellence, for, though it augments our power of acting absolutely, it does more in that it fosters (*fovet*) our nature and power, and so opens the way for growth.

6.2.4 Augmentation of power of acting II: existential feedback

It follows quite naturally from Spinoza's principles that insofar as each body acts on itself to construct its own body, and insofar as a second body is acted upon by itself and by that other within this dual field of essential consciousness, so the augmented power of this field has the capacity to work upon each body within it and cause some transition in its power of acting. Thus, we are quite conscious of the importance of our working together because the first thing that constitutes our enduring mind, the conatus, will transit to greater perfection and thus produce in us pleasure; we take pleasure in our acts, and the more so with greater success (EIIIP58). Note that here it is quite critical to understand the correct order of transition. If *A* acts with *B* and then feels pleasure, there must have been two augmentations in the power of acting. If these were equal, then *A* and *B* working together would have a recurrent power augmentation to infinity, which is absurd. It seems rather that the initial combination of right in the act, which is the greater 'stepping up' of power, does not of itself produce pleasure in any one person. This makes both experiential sense and avoids an absurd thesis. Rather, it is the affective *adequate* appreciation that *A*'s efforts succeeded because of *B*'s assistance, which produces the principle basis for the 'emotions insofar as we act' (EIIIP57 Sch.). Spinoza appears to be quite determined on this point: that joint effort produces no causally 'proximate' individual transition save insofar as a person adequately conceives that she has acted.[23] This follows through to the general tenor of the multi-body dynamics of EIVP29ff., where Spinoza places greater stress on the latent augmentative capacity of each pursuing his own benefit and thus providing useful works for others, than on pursuing the (seemingly more obvious) claim that endeavour in common produces a greater benefit to all involved, due to the nature of essential consciousness. This choice does have the advantage of explaining unwitting endeavour in common that produces actually existing imperia.

6.2.5 Augmentation of the power of acting III: human relations

The foregoing considerations naturally pose the question of which tools may be considered more useful and less likely to lead us into confusion about the nature we endeavour to express. The answer is by now quite obvious: we must seek out tools that are most like us, for by using them we express the most possible of our own nature and augment it to a great degree. This tool, if we may consider it such, is another human being:

> if [the human] dwells among individuals which are such that they agree with the nature of the human, by that very fact a man's power of acting is enlivened and fostered[24] [iuvabitur et fovebitur].
>
> (EIV App. §7)

And from §26 of the same Appendix:

> Apart from humans, we know of no particular thing in Nature whose mind we can delight, and with which we can join in friendship or in some kind of association.

There is a limited sense, therefore, in which working through another human being we are able to express most what is common between humans. The 'tool' concept, however, is slightly obscured in this relation, because the commonality of natures that two humans have, and which we will examine in section 6.3, first and foremost rests on a commonality of power. One may see this in EIVP40, discussed above, whereby differences in the power of humans introduce discord between similar natures, but this is already apparent from the structure of the imperium we have already set out. It is easily seen that the two powers placed in the ecliptic relation of circulation may not significantly differ in strength, for even by a power ratio of 4:1, we already see that, taken in isolation, we only have a relation of domination.[25] It is more likely, however, given the general similarity of powers of human individuals (within bounds of virtue) that any domination comes from without, or from a greater number of humans acting either rationally or passionately. The case of the human must be considered as providing three instances of utility:

(a) use through union;
(b) indirect utility; and
(c) common utility.

The first, use through union, is specified in TPII (and partially in EIVP31 Corol., and P37) and naturally follows from the combination of right of two individuals forming a common endeavour. As we have seen above, this can be seen as a summation of individual rights or the raising by a power of a projected power due to neither individual (an appearance of the multitude). In this sense, both individual humans use each other as tools in the technical sense described above, and by so doing express what is common between them with the sum of the power of each. The result of combination is the more virtuous expression of humanity. The second, indirect utility, can be found discussed in EIIP40, the related part of the TdIE, and partially also EIVP31 Corol. It follows from the similarity of natures thesis that if one or more humans with greater virtue expresses their human nature in some work, that work will also express the human nature of some third less virtuous individual, though they had no hand in it. Thus, the merchant by hearsay can derive the fourth proportional, though he knows not why the process is correct. Augmentative tools are created for the benefit of all. Finally, common utility arises from the creation of the imperium, which has the enveloping effect discussed above. While these three areas all rely on the as yet unexamined concept of common nature, it is this last that elucidates the meaning of '*fovere*' and the role it plays with respect to the imperium. It is to this concept that we now turn.

6.3 Right in common – Spinoza's theory of natural right in the imperium

6.3.1 The problematic of common natures

Spinoza's construction of a theory of natural right from the simplest bodes to the whole face of the universe must very quickly encounter the problem of complexity. Even within the PI, Spinoza already makes a virtue of this complexity in permitting the *forma* of a thing to be retained though the composite elements vary or are replaced. The realisation that this may be explained by reference to an absolute circulatory enveloping power that constitutes the formal essence for a thing's continued existence does not detract from the problematic of determining the relation between this infinite cause and the determinations to exist and act that derive from the finite world. Thus, Spinoza admits repeatedly in his political works that the natural right of humans must be defined by reference not to reason, but whatever passing fancy should impel that instant,[26] and infamously declares that *so far no one has determined what a body can do* (EIIIP2 Sch.).[27] This admission is necessary because for the greater part we must operate with what the second kind of reason can hypothesise in its deductions from our encounters and their commonalities. At this finite level, already it seems that one must divide between an active 'human' nature and a passive 'un-human' nature, which is rather the act of some third thing. Along this road surely lie Peripatetic essentialism, and the idea of natural laws among humans that characterises the Christianising neo-Stoicist tendencies of Grotius, Pufendorf and Butler. Under this model, reason is able to access the 'human' concept and thus judge whether cases conform, that is, are active and passive, according to this rational common notion.

Spinoza's response to this question 'what is a thing's nature?' unsurprisingly derives from a far more expressionist angle. To understand this, it is most helpful to consider a different interpretation of the early Stoic doctrine offered by Sambursky. Citing Chrysippos' example of the cylinder that is impelled to begin rolling down a hill, Sambursky notes[28] that Chrysippos' apparently hair-splitting distinction between passion to commence rolling and action to continue descent at greater speed may be understood in what we would call an entirely generative sense. Sambursky argues (in a manner that is creditable for its elucidation of reasons rather than strict adherence to false historicism)[29] that 'the logical consistency of Chrysippos' train of thought within the deterministic framework can be elucidated by comparing it with the formalism of Newtonian analytical dynamics'. The important point here is to understand that Chrysippos and Newton should be considered as approaching the same problematic of explaining events by assigning causes correctly to various bodies, but with radically different (and equally suppressed) means: geometrical and analytical, respectively. Sambursky continues[30] in an important passage:

> let us consider the simple act of motion of a body; it is causally determined by a differential equation into which enter the co-ordinates, their (first and second) derivatives with respect to time and certain material constants, and by the initial conditions, i.e. the data fixing the position and velocity of the body of the certain moment. The solution to the equation gives the orbit of the body in general terms.

The differential equation thus determines not only what a body will do, but it determines a family of infinite possible solutions, each of which determines the duration of the body for all time. For the simplest bodies, and composite rigid bodies, we thus are presented with a sense in which the body can be said to act. Whatever tribulations, as Sambursky writes, may have befallen the body before zeroth hour come together as the initial state for our consideration, in which a chain of causation collapses into the moment. Taking the body as it now is, persevering in existence, as Spinoza would say, we are now able to determine this body's actions by reference to the equation of motion appropriate to it. Whatever impulses it may passively suffer, it will convert them according to its equation of motion according to one of the infinitely many ways designated by that common nature. It will not, however, turn from a man to a horse, for that is not in its determinate reason. There is thus a sense in which action is giving effect to an impulse according to a specific nature. This nature is not considered as some abstract logical essence, but is rather expressed as the instantiations of this generative function according to determinate conditions.

This last point is the most critical for Spinoza, and more so because he offers no completely worked out quantitative analysis of the precise relations of determination that explain dynamic motion. From what we have established in our earlier chapters, however, the genetic definition of natural right suggests broadly how Spinoza could follow the Stoic division of active and passive nature. In the case of the simplest body, for example, can we not regard its particular nature as its locus relative to all simple bodies (which it expresses alone), and its common nature as that which it shares with all simple bodies (its current motion to rest)? It is these initial conditions – the nature of the thing[31] – that we feed into the *potentiae* impressed at the locus, both the impressed finite power and the formal essence as an additional free power. We compose these powers in the Cartesian fashion and assess, by considering some reference point, the expression of the power of this nature along a line. The broad structural logic of this model is readily transferable to composite bodies and incompressible fluids, though it will not help Spinoza with complex bodies (we suspect he intuits the difference, but his mechanics provides few answers). By this, we mean that the failure to determine a differential equation that explains human activity does not at all permit one to discard the central Cartesian thesis that all is explicable in terms of God or Nature, body, motion and rest, and in addition a proper appreciation of transitions. These same relations are at work, but now must be analysed in their effects so that one may continue to treat the human emotions geometrically, and that affects may be to the mind (and here the oblique reference to Descartes' *Météorologie* is problematic) as one attributes to the atmosphere the nature of heat, cold, storm, thunder (TPI[4]). This collapse into a kind of undifferentiated *Nichts* is, we believe, a direct consequence of Spinoza's over-reliance on the attributes as explaining power in its necessary form as *magnitude*, and leaving nothing back for 'substance' or whichever finite thing to explain. In simple terms, Spinoza and many who follow him would want a body without a skeleton, the skeletal being for him a product of a field of forces. Leibniz already spotted the flaw, and expresses it at the beginning of his *Principles of Nature and Grace* in geometric terms when he points out that magnitudes must collect together simple substances (points) as composite substances (i.e. magnitudes must 'hang' across more than one point).[32] The geometric terminology here is somewhat misleading for it is aimed at a wider audience; Leibniz is not simply taking the opposite position on geometric priority (what comes first, point or motion?) for Spinoza has actually covered both in the *causa sui*. Rather, Leibniz is making a distinction between space and place,[33] between the numeric and situational worlds, the former implicating the latter, the latter informing the former, and placing activity in the points over against power in the magnitudes. Thereby, he sunders geometry into its natural and historical aspects and overcomes the bounded dynamism of the Spinozan eternity with his own infinite 'progress'.

In any event, while Sambursky provides a useful mode of understanding the thinking of Chrysippos, in the latter's case, as well as with Spinoza, we must understand that the problem is now approached without the Newtonian tools to hand. How, then, does Spinoza propose to solve the problem of natures?

6.3.2 The principle of common right

We take the view that Spinoza brings two aspects of one methodological concept, common natures and the common notions, to bear on the problem of determining natures. This may be seen from a consideration of the inverse relation of the Newtonian formalism Sambursky deploys in the case of the cylinder. For we may consider that the continued existence of any thing is nothing other than an expression of its nature in some degree. In other words: whatever *b* does, active or passive, is a partial solution to the differential equation that determines its nature. Spinoza, lacking the tools yet also having the insight not to attempt the construction of such an equation in the case of complex bodies, proposes rather to trace back from the solutions to this nature using two threads: transitions and commonality.

We have already analysed how the transitions operate within this structure and are able to see that they are expressions of a change in the power of acting of a finite thing entirely related to that thing alone. The finite thing is, in its singularity, closer to its form through the transition. From the finite perspective of individual virtue, Spinoza is quite happy that pleasure is the ethical guide to salvation, in its coincidence with reason. This is not, however, sufficient for the foundation of collective human life, which is the means to that individual happiness. For this reason, the common notion, already playing a critical role in epistemology, is now required to play a role in the life of the city. It does so, however, not as a prior being of reason constructed according to the principles of the second kind of cognition, but as what one might term a concrete universal, that is, as the effect of the co-expression of individuals' natural right. In this sense, it is quite irrelevant that two individuals who form together a union in the state of nature should have an adequate idea of their common nature. Rather, there is a material reconfiguration of their mutual power of acting that arises come what may.

This is really nothing other than a repetition of the insistence that, in the case of finite things, it is insufficient to determine an essence, whole and complete, being formally in an attribute and that is only actualised by a characteristic relation. From each angle, as it were, variables are set by various series, each of which could, in the simplest cases, be brought together in a defining equation, but this is not the same as claiming, as some do, that there is a 'general function' that is involved in and expressed by a particular thing. It is not *a* difference that determines thinghood, but the relation of differences, expressed by more than one generating function, in a manner that 'points' in its instantiations back to a 'natural law', that is, it *projects* onto substance a being of reason. We do not deny, however, that the formal consciousness of a thing can be so determined; we are simply distinguishing between determination to exist and what that existing thing determines to do, between what a body does as cause, and what it could do as terminus of causes. Nor is this to deny the distinction that Spinoza seemingly refuses to abandon, namely between consciousness and union; in fact, it reinforces it. The paradoxical result of endeavouring to locate a formal 'soul' of a complete individual in the attributes is that it denies that very individuality in reducing all 'characteristic' relations to individuals or non-individuals depending entirely on philosophical bent. As we have said, rather each power determines a formal essence that may be filled by an infinite range of other powers, each of which determine and refine the resulting individuation within the relativistic parameters set by the hegemonic powers (what acts?). We cannot agree with Deleuze (1990a: 278) that 'Spinoza's common notions are biological, rather than physical or mathematical ideas.' We aver that Deleuze's claim that relations between visceral parts determine form places less stress than is required on Spinoza's complete divestiture of finitude from immediate divine creation, that is, on individuation of finite modes as opposed to common notions. It is because Spinoza refuses individuation at the level of the formal essences in favour of finite determination to exist as such, that he is able to advance a theory of common notions that overcomes that 'subjective' individuality Deleuze seeks to avoid. We say that Spinoza in fact wishes to use the common notions, and the common natures that found them, to express rather the sense in which relations between things nevertheless have epistemic and ethical value in the expression of commonality through union.

From this idea, it is possible to work backwards to the individual thing, while holding apart conceptually the formal essence it 'draws down', and complete our picture of natural right.

Whenever power is expressed, a common nature is expressed according to two variables: (a) the degree to which this common nature is able to express itself with respect to the power of each other thing that determines it to act; and (b) the complexity of the nature, down to a minimum of the simple body whose nature is a single quantum of motion and rest. Over and above this, the particular nature of the body in question should not be ignored; that which is not expressed in common, though also that which is peculiar to the thing's history. For the simplest body, this is nothing other than its current place and time in the universe relative to all else. These are the natures that make right natural, and Spinoza consistently describes natural right as flowing from its natural laws: 'whatever a thing does by the laws of its own nature, it does with sovereign right' (TTPXVI, Geb.III/190, Akkerman 506.14–15); 'each person, by the highest right of Nature, does what follows from necessity from his own nature' (EIVP37 Sch. 2); 'whatever man does form the laws of his own Nature, he does by sovereign right of Nature' (TPII[4]). And as we have already stated in Chapter 4, following Gueroult and Dreyfus in part,[34] it is this doctrine that feeds into a concept of will restricted to ideas that, in the Scholium to EIIP49, Spinoza carefully distinguishes from images (of imagination) and words that signify ideas. It is the concept that is an act of the mind, and in this act by definition the mind must, to a greater degree, express its nature, with the consequence that this thinking is by natural right. But a perception is a passion of the mind, and this passion by definition to a greater degree expresses the nature of some other thing, with the consequence that such thinking, insofar as it explicates another, contrary nature is not by natural right. It is a distinction that Chrysippos makes and may be found just as unsatisfying, but if Spinoza is defining natural right by reference to a thing's nature, then it follows that only those effects derived from a thing's *nature* and every other thing's *power* are involved in each case. The result remains the same; only one effect occurs as the powers are composed. The difference in endured experience is that the formal being of each thing's volition overlaps or better becomes mixed, and the line of actualisation determines the extent to which each thing has failed to obey the norm of the present, and so act under the power of another (the affects). So those who equate Spinoza to the Seldenians and have him approving of whatever passing fancy a person can get away with are dramatically wide of the mark. They are correct, however, in the sense that the Middle Academics were correct in attacking a similar thesis by Chrysippos: that actually unravelling which of two natures actively caused some effect is very difficult, and easily invites prejudices about what natures *should* be like (i.e. what is dutiful in man).

Returning, however, to the wider discussion of how we learn of common natures (and by subtraction of what is particular) 'union' in this context must not be seen as carving a real divide between consciousness producing singular things and mere associations. The physicality of Spinoza's conception, which determines thinghood by reference to the action of some relatively greater power, posits a continuum in which, as the mutual differentials of power approach zero, so the strength of persevering in being of each thing is reduced (for it is 'grasped' in its being by some hegemonic power(s)). Thus, union stands below a threshold of thinghood as the action together of things, which, however, is quickly disunited by multiple sources due to the lack of a power that works to combine. Without accepting this spectrum of union, one cannot account for the specificity of common endeavour in Spinoza's work and also the very transitory life with which it is plagued. As we shall see, 'as if with one mind' is a phrase that must be seen as approaching but never *constituting* thinghood because no material thing is created that could take over the role of hegemon of its parts. As with our example of the money form, for Spinoza the political multitude cannot locate a single formal essence in which it may become embedded; at best, the constituents can configure their essences in some kind of system of fostering.

This interpretation can be seen from our discussion of superposition of powers, both as circulation and in act. The act of two or more things *in union* can only be derived from the commonality of these acts, and it thus expresses that 'part' of each agent's nature that is in common. There is a sense, as we have seen, in which this union determines a centre of power that is not an actually existing singular thing, being rather the idea of a transcendent or universal power thrown out from its actualisation. Being an idea, and likewise grounded in the centre of power determined in Nature, but lacking thinghood *qua* individual thing, we thus find before us a mode that appears to reason to operate *as if* it were a real thing. The primary example of this for our purposes is the sovereign, or properly, the *finite mode of the imperium* – an idea over which Spinoza has struggled in his reading of Hobbesian social contract theory. We draw the reader's attention to the following definition of sovereignty in TPII[17]:

> Hoc ius, quod multitudinis potentia definitur, imperium appellari solet. Atque hoc is absolute tenet, qui curam reipublicae ex communi consensu habet . . .
>
> This right, which is defined by the power of the multitude, is usually called the imperium. It is held absolutely by whoever has oversight of the republic by common consensus.
>
> (my translation)

Spinoza thus settles upon the idea that the imperium is an expression of common power, that is, it is an expression of power of a group of individuals insofar only as they act as one. Notice that according to the principle of superposition of powers, we do not obtain a 'new' consciousness unless those powers determine the bodies on which they act to some existence. It is therefore appropriate to define this mode. We define:

> An *imperium* is a singularity of projection from particular things that would not appear in the field of right as an origin but for that projection.

In Spinozan terms of Extension, this amounts to saying that given any locality there is a transition occurring that is not due to difference of motion and rest at that point (i.e. there is no individual body in the sense of EIIP13 Lem. 1). From this we propose:

> *The principle of common right*: every act of $\beta_1, \beta_2 \ldots \beta_n$ in union is a partial solution to the aggregate natures of each of $\beta_1, \beta_2 \ldots \beta_n$, and each such act expresses their common nature as an imperium.

Given that the virtue of any number of humans is variable, it is likewise possible to posit a series of imperia, each of which express common right, that is, the common natures of each constituent, with greater reality. It seems that a form of this principle is readily adopted by Marx in his chapter of *Capital* on *Co-operation*, though following John Bellers, he is keen to notice that combination of power also generates a 'collective power' where 10 men straining to lift a ton is qualitatively not equivalent to 100 men each using a finger, an observation far beyond Spinoza's frame of reference.[35] It is this working hypothesis of a series of imperia, each with a common right appropriate to itself, which allows us to understand the flow of the *Tractatus politicus*, to which we now turn.

6.3.3 From substance to imperium

Gueroult famously established (1968) that Spinoza begins his derivation of the unique and infinite divine substance first by dividing existing and acting, and then constructing an infinite series of substances, each of which enacts a single infinite attribute. He then resolves each such substance into the One. The subtlety of Spinoza's move in part consists in the Socratic technique of granting one's contemporaries the commonplaces of their conception of God and Nature, and drawing from these notions the true nature of things. It is our conjecture that Spinoza deploys similar tactics in the *Tractatus politicus*, where he moves from a conception of a series of imperia, each with its common right and desire for security, towards one rational imperium that, if achievable at least in some degree, will ensure the longer endurance of the given civil society.[36]

6.3.3.1 The working definition of a state's aim as its security

Spinoza begins his construction of the imperium in his usual fashion with a definition, either directly, as in the *Ethics*, or by way of discussion of a common conception, as in TTPIV and here in TPI:

> Freedom of soul or strength of mind is the virtue of the private individual; the virtue of the imperium is security.
>
> (TPI[6])[37]

We take the view that this statement plays a similar role to EI Def. 6, where Spinoza defines God as an absolutely infinite entity, that is, a substance consisting of infinite attributes, each of which expresses eternal and infinite essence. The primary tactical purpose of both definitions appears to be Socratic, in that it posits a starting point with which Spinoza's contemporaries would have largely agreed had they not known what was coming down the chain of reasons. One of the most fascinating aspects of Spinoza studies is that whereas the sleight-of-hand Spinoza performs with the God concept is well known and comfortably accepted today as something quite shocking in the past, Spinoza's reworking of the imperium is still shocking for us. As Balibar contends,[38] it may even have been shocking for Spinoza too. The claim that the virtue of the state is security is either read as in tune with the Realpolitik of our own times or as an apology for it.[39] Insofar as Spinoza's treatise is understood as a kind of letter to the prince about statecraft, not unlike Seneca's *De Clementia*, the above definition falls on the side of being rather attractive, though perhaps also to Spinoza in his troubled times it was likewise a call for envelopment. Our point, however, is that this 'hook' of a definition should be treated with due caution, and that the flow of Spinoza's argument leads us to quite a different understanding of this beginning.

6.3.3.2 The existence of a multiplicity of imperia

The introductory chapter of the TP ends with the following claim, which flows from the conception of union of bodies and their right:

> Finally, since all men everywhere, whether barbarian or civilised, enter into relationships with one another and set up some kind of civil order, one should not look for the causes and natural foundations of the state in the teachings of reason, but deduce from the common nature or conditions of men.
>
> (TPI[7])[40]

As Wernham notes,[41] the decision that the foundations of the imperium cannot be deduced from the precepts of reason appears to be an acknowledgement of the failure of social contract theory to account for the very thing that renders a contract binding (*utilitas*). Rather, the statement not only introduces the following chapter's discussion of natural right, but already makes the general claim that *there exist* numerous imperia, indeed as many at any moment as express the conditions or common nature of humans. The addition of 'conditions' alerts us to the fact that Spinoza, as TPI[6] has already made clear, is particularly concerned with the variations in virtue of humans, which determines a difference of mutual condition and thus, juridically, a relative difference of natures that diminishes common right. Spinoza is not saying that all humans form an imperium solely by being human; they must act in union also. When powers or virtues are more alike, a mutual flow of essential consciousness is constituted that operates according to a summation of individual rights and discloses, at least in the common ecliptic, a union of appearance, rather than thinghood proper. We are thus asked to imagine the world as a confused flow of arbitrary unions of utility and common endeavour, with a great disunity of purpose between these endeavours, which just as much leads to a state of war as would the isolated existence of single conatuses according to the Hobbesian model of the state of nature. As Spinoza says, his state of nature is immanent to the imperium.

6.3.3.3 The action of a multiplicity of natural rights

Having determined the existence of multiple unions of convenience, each one an imperium, Spinoza now holds forth on his natural right theory. We have explored this theory of natural right in Chapters 4 and 5, and so propose to summarise only the essential aspects at work. The primary purpose of this discussion of natural right is to establish that each thing expresses the natural right of God or Nature, first as infinite rights expressed at local sources, second as finite rights within the general equilibrium, all of which combine up to the right of the whole of dynamic Nature itself. The first experience of this world is the endeavour to persevere in one's being as an existing thing, and derivatively to work according to one's nature. This endeavour is expressed foremost by the activity of every particular thing within the constraints of the whole. Finite Nature must be understood, as we have shown, not as partitioned between individuals and groups of individuals, but as immanently summed across existence such that individual powers are coerced and constrained from their fullest actualisation (the formal being of acts). The character of each individual right is thus as indefinite as its existence *but for* the existence and actions of each other thing.

6.3.3.4 The existence of a multiplicity of imperia, each with one right

We now have the basic ingredients of natural right: the existence of multiple imperia and the formally indefinite activity of finite natural rights. In TPII[13–15], Spinoza now combines the two. First, as we say in section 2 above, forces are united and the consequent right is in combination greater,[42] but this possibility of combination is diminished by a difference of virtue.[43] Second, Spinoza places such imperia in the context of the natural state as a whole, noting that the more humans that unite in this way, the more right they collectively possess, and can thus repel threats to their territories and body. Further, the greater this combined right, the greater the number of threats (the right of 'all') that can be repelled.[44] In other words, there endeavours to exist a multiplicity of imperia, each expressing a combined single natural right that is formally indefinite but actually restrained.

6.3.3.5 The particularity of each imperium's right

The right of each imperium may be considered as a kind of event, that is, the aggregate act of each such combined body. It is a partial solution to the common nature of the imperium's constituents, yet, reliant as it is on these constituents being in act, this partial solution will only express that nature according to the combined virtue of its constituents. Here, our mechanical reconstruction of Spinoza's thinking is quite helpful in unravelling the effect of this difference of virtue. One can see from our earlier combination of right that if we place a number of bodies in relation, sum across their rights (and any tools transforming them), then the effects of such combined right determine a projection towards a point that only has actually existing bodies as its source. Even in the case of two bodies, as a third, less virtuous body is affected, the result of summation of powers is that at that moment this third body proceeds in a direction that does not appear to be due to either. Descartes' parallelogram rule for summing forces shows this. Even with multiple bodies, this basic principle means that those effects that appear as due to one body are certainly due to all as all combined. If we thus imagine our combined group of bodies acting in union, the global movement may be rationally determined to some centre that may or may not be located in any one of the bodies. Indeed, it may be located outside of the group of bodies if their combined desire is towards something they do not possess.

Now, such desires are the bane of passionate existence for Spinoza, and he spends much time decrying greed and lusts as precisely those sorts of desires that, in combination, can lead whole imperia astray. These are the whims and fancies of the multitude that take on the geometrical form of a group of bodies endeavouring to attain what they imagine is their salvation. Their problem is, however, that given that such passionate pursuits are grounded in imagination, the actions of the united body are of necessity contrary to that unity, and as we approach the limit case the union will tear itself apart. This limit is but one extreme, the other being the limit of a city of the wise, and as with this latter, Spinoza regards them as more unlikely than not. His interest is in actually existing states that do last at least a few years and thus evidence a degree of common purpose. There is a spectrum of imperia, defined by natural right according to their virtue. This spectrum provides the variable basis that allows us to consider the existence of multiple imperia, each with their own interests according to their determinate right, here understood as their combined ability to express the common nature of their constituent bodies. In this case, our mechanical interpretation demands that the actions of each body project with a certain degree of regularity this common centre of purpose that appears as union.

From all this, we find we have little trouble understanding the infamous statement in TPII[16] that: 'where men have common rights . . . [they] are all guided as if by one mind'.[45] The degree of virtue of the imperium determines the *reality* of this united mind where reality is understood as the intensity, clarity and distinctness of the effects of the common endeavour of the bodies in that imperium.

The more power those individuals express, the more their common natures are expressed together, and thus the more this common nature, this common notion of the human as Spinoza's foremost ethical *ens rationis*, is expressed and projected into the world. This being of reason, though it be virtuously affirmed, does not have being except in the limit. By all means the imperium exists, but it is not a particular thing. It is a mode; an effect of particular things. It is also a mode of thought, and thus *qua* idea, it can be a tool that transforms an individual's power of acting. But the mode cannot cause this idea to enter an individual's mind; rather, other individuals in act must cause it to so enter, whether by hearsay or simply by the existence of the effects of common right. Every imperium is simply too mutable to meet Spinoza's strict static criterion of an enduring characteristic proportion of motion and rest. When we speak of imperium, the specific benefits to natural right it may be said to confer are properly derivative of the rights of its common constituents, and they alone. The imperium appears as if it were one mind, when in fact it is the result of many acting in common. Conversely, this common right, which the power of the multitude *defines*, is generally called the imperium (TPII[17]). Notice: (a) the explicit generative use of 'defines' that Spinoza deploys; and (b) the 'generally called' (*appellari solet*), indicating that the imperia Spinoza is discussing have a questionable nomenclature. We may be able to discern the reason in due course.

This being of reason forms the totem or anchor for a number of institutions that flow from the appearance of common consent. Spinoza completes TPII by repeating what he has already shown in EIVP37 Sch. 2, namely that justice, injustice, sin, blame, praise and merit are all things that are constructed within the imperium. At this stage, Spinoza prefers to relate these concepts, which are engendered by civil laws, back to the common consent of the imperium. It follows that the virtue ascribable to such laws and conceptions of justice are indexed to the virtue of the imperium, that is, their reality or power derives from the reality or power of the imperium such that all laws and related conceptions, though they contain the same signs, vary in their power according to the virtue of the imperium that expresses certain common natures. While the augmentation of power is simple, and so does not specify a 'true' justice, its ability to augment the power of enduring and working assists the ability to express a formal essence through work, and in the city one's common nature. This provides an interesting argument for human rights, for the fluidity of the imperium notion, which simply requires human common endeavour, means that contrary to positivists' view of the matter, the common endeavour of multiple individuals in various territories to uphold what they commonly consent to as human rights constitutes an imperium with a degree of reality in just the same way as a more classical territorial state. Indeed, human rights may be seen as having the reality (the power) that they do, in spite of their lack of enforcement power, precisely because of the unity of the mind of the individuals involved, which expresses their common nature in a greater degree. Spinoza at once raises the possibility of these arguments to the material plane, such that one could speak of an imperium of human rights, but in so doing is perfectly aware that on this 'level-playing field' of right, such an imperium is at the mercy of greater power, even if irrational. There is no claim in Spinozism that a concept *must* attain its self-realisation, except in the case of the first.

6.3.3.6 Inconsistency of multiple imperia each expressing one particular right

In TPIII, Spinoza now proceeds with what one might call a *reductio ad bellum* argument. In the *Ethics*, he sought to show that multiple attributes must either have nothing in common or lack the very infinity that defined them, and that it must be the case that substance expresses an infinity of mutually exclusive attributes, or absurdity results. This takes place first by a restriction on free thought and action to prevent disorder, which we discuss in this section, then by a counter-argument that prevention of disorder is less feasible depending on the order the imperium pretends to impose.

Now, at the finite level of imperia, Spinoza reprises his working definition of the virtue of the imperium as security in order to establish the problematic relation that must subsist between the multiple imperia expressing with varying virtue their respective combined right. It must be remarked that while Spinoza seems now, in TPII[17], to have formally redefined the imperium as the *potentia multitudinis*, this continues in no way to contradict his general thesis that an imperium can spring up anywhere that two or more humans combine to perform work. This is evident from the following discussion, where though a more 'state-like' imperium is now in play in the argument, with its corporate powers and common consent, Spinoza continues the state of nature into this imperium by allowing for dissent and riot as imperia within the same 'sphere'. Each such imperium expresses a certain degree of virtue according to the combination of the power of constituent rights, and as such expresses its constituent common nature as humanity. In TPIII[11], Spinoza somewhat elides the looseness of union that characterises the city when he determines that as between imperia, 'the two imperia are in the same relation to one another as are two people in the state of Nature' subject to the exception that an imperium can take better precautions against subjugation. Our mechanical interpretation, founded on common right, indicates why Spinoza treats the states of war and alliance (*foedus*) as oscillating in the way they do. It is only insofar as the commonwealths pursue a common purpose – fear of loss or hope of gain – that they project a commonality of right around which the citizens mutually circulate. As this purpose vanishes, so the commonality of projection vanishes in the minds of each, and the imperia pursue the next most advantageous purpose that constitutes themselves as imperium, and so, to the extent that these purposes divide the imperia, they are in a state of war again.

The Spinozan model thus has a tendency to collapse back into the state of nature, and for groups of citizens across boundaries to form imperia as they see fit, but this somewhat overlooks the stress Spinoza is placing on the 'nature' of officiating imperia specifically. By officiating, we mean the civil order that is entrusted to officers.[46] It is not the case that Spinoza is saying that notional transfers of natural right to officers occur, and that this constitutes an imperium, but rather that the 'most charitable' role of the officer 'is to safeguard peace and promote harmony' (TPIII[10]), which is most effectively achieved by fostering reason and easing the path to actualisation of the multitude's common purpose (TPIII[7]). We might compare this to Leibniz's definition of justice as '*charitativus sapientiformis*'.[47] We believe it is important to indicate the linkage back to Spinoza's 'fostering' of the multitude and the density of the meaning of 'charity' for both these thinkers, but to understand that, at least in outline, we must follow Spinoza's thinking about the natural right of the multiple imperia. As Spinoza's advice to the officer makes clear, the right of each imperium rests on its rationality of pursuing common purposes up to the limit case of an imperium governed in the most rational manner.

This argument is conducted in the space that exists between the right of multitude considered collectively and the right of each individual. The basic principle, self-evident for Spinoza, is that as this multitudinous right exceeds the individual's right, so the latter is restrained from acting in a manner not permitted by the imperium.[48] It is here, however, that our causal analysis of eternity and its role in essential consciousness plays an important role and helps us re-balance the fatalism that dogs interpretations of the *Tractatus politicus*. If we remember that to think in eternity is to appear to reorder the causal chain so that one, as it were, immediately completes to infinity one's act, then we can understand the faith Spinoza places in reason over against an irrational imperium. Thus, the very first cause of being is eternal and remains after death, but also each act of intuition is eternal and incapable of being undone by finite power. Even ideas of the second kind of cognition have a certain species of eternity that render them exemplary in the imperium. It is with this rather Stoic armoury that Spinoza proceeds to bear the worst of the imperium and to establish just how far its expressed communal power extends.

Having established that the imperium cannot leave all matters of judgement up to private individuals, lest it dissolve almost immediately according to whim, Spinoza argues that in matters of common decree, even the rational human must consider herself bound though she disagree with the rationality of that law. One wonders whether, in this, Spinoza has not been inspired by Grotius, whose *De veritate religionis christianae* discusses the issue of higher and middle goods, or Stoic goods and indifferents.[49] In this, we rely on the fascinating exposition of Grotius' view of middle goods by Besselink.[50] Grotius' *Meletius* offers an even more explicit consideration of indifferents, for it is here that we find a conception integral to Spinoza's own view, namely that there could be only the ultimate good: *Deo frui, sive beatitudo*.[51] Against beatitude, both Grotius and Spinoza argue, all other deemed goods are in fact indifferent. Where they differ, it is in Grotius' voluntarism in determining that what may be metaphysically indifferent under natural law falls under custom so that according to mores things may be declared good or bad, and that these are done so, Grotius adds, because they may help in the attainment of the ultimate good. Grotius' list of such middle goods is wide, ranging from life and learning to wealth and honour, with middle bads ranging over shame and poverty.[52] Spinoza places the stress of means to the ultimate good not on objects, but on common life, on combined consciousness. It is association that is the most useful thing, not wealth. Every other good, save perhaps learning as reason, is relegated to the status of derivative of the middle good of association, itself indifferent with respect to beatitude. With this demotion is taken the character of contingency and tradition, whereas common association is always good and is *always* to be sought in the state of nature. Though Spinoza may not have intended it, there is room to argue that from the Grotian perspective, the principle of association has become a natural law. Our major point, however, is that we can see how Spinoza may regard rational laws in relation to middle goods and bads as attracting the Stoic ethical response they deserve – indifference from the perspective of the *summum bonum.*

Spinoza now turns and begins to dismantle the juridical structure of absolute determination of law, declaring that he has explained how far the power, and consequently the right, of the imperium extends.

6.3.3.7 The unification of imperia under one right: towards the imperium intuitivum

In TPIII[7–9], Spinoza links together his arguments with three points, which we reconstruct as follows:

(a) The human that thinks and extends in eternity is in respect of those acts expressing the power of God or Nature. Such acts are incontrovertible and completed in and for eternity. Likewise, the rational human acts according to a certain species of eternity in having adequate ideas. Such a human, in respect of these acts, is most powerful and has the most right and virtue, and bears the finite restraints of the state of nature and the passionate imperium with equanimity, for duration fades in their thought. An imperium that harnessed such a human's power would thus express this virtue and would derive its own endurance from that right. That is, as with the human, the imperium expressing rational power would likewise be in greater possession of its right in the state of nature.[53] Remember that by endurance, Spinoza ultimately means lack of restraint from expressing one's nature; it is not remaining the same through time, but the condition of experiencing no time whatsoever. An imperium seeking security, that is, endurance, should endeavour to harness this virtue by creating the conditions in which all its bodies were able to attain such virtue.[54]

(b) The imperium's right is necessarily finite with respect to particular things:
    (i) No one can be induced to give up their judgement, and that, as such, the rational human cannot be forced to deny reason at the imperium's behest. Spinoza may or may not see the contradiction with his claim that the rational should obey irrational laws, though, if he holds the

Stoic/Grotian view of indifferents, this argument must distinguish between irrational laws about middle goods and bads, and irrational laws that threaten the *aim* of the imperium (i.e. threaten the possibility of communal life as the means to the highest good).

(ii) No one without hope or fear can be subjected to laws, for they either have no regard for threats and punishments, or they see no reason to love the political order (*statum*).

The interesting thing about both these points, though they appear to be aimed at the mad, criminal and free thinkers, is that Spinoza is perfectly aware that his own *Ethics* characterises the wise human as someone exercising reason in both guises and being un-swayed, thanks to the power of the *idea Dei*, by hopes and fears. The more explicit argument, which flows from (a), is that the imperium must understand that its power will only extend into the judgements of the wise if those very judgements are acts of love for the imperium. Again, the imperium must engage with reason or be doomed to have its right limited and its duration defined.[55] Liberal interpreters may seize on a possible distinction between laws pertaining to middle goods and those pertaining to the highest aim of the imperium to argue that Spinoza thereby leaves a liberal space for free exchange, which must be respected by all rational citizens. This misconstrues the aims, range and criticality of communal life in Spinoza's thought. So intrinsic is this conception to human endeavour, and so primary is it to the attainment of sufficient virtue, that communal life can in no way be limited to a public sphere. Every act must be subjected to the consideration of whether it furthers communal life. Thus, every act must first be determined worthy of indifference, rather than being assumed or predetermined as such.

(c) As if to hammer home the above two arguments, Spinoza asserts that the primary security risk for the imperium is its own constituents. Any decree that arouses general indignation will be subject to a conspiracy against it equal to the combined right of the conspirators. In other words, the imperium, by its irrationality, will have generated another imperium whose right may exceed its own and by which it will be replaced. To avoid this, the imperium must ensure that it tacks the closer to reason.[56]

In the depths of this argument is an idea that should not surprise us: that the commonality of humans derives from their virtue and is expressed by their reason; the more virtuous, the more humans have in common and the more they seek mutual company; this mutual company forms an imperium that, so constituted by higher virtue, is more powerful and expresses their common nature in a greater way; but reason is united in the Infinite Understanding; so if two imperia exist that are virtuous in this order, they will each act in the same manner and seek each other's company; they thus will form an imperium of combined natural rights, and so on until all humanity is thus combined in the state of fostering reason, though whether we can speak of humanity anymore is questionable, as we shall see. Spinoza thus recovers his argument for God's uniqueness also on the politico-juridical plane of natural right.

In view of the foregoing, we define:

> The imperium intuitivum is an imperium constituted by singular things each of whose right approaches the limit of beatitude.

This formal idea of an imperium intuitivum grounds the practical argument that the most enduring imperium, the one that is the most secure, is in fact the one that most fosters rationality and thus approaches its own overcoming in the imperium intuitivum. This is the social transition in Spinozism. Just as the machine was raised to its infinite limit, now the city as social machine is raised to its limit as the infinite right-producing machine. This is, as considered between its constituents, at once *cosmopolis* and eternal and infinite intellect of God. As Spinoza writes in EVP40 Sch.:

> our mind, in so far as it understands, is an eternal mode of thinking, which is determined by another eternal mode of thinking, and that again by another, and so on to infinity, in such a way that they all constitute simultaneously the eternal and infinite intellect of God.

The citizens of the imperium intuitivum are sources of an infinite power that is determined by their relations *inter se* in a manner that appears to confirm the 'higher' equilibrium of power at the level of the infinite machine, but, remember, which power is issuing forth transitions in the finite world of duration insofar as the formal essences of the imperium intuitivum are being expressed by appropriate relations in the finite level. To be clear, the finite imperia together constitute a general equilibrium of human relations expressing the aggregate of finite powers, but over above this there is already one imperium intuitivum that is constituted by each person to the extent that they express the infinite *potentia Dei.* It is this difference of imperia that makes ethics possible, insofar as natural right now derives also from infinite power and constitutes the means for fostering the citizen.

One can perhaps now guess the sense in which Spinoza uses 'charity' and understands the political office of the sage, office here being disconnected from any conferred title. Already with Aquinas[57] (drawing on Augustine), there is a tradition of constructing the relation between grace and nature such that grace (*charis*) derives from God and is experienced as the joy and perfection of the donee (hence, *charisma*), but that this perfecting also institutes charity as the grace of the faithful. Now, the Latin *caritas* translates the Greek *agape*, not *charis*, but the suggestive homophonic linkage is made by Aquinas, drawing on Augustine. As Badiou has observed, *charis* as envisaged by Paul 'names the event as condition of active thought'[58] because 'thought can only be raised from its impotence by something which exceeds its order'.[59] Distributed between the Stoic transition as intervention in the order of the world,[60] and the Spinozan transition of activity of the infinite power in the general equilibrium, we begin to perceive the outlines of how the sage, as 'officer' of the imperium intuitivum, is to act 'charitably'. Moreover, we see by virtue of the formal essence of every thing that each person already expresses in some degree this inalienable power to intervene in the ordered power of the world. Hence, Spinoza writes that:

> the true knowledge and love of God [which is His power] cannot be subject to anyone's jurisdiction, as is also the case with charity towards one's neighbour . . . and . . . the highest form of that charity . . . is to safeguard peace and to promote harmony . . .
>
> (TPIII[10])

This needs to be read in the light of EVP20; 'the more [the *amor Dei*] is fostered [*fovetur*] the more men we imagine to be joined with God in the same bond [*vinculum*] of love'. Spinoza, though he does not use this terminology, *formaliter* marks the transition that Aquinas and Suárez might describe as: from *lex* derived from *legere* to *lex* derived from *ligare*; from law as that which is read, to law as that which links together.[61] Descartes writes in his *Sixth Objections*: 'Rex est legis effector, etsi lex ipsa non sit res physice existens, sed tantum, ut vocant, ens morale.'[62] Yet, perhaps we find the closest jurisprudential expression in this move in the *Hieroglyphica* of Pierius, about which Armogathe writes:[63]

> [Book XIV of the *Hieroglyphica* is] a very significant document for the semiotics of early modern Europe, where the icon of the law is a crown, which returns to the political sense, but a braided crown (an allusion to the mystical sense of the crown of thorns), affirming thus at the same time the political law (*legere*) and the physical law (*ligare*), because 'it is interwoven by some links, which compel our life to be bound in some way' (certis est vinculis complicata, quibus vita nostra veluti religata coercetur).

The resonances with the Leibnizian irenic plan for both a universal characteristic and a linkage of all princes into one unified (Christian) state are striking, though their common Stoic roots should not go overlooked. The difference with Spinoza is that he regards this grander plan as unachievable, and prefers to construct its formal essence in the minds of his readers through his argumentation that common reason is the route to the imperium's endurance and thus the highest aim of society. Ultimately, the Leibnizian idea for the *Elementa iurisprudentiae universalis*[64] is derived from the human nature now expressed, whereas for Spinoza the imperium is derived from the variations of 'being human' that occur across the spectrum of communal virtue. Balibar has shown in his work on trans-individuality[65] how Spinoza's dictum in TPV that man is not born a citizen but is made, indicates just how fluid Spinoza's concept of the human is. In so doing, Balibar elucidates the generative aspects of social life in which each constituent grows towards virtue and thus expresses 'humanity' anew with every transmutation. There is no contradiction here with our argument that Spinoza solves the 'common nature problem' by reference to the solutions expressed by communal acts; rather, Balibar's close textual analysis of the immanent flow of social life confirms it from a different angle. If one is sensitive to Leibniz's concerns, one can see that he too believes that common activity expresses a human nature through particular cases (*ius naturale*). He departs from Spinoza in regarding sufficient of this so-expressed human nature to be unchanging so as to provide rational civil laws from which to craft a jurisprudence (TTPIV Geb.III/59). It is a question, between the two thinkers, of the threshold of juridical mutability, with Spinoza determining that civil laws, justice, sin and so forth fall very much on the side of the mutable.

We may remark on one significant point of distinction between these competing views of citizenship, which the quotation from Pierius raises. This is the conception of the *vinculum*, a term of art with particular resonance in the Early Modern Period following the underground circulation of Giordano Bruno's incomplete treatise *De vinculis in genere* (c.1588). Garrett[66] has attempted to draw certain parallels between Bruno and Spinoza on several matters, though he concedes: (a) there is no evidence that Spinoza had read anything of Bruno; and (b) it is just as likely (if not more so) that Spinoza and Bruno were drawing on the same Pre-Socratic and Hellene sources. We make no judgement on this matter; rather, we note that whereas Bruno appears to consider the binding agent as both that which constitutes a thing, such as a man or a dog,[67] it also is that which operates across things, say in the love between humans, depending on the character and the susceptibility of those involved. Bruno considers binding as comprising within itself the Heraclitan contradiction that marks the universal animus, stated as a highly relevant claim that light is nothing without the darkness that allows its measurement.[68] The process of being bound, therefore, is determined as much by dissimilarity, confusion and therefore beguilement, and Bruno clearly advances binding as a method of magic that may be deployed by rhetoricians and lovers. An examination of Spinoza's *Ethics* reveals a sparse use of the *vinculum*, but a deployment appearing to be quite consistent and deliberate. We thus find binding first discussed in EIIIP35, where Spinoza expressly describes a 'bond of friendship' as something that is *imagined* with respect to two other persons.[69] This seems to be the meaning of EIV App. §12, which also refers to the utility of binding between humans and thus strengthening friendship.[70] It could be argued that this statement refers back to EIVP35 and thus rests on the conception that it is reason alone that permits common life. Yet the immediately consequent statements of the Appendix (§§13–14) speak of both the passionate and active aspects of society, and argue that the negative effects of social passions are to be borne and that one should try to *apply those measures which lead to the formation of concord and friendship.*[71] By linking concord with friendship, we aver that Spinoza is tying the imagination (appearance) of a bond of friendship to the more fundamental relation of concord, with its metaphysical apparatus, which we have outlined. Support for the view that here the *vinculum* is a confused idea, also comes from EIVP54: Spinoza uses *vinculum* with respect to the mob, asking how otherwise they are to be bound (restrained) if they could not feel fear. It is just this sense of hope/fear as a restraining factor that motivates a similar statement with respect to alliances between states in TPIII[14].[72] The final occurrence of the *vinculum* in the *Ethics* is in EVP20, as we saw above. Yet again, it is related to imagination, in that the more the love of God is fostered, *the more humans we imagine to be joined with God by the same bond of love*.[73] It thus appears that Spinoza regards the *vinculum* as a creature of the imagination that, however, has its basis as an idea in the deeper system of concord advanced in the foregoing sections of this research. Spinoza does not discard the *vinculum*, regarding it as would Machiavelli as a passionate tool for introducing harmony and friendship, and thus places it in the same category as civil law, with its like power of imaginative restraint. Yet the *vinculum* is not an efficient cause of its own perception; rather, that is the union of common right in endeavour, which is such a cause. On this particular matter, *pace* Garrett, Spinoza thus seems opposed to a Brunian conception of binding as the true agent of, for example, love and hate. If there is a similarity to the tradition of the renaissance magus, it seems more likely to consist in the idea that compositions in the finite sphere of mind can call forth powers in the 'higher spheres' into the lower, though it is more probable still that such ideas in the renaissance share a common ancestor with Spinoza in early Stoicism, mediated in the former case by Neo-Platonism, in the latter by Cartesianism. It is the idea of calling on a 'higher power' that suggests that Spinozan Love as immanent version of that power may play some role in binding the imperium intuitivum, even among the ignorant. For as Spinoza argues of piety, it does not follow from ignorance of the fact that good food is sustaining that a person should prefer deadly food (EVP41 Sch.). Every particular thing is such through Love and, as we have shown, is not merely revealed, but nourished. All may be said to be bound in this way, by their very reality, their realisation.

Returning to our thread, the cosmic city thus proposed is not the substandard reworking of the Stoic conception that can be found throughout Early Modern thinking in different degrees (from Lipsius and Grotius through to Montesquieu and Smith), a city that is inhabited by rational human beings by reason of their possession of rationality. Rather, this city is expressed according to every eternal act in common and is brought forth by fostering. 'Hence in the Republic Zenon said: "Eros is the God which contributes to the city's security".'[74] That which is expressed is the eternity of the virtuous mind and it is insofar as any two particular things can think in common that the cosmic city is expressed eternally. We contend that Spinoza claims that formal essence of this imperium intuitivum:

(a) is radically democratic in that the first constituent of its eternity is the *idea Dei* eternally expressed in the very act of thinking of each particular thing;
(b) as such act of God, having the character of the immutable absolute;
(c) as absolute it stands in relation to all imperia, whose virtues are inherently mutable, as the immanent standard of civil attainment of its highest good; and

(d) it operates as a moment not so much as transition to *greater* intensity, though relevant, but as transition *towards* God; the former is relative and pleasure bound; the latter is necessarily the true idea.

Accordingly:

(e) a city in which citizens pursue greater intensity, or gain, is not a rational city, despite the many claims that each human rationally endeavours to pursue her private benefit;
(f) rather, a city in which citizens pursue the *summum bonum* are less interested in increases in intensity, save insofar as these correlate to the ultimately desired movement towards beatific intuition;
(g) insofar as we are thinking things we are *already* citizens of the imperium intuitivum, though we fail to see this through the common order of nature;
(h) thus the formal essence of the imperium intuitivum is actualised by and is involved in each thinking – that is, it is not coming, but is already 'here' with the highest degree of implication;
(i) as our power of thinking increases through our thinking in common and the construction of concepts, so a greater part of our mind pertains to eternity and we inhabit and thus actualise the contours of this city to a greater degree; and
(j) the core moments of the imperium intuitivum are: (i) the intuitive-charitable act of 'fostering' intended as an opening of the genetic power of formal essences as sites of the multitude's life; and (ii) the reciprocal passionate imagining of the bond of life with the *amor Dei*. The imperium intuitivum thus turns on itself through the types of cognition, and amounts to the concept of the city.

There is the almost Scotist judgement Spinoza makes from the very outset: to determine that the means or knowledge of salvation is already immanent to thought and extension, and thus self-evident to every thinking thing. There is no silent vigil for the Second Coming, no utopian dream of a New Jerusalem, but a radicalisation of natural right as the doctrine of consciousness at work – a consciousness, for there is only one consciousness, which seeks to raise its own actuality to the highest degree. Just as the real geometric point precedes the magnitude and the form; just as the case, understood as a real *instance*[75] of *ius*, precedes the law, which latter is inscribed on a series of cases, so it is for this formal essence of the highest imperium, actualised at least in the moment of thought, to precede every human imperium as not an ideal but a materially acting incorporeal 'formal imperium' within the life of each state. Remember, this is not Spinoza's political doctrine, which is aimed at ameliorating what he regards as the problematic of passionate life in the imperium. Rather, we seek to examine the juridical consequences of his theory of natural right, which echoes and even amplifies the radical fringes of rights theories in the seventeenth century, as Tuck has shown with respect to Selden, De la Court, and the infamous 'Constans'.[76]

As in those cases, the prescriptions for remedying the passions of the populace somewhat mask the work in favour of a 'republican régime of active citizens'.[77]

One final contemporary point of comparison for Spinoza is Grotius' *De imperio summarum potestatum circa sacra*,[78] which amounts to a treatise on the state's relation to the sacred. We first set Spinoza's 'this right, which is defined by the multitude, is often called an imperium'[79] in contrast to Grotius' equivalent 'This Supreme power [*Summa Potestatis*] so defined we call the Imperium, to be extended not just to the profane, but also to the sacred.'[80] By the '*summum potestatem*', Grotius understands persons or others who submit to the command that it is exclusively God's.[81] He thus speaks of the *Summa Potestatis* as 'not assumed by right, as is its sometimes taken to be, but held by right, in the manner that is customary for the Latins and Greeks to speak'.[82] Against Spinoza's *potentia*, as Negri has notably pointed out, this *summum potestatem* seems rather flimsy. Yet Spinoza's ownership of the Parisian 1648 edition of *De Imperio*, the structural similarity of the definition, and the appearance of a characteristic reworking in the *Tractatus politicus*, suggest at least the possibility that a line may be drawn from Grotius' divinely oriented imperium to Spinoza's own naturalist theory outlined above.

For Spinoza, this groundwork is intensely complicated, bound up as it is with his dynamic physics and astonishing temporal-spatial theory. We have endeavoured to bring this doctrine of natural right to the fore by stressing its mechanism over the customary content of irrational, rational and divine laws (TTPIV).

6.3.4 The highest aim of society – ethics and politics

In TPV, following a discussion of international politics and the rights of the office holder of the imperium, Spinoza returns to and summarises the thread of his argument. It is a recapitulation of the ideas that ultimately the *securest* imperium is the most *rational*, that is, the one that expresses the common nature of its citizens in the greatest way by virtue of the power it has aided them to develop. Spinoza sums up his theory with the following statement, whose language indicates the central importance of our reconstruction of the vortical model of natural right:

> Thus when I say that the best imperium is one in which humans live in concord, I understand human life, which is characterised not by the circulation of blood and other vital processes common to all animals, but primarily by reason, the true virtue and life of the mind.
>
> (TPV[5])

We are thus brought back to the fundamental linkage between the flux of natural right in its existential and essential guise and the flow of conscious life in common, insofar as this is permitted by Spinoza's conception of reason. Note, however, that in all this, reason must be understood according to its double aspects of rationality and intuition. We have already seen how the act of thinking and the idea that is thought are categorically distinct. Yet consciousness in itself is power, and given that power is natural right as far as it extends, we must be careful to clarify the difference between the power and its effect. It is because the norm of the present and that of the common will or intellect are situated in the action of the mind, not its effects, that the constitution of the imperium is, first and foremost, a matter of attributive analysis. The infinite understanding may provide us with the being of the adequate ideas, ideas that humans can share insofar as they express a commonality both between object and human, and between humans sharing this idea, but these common notions only present thought under a certain species of eternity. This is thought that has *rectitude*, but it is not intuition. The infinite understanding is a result of God's infinite thinking, not the cause of it, and so it is the product or creation of God's natural right. Insofar as humans likewise produce common notions and the rational civil laws and conceptions of justice that we are to suppose derive from them, these ideas are not *that* infinite natural right but only natural right resulting from finite power. And now perhaps must come the final moment of Spinozism, the meaning of infinite power on which the imperium intuitivum is, in a novel sense, 'grounded'. For the infinite immediate mode is the creation of God or Nature that it has completed for itself, but our finitude means that this is a creation that is yet to come; we are caught up in the act of creation, which has already been pursued to completion.

The modal level thus complements the level of attributes – their difference makes ethics possible. There is a view that the sum of the modes in the city, the clamour of the multitudes, suffices to compose a mode that will foster the greatest mutations of power. Simply by the revelation of this sum of powers by the infinite immediate mode, we have constituted all the formative potential adequately to distribute joy among the populous. The infinite mediate mode is simply the instant of the finite present as it rolls to this end. And what is this end? We have seen that it must be the resolution of all power down to a point that, in Nature's case, is a point that will bear an infinity of motion and rest, a point that physically can only be the celestial light at its most intense; in God's Thought the beatific vision of the 'Son'. Our view is that this is nothing other than a luminescent version the Stoic conflagration,[83] and it is this conflagration that forms the ultimate instance of natural right and the ground that is yet to come for the imperium intuitivum. It is this striking, ever recurring conclusion from which and to which the Spinozan sage eternally turns her mind, despite Spinoza's positive rejection of its finite corollary, the Stoic theory of suicide (EIVP20).

We cannot submit to this divine *consumption*. To permit power to be redistributed according solely to the form of the mode that is composed by the sum of the powers of the multitude may appear radical, but is to adopt the ethics of consumption, for:

(a) The thus composed mode takes on a form from below, but this below composes with the infinite immediate mode of substance – to be multitude it must not exclude (become in common), and by necessity takes within itself all present modal determinations including that of the One.

(b) The composed mode is an effect, not cause, of the distribution of the modes. Against this, formal essences are formative, the cause the modes that compose into multitudes.

Perhaps this drives Marx's assault on the Ricardians who believed value could be redistributed by market regulation (for the market is, dare we say it, also a multitude). As we noted in Chapter 1, a key difference from Hobbes is that Spinoza rejects the multitudes' muddled settlement on a political compromise in favour of a struggle of reason for social concord in the best imperium attainable. Who is the thinker of 'might is right' when it is Hobbes who would counsel as political goal the inevitable demise of the mass onto compromise, while it is Spinoza who counsels necessary resistance in favour of mutation towards the harmonious imperium? Even if we could agree that these positions are two parts of the same belief – that the political horizon of multitudes is bounded by the composition of their constituent powers – Hobbes argues for attaining the highly probable (commutative justice); Spinoza for the highly improbable (redistributive justice).[84] Or at least, Spinoza reminds us that the highly improbable is always a political possibility. For Marx – and Spinoza's influence appears strong here – the Ricardian reliance on commutative justice only attacking the cause of the problem, the cause nexus of *production*, will provide the basis for an effective reworking of industrial relations. Our question is whether this is unduly to limit the potential of Spinoza's thought. There is a role for the modes that multitudes compose insofar as we relate these back to the attributes. In this chapter, we have tried to indicate that the interaction between modal existence and the active attributive flux is key: introductions of motion and rest produce variations in the attributes; tensions in the attributes produce variations in motion and rest. This is the lesson of the infinite immediate mode as expression of the infinite machine. We must build machines that aim not directly at the production of modes, but at the production of formal essences. For by producing (or otherwise deepening and configuring) formal essences, we produce the conditions of natural right. These sources of natural right then become the crucible in which we consume the *authority* (*potestas*) of this world and forge the new. If Spinozan machines can be said to internalise rule-making at all, it is to dissolve the infinite series that bind machines and even *Deus sive Natura* – to unmake God through the intensive dissolution of Promethean chains. Only at the limit of the multitude, when we have invested it with the greatest possible *potestas* and *potentia*, do we find that all that was ontologically solid melts into air. This is a multitude of a different order altogether, in which the existence, essence and excess of things uncouple as if with one utterly material mind. Elsewhere, we have called this the *supermultitude* (2015). It follows readily enough from Spinoza's own doctrines, but it is a case derived at an impractical extremum. If it serves any utility, perhaps this is only experimentally insofar as it allows us to think of the unmaking of substance in act. So foster multitudes but do not let the ephemeral form of the mode supplant the formative role of the attribute, for only when each aspect of the living process is accounted for do we uncover through intuition the possibility of unpicking the absolute concept.

Insofar as we consider natural right in this intuitive sense, then, it is a theory about what categorically is not yet but is determined to come, about *this* work, a labour that forms a juridical surface across the mutilated world of political actuality. It is this surface that, with its eddies, flows and vortical tendencies, demands the analysis that Spinoza began to provide with the geometric tools available to him. He understood the tendency of law to point at what is present and provide a rule for all of it. And he accepted this simply because he knew this to be the first error of all ethics: the confusion of effects and decrees with causes and reasons.

Notes

1 'It is interwoven by some links, which constrain our life to be bound in some way.'
2 Cf. Ch. 5.
3 Cf. Ch. 3.
4 Where one draws the line between the fluid characteristics of the 'example' and proto-field characteristics at which the example is aiming being more than a little problematic.
5 Though physically impossible for a plenum.
6 Deleuze writes a not dissimilar thing, that 'rights are naturally additive' (1990a: 265–266), though he argues that this only applies to rational beings, whereas in the city people must be *forced* together. This seems to overlook Spinoza's grounding of human sociality in the commonality of their natures first of all, which even in strife must at some level require something in common to constitute even a painful encounter. Of course, if Deleuze in fact means that humans can become more 'in common' through reason, as Balibar argues (1997), then we agree that this is Spinoza's view.
7 Cf. *Le monde* A&T XI pp. 63–64.
8 Ibid., p. 54.
9 TPII[13].
10 'Cum ergo dicimus, illud imperium optimum esse, ubi homines concorditer vitam transigunt, vitam humanam intelligo, quae non sola sanguinis circulatione et aliis, quae omnibus animalibus sunt communia, sed quae maxime ratione, vera mentis virtute et vita definitur.'
11 Hobbes (1994) *Leviathan* VI, 1, and also *De Corpore* XXV, 5, Molesworth (1839–1845).
12 'Quae efficiunt, ut motus et quietis ratio, quam corporis humani partes ad invicem habent, conservetur, bona sunt; et ea contra mala, quae efficiunt, ut corporis humani partes aliam ad invicem motus et quietis habeant rationem.'
13 'Quae ad hominum communem societatem conducunt, sive quae efficiunt, ut homines concorditer vivant, utilia sunt, et illa contra mala, quae discordiam in civitatem inducunt.'
14 See the important chapter in Athusser (1965).
15 (1984).
16 (1984: 273ff.).
17 This understanding of Marx's reinterpretation of the Feuerbachian God is due to Balibar.
18 TTP17 Geb.III/203. TTP5, Geb.III/55, 75. HG4, Geb.I/295/20–23.
19 'Sed quemadmodum homines initio innatis instrumentis quaedam facillima, quamvis laboriose et imperfecte, facere quiverunt, iisque confectis alia difficiliora minori labore, et perfectius confecerunt, et sic gradatim ab operibus simplicissimis ad instrumenta, et ab instrumentis ad alia opera, et instrumenta pergendo eo pervenerunt, ut tot et tam difficilia parvo labore perficiant . . .'

20 '. . . sic etiam intellectus vi sua nativa (facit sibi instrumenta intellectualia, quibus alias vires acquirit ad alia opera) intellectualia, et ex iis operibus alia instrumenta seu potestatem ulterius investigandi; et sic gradatim pergit, donec sapientiae culmen attingat'.
21 The tool's power refers us to its capacity to endure and to work; its nature discloses the specific qualitative appearance of this power, as rigidity, sharpness, etc.
22 (1962: 96–97).
23 Proximate because it accompanies the act of working together. Spinoza rather suggests any joy comes from imagining the success of our joint act and the actual benefits derived from this labour. In working together, we are surprised, if anything, by our joint strength.
24 It should not go unnoticed that *fovere*'s past participle *fōtus* has etymological connotations over and above fostering.
25 Matheron (1969: 296) also discusses domination by reference to utilisation of another human.
26 TPI[5], II[5], V[2, 3].
27 See also Deleuze (1980).
28 (1959: 62).
29 Can one even write a history of Stoicism? Chrysippos was more Spinoza's contemporary than Pufendorf, or better, they are co-eternal.
30 Ibid.
31 We speak of here of nature considered by reference to the power relations of the attributes expressed at that moment of causation into the general equilibrium. This is not the same as the expression of this nature by a mode: the mode expresses the power only as extensive variation of time and intensity of modal 'form'.
32 (1989: 207).
33 Compare Hegel's *Enzyklopädie II* (1969) §§254–262.
34 Gueroult (1974: 503–504), affirming Dreyfus in n. 30. *Pace* Gueroult, we would place less emphasis on the truth of an idea as the enveloping volition, and more on the transition due to consciousness availing itself of a powerful tool.
35 (1976: 433) and for Bellers see n. 5 ibid.
36 TPI[6].
37 'Animi enim libertas seu fortitudo privata virtus est; at imperii virtus securitas.'
38 (1997: 1).
39 Curley in Garrett (1996: 315–342).
40 'Denique quia omnes hominess, sive barbari sive culti sint, consuetudines ubique iungunt et statum aliquem civilem formant, ideo imperii causae et fundamenta naturalia non ex rationis documentis petenda, sed ex hominum communi natura seu conditione deducenda sunt . . .'
41 (1958: 265 n. 5).
42 TPII[13].
43 TPII[14].
44 TPII[15].
45 The well-known 'una veluti mente ducuntur'.
46 Cf. Agamben's archeology of the office in *Opus Dei* (2012).
47 Cf. e.g. (1903: 331).
48 TPIII[2], but already stated in TPII[16].
49 (1755 [1627]) I, vii, 'Tum vero instituta quadam ita & homnibus communia, ut non tam naturae instinctui, aut evidenti rationis collectioni, quam perpetuae & vix paucis in locis per malitiam aut calamitatem interruptae traditioni, accepta ferri dabeant: qualis olim fuit victimarum in sacris mactatio, & nunc quoque pudor circa res Veneris, nuptiarum solemnia, & incestorum fuga.' Compare Kant's definition of marriage.
50 In Blom and Winkel (2004: 177–196).

51 *Meletius* [13], quoted in Besselink, ibid., p. 193.
52 *Meletius* [58], quoted in Besselink, ibid.
53 I.e. as against other imperia. TPIII concludes with a discussion of international politics and law.
54 TPIII[7].
55 TPIII[8].
56 TPIII[9].
57 *ST* Q.113 Art.10.
58 'nomme l'événement comme condition de la pensée active' (1997: 89).
59 'la pensée ne peut être relevée de son impuissance que par quelque chose qui exceed son ordre' (ibid.).
60 The difference between necessity and fate, consider SVF2.913 in the light of the difference general equilibrium/disequilibrium.
61 Here, we rely on Armogathe in Daston and Stolleis (2008: 277).
62 A&T VII p. 336.
63 Ibid., n. 45 *supra.*
64 Leibniz, *Akademie Ausgabe der Sämtlichen Schriften und Briefe* (1930–) vol.VI 4, 443, cf. also pp. 359–361.
65 Balibar (1997).
66 (2001: xlvii and lxxxix ff.).
67 *De vinculis in genere*, hereafter D.V., §1 'On bonding in general' (2001: 145–146).
68 (2001: 169) D.V. §8 'The measurement of bonds'.
69 'Si quis imaginatur rem amatam eodem vel arctiore vinculo amicitiae, quo ipse eadem solus potiebatur, alium sibi iungere, odio erga ipsam rem amatam afficietur, et illi alteri invidebit.'
70 'Hominibus apprime utile est, consuetudines iungere, seseque iis vinculis astringere, quibus aptius de se omnibus unum efficiant, et absolute ea agere, quae firmandis amicitiis inserviunt.'
71 'Quare satius est eorum iniurias aequo animo ferre et studium iis adhibere, quae concordiae et amicitiae conciliandae inserviunt.'
72 'Hac autem aut illo civitatum alterutri adempto, manet ipsa sui iuris . . . et vinculum, quo civitates invicem adstrictae erant, sponte solvitur.' Cf. also TPIX[4].
73 'Hic erga Deum amor neque invidiae neque zelotypiae affectu inquinari potest; sed eo magis fovetur, quo plures homines eodem amoris vinculo cum Deo iunctos imaginamur.'
74 SVF 1.263.
75 The concern here, which is that of Leibniz, is with the case as a real series of events (an unfolding concept, e.g. the life of Sextus Tarquin) and not case in the sense of decision or judgment. Laws swarm across the surface constituted by real cases (lives) and for Spinoza 'rational' laws are those that build upon these surfaces rather than simply pass across them, such that the case of the sage coincides with law as a 'lawlike' and *sui iuris* life. Otherwise, like the fury that drives Hercules, the law as body counsels and enrages and demands to be fed of its own account, and not for that of its 'host'. On this model, precedent might be defined thus: *the appropriation of a case to the body of law*. It is no wonder collections of laws are called 'digests'!
76 The latter the author of *Polityke Weeg-Schaal*, as discussed in Tuck (1979: 141–142).
77 *Per* De la Court, as quoted in Tuck (1979: 141).
78 (1970) Scientia Verlag, Aalen. Hereafter *De Imperio* with book and [paragraph].
79 'hoc ius, quod multitudinis potentia definitur, imperium appellari solet'.
80 'Hujus ergo *Summa* Potestatis ita definitae Imperium dicimus, non ad profana tantum, sed ad sacra quoque extendi.' *De Imperio* I [2], emphasis in original.
81 'cui imperium sit in populo Solius DEI imperio subditum'. Ibid.

82 'non pro iure sumimus, ut sumi interdum solet, sed pro ius habente, quomodo & Latinis mos est loqui & Graecis'. Ibid. (I[1]).
83 Cf. Plutarch's report SVF 2.605.
84 Probability, the reckoning of chances, becomes a factor as we cannot determine the precise activity of each constituent of a multitude.

Bibliography

Agamben, G. (2012) *Opus Dei – Archéologie de l'office – Homo Sacer Tome 5*, Seuil, Paris.

Althusser, Balibar, Establet, Macherey, Rancière (1965) *Lire le Capital*, Quadrige/PUF, Paris.

Aquinas, T. (1882) *Sancti Thomae Aquinatis (doctoris angelicae): Opera omni* (13 vols), Typographia Polyglotta, Rome.

—— (1947) *Compendium theologiae*, S.J. Cyril Vollert (trans.), B. Herder Book Co., St. Louis & London.

Arnim, J. von (1979) *Stoicorum veterum fragmenta* (4 vols), BG Teubner, Stuttgart.

Badiou, A. (1997) *Saint Paul – la fondation de l'uinversalisme*, Collège International de Philosophie, PUF, Paris.

Balibar, E. (1992) 'A note on "consciousness/conscience" in the *Ethics*' 8 *Studia Spinozana* 37–53.

—— (1997) 'Spinoza: from individuality to transindividuality' *Mededelingen vanwege het Spinozahuis*, Vol. 71, Eburon, Netherlands.

—— (2007) *Spinoza and Politics*, Verso, London.

Blom, H. and Winkel, L. (2004) *Grotius and the Stoa*, Van Gorcum, Assen.

Boulnois, O. (2012) 'From divine omnipotence to operative power', in A. Schütz and M. Traversino (eds), *'Epigenesis' in the History of Power and Laws*, Edizioni Studio, Domenico, Bologna, pp. 83–97.

Bruno, G. (2004) *Cause, Principle, and Unity, and Essays on Magic*, Cambridge University Press, Cambridge. Includes a translation of *De vinculis in genere*.

Connelly, S. (2015 forthcoming) 'Cosmopolitanism for the love of multitudes', in T. Caraus and E. Paris (eds), *Post-Foundational Cosmopolitanism*, Routledge, London.

Daston, L. and Stolleis, M. (eds) (2008) *Natural Law and Laws of Nature in Early Modern Europe: Jurisprudence, Theology, Moral and Natural Philosophy*, Ashgate, Farnham, UK.

Deleuze, G. (1990a) *Expressionism in Philosophy: Spinoza*, M. Joughlin (trans.), Zone Books, New York.

Deleuze, G. and Guattari, F. (1984) *Anti-Oedipus: Capitalism and Schizophrenia*, Athlone, London.

Garrett, D. (ed.) (1996) *The Cambridge Companion to Spinoza*, Cambridge University Press, Cambridge.

—— (2001) 'Introduction', which fronts a loose translation of the *Ethics*, Wordsworth, London.

Grotius, H. (1625) *De jure belli ac pacis libri tres, in quibus jus naturae & gentium, itme juris publici praceipua explicantur*, Nicolaum Buon, Paris.

—— (1755) [1627] *De veritate religionis christianae, cum notulis J. Clerici* (2 vols), J. Nourse, London.

—— (1970) [1648] *De imperio summarum potestatum circa sacra*, 1690 Frankfurt/M. edn, reprint Scientia Verlag, Aalen.

Gueroult, M. (1968a) *Descartes selon l'ordre des raisons: II – L'âme et le corps*, Aubier, Éditions Montaigne, Paris.

—— (1968b) *Spinoza: I – Dieu*, Aubier, Éditions Montaigne, Paris.
—— (1974a) *Spinoza: II – L'âme*, Aubier, Éditions Montaigne, Paris.
—— (1974b) *Études sur Fichte*, Aubier, Éditions Montaigne, Paris.
Hegel, G.W.F. (1969) *Werke in zwanzig Bänden*, Suhrkamp Verlag, Frankfurt am Main.
Heidegger, M. (1962) *Being and Time*, Blackwell, Oxford.
—— (1977–2007) *Gesamtausgabe: Veroffentlichte Schriften (16 Bände)*, Vittorio Klostermann, Frankfurt am Main.
Hobbes, Sir. T. (1994) *Leviathan*, Hackett, Indianapolis, IN.
Leibniz, G.W. (1903) *Opuscules et fragments inédits de Leibniz*, L. Couturat (ed.), Félix Alcan, Paris.
—— (1962) *G.W. Leibniz: Mathematische Schriften*, C.I. Gerhardt and Georg Olms (eds), Verlagsbuchhandlung, Hildesheim.
—— (1989) *Philosophical Essays*, R. Ariew and D. Garber (trans.), Hackett, Indianapolis, IN.
—— (2010) *Theodicy*, A. Farrer and E.M. Huggard (trans.), Cosimo, New York.
Marx, K. (1968) *Texte zu Methode und Praxis II: Pariser Manuskripte 1844*, Rowohlt, Reinbek bei Hamburg.
—— (1970) *A Contribution to the Critique of Political Economy*, Progress Publishers, Moscow.
—— (1976) *Capital* (3 vols.), Penguin & New Left Review, London.
Marx, K. and Engels, F. (1971–1990) *Marx-Engels Werke: Ergänzungsband*, Dietz Verlag, Berlin.
Matheron, A. (1985) '"Le droit du plus fort": Hobbes contre Spinoza' 110 *Revue Philosophique* 149–176.
—— (1988) *Individu et Communauté chez Spinoza*, Editions de Minuit, Paris.
Molesworth, Sir Wm. (ed.) (1839–1845) *The English Works of Thomas Hobbes of Malmesbury* (11 vols.), London.
Moreau, P.F. (1977) 'Ius et Lex: Spinoza devant la tradition juridique' (July) 43 *Raison Présente* 53–61.
—— (1984) 'Le fondement metaphysique du droit chez Spinoza' in J.J. Curiel (ed.), *Memoria del X Congreso Munidal Ordinario de Filosofía del Derecho y Filosofía Social Filosofía del derecho y problemas de filosofía social*, vol. X, Universidad Nacional Autónoma de México, Ciudad Universitaria, 04510, México.
'Pierius' (Ioannis Pierii Valeriani) (1678) *Bellunensis Hieroglyphica, sive de sacris Aegyptiorum aliarumque gentium litteris commentariorum*, t. LVIII, Christiani Kirchneri, Frankfurt am Main.
Sambursky, S. (1959) *Physics of the Stoics*, Greenwood Press, Westport, CT.
Schofield, M. (1991) *The Stoic Idea of the City*, Cambridge University Press, Cambridge.
Schütz, A. and Traversino, M. (eds) (2012) *The theology of 'potential dei' and the history of European normativity*, Divus Thomas, Bologna.
Tuck, R. (1979) *Natural rights theories: their origins and development*, Cambridge University Press, Cambridge.
Wernham, A.G. (1958) *Benedict de Spinoza: the political works*, Clarendon Press, Oxford.

Chapter 7

Conclusion

With the explication of the imperium intuitivum, we have attempted to show the formal limit of Spinoza's theory of natural right: the idea of a city as a right augmenting machine for its constituents. Combining a Stoic-inspired theory of the attributes with Cartesian statics and hydrostatics, we believe we have shown the physical principles that are the 'true codes' of Spinoza's thinking about natural right. As part of this endeavour, we have discovered many important results, including how the attributes need to be considered as incorporeal events of God or Nature, the role of Cartesian statics as an erroneous basis for kinematics in the PI, the possible Brunian meaning of 'rest', the reference point of the *Mechanica* and its theory of circulation, and the inspiration and questions initiated by the Cartesian celestial hypothesis. This helped us to establish how the definition of natural right that Spinoza finally settled on was not a reductive afterthought, dismissing legal theory as mistaken theology, but a full expression of a key principle of Spinoza's doctrine. Right then becomes formalised as a power of existing – the thing's immutability as it is constituted and subjected to transitions – and a power of working conceived as both finite effort and an inalienable right to foster (*fovere*) the world so that the multitude may thrive – the conatus to mutation. Consequently, when we speak of natural right, what we have shown in this book is that we are speaking in the simplest case about a rigorous equivalence between:

(A) Natural right =
  (a) finite and/or infinite power
  (b) extended along a line
  equals
(B) the transition (if any) of a certain proportion of:
  (a) motion to
  (b) rest
  (i.e. the power [*potentia*] of operating)
  of some machine defined by its willing of its:
  (a) common nature; and
  (b) particular nature
  (i.e. the power [*potestas*] of existing)
  to the extent that this produces some actual, quantitative effect.

The elements (B) are the *components of natural right*, and what is striking about them is how they integrate all the categorical elements of the Spinozan ontology that we attempted to reconstruct at the end of Chapter 3. Taken with respect to (A), natural right indeed amounts to a complete statement about Being, but what Spinoza is interested in is that which the components (B) inform us (as Spinoza has been reminding us through his *oeuvre*); that natural right tells us not only what a thing is, but what *work* it is doing, and conversely, that a thing which is not working lacks actuality, reality, perfection and virtue. The ethical task becomes work, the labour of the construction of concepts, of tools, which in their very construction must be expressed in the world to the extent they prevail. The Spinozan worker remains forever within the closure of Being, but always right at its limit, pushed up hard against that boundary, and it is perhaps this price Spinoza is willing to pay in exchange for fully resolving ethics (and so natural right) into physics and thereby raising the artisan above the priest. Marx, in his critique of Hegel, seems to implicate Spinoza (and perhaps also the Hellenes) on this very point when he damns 'the Master'[1] for believing that *Entäußerung* was a necessary stage of mind that obtained the absolute on condition only that it was the act of alienation of the products of work itself, which was the price of passage (i.e. mind must abstract itself from its world; from its work(ing)).[2] For all his alleged asceticism, Spinoza's theory of natural right, and the sage that most perfectly expresses it, is not some stage to be overcome, but is driven into the heart of the city as the condition of its existence and its continued survival. Where the multitude does not work, the city's aggregate virtue is correspondingly reduced. It was for Marx to show that it was possible for the multitude to work within the city, but for that labour (both finite and infinite) to be alienated nevertheless – *for the multitude to be deprived of their natural rights* – and for this process itself to call into question the city's sustainability. Yet Marx's core premise on this point was that the Spinozan artisan did not cease to be in the eighteenth century, but that it continued as a conceptual sphere within capitalism, just as the state of nature continued in the Spinozan city.[3] Indeed, we would venture to read Marx as regarding the Spinozan ethics of work as now operating as the ideological chain which *first* caused the worker (and the bourgeois economist) to see the sale of labour power as a fair bargain, and to be blind to the real source of profit,[4] and *second* operated to cast the general equivalence into the role of infinite substance, the boundary of all Being reaffirmed by the worker even as she constantly reconstructs it.[5] Is this the tragedy of Spinoza's central juridical theory of right: that even as this theory is considered bizarre and useless to the jurist, and so lacks the legal success of Hobbes' original, it has become the actually existing ethical perspective with which the worker confronts her condition? This is the condition of the C-M-C circuit that appears to the worker as the exchange of the commodity of her future labour for commodities produced by an equivalent amount of labour (in equilibrium conditions). How might the worker assess the just bargain? We suggest that, in Spinozan terms, this exchange appears as nothing other than the equivalence: *amount of work done (labour commodity)* = *amount of work done (commodity or monetised equivalent)* = *natural right*. After all, is not present natural right a scalar quantum derived from power extended as magnitude? If work is right by nature, what could be fairer than the market equivalence of natural rights? 'But how could anyone make a profit?' asked Marx. Perhaps it is because one can only see the success of Spinoza's theory of natural right from without this sphere, from having discovered its limitations in meditating on the *work of death*, that, for those jurists who remain within, it is absolutely necessary that Spinoza be judged to have failed.

Now, both powers of endeavouring to exist and endeavouring to work are subject to a limitation that they have right insofar as they prevail, but rather than a statement of acceptance of the brutality of the world, we have tried to show that this is the necessary and determinate moment of true freedom that mirrors that of God or Nature. It is because right cannot change in a given case that even through the second kind of knowledge we can establish how to augment it using tools and combining with others. Through the third, we can learn to arrange bodies to inflect formal essences and construct machines that express greater power.

The imperium is conceived as a somewhat mutable right augmenting machine that draws on the power of its multitude to increase the flow of conscious circulation and so increase experiences, and to augment the power of all. A doctrine of might is right with security at its heart, when understood through its physical principles, becomes a profound declaration in favour of concord through community and the highest right and security of that imperium, which most fosters reason in both its rational and intuitive (i.e. mutative) forms.

Such a model of right takes the Hobbist theory of miraculously willing atoms not as a starting point, but has a countervailing physical background of machines coupled together as the links in the great chain of causation. One can see in this the importance Cantor placed in Spinoza; not his theory of infinitude that was overturned, but in the brilliant idea that every whole is a machine constituted of parts that are themselves machines, all the way up and all the way down. Spinoza seeks to mechanise natural right theory, but in so doing he juridifies the entire universe from greatest to smallest, bringing all within one order of natural right. This naturally initiates the question of whether set theory is fatal for Spinozism. One possible avenue for research is to show how the set concept fails adequately to account for the incorporeal choice of parts, which ensures that, for Spinoza, not every possible may exist, but only those actually determined to exist by natural right.

Spinoza quite happily abandons the concept of natural laws to the new scientific meaning. Natural right, on the other hand, is the name for a way of thinking about the surface of consciousness, the endeavour that powers the norm of the present, and subject matter of a geometry of juridical forms from which we can endeavour to construct the conditions of a general will or intellect. Yet Spinoza did not go far enough. His natural right creaks under the weight of its determinism, which necessarily creates indeterminacy, as Vuillemin[6] has beautifully shown. He fails to realise that God or Nature's eternal act, given a new twist by modern authors who grant the *actio* its Aristotelian rather than Stoic meaning, is a being of reason – a useful way of comparing a unified world by reducing every mode to the act of something. To a certain degree, Spinoza is ahead of these modern (vital, energetic) interpretations because he only attempts to explain his physical world using actually observable events (body, motion and rest, transitions), rather than granting ontological status to what amounts to a way of thinking about such events in terms of total and systemic vitality. The One becomes ironically a Neoplatonic living form, for in its dissolution in 'pure action' it has no more, or precisely just as much, being as the number '1'. Even Spinoza doubted whether that was appropriate.[7] Against this tendency comes the need to consider attributes, and thus natural rights, as having their own peculiarities depending on the substantial or modal configurations which expressed them.

Spinoza's theory of natural right is not simply 'eccentric Hobbism'. Not only does it advance according to a physical model that stands in opposition to that deployed to Hobbes, but more importantly, even if Spinoza is taken as a corpuscular thinker of clashing atoms like Hobbes, he takes up all this power and folds even greater power into it. As a result, he can at once deny the liberty of Hobbes, which appears as empty and inexplicable desire, and yet rediscover hard-won liberty having passed through the demands of necessary power to attain the infinite. The power thus regained is now determinate freedom from determination, and as such becomes a differentiated object for the highest form of cognition, that is the *scientia intuitiva*. Spinoza's challenge to the jurist is to demand our acceptance of determinism, of the zeroth moment of power, as the condition of passage to a full understanding of his political theory. Did not the early Stoics also withhold Zenon of Kition's execrated *Republic* from acolytes until they had proven themselves to be true philosophers? When he is accused of declaring 'right is might', are these accusations more from fear, for perhaps it is only if one fully pursues this doctrine to its ends, if one is prepared to think so anti-juridical a thesis, that one can arrive at what is most rare because it is most difficult? Natural right is thus transformed into a trifold doctrine – of *potestas*, *potentia finita rei* and *potentia absoluta Dei* – which subsumes the struggle of finitude within itself in order to reveal an inalienable natural right. The too great a focus of jurists on but one half of conatus doctrine – an implicit attempt to shoehorn Spinoza into the safer legal strappings of the Sage of Malmesbury – obscures Spinoza's couplet of existing *and* working, and consequently seems to depart the *Ethics* early in its Third Part for the political works, only sparsely referencing the few political Scholia from the Fourth, and leaving much of the tripartite distinction of power that Spinoza's lays across EIII-V unconsidered. EV is practically abandoned, even though some of its last remarks discuss the divine law and the *sui iuris* sage[8] – imbued with infinite power – thus indicating the continued relevance of legal theory to Spinoza's ethical thesis.

This infinite right, if conceived within the unity of Spinoza's physics, bears with it those cautions and insights that the simple granting of atomic freedom cannot. Among these are the knowledge that the mind is a nexus between the pre-individual formal essence, which is far greater in possibility than our bodies, and the multitudes, which are nourished by our very power. 'Anarchic licence' might thus still apply, but it is the rationalist freedom of Godwin or Kropotkin, not the openness to the *Nichts* of Stirner and Bakunin. We now understand that immanent power must come into the world at determinate sources, and that in Thought we must work to construct bodies and inflect sources, the greater to express the tireless power as an exemplary, virtuous natural right.

The question that arises for us at the end of this book, in considering the routes from Spinoza, is whether particularly the analysis of the virtual, pursued by Deleuze, does not conflate three separate initiatives in Leibniz's thought. At the first level, we analyse power, seeking to determine its texture and singular points, in the manner in which Descartes and we say Spinoza also attempted in their theories of the celestial vortex (or city), though they could only discover absolute cases of existing things (machines in act). At the second level, we pass with Leibniz from *potentia* to *vis viva* and consider substance(s) in act, integrating duration into space while discovering that duration, too, has its singular points and lacunae – its points of transition. Our belief is that Leibniz, however, found both approaches still all too physical and continued through his life to pursue various strands of logic as a necessary complement: the *ars combinatoria* as science of logic. Leibniz maintained, as we have noted, that *le calcul des nombres* had as its necessary complement *l'analyse de la situation.* At the third level, then, of substance itself, Leibniz confronts Spinoza with the idea that in raising natural right (work) to the limit of God or Nature and so resolving it into simplicity (and for Hegel death), Spinoza celebrates the power of work and pays no attention either: (a) to the reason for its being carried out (i.e. not work itself, but *the* work); or (b) the possibility that the work might not belong to this substance, to this infinite understanding, and be distinguishable from it. Spinoza may feel that a natural right is nothing if it cannot be fulfilled, but Spinoza's natural right, even if carried out to infinity, is unfulfilling and unfulfillable: his physics literally *consumes* his logic. For Leibniz, this insight marks the entrance to his kingdom of ends, but we would remind our reader that Nature, before Spinoza, was once also such a kingdom.

On the other hand, however, within the ethics of the mode, there is a more fertile nexus from the perspective of the multitude. If the mode – as particulariser of things – is also first and foremost the condition of the situs of the multitude, and so the condition of ethics, then Deleuze has pinpointed the moment of expressionism in Spinoza and Leibniz. As we have noted at several points in this text, Spinoza's thinking of multitudes is restricted by his adherence to the theory of a fluid plenum, one that Leibniz critiques and goes beyond. Yet just as natural right stands as a necessary groundwork for ethics, so Spinoza's theory of multitude is not to be discarded, but provides already a useful framework for considering the multiplicity. The great merit of the Spinozan ethics is that the modes are synthesised from the fluctuations of the soul – from the discordant depths – and not played out harmoniously by the free One as a model for the world. It is not Being that clamours, but the modality of the clamour that in the limit *composes* present Being. So also the multitude presents its Being according to the composition of its discordant modes. In our 'Cosmopolitanism for the love of multitudes' (2015), we have analysed the Spinozan theory of multitude within the context of the cosmopolis. It perhaps suffices to say that the multitudinous point of view requires a new methodology, one determined by the intensive interaction of *potentia* and *potestas*, mediated by the attributes, which we believe allows to understand the difference of approach of the *Tractatus politicus*. At every moment, the multitude expresses its composition, and as the composition fluctuates as if with one mind, so the Being that is expressed mutates from Being to Being, from political form to political form, from the lowest to the highest pitch of human freedom.

Notes

1 The epithet Marx deploys in *Differenz* (1841) (1971–1990: 256–308).
2 Marx, *Kritik der Hegelschen Dialektik und Philosophie* §XXIII (1968: 113–114).
3 *Capital* (1976: 290) 'the labour process . . . is common to all forms of society . . .'
4 Ibid., p. 301.
5 Ibid., p. 302, where Leibniz's best possible world is attacked but *a fortiori* Spinoza's world.
6 (1990).
7 Letter 50.
8 We have only touched on these issues fleetingly, but the terminology and its links to Aristotle and Hobbes are discussed by us in our earlier Connelly (2011).

Bibliography

Connelly, S. (2011) 'Intuition beyond the law of the state' 7(2) *Utrecht Law Review* 29–41.
—— (2015 forthcoming) 'Cosmopolitanism for the love of multitudes', in T. Caraus and E. Paris (ed.), *Post-Foundational Cosmopolitanism*, Routledge, London.
Marx, K. (1968) *Texte zu Methode und Praxis II: Pariser Manuskripte 1844*, Rowohlt, Reinbek bei Hamburg.
—— (1970) *A Contribution to the Critique of Political Economy*, Progress Publishers, Moscow.
—— (1976) *Capital* (3 vols), Penguin & New Left Review, London.
Marx, K. and Engels, F. (1971–1990) *Marx-Engels Werke: Ergänzungsband*, Dietz Verlag, Berlin.
Vuillemin, J. (1990), 'Physique panthéiste et déterministe: Spinoza et Huygens' 6 *Studia Spinozana* 231–250.
Winter, T.N. (2007) *The Mechanical Problems in the Corpus of Aristotle*, Faculty Publications, University of Nebraska-Lincoln.

Appendix I

Spinoza's library

Part I: books officially forming part of Spinoza's estate at death

For ease of reference, we reprint here the contents of Spinoza's library at his death as noted by the notary v. Rooijen, from the text collated by Freudenthal in his (1899) *Die Lebensgeschichte Spinoza's in Quellenschriften, Urkunden und nichtamtlichen Nachrichten*, Veit & Comp., Leipzig (pp. 160–164). Footnotes are those of Freudenthal.

Folios:

1 Buxtorfii Biblia twee folumina(!) cum Tiberiade.
2 Tremellii NT cum Interpretatione Syr: typis Ebr. 1569.
3 Lexicon scapulae. 1652 Lugd.[1]
4 Tacitus cum notis Lipsii[2] Antverp. 1607.
5 Livius. 1609. Aureliae.
6 Longomontani Astronomia danica cum appendice de stellis Novis et Cometis. 1640. Amstel.
7 Nizolius. 1613. Francof.[3]
8 Aquinatis dictionarium Ebr. Chald. Talm. Lutet. 1629.
9 Diophanti Alexandrini Arithmeticum Libri 6 Paris 1621.
10 Fl. Josephus. Basil. 1540.
11 Biblia en lengua Espagnola. V.T.
12 Aristoteles. 1548. Vol. 2.
13 Nathanis Concordantiae. Ebr.
14 Tesoro de ka lengua Castellana. 1611. Madrid.
15 Vietae opera Mathematica. Lugd. 1646.
16 Hugenii Zulichemii Horologium Oscillatorium. Paris. 1673.
17 Epitome Augustini Operum omnium. 1539.
18 Pagnini Biblia. 1541.
19 Moreh nebechim. Venetiis. Rabb.
20 Sphaera Johannis de Sacrobosco.

21 Idem.
22 Don Johannis a Bononia de Praedestinatione.
23 Dictionarium Rabbinicum.
24 Precationes Paschales Rabb.

In Quarto:

25 Biblia Ebr. Cum Comment.
26 Dictionarium Lat: Gall. Hisp. 1599. Bruxell.
27 Calvini Institutiones Hisp. 1597.
28 Veslingii Syntagma Anatomicum. Patavii. 1647.
29 Biblia Junii et Tremellii.
30 Riolani Anatomica. Paris. 1626.
31 Descartes Brieven.[4]
32 Virgilus cum Notis Variorum. 1646. Amstel.
33 Kerckringii Specilegium(!) anatomicum. 1670.
34 Descartes Proeven.[5]
35 Politieke discoursen. 1662. Leyden.[6]
36 Obras de Quevedo. Vol.2. Bruxell. 1660.
37 Poësias de Quevedo. 1661.
38 Opere di Machiavelli. 1550.
39 Pagnorii Mensa Isiaca. Amstel. 1667.
40 Corona Gothica Hisp. 1658.
41 Grotius de Satisfactione Christi.
42 Sandii Nucleus Hist. Eccles. 1676 col. Cum Tractatu de Script. Vet. Eccles.
43 L'Empereur Clavis Talmudica.
44 Renatus Descartes de prima Philosophia.
45 _______________ de Geometria.
46 Renatus Descartes de Philosophia prima.
47 Blijenbergh tegen Tract. Theo. Polit.
48 Leon Abarbanel dialogos de amor.
49 Descartes de Geometria.
50 Descartes opera Philosophica. 1650.
51 ________ de Homine.
52 Vossius de arte Grammatica.
53 a Schooten Exercitationes Mathematicae.
54 Praeadamitae. 1655.
55 Sepher Tabnith Haical.
56 Joseph del medico abscondita sapientiae.
57 Een Rabbinish Mathematish boeck.
58 Explicatio 5 libr. Mosis.
59 Sepher dikduck.
60 Mori Utopia.
61 Snellii Tiphys Batavus.

62 Gregorii Optica Promota Lond. 1663.
63 Todas Las obras de de Gongora. Madrid. 1633.
64 a Schooten Principia Matheseos Univers. 1651.
65 Comedia Famosa del Perez de Montalvan.
66 Lansbergii Comm. In Motum Terrae. Middelb. 1630.
67 Mansvelt adversus anonymum Theol.-Pol.
68 Stenon de Solido. Flor. 1669.
69 Id.
70 Lansbergii Cyclometrii nova.
71 Fabricii Mannemium (!) et Lutrea Caesaria.
72 Algebra door Kinckhuysen.
73 Gront de Meetkunst door Kinckhuysen.
74 De Meetkunst door Kinckhuysen.
75 Scheiner Refractiones Caelestes.
76 Lansbergii Progymnasmata astron. Restituta.
77 I. Lansbergii Apologia pro P. Lansbergio.
78 Wouter Verstap. Arithmetica.
79 Bartholoni dioristice.
80 Keppleri Eclogae Chronicae.
81 Calepenus 8 Ling.

In Octavo:

82 Chiduschim.
83 J. ben Schemtob: Kalendarisches Lehrgedicht(?).[7]
84 Book by Isak ben Abraham Chajim Jessurum.
85 Lexicon Schrevilii. 1654. Gr. Lat.
86 Bartholini anatomia. 1651.
87 Machiavelli. Basil.
88 Hippocrates 2 vol. 1554.
89 Epicteti Enchiridion cum tab. Cebetis cum Wolfii annot.
90 Franciosini Vocabolario Ital. et Spagn.
91 Arrianus de Expedit. Alex. M. Amst. 1668.
92 Politycke Weegschael door V.H. 1661.[8]
93 Buxtorfii Thesaurus gramm.
94 Dictionarium Lat: Belg.
95 Petronius arbiter cum Comm. 1669. Amstel.
96 Metii Alemariani Instit. Astron. Libri. 3.
97 Novellas Exemplares de Savedra.
98 Las Obras de Perez. 1644.
99 Tulpii Observationes Med. 1672.
100 Boyle de Elatare et gravitate aeris. 1663. Lond.
101 Luciani mortuorum dialogi.
102 Pererius in Danielum. 1602. Lugd.

103 Julius Caesar.
104 Sandii Nucleus Hist. Eccles.
105 De brieven van Seneca.
106 Kekkermanni Logica.
107 Munsteri Gramm. Ebr. Eliae Levitae.
108 Pinto Delgado Poema de la Reyna Ester.
109 Rhenii Tyrocimium Ling. Gr.
110 Vossii. Instit. L.G.
111 Scioppi Grammatica Philos.
112 Grotius de Imperio Summarum Potestaum circa Sacra.
113 Metii Astrolabium.
114 De Graefs driehoeksmeting.
115 El Criticon Vol. 3.
116 Vossii Rud. Gr.
117 Raetken Spaense Grammatica.
118 Ben Israel Esparanca (!) de Israël.
119 Homeri Iliad. Gr.
120 Dialogues Francois.

In 12°:

121 Klauberghs uytbreiding van Descartes.
122 Velthusius de Liene et Generatione.
123 Neri ars vitraria. 1668. Amst. Cum fig.
124 Salustius.
125 Logique ou ou l'art de penser.
126 Voyage d'Espagne. 1666.
127 Claubergii Logica.
128 Senecae Epistolae.
129 Hobbes Elementa Philosophica.[9]
130 Clapmarius de arcanis Rerum pp.
131 Kerkring in currum Triumphalem.
132 Boyle Paradoxa Hydrostatica.
133 Baudii Epist. Et Orationes.
134 Martialis cum notis Farnabii.
135 Wolzogen de Scriptuarum interprete.
136 Plinii Secundi Episolae cum Panegyricis.
137 Senecae Tragedae.
138 Mostarts Sendbriefschrijver.
139 Johannis Secundi Opera.
140 Ovidius 3 Vol.
141 Verulamii Sermones fideles.[10]
142 Le Visioni Politique. 1671.
143 Curtius.

144 Virgilius.
145 Plautus. 1652.
146 Ciceronis Epistolae.
147 Petrarcha de Vita Solitaria.
148 Justinianus.
149 Velthusius de Usu rationis in Theologia.
150 Euclides.
151 Ovidii Metam. Tom.II.
152 Obra devote. La Cuna.
153 Stenonis Observ. Anat.
154 Phrases Virgil. Et Horat.
155 Virgilius.
156 Ephemerides.
157 Pharmacopaea Amstelred.
158 Historie van Karel de II.
159 Tacitus.
160 Elementa Physica.[11]
161 Obras de Gongora.

Part 2: extract from a letter by Schuller detailing a list of books found among Spinoza's things

[In Freudenthal, J. op. cit. (1899: 203), from a letter obtained by Stein in Zurich (5 Stein a. a. O. S. 287). Formatting has been altered to aid reading. Schuller reports that he checked Spinoza's bookcase for the books on the list but found none, suggesting the list was of desiderata. However, item 8 had been read by Spinoza, as Letter 44 to Jellis appears to attest, so it is possible that the list contained other works that Spinoza had borrowed from his friends (Jan Rieuwertsz after all being a bookseller). Clarificatory notes are our own.]
'Amstelodami, 29 Mart. 1677.
[. . .]
Pervelim ex Te discere, num ex sequentibus libris (quorum catalogum – cum hac inscription: libri rarissimi – inter posthuma reperi) unquam aliquos videris:

1 Florentinus de rebus sacris;
2 Joh. Beneventensis de nefandis christianae religionis erroribus;
3 Alius Beneventensis de Sodomiae laudibus;[12]
4 Averrois argumenta de aeternitate mundi;
5 Anonymous quidam Italus de commercio sanctorum et sanctarum;
6 Idem de stultitia gentium;
7 Idem de magia Mosis et Muhamedis;
8 Franciscus Datsii(!) homo politicus, liber rarissimus;[13]
9 Du Mas Abbas opuscula missoria;

10 A Sancto Bernardo monachus Hispanus de commercio daemonium. Idem de eorundem in hoc mundo politia et actionibus. Ejusdem cum ipsis familiaria colloquia. Idem de examine conquestionem Joh. XXII. Papae de existential Dei, animae immortalitate et inferno, opus rarissimum;
11 Vir de Religione Bona dictus, ubi de novis religionis christianae reformatoribus e. gr. Luthero, Calvino et Melanthone; idem de examine duorum regum Caroli V. et Francisci I., author Hispanus est;
12 Abavillus, Hispanus monachus Turca factus, de authoritate politices in eccles. Deque suae mutationis rationibus. Ejusd. Problemata politica. Ejusd. Dicta christiana;
13 Prophetiae Malachiae Hibern. Episcopi de Pontificibus.'

According to Freudenthal (1899: 296), he was only able to locate works 3, 8 and 13.

Notes

1 Joh. Scapula, born probably in Lausanne in the middle of the sixteenth century, published a quite destructive extract from Stephanus' *Thesaurus linguae graecae* under the above title first in 1579. The Elzevier edition of 1652, which Spinoza possessed, was one of the most beautiful of the much-used Lexikons.
2 Justus Lipsius, philologist and humanist, collected together Stoic sources in an attempt to rework Stoicism within a Christian context. His works *De Constantia* and *Manuductionis ad Stoicam philosophiam* inspired neo-Stoicism in the Low Countries, and at least provide an interesting confluential reading with the *Ethics.*
3 Freudenthal suggests this is Nizolius' *Thesaurus Ciceronianus*, given the folio edition and the publication of precisely this work in Frankfurt in 1613.
4 The 1661 Dutch translation of Descartes' *Letters*, by Spinoza's friend Jan Rieuwertsz.
5 Descartes' *Specimina philosophiae*, with the subtitle *De methodo.*
6 The author was Pieter van de Hove (de la Court).
7 The Hebrew transcription of the title suggests several works. Kaufman suggests this candidate.
8 I.e. van de Hove, specifying Jan de la Court.
9 I.e. Hobbes' *De Cive.*
10 I.e. Francis Bacon (1561–1626).
11 By van Rooijen (i.e. Willebroord Snell van Rooijen), which treats of optics.
12 These two works are by Giovanni Della Casa, Bishop of Beneventum, Italy. Della Casa's licentious poem *Il capitol sopra il forno* was widely known as *De Sodomiae laudibus* after the accusations by Della Casa's enemy, Vergerio, that the poem amounted to a defence of homosexual acts. This dispute, initially an internal power struggle in the Catholic Church, was seized on by militant Protestant writers as 'proof' of the corruption at the heart of Catholicism. Indeed, Della Casa was also Pope Alexander III's censor of books (for a fuller discussion, see Puff. H. (2003) *Sodomy in Reformation Germany and Switzerland: 1400–1600*, University of Chicago Press, Chicago, IL, p. 158ff.). One wonders whether the anti-Catholic tenor of Spinoza's letter to Alfred Burgh explains his interest in Della Casa's writings.
13 This work, written by Brandenburg councillor Christoph von Rappe, normally under the pseudonym 'Peter Oldenburger' is likely to be the *homo politicus* that Spinoza attacks in Letter 44 to Jelles.

Index

www.ingramcontent.com/pod-product-compliance
Ingram Content Group UK Ltd.
Pitfield, Milton Keynes, MK11 3LW, UK
UKHW011001180926
475701UK00004B/493

* 9 7 8 1 1 3 8 2 4 1 5 4 1 *